Fifth Edition

Write It

A Process Approach to College Essays, with Readings

Linda Strahan
University of California, Riverside

Kathleen Moore
University of California, Riverside

Michael Heumann
Imperial Valley College

Kendall Hunt
publishing company

Kendall Hunt
publishing company

www.kendallhunt.com
Send all inquiries to:
4050 Westmark Drive
Dubuque, IA 52004-1840

Table of Contents

Assignment 6: "Connectivity and Its Discontents"

Assignment 7: Arguments through Literature: "The Monkey Garden"

Part 3: Case Studies   553

Acknowledgments

We want to acknowledge the University Writing Program faculty and TAs at the University of California, Riverside, for their suggestions for this new edition. We are particularly indebted to the classroom instructors, whose exemplary teaching and careful assessments of the needs of their students have directly influenced much of this text. We have observed many of you in the classroom, impressively bringing the lessons in this book to life.

In particular, our warm thanks go to Benedict Jones for his tireless and skillful editing of the manuscript for this new edition, and for his contributions to its content. He has found and corrected a number of dropped or misspelled words, and dug up original sources for obscure references in several of the reading selections. His suggestions on content have been extremely useful. His skills as a researcher and proofreader have been invaluable.

We also thank Simon Lee and Kim Turner for incorporating two of the new lead essays into their English 4 course work. The sample student essays for Case Studies 2 and 3 have been collected from their students.

We are also indebted to the Kendall Hunt team whose work made this book possible. We especially thank our editorial and managerial team, Taylor Knuckey and Linda Chapman, for their good advice and consistent attention to detail. We are especially grateful for the tedious but important work that was done to clear the copyright permissions for the many articles included in this edition. Through five editions of *Write It*, the people at Kendall Hunt have been reliable, efficient, and professional. We value our working relationship with them.

Foreword

Engineers tell us that they spend half of their time on the job writing reports, proposals, and job-related messages to their colleagues. Much of that work is "writing on demand," which must be completed rapidly, accurately, and in a way that helpfully addresses the requirements of the task. In many walks of life, the ability to respond quickly in writing, doing that work in a way that truly addresses the issue at hand, is what eventually distinguishes the rising professional, entrepreneur, craftsman, teacher, and civic leader, as well as the effective employee. Writing on demand also prepares us to speak in job-related settings. It readies us to formulate and express our thoughts in spoken words that others find useful, informative, and persuasive.

Your work in this course will improve your chances of thriving at the University, which holds in high esteem the ability to compose thoughts with dispatch, accuracy, relevance, and verve. Your preparation will help you become a better reader, for good writers see more when they read. Conversely, the more you learn to read attentively, the better the writer you will become. What you learn in this class will also help you articulate your ideas and express yourself in aspects of your life that have little to do with the world of work or academics. A trained proficiency in writing and reading will give you greater access to the ideas and experiences of others.

Your lecture class, your workshop sessions, and your online studies will prepare you to succeed in this class and prepare you for Freshman English. You will need to be patient as well as dedicated; many students need more than one quarter to become proficient writers. Remember that the goal of this book is to help all students reach proficiency as quickly as possible. We look forward to seeing you in Freshman English.

Professor John Briggs
Director of the University Writing Program
University of California, Riverside

Preface

This book will introduce you to a form of academic writing that you will meet in many of your college classes across the disciplines. Each section of the book presents and gives you practice with a range of writing strategies that guide you through the writing process and show you how to use each stage to maximize its benefits. These strategies will help you gain the confidence and understanding you need to write effective academic essays. Students, especially those majoring in disciplines other than English, sometimes see introductory college writing courses as unnecessary and unimportant. However, you will be asked to read critically and give written responses in many of your college courses, and your professors will take for granted your ability to do these things. If you work through this book carefully, we believe that you will develop a process for writing that will allow you to effectively complete any college writing assignment you are likely to see that asks you to respond to an idea.

Producing a successful essay can be a daunting task because it requires not one but a series of skills: focused reading, critical thinking, careful analysis, marshaling of evidence, drafting, and editing. *Write It* offers exercises to guide you through each stage in the production of an essay, allowing you the opportunity to practice each skill one stage at a time. While the book goes through the writing process step by step, remember that writing is always a recursive activity, and when you begin a paper, you may not always begin at step one with your topic and proceed in a linear way, one step at a time, to proofreading. *Write It*, however, must examine the steps in the writing process sequentially, beginning with a reading and a follow-up writing topic, and continuing right through prewriting, drafting, and rewriting using a peer review. As you move through the guiding exercises *Write It* provides, new ideas will come to you. Don't set these discoveries aside; carry them forward into the remaining exercises. As you relate old and new information, you will explore each assignment's topic from several angles so that your ideas will build on one another. In this way the steps, though done in isolation, will come together in a unified perspective. The organization of this book is intended to help you come to see essay-building as a process rather than a formula, the stages as necessary steps to internalize until each becomes an intuitive part of writing itself.

Because no writers—in the real world or in the classroom—write in a vacuum, *Write It* provides readings and tasks for students to address. In each of seven writing assignment sections, you are first asked to attend to a reading selection and respond to a writing topic about that reading. The reading selection and writing topic are followed by structured writing tasks that help you develop and organize your ideas in order to answer that question in a successful way. *Write It* guides you through each stage in the process; you meet each unit's central reading and then move through a sequence of prewriting exercises, such as "Questions to Guide Your Reading," "Developing an Opinion and Working Thesis Statement," "Planning and Drafting Your Essay," and "Getting Feedback on Your Draft," that will help you develop, revise, and edit your essay. Each section also includes a series of related readings that lead you to consider the topic of each assignment in a larger context and to participate in an exchange of ideas about the topic each assignment unit addresses. Following the assignment units is a section that contains student essays, and you will be able to read and evaluate the essays other students have written in response to a few of the reading selections' writing topics. This process encourages you not just to become a writer of college essays but also to become a reader and writer in college. As you participate in the exchange of ideas with others in the academic community, you will both shape and be shaped by that community. Your experiences are unique to you, and your writing will reflect the knowledge you've accumulated from those experiences as you engage with others in defining the world in which we all live.

HERE IS HOW TO USE THIS SKILL-BUILDING BOOK

Write It is presented in three parts.

Part 1: Some General Guidelines

- steps for a thoughtful reading of an essay, with a sample annotated reading selection
- an explanation of plagiarism and copyright infringement
- an introduction to the benefits of a handbook
- a suggested structure for an argument essay, with an example
- two alternative essay structures, with examples
- a strategy for writing a timed essay

A Closer Look at the Elements of the Conventional Argument Essay

- an introduction in an argument essay
- guidelines for writing a directed summary
- strategies for developing your ideas
- a guide for writing a paragraph that supports your thesis statement
- an introduction to logical fallacies
- how to use transitions
- strategies for writing conclusions
- a sample scoring rubric

A Closer Look at Your Control at the Sentence Level

- a checklist for proofreading your essay
- grammar diagnostic tests
- sentence skills assessments

Part 2: SEVEN ASSIGNMENT UNITS that contain a central essay to read and analyze and a writing assignment to respond to with your own essay. For each of these, the book will lead you through the writing process as you:

- read for comprehension and learn to recognize and evaluate a writer's argument;
- develop your own position and supporting evidence;
- organize your ideas into an effective essay structure;
- revise and edit for coherence and clarity;
- incorporate supplemental readings to broaden the scope and complexity of your essay response.

Part 3: THREE CASE STUDIES that provide examples of students' writing to highlight strategies other students have used to construct essays. This section gives you an opportunity to practice applying criteria from the scoring rubric to evaluate others' essays. By evaluating the writing of others, you will become better at evaluating your own.

The step-by-step lessons in this skill-building workbook will provide you with a strong foundation for good writing. The book's techniques have been widely tested and proven successful. In a recent survey on our campus, students credited the lessons in this book for their success in their first college writing class. We are confident that this book will work for you, too.

Basic Information

The particular argument essay that you will study in *Write It*—one that responds to the essay of another writer—will help you gain practice in critically analyzing issues, formulating logical arguments, and persuasively expressing your opinions by using the conventional rules of written English and a clear essay structure. The thesis-centered essay is the most commonly assigned essay format in college. Its purpose is to persuade, and its formal parts are established by convention and provide a structure for presenting an argument. These parts include an introduction that orients the readers to the essay's subject, a thesis statement that presents the argument, body paragraphs that develop and support the argument, and a conclusion that closes the essay.

Part 1 is designed to be used as a writing reference section, as it gives you a basic set of directions for writing within the argument essay's conventional format. The section gives you an overview of the process of essay writing, and contains the following information:

Some General Guidelines

How to do a thoughtful reading of an essay

A brief explanation of plagiarism

Guidelines for using a handbook

An overview of the argument essay structure

A look at two alternative essay structures

Tips for writing a timed essay

Guidelines for drafting

Suggestions for writing the introduction and a well-developed thesis statement

Guidelines for writing a directed summary

Strategies for developing ideas

A basic structure for writing supporting paragraphs

How to recognize some common logical fallacies

Some ways to use transitions

Options for writing a conclusion

How to use a scoring rubric

Help with Revising and Editing

A guide for proofreading your essay

Diagnostic exercises for checking grammar skills

As you can see, Part 1 of this book contains guidelines for all of the essay's parts to help you work within the essay's conventional structure. The information in Part 1 is organized around the stages of the writing process and includes guidance on building each of the conventional essay parts that come together to form the essay's overall structure. Spend some time with these pages before moving to Part 2, where you will be asked to put them into practice. As you engage with the writing assignments in Part 2 and use the stages of the writing process to develop an essay within a particular writing context, you will want to turn back to Part 1 for guidance.

A Step-by-Step Strategy for Reading Thoughtfully

In order to respond appropriately to a reading selection, you will have to spend some time reading and analyzing the reading selection's argument and supporting material. Here are some guidelines to help you develop sound strategies for understanding. You will need to understand the reading selection before you can discuss its argument and respond with an argument of your own.

In our everyday lives, we read on a daily basis. We live in a literate society, so we read things like signs, e-mails, and menus without much effort and without thinking about them very much. In an academic setting, however, reading becomes an activity that requires effort and thought. Use the steps below to ensure that your reading is focused and productive.

1. **Consider the title given to the material you are to read.**

   It should suggest a particular topic or topics to you. Think about what you already know about the topic. Think about what else you need to know about the topic in order to have an informed opinion about it. Look at the title again and ask yourself what its wording suggests about the author's opinion and perhaps his or her reason for writing about the topic.

2. **Learn about the author.**

   If a short biography about the author is presented with the reading, look for biographical information that may have influenced the content and perspective of the reading. Sometimes you can better evaluate a writer's argument by taking into account his or her level of expertise or personal connection to the subject of the essay.

3. **Read through the material once quickly.**

   This first rapid reading gives you an overview of the subject, the author's attitude toward the subject, and the nature of the supporting evidence that the reading contains.

4. **Read again to identify the thesis.**

   For your second reading, you need a pen or highlighter as well as your eyes. Your first task on the second reading is to find and mark the thesis. The thesis states the author's position on the topic. Often, it is contained in a single sentence, but, in some cases, it takes several sentences to make clear the point of the work. There are times when the author does not state his or her thesis explicitly, but you should be able to state it after reading through the essay once. You might want to note the thesis in the margin.

5. **Read slowly and methodically through the rest of the material.**

Each paragraph has a topic sentence that expresses the main point of the para-graph. The topic sentence is usually found at the beginning of the paragraph, but it can be anywhere within the paragraph. You should note the point (or topic sentence) of each paragraph as you work through your second reading. The remainder of the paragraph contains evidence to support the topic sen-tence. While you read, your job is to evaluate this evidence for its logic and validity. For future reference, you may find it useful to make comments in the margins regarding the strength and weakness of the paragraph's evidence.

6. **Read again for review.**

Now that you have thought through the ideas and evidence supporting the ideas in your reading, read the whole thing again. Watch for any anomalies—statements or points that don't fit with your overall understanding of the mate-rial. If you find any, take time to determine whether the material is an authorial error or a misreading on your part. You may find that you need to go back to Step 4 and begin working through the reading again. Once you are certain that your reading is accurate, you are prepared to discuss, summarize, and respond to the reading with your own essay.

Look over the following essay and notice the way that one writer used Write It's *guidelines to underline main ideas and make notations in the margins. These notes help identify the essay's argument and supporting details.*

An Example:

Leadership: Facing Moral and Ethical Dilemmas   *Essay*

THE CENTER FOR BUSINESS AND ETHICS AT LOYOLA
MARYMOUNT UNIVERSITY

Last year in the U.S. alone, 257 public companies with $258 billion in assets declared bankruptcy. This was a huge increase over the previous year's record of 176 companies with $95 billion. This year will cer-tainly be worse in terms of big companies going bust. [outline of the problem] Big Fortune 500 companies aren't expected to collapse.

Taking a look at what went wrong and why these companies failed reveals moral and ethical [thesis statement] shortcomings. Other obvious factors contribute to a company's demise. A bad economy, financial risks that don't pay off, accounting manipulations that seemed smart at the time, loss of competitive advantage, and rapidly changing market preferences are undeniably strong negative factors. But to truly understand, one must look deeper, into the very hearts and souls of the leaders who guide corporate responsibility. <u>One must look at the moral and ethical stance of an organization and the role of leadership in creating a culture of values.</u>

restatement of the thesis

September 11th was a tragedy that brought harsh consequences for many businesses. One can blame terrorism. But the recent rash of bankruptcies is more frightening in that we brought this on ourselves. True, one can point fingers at the CEOs in charge. There is no doubt that some were in a position to know when to jump ship before the rest of us.

comparison to emphasize the seriousness of the situation

In 1986, the space shuttle Challenger exploded, causing the death of seven astronauts. A subsequent investigation of the culture at NASA revealed important lessons. Multiple mistakes, not just a single error, occurred, and neither did the managers intentionally commit wrongdoing. Yet it could have been prevented. The errors were years in the making. NASA engineers noticed damage to the crucial O-rings, yet they repeatedly convinced themselves the damage was acceptable. One analyst described it as "an incremental descent into poor judgment." The culture at NASA was extremely success-oriented. They had hired the best of the best and had highly complex and sophisticated performance goals. The pressure to succeed mounted gradually until minor violations of standards became standard. Nothing looked wrong until it was all over.

example: 1986 space shuttle explosion that resulted from managerial/engineering errors in judgment

The culture at Enron was very similar. They hired the brightest from graduate schools. Success was rewarded and non-performers shunned. The emphasis was on the numbers and immediate success rather than on long-term values. The company gradually descended into poor judgment, denial, greed, deceit, ego, wishful thinking, poor communications, and lax oversight. But this trend was apparent only in retrospect. No one noticed at the time, as everyone was immersed in the culture. The question to ask is not how did this happen at Enron, but how is it happening in one's own organization right now? Where are the corporate standards being violated? As a leader, in what ways is one contributing to a loosening of ethical and moral values? What does one need to do to improve organizational integrity?

example: Enron's culture of denial, deceit, etc.

Ethical and professional dilemmas are not new. In the past, people relied more on religious doctrine to guide standards; however, evil carried out in the name of religion has shaken confidence in religious traditions. These are difficult times in terms of people's ability to know what is the right thing to do and still remain successful in their professions. Is business ethics a contradiction?

explanation for the changing definition of business ethics

We seem to accept that modern businesses have morality and ethics different from social traditions. Robert Jackall (1997) suggests that the modern bureaucracy has created a "society within a society" in which the set of ethical standards may not be consistent with those of the larger society. This might help explain how certain corporate leaders could do what they did and still look at themselves in the mirror. Our current capitalistic society goes along with these special societies, as long as they are successful. Enron was touted as one of the most innovative organizations five years in a row by *Fortune* magazine. Only when there is a collapse do people cry "foul."

reference to authority to explain the modern ethical standard of corporations

In America, the Protestant work ethic at one time formed the basis of good business relationships. A person's word was his bond, and business could be counted on with a handshake. Personal integrity and reputation mattered. But in business, there is also a "dog eat dog" mentality. To the victor go the spoils. Somehow, when it comes to business, there is such an emphasis on success that morals and ethics take a back seat.

comparison of modern business ethics to Protestant work ethic

The larger an organization, the more complex the strategy and operations, and the easier it becomes to stretch standards and change the numbers to reflect what is desired rather than what is. Meeting the numbers seems more desirable than sticking to reality. Besides, one might reason that "reality" or "truth" is really just a question of which version, which perspective. Here's the way one cynical executive put it: "Let's be honest. We lie, and our colleagues lie to us. That's how human beings operate. People prefer to tell each other what they want to hear. . . . I don't need perfect people; I need successful people who can think for themselves and get the job done. If they need to tell a little white lie, I can live with that."

restatement of explanation, and a quotation for impact

An Explanation of Plagiarism and Copyright Infringement

You may be aware of the requirement that all work you turn in for credit must be your own, but sometimes students inadvertently commit plagiarism because they are unclear about what constitutes plagiarism or infringement of copyright laws. Review the following definitions and rules, and check to see that your own paper meets all the requirements of intellectual and academic honesty.

Copyright refers to the legal ownership of published material. Any writing—a play, an essay, a pamphlet, a website—is the intellectual property of the person who wrote it. If, in your paper, you borrow that property by quoting, summarizing, or paraphrasing, you must give credit to the original author. The *fair use* laws allow you to borrow *brief passages* without infringing on copyright, but you must credit the source and document it properly. Your handbook will show you the correct form to use for each and every source.

Plagiarism can occur in different ways. For example, some students make poor choices and turn in another student's work as their own. Institutions of higher learning have strict policies regarding this type of plagiarism, and the consequences for this action can be significant. Plagiarism may also be committed by oversight; a student may have forgotten where he or she found the particular material or even that the material was not his or her own. It is important during your research that you include all the source information in your notes so that you will not accidentally commit plagiarism and be held accountable for it.

Remember to acknowledge the following:

> *Ideas*—any idea or concept that you learned elsewhere that is not common knowledge
>
> *Words and Phrases*—exact reproduction of another author's writing
>
> *Charts/Tables/Statistic/Other Visuals*—other forms of work done by an author
>
> *Your Own Work*—work of your own done for a different assignment, class, or purpose

Intellectual property is the result of work done by a person with the head rather than the hands; nevertheless, the result of that work still belongs to the person who did it. If a carpenter made a chair, that chair is owned by its maker. You would consider taking that chair an act of theft. Try to think of printed material as a similar object, and show that property the same respect you would any other. By doing so, you will avoid plagiarism and copyright infringement.

How to Use a Handbook

Your handbook is a valuable tool and resource. Many students own a handbook but fail to use it. Others, however, keep their handbook next to them when they are writing and consult it when they have questions or when they need some prewriting activities to help develop their ideas. It is important to become familiar with some of the resources available in a handbook.

Writing is like a journey; it has a beginning and an end. To reach your final destination, it is best to have a map. Even with a good map, wrong turns and detours are to be expected, but without a map, the trip can be prolonged and frustrating. A handbook provides a useful map for any kind of writing.

A handbook helps at every stage of the writing process. It has sections that show you how to get started by defining your purpose and your audience. Your handbook has chapters that can aid you as you make a plan for your writing, and chapters that can lead you through the drafting process. When your rough draft is completed, your handbook will give you ideas and techniques for improving and revising the work you have done. Most importantly, a handbook contains all the information and explanations of the conventions of written English. You will want to consult your handbook extensively as you correct and edit your final draft.

You need to familiarize yourself with two important features of your handbook: the **table of contents** and the **index.** Learning how to use them and training yourself to consult them will save you time and improve your writing.

The Table of Contents

The table of contents appears at the beginning of your handbook. It gives the title (topic) of each chapter and lists the subtopics covered in each of the chapters. A page number follows each listing for easy access to the information.

Example: Your instructor has given a general assignment for your paper. You are to write a research paper on the novel *Beloved*, by Toni Morrison, but you are expected to come up with your own topic. You have no idea where to begin. Checking the table of contents reveals the following listing:

"How can I think through a writing topic?"
Turning to the page you are directed to, you find discussion and concrete suggestions that lead you through the following steps:
"Selecting a Topic"
"Broadening or Narrowing a Topic"

But you don't yet have a topic. You continue reading, however, and find sections that tell you exactly what to do to help yourself come up with ideas for your paper:

freewriting
brainstorming

mapping
questioning

You try them all, but the final technique, using the question words, produces the following:

Who? Sethe

What? escaped

When? pre-Civil War

Where? Sweet Home Plantation to a free state

Why? slavery

How? Underground Railroad

The final question, "How?" produces a relevant and researchable topic, *the Underground Railroad*. You can research that topic. Once you have gathered information, you are able to return to the section in the handbook on narrowing your topic and begin to refine your topic. Then you can formulate a thesis.

Index

The index appears at the very end of your handbook. It contains an alphabetical listing of every topic, concept, and problem addressed within the handbook's pages. A page number or a sequence of page numbers follows each listing. These numbers indicate pages where information on a particular listing can be found.

<u>Example</u>: You are writing about your family and want to discuss the origins of the family name. You have written the following sentence:

My family, the Taylors, got their name from an ancestor's occupation.

You are unsure about your pronoun choice. Should it be "their" or "its"? You know that "family" is a collective (group) noun. You look up collective nouns and find the following listing:

"Collective nouns"

"pronoun agreement with"
"verb agreement with"

You might first want to refresh your memory about collective nouns in general, but, if you feel confident about their definition, you can go directly to the index listing for pronoun agreement. There, you will discover that collective nouns like "family" can take both the singular and plural pronoun, depending on the content and meaning of the sentence. If the group (collective noun) functions as a whole, or one, the singular pronoun is correct. If the members of the group act individually, the plural pronoun is needed. In your sentence, the family is acting as a unit. Which pronoun would be correct?

The Conventional Academic Essay Structure

The structure of a thesis-centered essay is established by convention. That is, the thesis essay format has an introduction that contains the thesis statement, followed by body paragraphs that support it, and ending with a conclusion that gives closure to the essay.

An Introduction That Contains

an introductory sentence that introduces the reading selection's title, author, and subject.

a summary of the reading selection that includes an answer to the writing topic.

your THESIS STATEMENT in response to the writing topic.

Body Paragraphs That Include

a topic sentence that gives the paragraph's central point, one that supports your thesis statement.

concrete evidence, explained so that it supports the central point and the thesis statement.

A Conclusion That Gives

a reminder of the reading selection's argument and your argument.

a sense of closure for the essay.

An Example

Read the following essay written by a college freshman for a composition course. See if you can use the above diagram to identify the parts of her essay. Does she use the structure presented in the diagram? Do her paragraphs focus on one central point? See if you can state each paragraph's point in your own words. How effectively does she develop and support her position? Do you find her argument compelling? Why or why not? What position would you take if you were asked to write an essay on plagiarism?

Plagiarism: A Crime to Be Prevented

Essay

Vicki Xiong

Plagiarism is an ugly word; it is an ugly act to be caught in—to have next to your name. No matter how ugly the word, students all across America continue to resort to its tempting "benefits." With the modern advent of the World Wide Web and the accessibility of the home computer, the act of plagiarism has become an easier crime to commit. Growing up, children are taught that stealing is wrong; plagiarism is indeed just that, wrong—for it is the stealing of another's idea(s). The only way to combat the outbreak of plagiarism is through prevention. Prevention of plagiarism is our best hope in securing the honors of academia in the years to come.

Plagiarism occurs when someone represents someone else's creative or academic work, whether all of it or part of it, as one's own. There are several forms of plagiarism. It can be an omission, where someone fails to acknowledge or give credit to the creator of words, pictures, or ideas. Or it can be a case where a person uses someone else's ideas and gives credit, but invents the source.

Study after study has continued to show that plagiarism is a growing epidemic. Students, when surveyed anonymously, overwhelmingly admit without any reservation to having relied on plagiarism to complete their assignments. Many people have studied this growing problem, and some think that as many as ninety-five percent of today's students plagiarize with little hesitation.

Plagiarism is a problem because it harms all parties involved—the plagiarizer, fellow classmates, and even the entire student body. The plagiarizer, taking part in academic dishonesty, makes a conscious decision to cheat not only those involved but himself or herself as well. The logic is simple. The workload (assignments, tests, quizzes, projects, etc.) of a course is designed to aid students in learning the basic fundamentals of the course. When cheating is practiced, the student robs himself or herself of the true learning experience, and thus loses the chance of absorbing the knowledge that might have been drawn upon for future reference.

Likewise, fellow classmates are harmed as well (especially in the college setting). When classes are graded on a curve, plagiarism is unfair to the diligent students who dedicate time and effort to do their best only to be deprived of the full benefit of the curve, as the cheaters set the curve with their added advantage. As students learn that some are plagiarizing to improve their grades, they lose faith in the integrity of the school and may decide that they have to plagiarize, too, in order to compete. As long as plagiarism is allowed to go on with little, if any, penalty, students will eventually lose their belief that colleges are honorable institutions and that going to one is a privilege.

On the large scale, society is harmed as well. Society is harmed when plagiarizers don't get caught. When plagiarizers are praised for their work, when they get the promotion, or when they get accepted into a professional school based on their supposed merit, they are rewarded for their dishonesty. Society is harmed when incapable, lazy people get by on their cheating ways and, when push comes to shove, are unable to perform their job to the best of their abilities because they cheated themselves of the basic training that schooling was supposed to provide. Plagiarism benefits no one. Yet it is an ever-growing problem in our constantly advancing society, where lust after the newest gadgets and tools will lead people to continue to live dishonestly to get what they want. This is not one of the lessons college graduates should be learning.

Unfortunately, academic dishonesty and plagiarism are not foreign issues in our present-day academia, but so far little has been done to stop it. On the contrary, the act of plagiarism has become a means of survival in the hostile and aggressive realities of higher education. As college admissions and professional school admissions continue to become more and more competitive, students will only be drawn more to the temptations of cheating. Little is done by campus authority figures to combat this. They should discuss the harmful effects of plagiarism and offer alternative choices for students who are struggling and under pressure to succeed. Many times, students plagiarize because their friends all do and they just haven't thought about the seriousness of what they're doing. If this problem were discussed more openly, these students might make different choices. When students are caught plagiarizing, professors are usually lenient. They seem unwilling to confront students who cheat. As long as professors and others in authority remain unconcerned about their students relying on plagiarism to complete their assignments, it will continue to grow and will eventually destroy the integrity of higher education.

Educators should make a commitment and join forces with other fellow educators across America in the fight against plagiarism.

Teachers should make it a duty to teach all students what plagiarism is, and to drill the ethical consequences of plagiarism into each and every student before they enter college. The conditioning should start as soon as students enter grade school. In the first grade, little lessons on cheating should be taught, and as students progress each year from grade school to middle school to high school, lessons in cheating, academic dishonesty, and plagiarism should be reiterated in more detail and observed under a stricter set of guidelines. The common excuse of "I was never taught that" will instantly be eliminated, as all students will be informed from an early age. The repercussions of plagiarism should be on a no-tolerance basis. If students are assured that when caught, they will be punished to the maximum, this will undoubtedly stimulate a fear and thus draw students away from the lure of dishonesty and cheating. Teachers and professors alike must be firm on implementation of the consequences when occurrences do happen; they must carry out the punishment—not just let students go with a warning. Then instructors will become the role models for students that they should be.

In addition to annual lessons on plagiarism, teachers at the high school level should also spend time teaching students ways to manage time. This will directly aid in the lowering of the overwhelming shock students often experience upon entering college and will hopefully decrease the temptation of resorting to academic dishonesty. At the same time, teachers should teach students to think for themselves—allowing them to explore the possibilities of their imaginations. Assignments and projects should not be so strictly constrained—confined by guideline after guideline. In contrast, assignments should encourage students to think outside of the box; this will enable them to practice creative thinking and, in turn, will reduce dependency on other people's thoughts and ideas as they build confidence in their own ideas. In essence, teachers should teach students to think, not to regurgitate.

Plagiarism is a serious problem that is rapidly growing. Its appeal has drawn in students from all walks of life. The act of plagiarism is no laughing matter. It must be taken seriously. Our actions will eventually catch up with us. Excuses will eventually run out. Educators should not put off lessons in plagiarism, but begin the conditioning as soon as possible—for prevention is our best bet in ending today's academic dishonesty crisis.

Two Alternative Essay Structures

Although it is most common in an argumentative essay to place the thesis early—usually towards the end of the first paragraph—there are alternative structures that can be used in an argument essay. Each of the two essay examples in this section contains a clear thesis statement, but neither thesis can be found at the beginning of the essay. The first essay uses what we call the "hourglass structure," and the second uses what we call the "funnel structure." You might notice that several of the reading selections in this book use one of these alternative structures, in part because they were not written for an academic readership. In your own essays, however, we recommend that you use the conventional academic essay structure.

The Hourglass Structure

One alternative structure for an essay places the thesis statement somewhere in the middle of the essay. Here is a diagram of this type of essay.

An Introduction That Contains

> an ANECDOTE that is related to the subject of the essay.
>
> a HINT about the writer's position on the issue.

Body Paragraphs That Include

> TOPIC SENTENCES.
>
> concrete EVIDENCE that supports the writer's position.
>
> additional EXAMPLES that support the writer's position.
>
> A THESIS STATEMENT.

More Body Paragraphs That Include

> TOPIC SENTENCES.
>
> concrete EVIDENCE that supports the writer's position.
>
> added EXAMPLES that support the writer's position.

A Conclusion That Gives

> a REMINDER of the writer's position.
>
> a sense of CLOSURE for the essay.

With the hourglass structure, writers ask readers to read a fair portion of the essay before they come to the essay's central point. Writers begin talking about a subject, offering assertions, anecdotes, and observations whose significance isn't yet clear. These assertions and observations are meant to create a path to the central point—stated in a thesis statement—followed by more corroborating assertions and observations.

Writers might use this structure when their thesis is controversial and they do not want to risk losing dissenting readers up front. To persuade readers who disagree, a writer tries to draw them in by offering material more widely agreed upon and accessible. You will want to notice when a writer uses an alternative essay structure because it will help you to identify the argument and the linking ideas that support it.

Making Great Strides

Essay

N. J. GLEASON

N. J. Gleason is a community college English professor with interests in science writing, creative writing, and autobiography.

As a child, I often had peculiar ideas about many things. Walking, for instance: Boys, I felt, strode decisively in a single-minded bid to get where they were going; girls, on the other hand, were slower and more deliberate. Nothing illustrated this perception better than a trip to London when I was nine.

My family used various forms of locomotion while assiduously avoiding everything that was peculiarly English. To my lifelong regret, we never used the Underground, not once. I remember being fascinated by the double-decker buses and terribly disappointed when we finally mounted one but *stayed in the lower level*. What was the point? And, of course, we took taxis. But much of the time, we walked, for London is famous for being a walkable city.

I have a clear memory of moving purposefully down a rather quaint London street: My father, my teenage brother, and I marched along in an inconsiderate pack, while my mother lagged far behind, being, well, a girl. I never considered that perhaps she saw walking in a foreign city not as a method of transportation but as a way to relax and soak up the ambience. I never thought that on vacation, a person might be less concerned about *getting* somewhere and more interested in *being* somewhere. My father and brother outpaced her because they were tall and had long legs; I kept up with them because it was very important for me to be one of the men, and I took great pride in my ability to cover ground with greater success than my mother did. But I was so caught up in staying with the pack that I have unclear memories of that street. It wasn't like the streets at home, but what made it different? Did it have shops? Perhaps. Cobblestones? Surely they were only the stuff of movies. No, it had row houses. Or perhaps not.

Later in the trip, we visited Hyde Park, ambling because of the high density of foot traffic and because we were rather lost in the huge green expanse that, along with the contiguous Kensington Gardens, covers nearly a square mile. Being in unfamiliar territory is a boon to the casual walker. We appreciated the vibrant grass, shrubs, and trees; passed Speakers' Corner without quite realizing its significance; crossed the picturesque Serpentine Bridge; and marveled at the large tribes of colorfully uniformed schoolchildren on outings. However, I thought of this ramble as belonging to my mother, the slow one. If we had known where we were going, *we men* would have far outstripped her. The sheer rudeness of it all never occurred to me, nor did I ever stop to think that a woman isolated is a woman vulnerable.

For despite such literary luminaries as Little Red Riding Hood and Tess Durbeyfield—both of whom met their fates in the country—I see the urban landscape as a much more dangerous proposition for anyone, but especially women. In today's cities, why walk when you don't have to?

Even the suburbs seem much safer; on many evening walks in my old suburban neighborhood, I aroused no obvious alarm even from unknown women who were walking alone. But in the city, where I have recently relocated, I am seen as a potential predator. One woman, noticing me behind her, whipped out her cell phone and reached her party in record time, far faster than she could possibly have speed-dialed and actually connected. She knew that she was safer if I thought she was talking to someone. Another yanked her child nearer to her as I approached. Other women have simply been startled or fearful, their apprehension all too plain even in the dim glow of streetlights.

An experience of my own a couple of years ago drives home the danger of walking alone at night in the city. After an evening social event, my friends and I visited a convenient coffeehouse and lounged on the patio, watching the pedestrians go by. One man, moving slowly down the sidewalk with his friend, gave me a shiver as I saw the expression—or lack of it—in his eyes: not the faraway mien of a man in thought, not the glazed or swimmy look of a man under the influence, but a chilling deadness that made me glad that he would be long gone after I had finished my decaf.

I was wrong. After I took leave of my friends, I crossed the street and headed home on foot, declining a ride because I wanted the exercise. Unemployed at that time, I had left my own car at home to save on gas and justify my cup of coffee. I passed the church, the attorney, and the dentist, becoming aware that two men were pacing me on the opposite side of the street. As I approached the intersection where I would normally turn right, the two men split up. One, whom I recognized as the man with the dead eyes, strode diagonally across the street as if to cut me off. His companion split off and crossed the street as if to flank me. I was in trouble.

I had moments to think. Turning around, obviously, was not an option. I couldn't go left, of course, since I would be thrown into the path of my would-be attackers. But if I turned right at the approaching intersection, I would be on a residential street with spotty streetlight coverage, where the men could converge upon me. Similarly, if I stopped at the menacing red DON'T WALK signal and waited politely on the curb to go straight, they would be on me in seconds. If I ran, I would tip them off.

I saw only one alternative to reach a well-lighted and busy intersection only minutes away. I quickened my pace, practically bolted through the ominous crossing signal, and forged ahead of the dead-eyed man, who (despite his long diagonal trajectory) had nearly crossed the multi-lane street by this time. Glancing behind me, I saw that his friend had already crossed but was well behind me, thanks to my swift stride. They could catch me only if they started running, but then I would start to run and likely reach safety ahead of them. I continued my trek to the major intersection, and they fell away harmlessly, perhaps to await some other hapless victim. I had made myself more trouble than I was worth.

I still don't know for sure that those men intended me harm, but I believe that they did. I feel that I was safe because I was a strong walker, as I had demonstrated as a child on a London thoroughfare many years before. I sometimes imagine how ill-equipped my mother would have been in such a situation. A well-off woman with a husband to protect her wouldn't be out alone in the city at ten o'clock at night, of course, but many women—and men as well—have fewer options and are often hamstrung by odd working hours, financial straits, and the lack of a vehicle. They run a higher risk of being targeted by predators.

In my new neighborhood, I no longer walk for any reason after dark—not for transportation, nor for pleasure, nor for exercise as I used to do in my old neighborhood in the suburbs. The city is a place to be watchful. Ever since my close shave, I see the evening stroll as a suburban luxury that many people simply do not have.

The Funnel Structure

Another alternative structure for an argument essay is one that places its thesis somewhere within the conclusion of the essay. Here is a diagram of this type of essay structure.

An Introduction That Contains

One of the following:

an ANECDOTE

an EXAMPLE

a SUMMARY of the topic

INFORMATION related to the topic

Body Paragraphs That Include

TOPIC SENTENCES

other ANECDOTES that point toward a position on the subject

facts, statistics, or other INFORMATION that points toward a particular position on the subject

additional EXAMPLES that point toward a particular position on the subject

concrete EVIDENCE that points toward a particular position on the subject

A Conclusion That Gives

a clear statement of the author's THESIS

a sense of CLOSURE for the essay

With the funnel structure, writers pile up the evidence piece by piece but do not state the significance of this evidence until the end. Writers might use this structure to present the reasonableness of their argument to a hostile audience, to lead an uninformed audience to form the writer's desired conclusion on an issue, or simply to prepare readers to accept a surprising conclusion.

An Example

Read "When Volunteerism Isn't Noble" and locate the thesis statement. Then use the diagram above to see how this essay's parts are organized. Why do you think this writer chose the funnel structure for her argument?

When Volunteerism Isn't Noble

Essay

LYNN STEIRER

Lynn Steirer was a student at a community college when she wrote this essay. It was published on the op-ed page of the New York Times *in 1997.*

Engraved in stone over the front entrance to my old high school is the statement "No Man Is Free Who Is Not Master of Himself." No surprise for a school named Liberty.

But in 1991, the Bethlehem school board turned its back on the principle for which my school was named when it began requiring students to perform community service or other volunteer work. Students would have to show that they had done sixty hours of such service, or they would not receive their high school diploma.

That forced me to make a decision. Would I submit to the program even though I thought it was involuntary servitude, or would I stand against it on principle? I chose principle and was denied a diploma.

Bethlehem is not alone in requiring students to do volunteer work to graduate. Other school districts around the country have adopted such policies, and in the state of Maryland, students must do volunteer work to graduate.

Volunteerism is a national preoccupation these days. Starting on Sunday, retired General Colin Powell, at President Clinton's request, will lead a three-day gathering in Philadelphia of political and business leaders and many others. General Powell is calling for more people to volunteer. That is a noble thought.

But what President Clinton has in mind goes far beyond volunteering. He has called for high schools across the country to make community service mandatory for graduation—in other words, he wants to *force* young people to do something that should be, by its very definition, voluntary.

That will destroy, not elevate, the American spirit of volunteerism. I saw firsthand how many of my classmates treated their required service as a joke, claiming credit for work they didn't do or exaggerating the time it actually took.

Volunteering has always been important to me. As a Meals on Wheels aide and a Girl Scout, I chose to give hundreds of hours to my community, at my own initiative. While my family and I fought the school's mandatory service requirement, I continued my volunteering, but I would not submit my hours for credit. Two of my classmates joined me in this act of civil disobedience. At the same time, with the assistance of the Institute for Justice, a Washington legal policy group, we sued the school board.

As graduation neared, a school official pulled me aside and said it was not too late to change my mind. That day, I really thought about giving in. Then he asked the question that settled it for me. "After all," he said, "what is more important, your values or your diploma?" I chose to give up my diploma, eventually obtaining a graduate equivalency degree instead. The courts decided against us, and, unfortunately, the Supreme Court declined to hear our case. The school has continued the program.

Volunteering is important. But in a country that values its liberty, we should make sure that student "service" is truly voluntary.

A Strategy for Writing a Timed Essay

When writing an essay under time constraints, you need a clear and thoughtful strategy. Look over the following suggestions, and then write a plan of your own that takes into consideration your particular strengths and weaknesses.

1. **Read the questions in the writing topic.** Circle the interrogatives (question words: who, what, where, when, why, and how) in the first part of the writing topic.

2. **Read the essay** and underline the information that specifically answers the question(s). Make margin notes.

3. **Write your summary** in a manner that responds directly to the question(s) asked.

4. **Reread the writing topic.** Determine which point of the author's argument you are being asked to take a position on. Think about what you believe and why you believe the way you do. Write your thesis to express that position clearly.

5. **Write a series of paragraphs** that offer developed reasons and concrete examples that support your thesis. In each paragraph, be sure to show the connection between your reasons, your examples, and your thesis.

6. **Write a conclusion.** It should provide a sense of closure for your essay. It can be a restatement of your thesis or a recalling of certain important information in your summary. It must, however, leave no doubt as to your own position on the topic.

7. **Proofread your complete essay.** Then double-check grammar and spelling by reading from the end of your essay to the beginning. Read your essay again to check that your ideas are fully developed and logically connected.

One Way You Might Budget Your Time:

Here is one person's time plan for a timed final essay exam. You should arrange your own time plan in a way that works best for your particular skills and the time you have.

Step 1: Reading the question—5 minutes

Step 2: Reading/marking the reading selection—20 minutes

Step 3: Writing the summary—15 minutes

Step 4: Writing the thesis—10 minutes

Step 5: Supporting the thesis—60 minutes

Step 6: Writing the conclusion—10 minutes

Step 7: Proofreading the essay—45 minutes

When creating your own time schedule, carefully consider your strengths and weaknesses. If you need more time for, say, understanding the reading selection but are generally strong when it comes to writing clear, correct sentences, you might plan to spend thirty or more minutes examining and marking the reading selection, and thirty or less on proofreading your essay.

Once you create your time schedule, try to stick with it so that you take advantage of all of the stages of the writing process yet still finish on time. If you use your schedule, you won't run out of time, but neither will you waste some of the time you are given because you rushed through and neglected some important elements related to relevance, development, support, or sentence clarity and correctness. You may discover that you left something out, or that you made a mistake in the way you presented an idea or used a vocabulary word. We tend to hurry when doing timed writing, and often our hand struggles to keep up with our thoughts. Mistakes are easily made, and they can make an impact on how the essay is received by evaluators.

A CLOSER LOOK AT THE ELEMENTS OF THE CONVENTIONAL ARGUMENT ESSAY

An Introduction in an Argument Essay

Use the guidelines below to shape an introduction appropriate for your paper. Be sure to look back at the introduction once your draft is completed because you may want to revise it after you have worked through your ideas more systematically; at that point, you are more likely to understand your argument better than when you began to draft. For this reason, many writers draft their introduction after they have written their body paragraphs.

The introduction is often the most difficult part of an essay to draft. A paper's opening creates a first impression for readers, and deciding how to begin can be difficult. The introduction should do three things: capture readers' attention, set the stage for the paper's argument, and present the thesis statement. Length is also an important consideration: An introductory paragraph should be only as long as necessary to provide a context for the argument that the paper will develop. Too much detail or background information will bog down your introduction and leave readers feeling confused. Save the details for the paper's body.

Customarily, the last sentence of the introduction is the **thesis statement**. A strong thesis statement is essential to developing, organizing, and writing a successful persuasive paper. An essay isn't successful simply because its grammar is correct or because it has an introduction, a set of body paragraphs, and a conclusion. These components must have a thesis statement to tie them together and give them significance. The thesis statement is an important part of the introduction because it unifies the essay and gives it a purpose. Including it at the end of the introduction ensures that readers clearly understand the paper's purpose at the outset.

Hints

- **Don't offer a flat explanation of what you will cover in the paper:**
  "This essay will discuss…," for example.
- **Avoid clichés:**
  "It is certainly true that love is blind."
- **Avoid meaningless platitudes:**
  "People often find it difficult to get along with others in this world."
- **Do not resort to overly broad statements:**
  "Since the beginning of time, humans have tried to live peacefully."

The essays in *Write It* follow the same format, and the introduction for each essay assignment will be effective if you follow these steps:

1st: Introduce the reading selection by giving the author's first and last name and the selection's title.

2nd: Give a directed summary of the reading selection (see the next page).

3rd: Present your thesis statement (be sure it answers the second part of the writing topic).

Guidelines for Writing a Directed Summary

Writing a successful summary of a reading selection can be challenging because it requires a thorough understanding of the reading's argument and supporting material. Before attempting to summarize a reading, be sure to spend time analyzing it using "A Step-by-Step Strategy for Reading Thoughtfully."

The summary guidelines we give are based on a specific type of writing assignment. In other words, *Write It* works solely with a particular type of writing assignment—one that asks you to read another writer's essay and respond to its argument in an essay of your own. With this kind of writing assignment, you will be required to write a focused summary of a particular aspect of the assigned reading selection. That focus will be determined by the first question in the writing topic that follows the reading selection. The summary you write will be limited in scope to the focus established in the writing topic question. The directed summary will also set the context and terms of the argument you will have to address in your response.

A directed summary is a summary that requires a specific answer. The goal is not necessarily to summarize an entire essay but to summarize the parts of the essay that are relevant to the first question in the writing topic. To write a directed summary that is complete and correct, follow the steps below:

Preparation

Step 1: Carefully read through the reading selection and the writing topic questions that follow it.

Step 2: Underline the key terms in the first question.

Step 3: Locate in the essay the specific sentences that provide information relevant to answering the first question.

Step 4: Decide on the answer to that question. Be sure you have read through the essay more than once and are ready to provide a thorough and correct response.

Writing

Step 1: In or near the opening sentence, include the title of the essay (in quotation marks) and the full name of the author (after the first mention, the author should be referred to by last name only).

Step 2: Use direct quotation sparingly and only when appropriate, to emphasize the answer the author provides to the question.

Step 3: In your own words, fully answer the first question in the writing topic.

Step 4: Explain this answer using careful reasoning.

Hints

- Do not include minor details or points.
- Do not insert your own opinions or ideas and attribute them to the author.
- Do not ordinarily include examples.

Strategies for Developing Your Ideas

Students often say that they know *how* to write an essay—that is, they know it should have an introduction, a thesis statement, supporting body paragraphs, and a conclusion—but they don't have anything to write *about*. They don't know what to say, and they can't think of any experiences they have had that they can use. Consider using the techniques below for exploring your thoughts and finding strategies that work.

Time is the crucial element here. It takes time to think carefully and systematically about a subject. You will have to focus your thoughts and have patience in order for your mind to work, to develop insights that go beyond surface impressions and quick, easy judgments. You should do much of your thinking in writing—this aspect is very important. Writing your thoughts down will give them definition and clarity.

If you find yourself without good ideas about a subject, try these strategies. You might not use all of them for any given assignment. Instead, look them over and choose those that seem most promising for the particular piece of writing you are developing:

1. *Focus*: Write down the issue of the reading selection that you want to explore; a simple phrase may be enough.

2. *Response*: Look over the selection again (and the reading and summary questions you have answered) and list its ideas. Write down:
   a. any questions and/or doubts you have about these ideas, and list your reasons;
   b. any points the writer makes that you find persuasive, and the reasons you find them convincing;
   c. your thoughtful impression of the reading selection;
   d. a final conclusion about the selection's argument, its weaknesses, and its strengths.

Hint

Your responses here do not have to be polished. Allow yourself to write freely, putting down all ideas that come to you. You will sort them out later.

3. *Reflection*: Now you need some data, some basic observations from your own experiences that you can examine and use to draw conclusions or insights. First write down, in a rough list, any personal memories you have that seem to relate to the subject you are writing on. Do a few minutes of freewriting to explore these memories. Try some *focused freewriting*, whereby you keep the

essay's general subject in mind, but write down everything that you can, even things you roughly associate with the subject. Stay with it until you feel you have something substantial, something your readers will find thoughtful and compelling.

If you need more structure, try using these general guidelines for each incident:

a. Begin by simply recounting what you remember: Make it as brief as possible, but don't omit anything that seems important.

b. Now expand your thinking: Try to speculate about the importance of the memory and its relevance to the subject you are exploring.

c. Look over what you have written: Underline the ideas that seem to be important. Think about the way they relate to the reading selection's ideas. How are your ideas like the selection's? How are they different?

d. Take note: Consider any judgment words in your freewriting, such as "sometimes," "always," "seems to," "might mean," "only when," and "but if." These will help you formulate the position you want to take in your thesis statement.

4. *Expansion*: Keeping the subject in mind, write down any relevant experiences you can think of from the world at large. Do you know of any examples from books, the news, movies, and your cultural awareness in general? Freewrite for each example that comes to mind.

5. *A Reconsideration of Your Freewriting*

a. First, begin by simply recounting the event or text, summarizing its main elements as briefly as you can without omitting important elements

b. Now move beyond the basic facts and try to explore the implications of each for the subject. What thoughts come to mind as you reflect on the event or text? What do those thoughts suggest about the subject? Take your freewriting as far as you can for each event or text you listed.

c. Then, look over all that you have written. Underline the ideas that seem to you to be important. Try to explain in writing how they relate to the reading selection's ideas. How are they like the reading selection's? How are they different?

d. Finally, look for the judgment words. These will help you formulate the position you want to take in your thesis statement. What seems to be your strongest feeling about the subject, the one most dominant in your freewriting?

6. *Shape*: Consider what you have underlined and the judgment words you found. What significance do they have once you consider them all together? What do they "add up to"?

a. Group parts of your freewriting together. Find some main ideas that you came back to two or three times using different experiences, examples, or texts. Try to identify all of the main ideas you find, and write out the connection between them and the underlined portions of your freewriting.

b. Explore the parts you underlined and the implications you noted by asking yourself the following questions:

§ Which parts seem important, and why?

§ How do the lists you made fit together, or what do they add up to?

§ Do any parts of your freewriting contradict other parts, or do parts have similar ideas?

§ What do either the contradictions or the similarities suggest?

c. Identify the ideas that you feel strongly about. Write about the reasons they are important and the way they relate to the subject you are exploring.

Hint

Sometimes it is too restrictive to think in terms of "for or against" the reading selection's issue. There are often more than two positions on a topic, and disagreeing with the position taken in the reading selection may mean that, while the selection's ideas may be sound, the conclusions drawn are not as convincing, in your mind, as the conclusions you want to draw.

Once you've done some freewriting and located important topics and supporting details, you have the foundation pieces to create an outline.

Hint

Your goal is to uncover what you know and develop it so that you can show your readers how you arrived at your main ideas and how your ideas led to your thesis statement.

Writing a Supporting Paragraph for Your Thesis Statement

The body paragraphs make up the largest part of an essay, and each paragraph should develop one important point in support of the thesis statement. Paragraphs should be unified around a central point and should contain concrete evidence that clarifies and supports that central point. Readers need concrete evidence as examples that help them to understand your ideas. Therefore, body paragraphs usually open with a topic sentence and include evidence, a discussion of the evidence, and an explanation of how the paragraph's subject matter connects to your thesis claim. Writing a well-developed paragraph can be easy once you understand the paragraph's conventional structure. Here is a useful memory device that will help you construct well-developed body paragraphs:

Remember the 4Cs:
Controlling idea sentence
Corroborating details
Careful explanation of why the details are significant
Connection to the thesis statement

Once you determine your thesis statement, you can develop your supporting paragraphs using the following guidelines:

Controlling idea sentence

First, write a topic sentence that announces the point you want to make in the paragraph.

Corroborating details

Then, think of specific examples that will help you explain and prove the point.

Careful explanation of why the details are significant

Now, carefully explain how each example proves the point you are making in the paragraph.

Connection to the thesis statement

Be sure to connect your examples and explanation to the position you have taken in your thesis statement. Tell your reader what the paragraph's point and examples have to do with your argument.

Here's an example: Thesis: The violence on television desensitizes viewers to real violence and can ultimately lead to a thoughtless and uncaring society.

Controlling idea sentence for a paragraph supporting the thesis statement
Write a sentence stating the point you want to make in the paragraph:
After seeing casual violence repeatedly on television, viewers come to see real-life violence in terms of entertainment rather than real human tragedy.

Corroborating details
Think of some examples that will show that people see violence in terms of entertainment rather than real tragedy. Here are some sample sentences:

- A couple of weeks ago, there was a pause in the traffic flow because there was an accident on the freeway and people always want to slow down and look.
- The last time I watched the evening news, reporters spent most of the time reporting on acts of violence in our society rather than on more positive events, I think because more people want to hear about violence.

Careful explanation of why the details are significant
Explain how these examples show that people see violence in terms of entertainment rather than real-life tragedy.

Connection to the thesis statement
Explain how we can understand this view of violence as an indication of society's growing lack of thought and care (paragraph's controlling idea), and how this is a direct result of television violence (tie to thesis statement).

Here is a sample body paragraph from a student paper on George Orwell's *Down and Out in Paris and London*. See if you can follow the 4Cs paragraph development.

The paper's thesis statement: In *Down and Out in Paris and London*, George Orwell shows the poor not as criminals but as people with no options.

(***Controlling idea/topic sentence***) Orwell's novel shows that poverty ultimately degrades character because the poor cannot afford ethics. (***Corroborating details***) As a *plongeur* at Hotel X, Orwell is forced to exist in an environment where almost anything goes, and he has to adapt in order to be accepted and keep his job. He recounts how, even to be hired for work, he must lie about his intentions. He is told by his friend Boris that "a *plongeur* can[not] afford a sense of honour" (60), and so the narrator hides the fact that he intends to break his contract with the hotel by walking away as soon as his job at the Auberge is available. He says that later he realizes how "foolish it had been to have any scruples" (60) because the hotels do not act honorably toward their employees, and the system seems to be every man for himself. Orwell also tells of thieves among the staff, and of how the doorkeeper regularly robs him of his wages. (***Careful explanation of why the details are significant***) The social order of the workers at the Hotel X operates openly by dishonesty and drunkenness, and Orwell cannot avoid joining this order if he wants to earn money to live. (***Connection to the thesis statement***) Given a choice between honor and the necessities of life, the poor in the novel often seem to have little choice but to do whatever is necessary to earn their keep. Dignity and honor are luxuries that they cannot always afford.

An Introduction to Logical Fallacies

A writer's job is to provide as much evidence and support as possible for his or her thesis. It is important, however, that the arguments a writer offers to defend that thesis be sound. If some of the arguments the writer presents are illogical or unfair, the writer will undermine his or her own position and lose credibility with readers.

Arguments that lack reason or justice are called *fallacies*. Fallacies are simply false arguments. Often, writers are so enthusiastic about their own position that they make false claims, unethical arguments, or assertions that cannot be proven by the evidence at hand. The best way to guard against spurious arguments is to become familiar with some of the most common types of fallacies and learn to recognize them in your own writing and the writing of others.

Fallacies fall into two categories. The first category contains unethical arguments. These arguments attempt to manipulate the reader emotionally or attack the opposing position in some way that is unjust. Here are some examples of fallacies that are manipulative or unfair:

1. *Ad hominem*—using a personal attack on the person rather than the argument itself

    example: The members of the Glee Club are a bunch of prima donnas, so, of course, they would oppose spending money to charter a bus instead of using cars to go to Disneyland for Senior Ditch Day.

2. *Birds of a feather*—using guilt by association to blame the person for actions of friends or family

    example: John Smith's sister has a drug problem, so even though he is a qualified nurse, he shouldn't be trusted in a job that requires him to administer prescribed narcotics to dying patients.

3. *Sob story*—using a sad situation or dramatic case to manipulate the readers' emotions

    example: Santiago Cortez was the only member of his family to survive a horrific plane crash, so he is the best candidate for mayor of our town.

The majority of fallacies are illogical because the thinking behind their arguments is flawed; the conclusions offered by these fallacies follow neither inductive nor deductive reasoning. Here are some examples of false reasoning:

1. *Circular reasoning*—restating the same argument in other words instead of giving evidence or proof

    example: The president has thought a lot about health care, so his plan is the most well-thought-out plan available.

2. *Post hoc, ergo propter hoc* (Latin for "after this, therefore because of this")—assuming because one event follows another, the second is caused by the first

    example: On Saturday night, Eun Hee went to the movies with her girl-friends, and on Sunday her boyfriend Jun Ho broke up with her. Jun Ho ended his relationship with Eun Hee because she went out with her friends.

3. *False dichotomy*—assuming an either/or choice so that the writer's position seems the only correct one

    example: Either we eradicate the Pit Bull breed altogether, or children playing outside will not be safe from dog attacks.

4. *Hasty generalization*—basing a conclusion on limited evidence

    example: My dog leaves the carrots in his bowl when I give him my leftover beef stew. Therefore, dogs do not eat vegetables.

5. *False authority*—citing a source that has no validity in terms of the subject

    example: Li'l' Hound, a popular rapper, took his mother to Mexico for expensive cancer drug treatments unapproved by the FDA, so the medicine must really work.

Transitions

Connect *or* Correct

Essays need transitions to link the ideas in individual sentences to each other and to tie paragraphs together. Transitions are the words or phrases that help relate thoughts and ideas to each other. Without transitions, sentences are merely lists, and paragraphs can seem disconnected from each other.

Transitions link concepts in one of two ways: They can signal that individual sentences or paragraphs extend a train of thought (***connect***), or they can predict for the reader that whatever follows will change the direction of thought (***correct***). Careful use of transitions improves the overall coherence of your essay.

A number of categories of transitional words ***connect*** sentences and paragraphs. Here are some of the kinds of transitions and some examples of words and phrases that ***connect***:

1. *time*—afterward, later, meanwhile, next, now, suddenly, then
2. *continuation*—also, finally, furthermore, in addition, secondly
3. *reasons*—for this reason, to this end, because of that
4. *examples*—for example, for instance, to illustrate,
5. *assertion*—in fact, indeed, to tell the truth
6. *repetition*—as already noted, in other words
7. *similarity*—in the same way, likewise, similarly
8. *space*—here, nearby, opposite
9. *linking*—consequently, therefore, as a result

Here are some kinds of transitions and some examples of words and phrases that ***correct***:

1. *alternative*—besides, instead, or
2. *contrast*—however, in contrast, on the other hand, on the contrary

Smooth transitions between sentences and paragraphs can be achieved in other ways besides the use of particular transitional words and phrases. Some other ways to link ideas and thoughts are:

1. *repetition*—Intentionally repeating a word or phrase from the previous sentence or paragraph in the new construction
2. *parallelism*—Using a similar structure in consecutive sentences or paragraphs. In other words, begin paragraphs with very similar sentences or with sentences noticeably similar in structure. Within a paragraph, repetition of sentence structure can be used for emphasis and to draw attention to connected ideas.

An Application Exercise

Here is a paragraph taken from Vicki Xiong's argument on plagiarism, which appears on pages 12–14. For each of the blank spaces in the paragraph, rewrite the sentence that follows it and include one of the transitions listed above. Be sure to check your sentences to be sure you have capitalized and punctuated them correctly. _____ Educators should make a commitment and join forces with other fellow educators across America in the fight against plagiarism. Teachers should make it a duty to teach all students what plagiarism is and to drill the ethical consequences of plagiarism into each and every student before they enter college. _____ The conditioning should start as soon as students enter grade school. In the first grade, little lessons on cheating should be taught, and as students progress each year from grade school to middle school to high school, lessons in cheating, academic dishonesty, and plagiarism should be reiterated in more detail and observed under a stricter set of guidelines. _____ The common excuse of "I was never taught that" will instantly be eliminated, as all students will be informed from an early age . _____ The repercussions of plagiarism should be on a no-tolerance basis. If students are assured that when caught, they will be punished to the maximum, this will undoubtedly stimulate a fear and thus draw students away from the lure of dishonesty and cheating. Teachers and professors alike must be firm on implementation of the consequences when occurrences do happen; they must carry out the punishment—not just let students go with a warning. Then instructors will become the role models for students that they should be.

Conclusions

The conclusion's primary purpose is to provide closure for your essay, but there are several effective ways to accomplish that goal. Consider the strategies below so that you can call on the most appropriate one for every essay you write.

Any essay that includes discussion of more than one point, idea, or example requires a conclusion. Without a conclusion, the reader has no sense of closure, no certainty that you have come to the end of your argument. It is important that you let the reader know that your essay is complete, not because you have run out of things to say or time to say them, but because you have fully explored and supported your thesis. The conclusion of the essay is also the place for you to impress upon the reader the importance of considering your ideas.

A good conclusion accomplishes two tasks:

1. It makes the reader aware of the finality of your argument.
2. It leaves the reader with an understanding of the significance of your argument.

Hint

Check to see that the conclusion of your essay fulfills the promise suggested by your introduction.

Writing the conclusion of your essay will offer you many choices and many challenges. You may choose a simple, formal ending, or you may choose to be somewhat creative and less conventional. Familiarize yourself with the possibilities below, and then decide which works best for your particular essay:

TYPES OF CONCLUSIONS

Brief Summary	"In conclusion . . . "To summarize briefly . . .
Significance of Subject	"All these matters need to be understood because . . .
Most Important Point	"Lastly, remember that . . .
Request for Action or Opinion	"X must be changed . . .
Useful Quotation	"In the words of . . .
Emotional Statement	an outcry, appeal, or plea such as "Let's all move to . . . " or "Please . . ."
Interesting Anecdote	a short, relevant story, or a reference to a story mentioned in the introduction . . .
Directive	"In the future" or "From now on" . . .

Sample Scoring Rubric

High Pass (A, A-, B+)

This score indicates superior writing skills. An essay receiving a high pass has a sophisticated style marked by variety in sentence structure, effective word usage, and mastery of the conventions of written English. The content of the essay responds directly to the writing topic with a persuasive argument and reasoned examples that address and explore the issue in a focused, organized, and thoroughly developed manner.

Pass (B, B-)

This score indicates strong writing skills. A passing essay characteristically shows some variety of usage in syntax and vocabulary and demonstrates competence in grammar, punctuation, and mechanics. It presents a response to the writing topic that is thoughtful and appropriate. Its argument is well developed with relevant examples and clear reasoning.

Low Pass (C+, C)

This score indicates satisfactory writing skills, which may be marginal in some areas. It often has some sentence-level errors, but these errors do not interfere with comprehension, and, for the most part, there is control of grammar, punctuation, and mechanics. The content provides an appropriate but sometimes partial or somewhat abbreviated answer to the writing topic. There is an attempt to focus and organize, but ideas and examples may not be logically sequenced or may be so brief as to lack clarity.

High Fail (C-)

This score indicates a problem in one or more of the following areas. Sentences may lack variety, may use vocabulary in an imprecise manner, or may contain an unacceptable number of errors in grammar, punctuation, and mechanics. The content of the essay might not adequately respond to the writing topic due to some misreading of the topic, or it may fail to develop its ideas with logic and/or examples. The essay may lack focus because it offers no thesis or central idea, it digresses, or it provides no discernible pattern of organization.

Fail (D+, D)

This score indicates clearly inadequate writing skills. Sentences tend to be simplistic and structurally repetitive. Errors in grammar, punctuation, mechanics, and word choice are numerous. The essay's content reveals a misunderstanding of the writing topic itself. There are not sufficient examples or any other details or ideas relevant to the topic. Paragraphs are disconnected, and the point, or thesis, of the essay is not clear.

Low Fail (D-, F)

This score indicates a complete lack of familiarity with the conventions of written English. There is no control of grammar, punctuation, mechanics, or vocabulary, and the sentences may be unintelligible. The content of the essay fails to respond to the writing topic in any logical manner, and it ordinarily fixates on a single idea or detail. There is no organizational pattern, and what development there is comes from repetition of a digression stemming from the single idea or detail.

A CLOSER LOOK AT YOUR CONTROL AT THE SENTENCE LEVEL

Proofreading Your Essay for Mistakes in Grammar, Punctuation, and Mechanics

Students often feel that their work is completed once they have revised their rough draft by honing the content and arguments it contains, but they should still carefully examine their sentences to eliminate any errors. Frequently, errors in the rough draft are overlooked during the revision process because writers are focused on idea development and structure. Any writer should review one last time for errors in grammar, punctuation, spelling, or word choice. While word processing programs can be helpful in finding some mistakes, computers are limited in this area. It is, therefore, the writer's responsibility to proofread and edit before printing out a final draft.

Examine the following ten errors commonly made by writers. Becoming familiar with these errors will help you to avoid them.

1. Underline the verbs and then
   * check to see that they agree with their subjects. (For help, consult a handbook.)
   * make sure you have used the correct verb tense. (For help, consult a handbook.)
   * when possible, change "to be" verbs (is, are, was, etc.) to action words.
     Flat: Gloria Watkins is a good writer.
     Active: Gloria Watkins writes brilliantly.

2. Mark sentences that contain informal language or slang. Rewrite them using more formal language.
   No: Kids' fairy tales are, like, really great to hear when you're a kid.
   Yes: We all enjoyed listening to fairy tales when we were young.

3. Circle all the pronouns in your draft and then
   * Check to be sure that they clearly refer to specific nouns; change any unclear pronouns to nouns.
   * be sure that the pronouns agree with what they refer to.
     No: Even though a person may witness an accident, they will not be able to remember exactly what happened.
     Yes: Even though a person may witness an accident, he or she will not be able to remember exactly what happened.

4. Identify sentences close to one another in the paper that use the same word two or more times (ignoring common words such as "the" or "to"). Eliminate the repetition by
   - looking for synonyms to replace repeated words.
   - seeing if you can combine two sentences into one and eliminate repetition that way.

5. To vary the pace of your sentences, try changing the construction of three or four of your sentences. For example, you can reorder the word(s) or turn clauses into phrases.

   Every culture has its own celebrations and rituals to mark special days.

   Celebrations and rituals mark special days in every culture.

   A writer might revise a paper several times before he or she submits it for a class.

   Before submitting a paper for a class, a writer might revise it several times.

6. Be sure there are no commas joining two complete sentences. For each comma splice, use one of the following methods to correct the error:

   comma splice error: Barbara decided to run for public office, however, she knew that the odds were against her winning.
   - Change the comma to a semicolon.

     Barbara decided to run for public office; however, she knew that the odds were against her winning.
   - Change the comma to a period and a capital letter.

     Barbara decided to run for public office. However, she knew that the odds were against her winning.
   - Link the sentences with a coordinating conjunction (for, and, nor, but, or, yet, so)

     Barbara decided to run for public office, but she knew that the odds were against her winning.
   - Turn the second sentence into a dependent clause or a phrase.

     Although she knew that the odds were against her winning, Barbara decided to run for public office.

7. Rewrite any sentence where "you" is used; eliminate "you" by replacing it with "I," "we," or another noun or pronoun.

   No: You can always identify a person who is wearing a uniform.

   Yes: We can always identify a person that is wearing a uniform.

   Yes: Everyone can identify a person that is wearing a uniform.

8. Use a dictionary to look up words you are unsure of and to make sure you've used them correctly.

9. Use spell check to eliminate misspelled words.

10. Be sure all sentences begin with a capital letter and have the appropriate punctuation mark at the end.

Assessing Your Grammar Mastery

Below are two diagnostic tests that check grammar mastery. Take Test #1. Next, check your answers with an answer key (your instructor will supply one) and mark those you got wrong. Then, fill in the assessment sheet to identify your grammar weaknesses. The assessment sheet will give you a focus for further study. You might, for example, use the index in your handbook to find out why you made the errors you made and how to correct them.

Diagnostic Test 1

In exercises 1–10, circle the correct word in each set of parentheses

Regular/Irregular Verbs

1. Clive Staples Lewis is best known as C. S. Lewis, the man who (brang / brung / brought) us the Narnia books.
2. His legal name was Clive, but his friends and family (knew / knowed / known) him as Jack.
3. Millions of children and adults love the Narnia books and are familiar with their illustrations (drew / drawed / drawn) by Pauline Baynes.
4. Lewis, who had already (wrote / writed / written) a science-fiction trilogy, (begun / began / begin) the first Narnia volume in the 1940s.
5. *The Lion, the Witch and the Wardrobe* first (come / came) out in 1950.

Subject-Verb Agreement

6. *The Lion, the Witch and the Wardrobe* (begin / begins) in 1940, when the four Pevensie children go to stay with an elderly and eccentric professor.
7. The group of children (have / has) been sent to the country because of Nazi air raids on London.
8. One of the children (hide / hides) in an old wardrobe during a game of hide and seek; pushing her way to the back, Lucy finds herself next to a lamppost in the middle of a forest.
9. She meets a faun named Mr. Tumnus. He and she (sips / sip) tea in his comfortable cave.
10. Neither she nor the faun (seem / seems) surprised that they both speak the same language.

For exercises 11-17, write a C next to any passage that is clear and correct. Write an X next to any incorrect passage, and <u>underline</u> any pronouns with disagreement or reference problems.

Pronoun Agreement and Reference

____ 11. Lucy is intrigued by the faun and enjoys their stories, but then Mr. Tumnus begins to cry.

____ 12. Mr. Tumnus admits to Lucy that he is employed by an evil queen, the White Witch. She keeps Narnia in perpetual winter and has told him to capture any humans he finds, but he is kind-hearted and allows her to go back through the wardrobe to England.

____ 13. Peter, Susan, and Edmund do not believe that Narnia exists, and he begins to tease Lucy.

____ 14. Lucy has no evidence because, instead of opening up onto a forest, the wardrobe has become an ordinary piece of furniture with a solid back panel; this is how Lucy originally got into Narnia.

____ 15. Next, Edmund hides in the wardrobe, meets the White Witch, and eats her enchanted food. As a result, he falls under her spell.

____ 16. After Edmund returns, he refuses to admit that Lucy was right. If anyone has read this far, you will realize that Edmund is a sulky and spiteful boy.

____ 17. Sometimes, children in a large family will adopt negative behaviors so he or she will receive more attention.

In 18-21, write a C next to any correct passage. Write an X next to any incorrect passage, and underline any dangling or misplaced modifiers.

Dangling/Misplaced Modifiers

____ 18. Peter and Susan, the two oldest children, approach the professor with worries that Lucy is mentally unstable. But the professor says that Lucy might be telling the truth.

____ 19. A historical landmark, the professor allows sightseers to tour his house.

____ 20. Trying to avoid a group of tourists, the wardrobe once again becomes a passageway to Narnia.

____ 21. Excited to be in Narnia together, the four children decide to visit Mr. Tumnus.

In 22-40, write a C next to any correct passage and an X next to any incorrect passage.

Run-On Sentences

____ 22. A terrible surprise awaits them Mr. Tumnus has been arrested by the White Witch.

____ 23. Lucy is sad because she knows that Mr. Tumnus was arrested for not betraying her.

____ 24. The children decide to help Mr. Tumnus if they can. Soon a friendly beaver approaches them.

____ 25. Mr. Beaver introduces the children to Mrs. Beaver they all have a fine meal and begin to plan.

____ 26. Mr. Beaver tells the children that the White Witch may have turned; Mr. Tumnus into a statue the beaver also informs them that they cannot save the faun by themselves.

Comma Splices

____ 27. The children learn about Aslan, a great lion who is the King of Narnia.

____ 28. Mr. Beaver says the children must have help, they must meet Aslan at the Stone Table.

____ 29. Mr. Beaver recites an old rhyme, according to the prophesy, humans, also known as Sons of Adam and Daughters of Eve, will sit on the throne at Cair Paravel and overcome the evil in Narnia.

____ 30. The White Witch knows that the four children can put an end to her wicked reign, so she wants to make sure that the prophecy is never fulfilled.

____ 31. Edmund quietly leaves, Mr. Beaver knows that the boy has gone to the White Witch.

Fragments

____ 32. Because Edmund has eaten enchanted food provided by the White Witch, he plans to betray his family to her.

____ 33. Which frightens everyone.

____ 34. Assembling food for the journey and making up a pack for each of them by Mrs. Beaver.

____ 35. When the children and beavers are partway through the journey and are given presents by Father Christmas, whom Americans know as Santa Claus.

Parallelism

____ 36. Father Christmas gives Lucy a dagger and a vial of healing potion, Peter a sword and shield, and Susan receives a bow and arrows, as well as an ivory horn.

____ 37. In true English fashion, Father Christmas also provides a pot of tea, a bowl of sugar, and some cream.

____ 38. Meanwhile, Edmund is having a terrible time. The Queen has interrogated him, he is put into a cell, and gets only bread and water.

____ 39. Edmund is not only hungry but also fears the White Witch.

____ 40. She takes Edmund on a long sleigh journey, and he wishes he were warm, well-fed, and that he is having a bad dream.

In 41-55, circle the correct word in each set of parentheses.

Adjectives/Adverbs

41. Spring is finally coming to Narnia, so the sleigh must be abandoned. This necessity makes the White Witch very (angry / angrily).

42. The other three children and the beavers arrive at the Stone Table, where the (patient / patiently) Aslan waits.

43. The White Witch prepares to kill Edmund. Clearly, she does not feel (badly / bad) for him.

44. She thinks that she can thwart the prophecy if she kills a Son of Adam, but she does not realize that Aslan has a (more deeply / deeper) knowledge of magic.

45. Aslan (willing / willingly) offers his own life instead. The White Witch agrees to his bargain.

Apostrophes

46. That night, Lucy and Susan cannot sleep. They probably (should'nt / shouldn't) leave their tent and wander around, but they do anyway.

47. Aslan (let's / lets / lets') the girls walk with him before he surrenders to the White Witch.

48. After she kills Aslan, the Witch thinks that victory is (hers / hers' / her's).

49. But (Aslans' / Aslan's) magic is stronger than the (Witch'es / Witch's / Witches'), so he comes back to life.

50. While the White Witch is in the field, preparing for battle, Aslan heads to her castle. His breath turns the statues into flesh again. He also breathes on Mr. (Tumnus / Tumnus's / Tumnuses) statue.

Capital Letters

51. Before rejoining Peter and Edmund in their battle against the White Witch, Aslan liberates many creatures, some of which do not exist in the (english / English) countryside.

52. Speaking of Edmund; Peter says, ("We'd / "we'd) have been beaten if it hadn't been for him."

53. Using her potion on Edmund, Lucy heals his wounds, but Aslan reminds her that others are waiting. "Yes, I know," (replies / Replies) Lucy, and she moves on to someone else.

54. Now that the White Witch is defeated, the children live long and eventful lives as kings and queens in Narnia. As adults, they encounter a familiar lamppost in the woods. In a later book, this location is a well-known geographical landmark called (Lantern Waste / lantern waste).

55. The four siblings keep walking and emerge from the wardrobe into the house of their old friend, the eccentric professor. No time has passed, and they are children again. Here the story ends. But fortunately, there are six more books in the (series / Series).

Sentence Skills Assessment for Diagnostic Test 1

Problem	Needs Review	Needs Study	Completed
Regular/ Irregular Verbs			
Subject-Verb Agreement			
Pronoun Agreement and Reference			
Dangling/ Misplaced Modifiers			
Run-On Sentences			
Comma Splices			
Fragments			
Parallelism			
Adjectives/ Adverbs			
Apostrophes			
Capital Letters			

Diagnostic Test 2

Write X in the answer space if you think a mistake appears in the sentence. Write C in the answer space if you think the sentence is correct.

Fragments

_____ 1. *The Lord of the Rings*, a work by J. R. R. Tolkien that is made up of three parts: *The Fellowship of the Ring*, *The Two Towers*, and *The Return of the King*.

_____ 2. In the first part of the trilogy, *The Fellowship of the Ring*, a young hobbit, Frodo Baggins, inherits from his uncle Bilbo a ring of great importance.

_____ 3. The ring, an instrument of absolute power, was lost by the evil Sauron.

_____ 4. When Gandalf, a wizard, warns Frodo that he should leave the Shire and keep the ring out of Sauron's hands.

_____ 5. While Frodo and his fellow travelers must carry the ring across Middle-earth to the Cracks of Doom, in the kingdom of Mordor, where they can destroy it forever.

Run-On Sentences and Comma Splices

_____ 6. They must cross Sauron's kingdom, where Sauron, the dark Lord of Mordor, is amassing an army of orcs he hopes to take the ring and control the world.

_____ 7. The ring's ability to endow its possessor with absolute power exerts a corrupting influence on those who come in contact with it.

_____ 8. Frodo takes the responsibility of carrying the ring to Mordor, he must have the strength and ability to resist the constant temptation of its power.

_____ 9. In addition to his strength of character, Frodo relies on the help of three hobbit friends, Sam, Pippin, and Merry, who join him on his journey, and their loyalty and bravery are put to the ultimate test as they try to fulfill their quest.

_____ 10. Sam is decent, simple, and honest, Pippin is homespun and optimistic, Merry is clever, fun-loving, and brave.

Standard Verbs

_____ 11. Hobbits are gentle, and they enjoy the simple things in life, such as smoking pipes, eating, and storytelling.

_____ 12. Hobbits reach an average height of three and a half feet and lives to be about one hundred years old.

_____ 13. The humans Aragorn and Boromir, both valiant and skilled at fighting, officially joins the Fellowship at the Council of Elrond.

_____ 14. An elf named Legolas and a dwarf named Gimli also join the Fellowship and accompanies Frodo for a part of his journey to Mordor.

_____ 15. Legolas is the son of an elf king, and, in the many dangerous confrontations the Fellowship faces, he will prove his skill as a superior archer.

Irregular Verbs

_____ 16. Gimli represents the dwarfs of Middle-earth and fighted with an axe, and Legolas and Gimli grow to respect each other's differences and rely on each other in battle.

_____ 17. The evil Saruman, once the head of the Council of the Wise, has gave in to the dark temptations of the ring and is willing to use his grotesque, savage Uruk-hai army to get the ring from Frodo and seize control of the world.

_____ 18. When Frodo is wounded, Aragorn (called Strider) leads the group safely to the country of the elves, where Elrond heals Frodo's wound, and everyone gets needed rest.

_____ 19. The group leaves elf country and heads south, but it be December when they depart, and a heavy snow begins to fall.

_____ 20. The snow becomed overwhelming as they cross Mount Caradhras, so they dig their way out and turn back.

Subject-Verb Agreement

_____ 21. Gandalf decide to pass through the mountains by traveling below them through the caves of Moria, but the caves are dangerous and the group resist.

_____ 22. Gandalf is the only one who knows his way through the caves, and he lead them along safely for two nights.

_____ 23. Then the group are attacked by orcs, and, as they run for the bridge leading out of the caves, the evil Balrog confronts them with a sword of fire.

_____ 24. Gandalf destroys the bridge and sends the Balrog to its death, but in the battle Gandalf loses his footing and falls to the bottomless depths below.

_____ 25. The remaining members of the Fellowship escapes to safety on the other side, but with Gandalf gone, they are thrown into despair and turn to Aragorn for leadership.

Parallelism

_____ 26. They spend ten days walking along the Anduin River, eating lightly, and to watch for orcs and the Dark Riders.

_____ 27. Sam spots Gollum, who has followed them since they left the caves of Moria, and he feels worried, protective of Frodo, and suspicion.

_____ 28. The conclusion of *The Fellowship of the Ring* recounts Frodo's decision about which path to take to Mordor and Boromir's attempt to take the ring from him.

_____ 29. Frodo finally decides to go to Mordor alone; he does not want his friends to suffer, he knows that they will try to protect him from the danger of Mordor, and the ring must be destroyed.

_____ 30. As the first book of the trilogy ends, Frodo steals away from the group with Sam, who refuses to leave his side, and the two hobbits set out alone looking for a path to Mordor.

Illogical Shifts

_____ 31. *The Fellowship of the Ring* portrays a variety of cultures that will make up Middle-earth, such as hobbits, elves, dwarfs, humans, wizards, orcs, Dark Riders, and Uruk-hai.

_____ 32. Each culture has its own way of life, customs, myths, ways of dress, and even style of fighting that the story develops for you.

_____ 33. *The Fellowship of the Ring* teaches readers that, in spite of our personal and cultural differences, you can be stronger by working together.

_____ 34. The first book of the trilogy keeps readers in suspense and looking forward to the second book to find out if evil Sauron, the Dark Lord, can reclaim the ring and reestablish his power over Middle-earth.

Sentence Skills Assessment for Diagnostic Test 2

Problem	Needs Review	Needs Study	Completed
Fragments			
Run-On Sentences and Comma Splices			
Standard Verbs			
Irregular Verbs			
Subject-Verb Agreement			
Parallelism			
Illogical Shifts			

Writing Assignments

Composition studies have identified four basic stages of the writing process—prewriting, drafting, revising, and editing. Research has taught us that writers use these stages either explicitly or implicitly whenever they write. These stages, however, do not necessarily progress one after the other, step by step, from first to last in a linear fashion. Instead, they are recursive, meaning that you will turn back to each stage again and again as you need it over the course of a writing project. Becoming skilled in using the writing process demands time and effort. But *Write It* will support that effort by giving you clear strategies for writing, strategies that you can use each time you are asked to complete an argument essay. You will find that the more deliberate you become at making use of the recursiveness of the process, the stronger your writing will become in both form and content. Giving you practice with this aspect of writing is one of the goals of this book.

A note on the organization of Part 2: For each essay assignment, additional reading material is provided in the "Extending the Discussion" section. These supplemental readings are meant to fill in a context for the argument in the main reading selection and help you explore the subject of that selection in greater depth. You will be encouraged to think about these supplemental readings as you develop your own ideas, formulate your thesis statement, and support it with discussion and evidence. We encourage you to continue using all of the prewriting activities provided. They will ensure that you develop your thoughts and organize them within an effective essay format.

Assignment #1

"Reading and Thought"

We hope you make systematic use of the prewriting exercises presented in this unit. As you move through the assignment units in *Write It* and gain experience with the writing process, you will be able to customize these strategies to fit your own strengths and weaknesses. But for now, rely on the ones provided to ensure that you fully understand Dwight Macdonald's argument and are able to present your own position clearly and compellingly.

Macdonald is concerned about the reading matter that surrounds us in today's world, and the reading habits that he believes such reading matter encourages. As you work with his ideas, be sure to keep an open mind as you consider his argument. Explore your own experience and knowledge carefully and thoughtfully before you take a position on the issue his essay presents. Also, keep in mind the importance of responding directly to the writing topic that follows his essay, and the importance of having a clear and well-supported thesis statement as you develop, shape, and revise your own essay.

Reading and Thought

Dwight Macdonald

Dwight Macdonald (1906-82), was a part of the New York intellectuals of his time, and became famous for his attacks on middlebrow culture. He frequently carried on his debate in essays published in magazines such as the Partisan Review, *the* New Yorker, Esquire, *and the magazine he edited in the 1940s,* Politics.

Henry Luce[1] has built a journalistic empire on our national weakness for being "well informed." *Time* attributes its present two-million circulation to a steady increase, since it first appeared in 1925, in what it calls "functional curiosity." Unlike the old-fashioned idle variety, this is a "kind of searching, hungry interest in what is happening everywhere—born not of an idle desire to be entertained or amused, but of a solid conviction that the news intimately and vitally affects the lives of everyone now. Functional curiosity grows as the number of educated people grows."

The curiosity exists, but it is not functional since it doesn't help the individual function. A very small part of the mass of miscellaneous facts offered in each week's issue of *Time* (or, for that matter, in the depressing quantity of newspapers and magazines visible on any large newsstand) is useful to the reader; they don't help him make more money, take some political or other action to advance his interests, or become a better person. About the only functional gain (though the *New York Times*, in a recent advertising campaign, proclaimed that reading it would help one to "be more interesting") the reader gets out of them is practice in reading. And even this is a doubtful advantage. *Time*'s educated people read too many irrelevant words—irrelevant, that is, to any thoughtful idea of their personal interests, either narrow (practical) or broad (cultural).

Imagine a similar person of, say, the sixteenth century, confronted with a copy of *Time* or the *New York Times*. He would take a whole day to master it, perhaps two, because he would be accustomed to take the time to think and even to feel about what he read; and he could take the time because there *was* time, there being comparatively little to read in that golden age. (The very name of Luce's

---

[1] The publisher of *Time* magazine until his death in 1967.

magazine is significant: *Time*, just because we don't have it.) Feeling a duty—or perhaps simply a compulsion—at least to glance over the printed matter that inundates us daily, we have developed of necessity a rapid, purely rational, classifying habit of mind, something like the operations of a Mark IV calculating machine, making a great many small decisions every minute: read or not read? If read, then take in this, skim over that, and let the rest go by. This we do with the surface of our minds, since we "just don't have time" to bring the slow, cumbersome depths into play, to ruminate, speculate, reflect, wonder, *experience* what the eye flits over. This gives a greatly extended coverage to our minds, but also makes them, compared to the kind of minds similar people had in past centuries, coarse, shallow, passive, and unoriginal.

Such reading habits have produced a similar kind of reading matter, since, except for a few stubborn old-fashioned types—the handcraftsmen who produce whatever is written today of quality, whether in poetry, fiction, scholarship, or journalism—our writers produce work that is to be read quickly and then buried under the next day's spate of "news" or the next month's best seller; hastily slapped-together stuff that it would be foolish to waste much time or effort on either writing or reading. For those who, as readers or as writers, would get a little under the surface, the real problem of our day is how to *escape* being "well informed," how to resist the temptation to acquire too much information (never more seductive than when it appears in the chaste garb of duty), and how in general to elude the voracious demands on one's attention enough to think a little.

Essay Topic

According to Macdonald, what is the nature of the "printed matter that inundates us daily," and what connection does this kind of reading have with thought? What do you think about the position he takes here? Be sure to support your argument with specific examples based on your observations and experiences as well as on your reading, especially the supplemental essays in this unit.

Vocabulary Check

You will want to be sure that you understand the key vocabulary terms below and the way they are used by Macdonald in "Reading and Thought." Words can have a variety of meanings, or they can have specialized meanings in certain contexts. Look up the definitions of the following words. Then, choose the meaning that you think Macdonald intended when he selected that particular word. Explain the way the meaning or concept behind the definition is key to understanding his argument.

1. *curiosity*

   definition: _____

   _____

   explanation: _____

   _____

   _____

   _____

2. *miscellaneous*

   definition: _____

   _____

   explanation: _____

   _____

   _____

   _____

3. *inundate*

   definition: _____

   _____

explanation: _____

_____

_____

_____

4. *ruminate*

definition: _____

_____

explanation: _____

_____

_____

_____

5. *speculate*

definition: _____

_____

explanation: _____

_____

_____

_____

6. *coarse*

definition: _____

_____

explanation: _____

_____

_____

_____

7. *passive*

definition: _____

_____

explanation: _____

_____

_____

_____

8. *chaste*

definition: _____

_____

explanation: _____

_____

_____

_____

9. *garb*

definition: _____

_____

explanation: _____

_____

_____

_____

Questions to Guide Your Reading

Answer the following questions so you can gain a thorough understanding of "Reading and Thought."

Paragraph 1

What is "functional curiosity," and how does Henry Luce believe it relates to the circulation of *Time*?

Paragraph 2

Why does Macdonald say that the kind of curiosity Luce is talking about should not be called functional?

Paragraph 3

Explain the difference between the way people today read *Time* and the way a sixteenth-century person would read it, according to Macdonald. Why is there a difference?

Paragraph 4

What is the problem, according to Macdonald, that today's reading habits have produced? Would you call this situation a problem? Why or why not?

Prewriting for a Directed Summary

The first part of the writing topic that follows "Reading and Thought" asks you about a central idea from Macdonald's essay. To answer this part of the writing topic, you will want to write a *directed* summary, meaning one that responds specifically to the writing topic's first question.

first part of the writing topic:

According to Macdonald, what is the nature of the "printed matter that inundates us daily," and what connection does this kind of reading have with thought?

Hint:

Don't forget to look back to Part 1's Guidelines for "Writing a Directed Summary".

Focus Questions

1. What is meant by the term "functional curiosity"?

2. What is the relationship Macdonald finds between functional curiosity and the reading habits of educated people of today?

3. What, according to the author, is the only thing readers gain from reading out of functional curiosity?

4. According to Macdonald, if a sixteenth-century person were confronted with an issue of one of today's magazines or newspapers, how much time would he or she likely devote to reading it? Why would it take so long?

5. What difference does Macdonald find between skimming and reading?

6. According to Macdonald, how can being "well informed" contribute to shallow thinking?

Developing an Opinion and Working Thesis Statement

The second part of the writing topic for "Reading and Thought" asks you to take a position of your own on the issue Macdonald addresses. Your response to this part of the writing topic will become the thesis statement of your essay, so it is important to spend some time ensuring that it reflects the position you want to take. Do you think that it is important to read more deeply, even if it means reading more slowly and therefore reading less?

> writing topic's second part:
>
> *What do you think about the position he takes here?*

Do you think his position on the connection between reading and thought applies to the reading many of us do on a daily basis? In order to make your position clear to readers, state it early in your essay, preferably at the end of your introductory paragraph. A clear thesis statement, one that takes a position on the importance of the kind of reading we do and its influence on our thinking, will unify your essay and allow it to effectively communicate with readers.

It is likely that you aren't yet sure what position you want to take in your essay. If this is the case, go on to the next section and work on developing your ideas through specific evidence drawn from your experience. Then you will be asked to reexamine the working thesis statement you write here to see if you want to revise it based on the discoveries you made when you explored your ideas more systematically.

1. Use the following thesis frame to identify the basic elements of your working thesis statement:

    a. What is the issue of "Reading and Thought" that the writing topic asks you to consider?

    _____

    b. What is Macdonald's opinion about that issue?

    _____

    c. What is your opinion about the issue, and will you agree or disagree with Macdonald?

    _____

    _____

    _____

2. Now use the elements you isolated in the thesis frame to write a thesis statement. You may have to revise it several times until it captures your idea clearly.

_____

_____

Prewriting to Find Support for Your Thesis Statement

The last part of the writing topic asks you to support the position you put forward in your thesis statement. Well-developed ideas are crucial when you are making an argument because you will have to be clear, logical, and thorough if you are to be convincing. As you work through the exercises below, you will generate much of the 4Cs material you will need when you draft your essay's body paragraphs.

writing topic's last part:

Be sure to support your argument with specific examples based on your observations and experiences, as well as on your reading, especially the supplemental essays in this unit.

Complete each section of this prewriting activity; your responses will become the material you will use in the next stage—planning and writing the essay.

1. As you begin to develop your own examples, consider the kinds of reading you've done and its effect on your own thinking. Perhaps make a list of the things you have read in recent weeks and the way that you read them. Then, consider how this reading influenced your thinking.

   Once you've listed your specific examples and done some speculative freewriting about the meaning or significance of each, carefully look over all that you have written. Try to group your ideas into categories. Then, give each category a label. In other words, cluster ideas that seem to have something in common and, for each cluster, identify that shared quality by giving it a title.

2. Now broaden your focus; list or freewrite about examples of reading material available on a regular basis for large numbers of people—for example, newspapers, popular Internet sites, popular magazines, or any other sources with which you are familiar. Do you think these sources influence people's ideas? Explore your thoughts.

Once you've written your ideas, look them over carefully. Try to group your ideas into categories. Then give each category a label. In other words, cluster ideas that seem to have something in common and, for each cluster, identify that shared quality by giving it a name.

3. Once you've created topics by clustering your ideas into categories, go through them and pick two or three specific ones to develop in your essay. Make sure that they are relevant to your thesis and that they have enough substance to be compelling to your reader. Then, in the space below, briefly summarize each item.

   Once you've decided which items/categories on your lists you will use in your essay, take some time to explain below how each category and its items connect to your thesis statement. You will use these details for the next stage.

Revising Your Thesis Statement

Now that you have spent some time working out your ideas more systematically and developing some supporting evidence for the position you want to take, look again at the working thesis statement you crafted earlier to see if it is still accurate. As your first step, look again at the writing topic, and then write your original working thesis on the lines that follow it.

Writing Topic:

According to Macdonald, what is the nature of the "printed matter that inundates us daily," and what connection does this kind of reading have with thought? What do you think about the position he takes here? Be sure to support your argument with specific examples based on your observations and experiences as well as on your reading, especially the supplemental essays in this unit.

Working Thesis Statement:

_____

_____

_____

Take some time now to see if you want to revise your thesis statement. Remember that your thesis statement must respond to the second part of the writing topic, but also take into consideration the writing topic as a whole. The first part of the writing topic identifies the issue that is up for debate, and the last part of the writing topic reminds you that, whatever position you take on the issue, you must support it with specific evidence.

There is a good chance that some revision of your thesis is necessary. Take some time now to see if you want to revise your thesis statement. Often, after extensive prewriting and focused thought, you will find that the working thesis statement is no longer an accurate reflection of what you plan to say in your essay. You may need to add or change a word or phrase in the subject or the claim. Or you may decide that the thesis statement must be completely rewritten so that it takes a very different position on the issue.

Use the following questions to reexamine it now to ensure that it is fully developed, clear, and accurate:

a. Does the thesis directly identify Macdonald's argument about the way much of our reading today affects thought?

b. Do you make clear your opinion regarding this connection?

c. Is your thesis well punctuated, grammatically correct, and precisely worded?

Add any missing elements, correct the grammar errors, and refine the wording. Then, write your polished thesis on the lines below. Try to look at it from your readers' perspective. Is it strong and interesting?

_____

_____

_____

Hint:

Be sure that your thesis presents a clear position; it should not be a statement that shows you haven't yet made up your mind and are still considering two or more options or possibilities.

Planning and Drafting Your Essay

Now that you have examined Macdonald's argument and thought at length about your own views, draft an essay that responds to all parts of the writing topic. Use the material you developed in the above activities to compose your draft, and then exchange drafts with a classmate and use the peer review activity to revise your draft.

Getting started on the draft is often the hardest part of the writing process because this is where you move from exploring and planning to getting your ideas down in a unified, coherent shape. You may not be in the habit of outlining or planning your essay before you begin drafting it, and some of you may avoid outlining altogether. If you haven't been using an outline as you move through the writing process, try using it this time. Creating an outline will give you a clear and coherent structure for incorporating all of the ideas you have developed in the preceding pages. It will also show you where you may have gone off track, left logical holes in your reasoning, or failed to develop one or more of your paragraphs.

Your outline doesn't have to use Roman numerals or be highly detailed. Just use an outline form that suits your style and shows you a bird's-eye view of your argument. Below is a form that we think you will find useful. Consult the academic essay diagram in Part 1 of this book, too, to remind yourself of the conventional form of a college essay and its basic parts.

I. Introductory Paragraph

A. An opening sentence that gives the reading selection's title and author and begins to answer the first part of the writing topic:

_____

_____

B. Main points to include in the directed summary:

1.

2.

3.

4.

C. Write out your thesis statement. (Look back to "Revising Your Thesis Statement," where you reexamined and refined your working thesis statement.) It should clearly state whether you agree with Macdonald's claim about the connection between the way we read and the development of our minds.

_____

_____

_____

II. Body Paragraphs

A. The paragraph's one main point that supports the thesis statement:

_____

1. Controlling idea sentence:

_____

_____

2. Corroborating details:

_____

_____

_____

_____

3. Careful explanation of why the details are relevant:

_____

_____

_____

_____

_____

4. Connection to the thesis statement:

_____

_____

_____

B. The paragraph's one main point that supports the thesis statement:

_____

1. Controlling idea sentence:

_____

_____

2. Corroborating details:

_____

_____

_____

_____

3. Careful explanation of why the details are relevant:

_____

_____

_____

_____

4. Connection to the thesis statement:

_____

_____

_____

C. The paragraph's one main point that supports the thesis statement:

_____

1. Controlling idea sentence:

_____

_____

2. Corroborating details:

_____

_____

_____

_____

3. Careful explanation of why the details are relevant:

_____

_____

_____

_____

_____

4. Connection to the thesis statement:

_____

_____

_____

D. The paragraph's one main point that supports the thesis statement:

_____

1. Controlling idea sentence:

_____

_____

2. **C**orroborating details:

_____

_____

_____

_____

3. **C**areful explanation of why the details are relevant:

_____

_____

_____

_____

_____

4. **C**onnection to the thesis statement:

_____

_____

_____

Repeat this form for any remaining body paragraphs.

III. Conclusion

A. Type of conclusion to be used (see "Conclusions" in Part 1):

_____

B. Key words or phrases to include:

_____

Getting Feedback on Your Draft

Use the following guidelines to give a classmate feedback on his or her draft. Read the draft through first, and then answer each of the items below as specifically as you can.

Name of draft's author: _____

Name of draft's reader: _____

The Introduction

1. Within the opening sentences:

   a. Macdonald's first and last name are given.   yes   no
   b. The reading selection's title is given and placed within
      quotation marks.   yes   no

2. The opening contains a summary that:

   a. explains the connection Macdonald believes exists between
      reading and thought   yes   no
   b. identifies the specific example Macdonald uses to illustrate
      this connection   yes   no
   c. explains the reason Macdonald believes Luce is wrong in
      calling this example one of "functional curiosity"   yes   no

3. The opening provides a thesis that makes clear
   the draft writer's opinion regarding Macdonald's claim.   yes   no

If you circled yes in #3 above, copy the thesis below as it is written. If you circled no, explain to the draft writer what information is needed to make the thesis complete.

_____

_____

_____

The Body

1. How many paragraphs are in the body of this essay? _____

2. To support the thesis, this number is   sufficient   not enough

3. Do body paragraphs contain the 4Cs?

Paragraph 1	Controlling idea sentence	yes	no
	Corroborating details	yes	no
	Careful explanation of why the details are relevant	yes	no
	Connection to the thesis statement	yes	no
Paragraph 2	Controlling idea sentence	yes	no
	Corroborating details	yes	no
	Careful explanation of why the details are relevant	yes	no
	Connection to the thesis statement	yes	no
Paragraph 3	Controlling idea sentence	yes	no
	Corroborating details	yes	no
	Careful explanation of why the details are relevant	yes	no
	Connection to the thesis statement	yes	no
Paragraph 4	Controlling idea sentence	yes	no
	Corroborating details	yes	no
	Careful explanation of why the details are relevant	yes	no
	Connection to the thesis statement	yes	no
Paragraph 5	Controlling idea sentence	yes	no
	Corroborating details	yes	no
	Careful explanation of why the details are relevant	yes	no
	Connection to the thesis statement	yes	no

(Continue as needed.)

4. Identify any of the body paragraphs that are underdeveloped (too short).

_____

5. Identify any of the body paragraphs that fail to support the thesis.

_____

6. Identify any of the body paragraphs that are redundant or repetitive.

_____

7. Suggest any ideas for additional body paragraphs that might improve this essay.

_____

The Conclusion

1. Does the final paragraph avoid introducing new ideas
   and examples that really belong in the body of the essay?   yes   no

2. Does the conclusion provide closure (let readers know
   that the end of the essay has been reached)?   yes   no

3. Does the conclusion leave readers with an
   understanding of the significance of the argument?   yes   no

   State in your own words what the draft writer considers to be important about
   his or her argument.

   _____

   _____

   _____

4. Identify the type of conclusion used (see the guidelines for conclusions in Part 1).

   _____

Editing

1. During the editing process, the writer should pay attention to the following problems in sentence structure, punctuation, and mechanics:

   fragments

   misplaced and dangling modifiers

   fused (run-on) sentences

   comma splices

   misplaced, missing, and unnecessary commas

   misplaced, missing, and unnecessary apostrophes

   incorrect quotation mark use

   capitalization errors

   spelling errors

2. While editing, the writer should pay attention to the following areas of grammar:

   verb tense

   subject-verb agreement

   irregular verbs

   pronoun type

   pronoun reference

   pronoun agreement

   noun plurals

   prepositions

Final Draft Checklist

Content:

- My essay has an appropriate title.
- I provide an accurate summary of Macdonald's argument concerning the connection between what and how we read, and their effects on how we think.
- My thesis states a clear position that can be supported by evidence.
- I have enough paragraphs and argument points to support my thesis.
- Each body paragraph is relevant to my thesis.
- Each body paragraph contains the 4Cs.
- I use transitions whenever necessary to connect ideas.
- The final paragraph of my essay (the conclusion) provides readers with a sense of closure.

Grammar, Punctuation, and Mechanics:

- I use the present tense to discuss Macdonald's argument and examples.
- I use verb tenses correctly to show the chronology of events.
- I have verb tense consistency throughout my sentences and paragraphs.
- I have checked for subject-verb agreement in all of my sentences.
- I have revised all fragments and mixed or garbled sentences.
- I have repaired all fused (run-on) sentences and comma splices.
- I have placed a comma after introductory elements (transitions and phrases) and all dependent clauses that open a sentence.
- If I present items in a series (nouns, verbs, prepositional phrases), they are parallel in form.
- If I include material spoken or written by someone other than myself, I have correctly punctuated it with quotation marks, using the MLA style guide's rules for citation.
- If I include material spoken or written by someone other than myself, I have included a works cited list that follows the MLA style guide's rules for citation.

Reviewing Your Graded Essay

After your instructor has returned your essay, you may have the opportunity to revise your paper and raise your grade. Many students, especially those whose essays receive nonpassing grades, feel that their instructors should be less "picky" about grammar and should pass the work on content alone. However, most students at this level have not yet acquired the ability to recognize quality writing, and they do not realize that content and writing actually cannot be separated in this way. Experienced instructors know that errors in sentence structure, grammar, punctuation, and word choice either interfere with content or distract readers so much that they lose track of content. In short, good ideas badly presented are no longer good ideas; to pass, an essay must have passable writing. So even if you are not submitting a revised version of this essay to your instructor, it is important that you review your work carefully in order to understand its strengths and weaknesses. This sheet will guide you through the evaluation process.

You will want to continue to use the techniques that worked well for you and to find strategies to overcome the problems that you identify in this sample of your writing. To recognize areas that might have been problematic for you, look back at the scoring rubric in this book. Match the numerical/verbal/letter grade received on your essay to the appropriate category. Study the explanation given on the rubric for your grade.

Write a few sentences below in which you identify your problems in each of the following areas. Then, suggest specific changes you could make that would improve your paper. Don't forget to use your handbook as a resource.

1. Grammar/punctuation/mechanics

My problem:

My strategy for change:

2. Thesis/response to assignment

My problem:

My strategy for change:

3. Organization

My problem:

My strategy for change:

4. Paragraph development/examples/reasoning

My problem:

My strategy for change:

5. Assessment

In the space below, assign a grade to your paper using the rubric in Part 1 of this book. In other words, if your instructor assigned your essay a grade of *High Fail*, you might give it the letter grade you now feel the paper warrants. If your instructor used the traditional letter grade to evaluate the essay, choose a category from the rubric in this book, or any other grading scale that you are familiar with, to show your evaluation of your work. Then, write a short narrative explaining your evaluation of the essay and the reasons it received the grade you gave it.

Grade:_____

Narrative:_____

_____

_____

_____

Extending the Discussion: Considering Other Viewpoints

Reading Selections

Is Google Making Us Stupid?
What the Internet Is Doing to Our Brains

NICHOLAS CARR

Nicholas Carr holds a BA from Dartmouth College and an MA in English and American literature and language from Harvard University. Carr has been a speaker at MIT, Harvard, Wharton, the Kennedy School of Government, and NASA, as well as at many industry, corporate, and professional events throughout the Americas, Europe, and Asia. He writes on the social, economic, and business implications of technology. He is the author of Does IT Matter *(2004),* The Big Switch: Rewiring the Word, from Edison to Google *(2008), and his latest book* The Shallows: What the Internet Is Doing to Our Brains *(2010). The following essay is an excerpt from his most recent book,* The Shallows.

"Dave, stop. Stop, will you? Stop, Dave. Will you stop, Dave?" So the supercomputer HAL pleads with the implacable astronaut Dave Bowman in a famous and weirdly poignant scene toward the end of Stanley Kubrick's *2001: A Space Odyssey*. Bowman, having nearly been sent to a deep-space death by the malfunctioning machine, is calmly, coldly disconnecting the memory circuits that control its artificial brain. "Dave, my mind is going," HAL says, forlornly. "I can feel it. I can feel it."

I can feel it, too. Over the past few years, I've had an uncomfortable sense that someone, or something, has been tinkering with my brain, remapping the neural circuitry, reprogramming the memory. My mind isn't going—so far as I can tell—but it's changing. I'm not thinking the way I used to think. I can feel it most strongly when I'm reading. Immersing myself in a book or a lengthy article used to be easy. My mind would get caught up in the narrative or the turns of the argument, and I'd spend hours strolling through long stretches of prose. That's rarely the case anymore. Now my concentration often starts to drift after two or three pages. I get fidgety, lose the thread, begin looking for something else to do. I feel as if I'm always dragging my wayward brain back to the text. The deep reading that used to come naturally has become a struggle.

I think I know what's going on. For more than a decade now, I've been spending a lot of time online, searching and surfing and sometimes adding to the great databases of the Internet. For me, as for others, the Net is becoming a universal medium, the conduit for most of the information that flows through my eyes and ears and into my mind. The advantages of having immediate access to such an incredibly rich store of information are many, and they've been widely described and duly applauded. "The perfect recall of silicon memory," *Wired*'s Clive Thompson has written, "can be an enormous boon to thinking."[1] But that boon comes at a price. As the media theorist Marshall McLuhan pointed out in the 1960s, media are not just passive channels of information. They supply the stuff of thought, but they also shape the process of thought. And what the Net seems to be doing is chipping away my capacity for concentration and contemplation. My mind now expects to take in information the way the Net distributes it: in a swiftly moving stream of particles. Once I was a scuba diver in the sea of words. Now I zip along the surface like a guy on a Jet Ski.

I'm not the only one. When I mention my troubles with reading to friends and acquaintances—literary types, most of them—many say they're having similar experiences. The more they use the Web, the more they have to fight to stay focused on long pieces of writing. Some of the bloggers I follow have also begun mentioning the phenomenon. Scott Karp, who writes a blog about online media, recently confessed that he has stopped reading books altogether. "I was a lit major in college, and used to be [a] voracious book reader," he writes. "What happened?" He speculates on the answer: "What if I do all my reading on the web not so much because the way I read has changed, i.e. I'm just seeking convenience, but because the way I THINK has changed?"[2]

Bruce Friedman, who blogs regularly about the use of computers in medicine, also has described how the Internet has altered his mental habits. "I now have almost totally lost the ability to read and absorb a longish article on the web or in print,"[3] he wrote earlier this year. A pathologist who has long been on the faculty of the University of Michigan Medical School, Friedman elaborated on his

---

[1]Clive Thompson, "Your Outboard Brain Knows All," *Wired*, October 2007.
[2]Scott Karp, "The Evolution from Linear Thought to Networked Thought," *Publishing 2.0* blog, February 9, 2008, http://publishing2.com/2008/02/09/the-evolution-from-linear-thought-to-networked-thought.
[3]Bruce Friedman, "How Google Is Changing Our Information-Seeking Behavior," Lab *Soft News* blog, February 6, 2008, http://labsoftnews.typepad.com/lab_soft_news/2008/02/how-google-is-c.html.

comment in a telephone conversation with me. His thinking, he said, has taken on a "staccato" quality, reflecting the way he quickly scans short passages of text from many sources online. "I can't read *War and Peace* anymore," he admitted. "I've lost the ability to do that. Even a blog post of more than three or four paragraphs is too much to absorb. I skim it."

Anecdotes alone don't prove much. And we still await the long-term neurological and psychological experiments that will provide a definitive picture of how Internet use affects cognition. But a recently published study of online research habits, conducted by scholars from University College London, suggests that we may well be in the midst of a sea change in the way we read and think. As part of the five-year research program, the scholars examined computer logs documenting the behavior of visitors to two popular research sites, one operated by the British Library and one by a U.K. educational consortium, that provide access to journal articles, e-books, and other sources of written information. They found that people using the sites exhibited "a form of skimming activity," hopping from one source to another and rarely returning to any source they'd already visited. They typically read no more than one or two pages of an article or book before they would "bounce" out to another site. Sometimes they'd save a long article, but there's no evidence that they ever went back and actually read it. The authors of the study report:

> It is clear that users are not reading online in the traditional sense; indeed there are signs that new forms of "reading" are emerging as users "power browse" horizontally through titles, contents pages, and abstracts, going for quick wins. It almost seems that they go online to avoid reading in the traditional sense. [4]

Thanks to the ubiquity of text on the Internet, not to mention the popularity of text-messaging on cell phones, we may well be reading more today than we did in the 1970s or 1980s, when television was our medium of choice. But it's a different kind of reading, and behind it lies a different kind of thinking—perhaps even a new sense of the self. "We are not only *what* we read," says Maryanne Wolf, a developmental psychologist at Tufts University and the author of *Proust and the Squid: The Story and Science of the Reading Brain*. "We are *how* we

---

[4] University College London. "Information Behaviour of the Researcher of the Future," January 11, 2008, www.ucl.ac.uk/slais/research/ciber/downloads/ggexecutive.pdf.

read."[5] Wolf worries that the style of reading promoted by the Net, a style that puts "efficiency" and "immediacy" above all else, may be weakening our capacity for the kind of deep reading that emerged when an earlier technology, the printing press, made long and complex works of prose commonplace. When we read online, she says, we tend to become "mere decoders of information." Our ability to interpret text, to make the rich mental connections that form when we read deeply and without distraction, remains largely disengaged.

Reading, explains Wolf, is not an instinctive skill for human beings. It's not etched into our genes the way speech is. We have to teach our minds how to translate the symbolic characters we see into the language we understand. And the media or other technologies we use in learning and practicing the craft of reading play an important part in shaping the neural circuits inside our brains. Experiments demonstrate that readers of ideograms, such as the Chinese, develop a mental circuitry for reading that is very different from the circuitry found in those of us whose written language employs an alphabet. The variations extend across many regions of the brain, including those that govern such essential cognitive functions as memory and the interpretation of visual and auditory stimuli. We can expect as well that the circuits woven by our use of the Net will be different from those woven by our reading of books and other printed works. Never has a communications system played so many roles in our lives—or exerted such broad influence over our thoughts—as the Internet does today. Yet, for all that's been written about the Net, there's been little consideration of how, exactly, it's reprogramming us. The Net's intellectual ethic remains obscure.

Google's headquarters, in Mountain View, California—the Googleplex—is the Internet's high church, and the religion practiced inside its walls is Taylorism.[6] Google, says its chief executive, Eric Schmidt, is "a company that's founded around the science of measurement," and it is striving to "systematize everything" it does.[7]

---

[5]Maryanne Wolf, *Proust and the Squid: The Story and Science of the Reading Brain*. New York: Harper Collins Pub, 2007, 142-146.

[6]from Frederick Winslow Taylor, *The Principles of Scientific Management*. New York: Harper, 1911. "Taylorism" is another term for "scientific management" and refers to a science-inspired management system that attempts to rectify labor inefficiencies in the workplace.

[7]Google Inc. Press Day Webcast, May 10, 2006, http://google.client.shareholder.com/Visitors/event/build2/MediaPresentation.cfm?MediaID=20263&Player=I.

Drawing on the terabytes of behavioral data it collects through its search engine and other sites, it carries out thousands of experiments a day, according to the *Harvard Business Review*,[8] and it uses the results to refine the algorithms that increasingly control how people find information and extract meaning from it. What Taylor did for the work of the hand, Google is doing for the work of the mind.

The company has declared that its mission is "to organize the world's information and make it universally accessible and useful." It seeks to develop "the perfect search engine," which it defines as something that "understands exactly what you mean and gives you back exactly what you want."[9] In Google's view, information is a kind of commodity, a utilitarian resource that can be mined and processed with industrial efficiency. The more pieces of information we can "access" and the faster we can extract their gist, the more productive we become as thinkers.

Where does it end? Sergey Brin and Larry Page, the gifted young men who founded Google while pursuing doctoral degrees in computer science at Stanford, speak frequently of their desire to turn their search engine into an artificial intelligence, a HAL-like machine that might be connected directly to our brains. "The ultimate search engine is something as smart as people—or smarter,"[10] Page said in a speech a few years back. "For us, working on search is a way to work on artificial intelligence."[11] In a 2004 interview with *Newsweek*, Brin said, "Certainly if you had all the world's information directly attached to your brain, or an artificial brain that was smarter than your brain, you'd be better off."[12] Last year, Page told a convention of scientists that Google is "really trying to build artificial intelligence and to do it on a large scale."[13]

Such an ambition is a natural one, even an admirable one, for a pair of math whizzes with vast quantities of cash at their disposal and a small army of computer scientists in their employ. A fundamentally

---

[8]Bala Iyer and Thomas H. Davenport, "Reverse Engineering Google's Innovation Machine," *Harvard Business Review*, April 2008.

[9]Google Inc. Press Day Webcast, May 10, 2006, http://google.client.shareholder. com/Visitors/event/build2/MediaPresentation.cfm?MediaID=20263&Player=I

[10]Rachael Hanley, "From Googol to Google: Co-Founder Returns," *Stanford Daily*, February 12, 2003.

[11]Larry Page, keynote address before AAAS Annual Conference, San Francisco, February 16, 2007, http://news.cnet.com/1606-2_3-6160334.html.

[12]Steven Levy, "All Eyes on Google," *Newsweek*, April 12, 2004.

[13]Larry Page, keynote address before AAAS Annual Conference, San Francisco, February 16, 2007.

scientific enterprise, Google is motivated by a desire to use technology, in Eric Schmidt's words, "to solve problems that have never been solved before,"[14] and artificial intelligence is the hardest problem out there. Why wouldn't Brin and Page want to be the ones to crack it?

Still, their easy assumption that we'd all "be better off" if our brains were supplemented, or even replaced, by an artificial intelligence is unsettling. It suggests a belief that intelligence is the output of a mechanical process, a series of discrete steps that can be isolated, measured, and optimized. In Google's world, the world we enter when we go online, there's little place for the fuzziness of contemplation. Ambiguity is not an opening for insight but a bug to be fixed. The human brain is just an outdated computer that needs a faster processor and a bigger hard drive.

The idea that our minds should operate as high-speed data-processing machines is not only built into the workings of the Internet, it is the network's reigning business model as well. The faster we surf across the Web—the more links we click and pages we view—the more opportunities Google and other companies gain to collect information about us and to feed us advertisements. Most of the proprietors of the commercial Internet have a financial stake in collecting the crumbs of data we leave behind as we flit from link to link—the more crumbs, the better. The last thing these companies want is to encourage leisurely reading or slow, concentrated thought. It's in their economic interest to drive us to distraction.

Maybe I'm just a worrywart. Just as there's a tendency to glorify technological progress, there's a countertendency to expect the worst of every new tool or machine. In Plato's *Phaedrus*, Socrates bemoaned the development of writing. He feared that, as people came to rely on the written word as a substitute for the knowledge they used to carry inside their heads, they would, in the words of one of the dialogue's characters, "cease to exercise their memory and become forgetful."[15] And because they would be able to "receive a quantity of information without proper instruction," they would "be thought very knowledgeable when they are for the most part quite ignorant." They would be "filled with the conceit of wisdom instead of real wisdom." Socrates wasn't wrong—the new technology did often have the effects he

---

[14]See Richard MacManus, "Full Text of Google Analyst Day Powerpoint Notes," *Web 2.0 Explorer* blog, March 7, 2006, http://blogs.zdnet.com/web2explorer/?p=132.
[15]Quotations from *Phaedrus* are taken from the translations by Reginald Hackforth and Benjamin Jowett.

feared—but he was shortsighted. He couldn't foresee the many ways that writing and reading would serve to spread information, spur fresh ideas, and expand human knowledge (if not wisdom).

So, yes, you should be skeptical of my skepticism. Perhaps those who dismiss critics of the Internet as Luddites or nostalgists will be proved correct, and from our hyperactive, data-stoked minds will spring a golden age of intellectual discovery and universal wisdom. Then again, the Net isn't the alphabet, and although it may replace the printing press, it produces something altogether different. The kind of deep reading that a sequence of printed pages promotes is valuable not just for the knowledge we acquire from the author's words but for the intellectual vibrations those words set off within our own minds. In the quiet spaces opened up by the sustained, undistracted reading of a book, or by any other act of contemplation, for that matter, we make our own associations, draw our own inferences and analogies, foster our own ideas. Deep reading, as Maryanne Wolf argues, is indistinguishable from deep thinking. If we lose those quiet spaces, or fill them up with "content," we will sacrifice something important not only in our selves but in our culture. In a recent essay titled "The Pancake People," the playwright Richard Foreman eloquently describes what's at stake:

> I come from a tradition of Western culture, in which the ideal (my ideal) was the complex, dense and "cathedral-like" structure of the highly educated and articulate personality—a man or woman who carried inside themselves a personally constructed and unique version of the entire heritage of the West. [But now] I see within us all (myself included) the replacement of complex inner density with a new kind of self—evolving under the pressure of information overload and the technology of the "instantly available." [16]

As we are drained of our "inner repertory of dense cultural inheritance," Foreman concludes, we risk turning into "'pancake people'—spread wide and thin as we connect with that vast network of information accessed by the mere touch of a button."

I'm haunted by that scene in *2001*. What makes it so poignant, and so weird, is the computer's emotional response to the disassembly of its mind: its despair as one circuit after another goes dark, its

---

[16]Richard Foreman, "The Pancake People, or, 'The Gods Are Pounding My Head,'" *Edge*, March 8, 2005.

childlike pleading with the astronaut—"I can feel it. I can feel it. I'm afraid."—and its final reversion to what can only be called a state of innocence. HAL's outpouring of feeling contrasts with the emotionlessness that characterizes the human figures in the film, who go about their business with an almost robotic efficiency. Their thoughts and actions feel scripted, as if they're following the steps of an algorithm. In the world of *2001*, people have become so machinelike that the most human character turns out to be a machine. That's the essence of Kubrick's dark prophecy: As we come to rely on computers to mediate our understanding of the world, it is our own intelligence that flattens into artificial intelligence.

Discussion Questions

1. Discuss the types of evidence that Nicholas Carr cites to support his contention that the kind of deep reading that used to come naturally has now become difficult. Which type did you find most interesting or convincing? Explain.

2. What abilities does Maryanne Wolf suggest are being lost due to the proliferation of Internet reading and its effect on the brain? Do you think that these abilities are important to retain? Explain.

3. How do you feel about the assertion of Sergey Brin and Larry Page, the founders of Google, that we would all "be better off" if our human brains were somehow replaced by artificial intelligence?

4. Explain the reasons you think Carr, Macdonald, and Johnson would each have for agreeing or disagreeing with Richard Foreman's concept of "Pancake People."

5. Skim Carr's essay again, this time circling any words that you cannot define—we recommend including "media," "phenomenon," and "discrete." Look them up in the dictionary. Then, discuss with a classmate how this activity has affected your understanding of this reading selection.

Yes, People Still Read, but Now It's Social

Essay

STEVEN JOHNSON

Steven Johnson is a widely read author who writes on urgent cultural issues in ways that offer new perspectives. His books have been critically acclaimed, and two were chosen as New York Times *Notable Books. His newest book is titled* Where Good Ideas Come From: The Natural History of Innovation *(2010).*

"The point of books is to combat loneliness," David Wallace observes near the beginning of *Although of Course You End Up Becoming Yourself*, David Lipsky's recently published, book-length interview with him. If you happen to be reading the book on the Kindle from Amazon, Mr. Wallace's observation has an extra emphasis: a dotted underline running below the phrase. Not because Mr. Wallace or Mr. Lipsky felt that the point was worth stressing, but because a dozen or so other readers have highlighted the passage on their Kindles, making it one of the more "popular" passages in the book. Amazon calls this new feature "popular highlights."

The "popular highlights" feature may sound innocuous enough, but it augurs even bigger changes to come. Though the feature can be disabled by the user, "popular highlights" will no doubt alarm Nicholas Carr, whose new book, *The Shallows*, argues that the compulsive skimming, linking, and multitasking of our screen reading is undermining the deep, immersive focus that has defined book culture for centuries. With "popular highlights," even when we manage to turn off Twitter and the television and sit down to read a good book, there will be a chorus of readers turning the pages along with us, pointing out the good bits. Before long, we'll probably be able to meet those fellow readers, share stories with them. Mr. Carr's argument is that these distractions come with a heavy cost, and his book's publication coincides with articles in various publications—including the *New York Times*—that report on scientific studies showing how multitasking harms our concentration. A study reported on early this month (see "Your Brain on Computers," *New York Times*, 6 June 2010) found that heavy multitaskers performed about 10 to 20 percent worse on most tests than light multitaskers.

These studies are undoubtedly onto something—no one honestly believes he is better at focusing when he switches back and forth between multiple activities—but they are meaningless as a cultural indicator without measuring what we gain from multitasking. Thanks to e-mail, Twitter, and the blogosphere, I regularly exchange information with hundreds of people in a single day: scheduling meetings, sharing political gossip, trading edits on a book chapter, planning a family vacation, reading tech punditry. How many of those exchanges could happen were I limited exclusively to the technologies of the phone, the post office, and the face-to-face meeting? I suspect that the number would be a small fraction of my current rate. I have no doubt that I am slightly less focused in these interactions, but, frankly, most of what we do during the day doesn't require our full powers of concentration. Even rocket scientists don't do rocket science all day long.

To his credit, Mr. Carr readily concedes this efficiency argument. His concern is what happens to high-level thinking when the culture migrates from the page to the screen. To the extent that his argument is a reminder to all of us to step away from the screen sometimes, and think in a more sedate environment, it's a valuable contribution. But Mr. Carr's argument is more ambitious than that: The "linear, literary mind" that has been at "the center of art, science and society" threatens to become "yesterday's mind," with dire consequences for our culture. Here, too, I think the concerns are overstated, though for slightly different reasons. Presumably, the first casualties of "shallow" thinking should have appeared on the front lines of the technology world, where the participants have spent the most time in the hyperconnected space of the screen. And yet the sophistication and nuance of media commentary have grown dramatically over the last fifteen years. Mr. Carr's original essay, published in the *Atlantic*—along with Clay Shirky's more optimistic account, which led to the book *Cognitive Surplus*—were intensely discussed throughout the Web when they first appeared as articles, and both books appear to be generating the same level of analysis and engagement in long form. The intellectual tools for assessing the media, once the province of academics and professional critics, are now far more accessible to the masses. The number of people who have written a thoughtful response to Mr. Carr's essay—and, even better, published it online—surely dwarfs the number of people who wrote in public about *Understanding Media*, by Marshall McLuhan, in 1964. Mr. Carr spends a great deal of his book's opening section convincing us that new forms of media alter the way the brain works, which I suspect most of his readers have long ago accepted as an obvious truth. The question is not whether our brains are being changed. (Of course new experiences change your brain—that's what experience is, on some basic level.) The question is whether the rewards of the change are worth the liabilities.

The problem with Mr. Carr's model is its unquestioned reverence for the slow contemplation of deep reading. For society to advance as it has since Gutenberg, he argues, we need the quiet, solitary space of the book. Yet many great ideas that have advanced culture over the past centuries have emerged from a more connective space, in the collision of different worldviews and sensibilities, different metaphors and fields of expertise. (Gutenberg himself borrowed his printing press from the screw presses of Rhineland vintners, as Mr. Carr notes.) It's no accident that most of the great scientific and technological innovation over the last millennium has taken place in crowded, distracting urban centers. The printed page itself encouraged those manifold connections, by allowing ideas to be stored and shared and circulated more efficiently. One can make the case that the Enlightenment depended more on the exchange of ideas than it did on solitary, deep-focus reading. Quiet contemplation has led to its fair share of important thoughts. But it cannot be denied that good ideas also emerge in networks.

Yes, we are a little less focused, thanks to the electric stimulus of the screen. Yes, we are reading slightly fewer long-form narratives and arguments than we did fifty years ago, though the Kindle and the iPad may well change that. Those are costs, to be sure. But what of the other side of the ledger? We are reading more text, writing far more often, than we were in the heyday of television. And the speed with which we can follow the trail of an idea, or discover new perspectives on a problem, has increased by several orders of magnitude. We are marginally less focused, and exponentially more connected. That's a bargain all of us should be happy to make.

Discussion Questions

1. Why does Steven Johnson feel that Nicholas Carr's complaint about multitasking is "meaningless"? How much time do you spend in a day multitasking? Do you feel that the quality of your work improves or decreases when you are multitasking? Give some examples to support your evaluation.

2. What evidence does Johnson use to suggest that Carr's concerns are overstated? Evaluate the strengths and weakness of this evidence.

3. Explain your inclination for siding with either Carr or Johnson on the issue of the importance of slow reading.

4. Why do you think Dwight Macdonald would or would not appreciate the ideas Johnson presents in this essay?

The Tomes They Are A-Changing

Essay

BENEDICT JONES

Benedict Jones earned an MA in English from the University of California, Riverside, and teaches in UCR's University Writing Program. He special- izes in pre-WWII evolutionary fiction and has given conference papers on prehistoric fiction. He also writes on a variety of other topics.

Older generations have probably always criticized the up-and-coming era. Thousands of years ago, even Socrates (if Plato's *Republic* is to be believed), indulged in a now-legendary diatribe in which he declared that the youth of his day were lazy, ill-mannered, and rude to their elders. In a similar vein, many critics have found fault with the latest technological developments, saying, for example, that automobiles wouldn't last or that talking pictures were a flash in the pan.

Likewise, the critical lens has often focused on the value of literacy and certain types of reading material. For example, another of Plato's works, *Phaedrus* (again featuring Socrates), skeptically contemplates the appropriateness of the newfangled written word as opposed to the oral tradition, a venerable institution that still held sway in Greece (Carr). Nowadays, we are likely to compare Twitter with *To Kill a Mockingbird* and conclude, with good reason, that the former is less likely to be cognitively nourishing than the latter. On the flip side, I sometimes expect that the technophiles are investigating a way to render Harper Lee's great classic into textspeak because the original is just too long and hard to read. Between the two extremes of, shall we say, the Greeks and the TechnoGeeks, a battle still rages over what people should read in their spare time and how they should read it.

For many hundreds of years, literacy or access to it was reserved for special classes of people. Only the rise of universal literacy could level that playing field; only quite recently has print culture taken hold and rendered reading indispensable for most people in the Western world and in the new global community. But it seems that, no matter what the circumstances, literacy always invites judgment. Whereas for a long time, people's sheer *ability* to read (or their easy access to literate intermediaries) illustrated their social class, now our choice of reading material is likely to reflect what other people think of us. If we choose to spend hours slowly ruminating over *Crime and Punishment*, we are likely to be labeled an intellectual or a highbrow.

If, on the other hand, we devour and praise *The Hunger Games* in our spare time, highbrow observers are apt to think us uncultured because we read popular pap intended for the unwashed masses. And if we do not read at all, some will think us barely human. But although I'm just as bad as the next literary snob when it comes to the educational arena, I believe that in their off time, people should read whatever they are drawn to, even if others consider it to be trash.

We should not confuse what we read in school with what we read during our leisure hours; the two can be quite different. Educators should still teach good literature, but we shouldn't expect people to read it in their free time, nor should we criticize them if they don't. Free time is exactly that—a period during which we should be free to read (or do) what we choose. After all, we don't expect people to work calculus problems or run science experiments for pleasure unless that is what they like to do. While I liked biology and physics in school, I wouldn't enjoy a summer vacation during which I felt compelled to design a science fair project just because it's good for me. Similarly, I wouldn't expect other people to read great poems and novels just to expand their minds unless that's what they would choose to do in the first place. We can't force people to like something just because we think they should like it.

We certainly cannot compare past reading habits with those of the present, either, because the last century or so is the first time the people of this country have come close to universal literacy. It is all very well to say that the people of 150 years ago had better taste and voraciously read masterpieces of Western literature, but what of the millions who still could not read at all? There's no comparison. Furthermore, knowledge of the Greek and Latin classics served as a wedge between the privileged elite and the less fortunate. A man who could quote chunks of Cicero at the drop of a hat probably did not have to worry about where his next meal was coming from, and a man who couldn't was generally barred from certain desirable professions. In the nineteenth century and earlier, college and even high school were class-based luxuries for most, and literacy was far from universal. While it is undoubtedly true that the American educational system has been dumbed down in recent decades, we must bear in mind that high school is now required, and a majority of all Americans attend college. This means that a high percentage of Americans, more than ever before, are being exposed to literature.

And another thing: We are apt to forget that much of what we call high literature now was most decidedly literature for the masses in its day. Classics do not start out as classics but become so over time. As respected children's literature scholar Alison Lurie notes in "The Oddness of Oz," L. Frank Baum's insanely popular Oz books were for decades eschewed by teachers and librarians, to the extent that libraries even refused to stock the books (44). The series, often indifferently written, is hardly high art, but the books have become classics because of their charm, their ingenuity, and their ability to spark the imaginations of children and adults alike. The staid librarians of the past clearly had a different opinion, but opinions change over time.

A more appropriate example of popular-turned-classic might be Charles Dickens, who appealed to the taste of a large cross section of Victorian-era readers. I expect that people reacted to his work in much the same way as readers of recent years have responded to the novels of Stephen King or J. K. Rowling. In the nineteenth century, readers breathlessly awaited the latest magazine installment of a Dickens opus that had not yet seen novel publication; people of our day lined up in droves for the latest Harry Potter book. I do not consider Stephen King to be high art, but I venture to say that Rowling's works will still invite critical attention in a hundred years. Perhaps Harry Potter will even be considered highbrow and reserved for the smugly superior and members of the intelligentsia. It's impossible to be sure, but I do know that what starts out as popular does not always stay that way.

I've also found that "trashy" books can lead a reader to classic treasure. We should not criticize a reluctant reader for favoring popular fiction over Shakespeare; we simply cannot know what doors popular works will open for them. Some people will stop with *Twilight* and never know *Twelfth Night*, but others may find that Stephenie Meyer and her kind become a stepping stone to other fantastic works, perhaps even *The Tempest* by way of *Harry Potter and the Sorcerer's Stone*. I doubt that many people start out reading literary greats at the age of five and never look back. For example, when I was a small child, I began my long literary journey very modestly with a volume of Mother Goose rhymes and Dr. Seuss's *Horton Hatches the Egg*. Only a few years later, I had graduated to *The Hobbit* and *The Lord of the Rings*, and my high school taste expanded to include thought-provoking offerings such as *Brave New World*, *1984*, and *Fahrenheit 451*. These works led me to contemplate H. G. Wells, Mary Shelley, and Edgar Allan Poe. My love of speculative works—at first, children's fantasies—led me to great works of dystopia and science fiction. In the same way, other people might find that less difficult novels will eventually lead to more challenging selections in the same genre. But why should these readers be expected to conform to someone else's timetable? Reading was what I did, what I loved, so I graduated to classic works relatively quickly. Other people may require more time.

And if they never get there, so what? People should enjoy what they read and read what they enjoy. Light or superficial reading is pleasurable and fun, and even literary snobs like me indulge in it from time to time. A number of years ago, I went through phases of obsession over Robin Cook thrillers and Jonathan Kellerman mysteries. I used to devour both like candy, but if someone asked me to relate one of those plots now, I wouldn't remember the first thing about it even though I enjoyed it immensely at the time. And I would have laughed in the face of anyone suggesting that I should have spent hours and hours contemplating the plot points and writing style of those bestsellers. They were chewing gum, designed to entertain me for a short time and be traded or donated as soon as I had sucked the flavor from them. I did the same thing as a child, zooming through series books with wild abandon. And yet I could—and still can—take time to mull over the deep themes in a truly classic novel. My occasional bursts of light reading have never prevented me from languidly savoring the classics. The two pursuits are completely distinct, and the existence of one does not automatically preclude the other.

I have also noticed that certain well-written popular works have excited the same careful attention from other people as an H. G. Wells classic incites in me; just look at the Harry Potter fans who linger for hours over their beloved volumes and gather, online or in person, with fellow enthusiasts to discuss the finer points of plot and character. Websites such as *Goodreads* with its 25 million members encourage discussion and sharing, and reading campaigns such as my hometown's One Book, One San Diego (modeled on a similar program started in Seattle in 1998) promote cultural literacy and unify readers from across the entire city. San Diego's 2013 nominations were an eclectic mix ranging from *To Kill a Mockingbird* to T. C. Boyle's *Tortilla Curtain* and, yes, Stephenie Meyer's *Twilight*. None of them made the cut, but the sheer number of nominations (177) indicates that reading, whether deep or superficial, is alive and well in San Diego ("Books"). Many major cities have similar programs.

Other types of "disposable" reading have value as well. We live in an increasingly international universe now; what could be more natural than to be curious about the state of the world as detailed in publications such as *Time, Newsweek,* and *US News & World Report*? Some pundits may criticize the constant barrage of weekly and biweekly issues, but these magazines raise awareness of what is going on in the world and act as only one component in a larger interactive web of radio, television, and other news media that help us to stay connected to a huge, global community of seven billion people and counting.

In a similar vein, the eclectic offerings of general interest magazines such as *National Geographic* and *Smithsonian* can be pure gold for people with diverse interests. Both publications contain well-written and thoughtful presentations of subjects ranging from the Kalahari Bushmen and the inhabitants of the Shetland Isles to the art of Jackson Pollock and the delights of the old Tom Swift book series for boys. It is soothing and enjoyable to read about such things. I do not claim that everyone who reads these articles comes away highly educated on their subject matter, but these pieces have the power to open people's eyes by exposing them to other cultures, art, and literature and, perhaps most important of all, provide that all-important nudge to find out more and perhaps discover a new passion that can be indulged in some depth. If we have never heard of a subject, we never have the opportunity to find out more and think deeply about it. Just as popular fiction can provide a springboard into more sophisticated literature, so, too, can popular magazines impel readers to read and contemplate nonfiction.

However, our print culture is currently being eclipsed by the electronic word; this I do worry about. More and more of my students seem to be losing the ability to write focused and unified paragraphs, and I have a theory that the constant texting and snippet-writing on Twitter and Facebook are responsible. But as long as higher education insists on upholding a high standard of thinking and writing, students will be forced to struggle against their impulse to read and think only superficially. As long as employers continue to value strong writing skills, the possibly harmful effects of snippet-writing will be kept at bay. And perhaps, once exposed in the classroom to the delights of reading, people will still indulge in the pursuit during their time off. Frankly, I would be thrilled if most of my students indulged in more light reading; deep reading would merely be a wonderful bonus.

I don't know where it will all end, but even from my exalted status as a lover of Good Books, I do not think that popular fiction and magazines are the evil influence that many think them to be. Deep reading may be an essential skill for a culture, but it is not an essential skill for every individual, and it never has been.

Works Cited

"Books." *Goodreads.* Goodreads Inc., n.d. Web. 5 May 2014. <https://www.goodreads.com/review/list/18560694-onebook-onesandiego?shelf=2013-nominated-books%3C/a>.

Carr, Nicholas. "The Oral World vs. the Written Word." *Poems out Loud.* W. W. Norton & Company, 18 June 2010. Web. 3 May 2014. <http://poemsoutloud.net/columns/archive/oral_world_written_word/>.

Lurie, Alison. "The Oddness of Oz." *Boys and Girls Forever: Children's Classics from* Cinderella *to* Harry Potter. New York: Penguin, 2003. 25-46. Print.

Discussion Questions

1. According to Benedict Jones, how do some people judge others by their reading material?

2. What distinction does Jones make between what we read in school and what we read in our spare time? Do you agree with his contrast of the two? Why or why not?

3. How does Jones compare his own youthful reading experiences with those of adults who currently read popular fiction? What lesson does he think we should take away from this comparison? Do you agree? Why or why not?

4. What arguments does the author make in favor of light reading and "disposable" reading material? Do you agree with him? How do you think Macdonald would respond to these arguments? Explain.

Why Literature Matters: Good Books Help Make a Civil Society

DANA GIOIA

Dana Gioia is an American writer and poet. He earned a BA from Stanford, an MA from Harvard, and an MBA from Stanford Business School. He has written or co-written several literary anthologies and college textbooks, a number of essays and book reviews, and four books of poetry; his first, titled Daily Horoscope *(1986), established him as one of the leading poets of his time. He has served as chairman of the National Endowment for the Arts. He teaches at the University of Southern California, and he became the California State Poet Laureate in December of 2015.*

In 1780 Massachusetts patriot John Adams wrote to his wife, Abigail, outlining his vision of how American culture might evolve. "I must study politics and war," he prophesied, so "that our sons may have liberty to study mathematics and philosophy." They would add to their studies geography, navigation, commerce, and agriculture, he continued, so that *their* children might enjoy the "right to study painting, poetry, music . . . " Adams's bold prophecy proved correct. By the mid twentieth century, America boasted internationally preeminent traditions in literature, art, music, dance, theater, and cinema.

But a strange thing has happened in the American arts during the past quarter century. While income rose to unforeseen levels, college attendance ballooned, and access to information increased enormously, the interest young Americans showed in the arts—and especially literature—actually diminished.

According to the 2002 Survey of Public Participation in the Arts, a population study designed and commissioned by the National Endowment for the Arts (and executed by the US Bureau of the Census), arts participation by Americans has declined for eight of the nine major forms that are measured. (Only jazz has shown a tiny increase—thank you, Ken Burns.) The declines have been most severe among younger adults (ages 18-24). The most worrisome finding in the 2002 study, however, is the declining percentage of Americans, especially young adults, reading literature.

That individuals at a time of crucial intellectual and emotional development bypass the joys and challenges of literature is a troubling trend. If it were true that they substituted histories, biographies, or political works for literature, one might not worry. But book reading of any kind is falling as well.

That such a longstanding and fundamental cultural activity should slip so swiftly, especially among young adults, signifies deep transformations in contemporary life. To call attention to the trend, the Arts Endowment issued the reading portion of the Survey as a separate report, "Reading at Risk: A Survey of Literary Reading in America."

The decline in reading has consequences that go beyond literature. The significance of reading has become a persistent theme in the business world. The February issue of *Wired* magazine, for example, sketches a new set of mental skills and habits proper to the twenty-first century, aptitudes decidedly literary in character: not "linear, logical, analytical talents," author Daniel Pink states, but "the ability to create artistic and emotional beauty, to detect patterns and opportunities, to craft a satisfying narrative." When asked what kinds of talents they like to see in management positions, business leaders consistently set imagination, creativity, and higher-order thinking at the top.

Ironically, the value of reading and the intellectual faculties that it inculcates appear most clearly as active and engaged literacy declines. There is now a growing awareness of the consequences of nonreading to the workplace. In 2001, the National Association of Manufacturers polled its members on skill deficiencies among employees. Among hourly workers, poor reading skills ranked second, and 38 percent of employers complained that local schools inadequately taught reading comprehension.

Corporate America makes similar complaints about a skill intimately related to reading—writing. Last year, the College Board reported that corporations spend some $3.1 billion a year on remedial writing instruction for employees, adding that they "express a fair degree of dissatisfaction with the writing of recent college graduates." If the twenty-first-century American economy requires innovation and creativity, solid reading skills and the imaginative growth fostered by literary reading are central elements in that program.

The decline of reading is also taking its toll in the civic sphere. In a 2000 survey of college seniors from the top 55 colleges, the Roper Organization found that 81 percent could not earn a grade of C on a high-school-level history test. A 2003 study of 15– to 26-year-olds' civic knowledge by the National Conference of State Legislatures concluded, "Young people do not understand the ideals of citizenship . . . and their appreciation and support of American democracy is limited."

It is probably no surprise that declining rates of literary reading coincide with declining levels of historical and political awareness among young people. One of the surprising findings of "Reading at Risk" was that literary readers are markedly more civically engaged than nonreaders, scoring two to four times more likely to perform charity work, visit a museum, or attend a sporting event. One reason for their higher social and cultural interactions may lie in the kind of civic and historical knowledge that comes with literary reading.

Unlike the passive activities of watching television and DVDs or surfing the Web, reading is actually a highly active enterprise. Reading requires sustained and focused attention as well as active use of memory and imagination. Literary reading also enhances and enlarges our humility by helping us imagine and understand lives quite different from our own.

Indeed, we sometimes underestimate how large a role literature has played in the evolution of our national identity, especially in that literature often has served to introduce young people to events from the past and principles of civil society and governance. Just as more ancient Greeks learned about moral and political conduct from the epics of Homer than from the dialogues of Plato, so the most important work in the abolitionist movement was the novel *Uncle Tom's Cabin*.

Likewise, our notions of American populism come more from Walt Whitman's poetic vision than from any political tracts. Today, when people recall the Depression, the images that most come to mind are of the travails of John Steinbeck's Joad family from *The Grapes of Wrath*. Without a literary inheritance, the historical past is impoverished.

In focusing on the social advantages of a literary education, however, we should not overlook the personal impact. Every day, authors receive letters from readers that say, "Your book changed my life." History reveals case after case of famous people whose lives were transformed by literature. When the great Victorian thinker John Stuart Mill suffered a crippling depression in late adolescence, the poetry of Wordsworth restored his optimism and self-confidence—a "medicine for my state of mind," he called it.

A few decades later, W. E. B. DuBois found a different tonic in literature, an escape from the indignities of Jim Crow into a world of equality. "I sit with Shakespeare and he winces not," DuBois observed. "Across the color line I move arm in arm with Balzac and Dumas, where smiling men and welcoming women glide in gilded halls." Literature is a catalyst for education and culture.

The evidence of literature's importance to civic, personal, and economic health is too strong to ignore. The decline of literary reading foreshadows serious long-term social and economic problems, and it is time to bring literature and the other arts into discussions of public policy. Libraries, schools, and public agencies do noble work, but addressing the reading issue will require the leadership of politicians and the business community as well.

Literature now competes with an enormous array of electronic media. While no single activity is responsible for the decline in reading, the cumulative presence and availability of electronic alternatives increasingly have drawn Americans away from reading.

Reading is not a timeless, universal capability. Advanced literacy is a specific intellectual skill and social habit that depends on a great many educational, cultural, and economic factors. As more Americans lose this capability, our nation becomes less informed, active, and independent-minded. These are not the qualities that a free, innovative, or productive society can afford to lose.

Discussion Questions

1. Why does the author find the comparison between the percentage of young people attending college and the percentage of young people reading books to be strange? How would you explain these statistics?

2. What are some examples of the kinds of activities the author considers to be cultural? If young people are not participating in these activities, how do you think they are spending their leisure time?

3. What are some of the consequences that the article discusses in relation to the decline in reading? Did any of them surprise you? Explain your answer.

4. After reading the selections given so far in this assignment unit, which of them most made you want to change your reading habits? Why?

Writing without Reading

Essay

JOHN BRIGGS

John Briggs did his undergraduate studies at Harvard and received his PhD from the University of Chicago. He is the author of Francis Bacon and the Rhetoric of Nature *(1988), which won the Thomas J. Wilson Award from Harvard University Press,* Lincoln's Speeches Reconsidered *(2005), and numerous articles, primarily on Shakespeare. At the University of California, Riverside, where he is a professor, he teaches courses in Renaissance literature, Shakespeare, Milton, and the history and theory of rhetoric. He also directs the University Writing Program. The following reading selection is an excerpt.*

Although grammar handbooks continue to be a staple of the composition curriculum, professional studies of grammar, style, imitation, and the relation of literature to composition are now rare in the flagship journals of composition and rhetoric. Up to the mid 1960s, they were fairly common. As the professional literature has grown more sophisticated, grammar has become associated with the specialized study of linguistics or with troublesome disputes over the status of nonstandard English. Mina Shaughnessy's pioneering 1977 study of the grammatical and rhetorical intricacies of basic writers' prose is steeped in literary reference, and draws from her thinking about literary composition. Yet in recent years the annual Mina Shaughnessy prize has gone to professional articles on a wide range of subjects unrelated to much of the spirit or content of her work.[1] Style has taken on its own stigma as an elite literary subject, though the textbooks and professional scholarship of Joseph Williams (*Style: Ten Lessons in Clarity and Grace*) and Richard Lanham (*Revising Prose*) continue to be cited with respect. Despite the substantial contributions over the past fifty years of major scholars and teachers who have bridged the gap between literature and composition—Wayne Booth, Kenneth Burke, Frederick Crews, E. D. Hirsch, James Murphy, and James Kinneavy, to name a few in addition to Williams and Lanham—discussion about the relation between composition and literature as academic pursuits, not simply as conflicting institutions,

---

[1]Mina Shaughnessy, *Errors and Expectations* (New York, Oxford University Press, 1977).

is now remarkably rare.[2] What follows is a brief review of some of the philosophical reasons for this change in the professional literature.[3]

To understand what is happening today to composition and English, it is useful to put the new professional literature in the context of the influential Dartmouth Conference of 1966, in which fifty prominent academics (half from Britain and half from the US) met for a month to discuss the state of English education in schools and colleges. Participants included faculty from British schools of education, American literary scholars such as Wayne Booth, Charles Muscatine, James E. Miller, Benjamin DeMott, and Arthur Eastman, and several academics who played major roles in the study and teaching of composition: Albert Kitzhaber, James Squire, James Moffett, and others. Walter Ong was among several dozen visiting consultants.

According to the two book-length reports published immediately afterward, the seminar's participants endorsed literature as one of the most valuable parts of the English curriculum. But they also failed to reach a consensus about literature's function in the English classroom, specifically with regard to the teaching of writing. One report on the conference, written by a British participant, places literature deep in the background. Students' own writings are the more prominent points of interest, as are pedagogical methods that help cultivate many kinds of writing. Yet the function of literature is evident at every point. It enhances students' creativity by giving them ways to think about and express their interests and experiences: "[L]anguage

---

[2]Christopher Gould, "Literature in the Basic Writing Course: A Bibliographic Survey," *College English* 49 (1987): 558-574; Marie Ponsot, "Total Immersion," *Journal of Basic Writing* 1.2 (1976): 31-43; Marie Ponsot, *Beat Not the Poor Desk: Writing: What to Teach, How to Teach It and Why* (Upper Montclair, NJ: Boynton, 1982). A popular textbook that combines literature and composition is Robert Scholes's *Text Book* (New York: St. Martin's, 1988). But Scholes is extremely careful not to seem to distinguish literature too much from other forms of discourse. Discourse and "texts," he argues in *The End of English* (New Haven: Yale University Press, 1998), should be the real subject of composition and the discipline of English. *Text Book* remains a useful source of ideas for incorporating literature into the composition course, even though it is directed toward the introductory literature course.

[3]For a prescient analysis of the hazards and possible benefits of this trend, see David Bartholomae's address as 4Cs chairman to the 1988 CCCC convention: "Freshman English, Composition, and CCCC," *CCC* 40 (February, 1989): 38-50. The danger of ignoring the departmental structure of the modern university is amply documented in John Heyda's study of the post-war communications movement: "Fighting Over Freshman English: CCCC's Early Years and the Turf Wars of the 1950s," *CCC* 50 (June, 1999): 663-681.

is learnt in operation, not by dummy runs. In English pupils meet to share their encounters with life, and to do this effectively they move freely between dialogue and monologue—between talk, drama, and writing; and literature, by bringing new voices into the classroom." This process "adds to the store of shared experience. Each pupil takes from the store what he can and what he needs."[4]

From the American side, the historian Herbert Muller argued that literature was crucial to students' intellectual and emotional growth. It was the lynchpin of all areas of English study. "Proficiency" in reading was not enough; "a lasting desire to read books" was what was needed. Teachers needed to foster a "love of literature" in the earliest grades. An attachment to reading—not mere proficiency—would need to become one of the goals, if not the main goal, of English instruction.[5] Students learning to write needed to draw from, and add to, this desire for literate experience.

The irony of Dartmouth's legacy is that even though there was a good deal of consensus on the place of literature in the general curriculum, the occasion marked, in the memory of many American compositionists, a turning away from external models and inspiration, and toward forms of personal experience in which reading plays only an implicit (if not incidental) role. The British assumed that reading would continue to have a deep influence on students' learning how to write, but many Americans concluded that students' writing, without regard for its relationship to reading, must determine the focus of instruction. Reading was still considered to be important, but it was left to drift. Students were supposed to choose books for themselves. Reading was an instrument for extending their curiosity and their drive toward self-realization; it was not to be prescribed, or made a focus of instruction. It was certainly not to be used to make organized exercises in imitation and variation.

The new approach to writing did not clearly exclude, at least in principle, the use of literature in the teaching of writing. James Moffett and Peter Elbow were interested in the ways in which individual works and genres could stimulate imitation and originality, as long as the focus of instruction remained on students as writers.[6] Inspired by

---

[4]John Dixon, *Growth through English* (Oxford: Oxford University Press, 1967), xii and 13.
[5]Herbert J. Muller, *The Uses of English* (New York: Holt, Rinehart and Winston, Inc., 1967), 78-79
[6]James Moffett, *Teaching the Universe of Discourse* (Boston: Houghton Mifflin, 1968); Peter Elbow, *Embracing Contraries* (Oxford: Oxford University Press, 1986).

the example of the British, these and other American composition-ists wanted to encourage students to seek out literary examples that would help them deepen and polish their work. But such shifts of emphasis did not reverse the overall narrowing of literature's role in the composition classroom. In fact, the dominance of such views in the sixties and seventies, when literature's role in composition became increasingly problematic, made composition instruction more vulner-able to conflicting demands for self-expression and for training in mechanical skills and technical writing. As less attention was being paid to the particular ways in which particular kinds of literature could contribute to the mastery of written English, composition increasingly became a field apart from literary studies—not only in terms of its methods but also in its attitude toward letters.

Of course, this philosophical resistance to literature in the com-position classroom has had much to do with academic politics. Since the end of World War II, when unprecedented numbers of stu-dents began entering American colleges and universities, the sudden demand (and need) for instruction in composition has strained the financial and intellectual resources of English departments, divisions, and entire campuses, increasingly dividing English departments into those who teach lower-division composition and those who teach (and pursue scholarship in) literature and other fields the department deems worthy of specialized study. Typically composed of part-timers and graduate students, and so not a faculty in the strict sense, the first group is responsible for teaching the majority of English classes but rarely receives the recognition and professional advancement that they believe they deserve. On the other side of the divide has been the lit-erature faculty, which has periodically expressed a distrust of financial and intellectual investments in composition when those investments seem to threaten the integrity of established studies. Many English faculty have resisted an obligation to teach what they consider to be a remedial or merely practical art. Or conversely, they have taught com-position courses in such a way that they became literature or theory courses unconcerned with students' progress as writers.

In the often stratified society of higher education, what seems to be disciplinary excellence to one group smacks of elitism to the other; what seems to be deleterious to serious education at the college level is, in the eyes of the second group, a chance to learn a skill without which higher education must fail. Each side suspects the other of lack-ing rigor. The presence or absence of literature in the composition classroom has often become a sign of instructors' sympathy for one view or the other.

Aggravating this conflict is the division among non-composition scholars over the literary status of nonfiction, which is a staple of instruction in writing courses. For literary scholars inheriting the legacy of the New Criticism, nonfiction tends to be suspect. On the other hand, for faculty who see themselves as teachers and scholars of cultural criticism, the question of nonfiction's status seems to be settled by broad new definitions of text. Caught in the middle, compositionists defend the teaching of nonfiction but are divided over the pedagogical value of esoteric or politicized approaches to textual studies. The professional literature of composition has unfortunately not taken up the question of what makes a particular kind of nonfiction—literary nonfiction—worth teaching.[7]

Amid such disagreements, Stephen Witte's prize-winning 1983 study of student writing focused attention on the connection between students' ability to write and their capacity to read their own writing for the gist of their thought:

> How students decide to revise a text is largely dependent on their understanding of the text. . . . [Unskilled writers] have never learned how to read and evaluate texts in their entirety, to respond to the overall semantic structure of texts, or to evaluate semantic structure against their intentions.[8]

---

[7]For a broad survey of post-Dartmouth attempts to combine critical theory with composition theory and pedagogy, see John Clifford and John Schilb, "Composition Theory and Critical Theory," in *Perspectives on Research and Scholarship in Composition*, ed. Ben W. McClelland and Timothy R. Donovan (New York: MLA, 1985), 45-67. The 1994 MLA anthology of essays edited by Clifford and Schilb shows how the interests of many leading compositionists have shifted decidedly toward new theory, which unlike the 1985 studies avoids poetics and the rhetoric of persuasion and eloquence. Robert Scholes's essay in that collection, "My Life in Theory", records a similar transition: from a desire to ameliorate the conflict between literature and composition to a conviction that only a theoretical and pedagogical revolution can join them. John Gage, an early questioner of this trend, warned of the regrettable influence of deconstructionism on composition pedagogy. See his essay "Conflicting Assumptions about Intention in Teaching Reading and Composition," *College English* 40 (1978): 255-263. Another moderate view can be found in James C. Raymond's analysis of publication patterns in "*College English*: Whence and Whither," *College English* 49 (1987): 553-557.
[8]Stephen P. Witte, "Topical Structure and Revision: An Exploratory Study," reprinted in *On Writing Research: The Braddock Essays 1975-1998*, ed. Lisa Ede (Boston: St. Martin's Press, 1999, 132-155.

Unskilled writers are frequently poor readers. Lacking experience with the ways other writers shape ideas, they cannot revise their work because they cannot read it for significance. Since literature draws readers into these worlds of meaning more fully and effectively than other kinds of texts, it would seem that some form of literary education is crucial to the task of learning to write, especially for struggling students. These findings are probably no surprise to college faculty who work with incoming students, but their implications are difficult for many advocates on the various sides of the composition debates to accept.

New forms of composition instruction have weakened students' ability to gain access to literature by reading sympathetically and identifying with views other than their own. Virginia Anderson has observed that an emphasis on a confrontational style of cultural critique diminishes their ability to see complexity, to sense the predispositions of their audiences, and to understand the purposes of their opponents. Students, she says, are sometimes pressured to identify with the instructor as an "embodiment" of a "political agenda" rather than as a coach or a model for the educated person.[9] A similar hazard awaits inexperienced students when the apparatus of critical theory, in the hands of unpracticed teachers, transports undergraduates into the matrix of a graduate seminar. Under the pressure of such theoretical and political imperatives, the professional literature pays less and less attention to finding useful literary texts, or engaging in the practical and intellectual challenge of teaching the analysis, imitation, and variation of sentences, paragraphs, and entire passages.

Nevertheless, despite these negative trends, our surveys suggest that a deep-seated antagonism toward anything resembling traditional literary education, though it is occasionally supported in the professional literature, is still far from the norm in most composition programs. The great majority of composition courses seem to be taught along quasi-traditional lines, though often without sufficient grounding in an intellectual tradition or literary studies. Erika Lindemann, writing in the March 1993 issue of *College Composition and Communication*, expresses a broader, more deliberate consensus among many compositionists: the view that literature's role in the

---

[9]Virginia Anderson, "Confrontational Teaching and Rhetorical Practice," *CCC* 48 (May, 1997): 200 and *passim*.

composition classroom is problematic, and ought not to be endorsed without thoughtful consideration. The following schematization attempts to identify her main assumptions.[10]

1. As a required course sanctioned by the full faculty, composition is uniquely suited to preparing students to write in the various discourses of the academy, not just in response to literature.

2. Writing about literature is a specialized activity. Students should be taught to write a variety of specialized discourses, not just one. Therefore, their work should not be restricted to the humanities. The course should help them learn how to interpret data as well as texts.

3. The literary essay is not the best kind of writing to teach in the academy. It is not sufficiently specialized to be a genre of academic discourse.

4. A focus on "Great Ideas" associated with the traditional study of literature wrongly deflects attention from learning to write, which requires the class to concentrate on working out the students' own ideas, arranging them effectively, and other aspects of the writing process. Since students must learn to write by writing, a significant portion of that process must be the subject of instruction in the classroom. Theme-based coursework in composition, which the study of literature encourages, is often dilatory for the same reasons. Moreover, literature-based courses that rely upon lecture rather than group work and workshops lack the practical intensity of good composition instruction. Most importantly, literature-based courses "focus on consuming texts, not producing them."[11] They do not teach style except as a thing to be appreciated.

5. Students do not need to read literature in a composition class to benefit from critical theory's insights, which can be applied to a wide variety of texts.

6. Aesthetic appreciation, which literary reading tends to encourage, should not be a high priority in the composition classroom. Practical goals should rule.

---

[10]Erika Lindemann, "Freshman Composition: No Place for Literature," *CCC* 55 (March, 1993): 311-315.
[11]Lindemann, 313.

7. Literature faculty say "too much" while their students write "too little."[12]

To one or more of these objections, Gary Tate, Wayne Booth, E. D. Hirsch, Frederick Crews, Richard Marius, and others have provided parts of the following responses[13]:

1. The mandate given to English departments to teach composition does not dictate that literature should be excluded or minimized. Greater attention should be given to teaching writing with the help of literature, including nonfiction prose works that have literary magnitude.

2. Writing about literature in a course that combines composition and literature is not necessarily specialized, and indeed should aspire to be something more than the specialized writing for a major or a job. The writing in such a course ought to have something to do with what it means to be human, including what it means to seek out the varieties of human excellence.

3. Indeed, the essay is not a specialized form of discourse. It often borders on literature, and combines many kinds of writing in its malleable form. Paradoxically, it is one of the best ways for specialists to communicate with generalists (the public), and with specialists in other areas. [14]

---

[12]Lindemann, 316.

[13]Wayne Booth, "Imaginative Literature Is Indispensable," *College English* 7 (1956): 35-38; E. D. Hirsch, "Remarks on Composition to the Yale English Department," in *The Rhetorical Tradition in Modern Writing* (New York: MLA, 1982), 13-18; Frederick Crews, "Composing Our Differences: The Case for Literary Readings" and Wayne Booth, "LITCOMP,' both in *Composition and Literature*, ed. Winifred Bryan Horner (Chicago: University of Chicago Press, 1983), 159-167. (See the entire collection.) See also Richard Marius, "Composition Studies," in *Redrawing the Boundaries*, eds. Stephen Greenblatt and Giles Gunn (New York: MLA, 1992), 466-481. A 1973 study by Thomas W. Wilcox indicates that many similar opinions were being heard a generation ago. See *The Anatomy of College English* (San Francisco: Jossey-Bass, 1973), 82 and 62-102. For other treatments of the topic, see James J. Murphy, *The Rhetorical Tradition and Modern Writing* (New York: MLA, 1982), and James Kinneavy, *A Theory of Discourse* (Englewood Cliffs: Prentice Hall, 1971).

[14]William C. Rice has noted that when writing instruction focuses on mastery of the specialized discourses of various disciplines in the academy, it ignores the absence of highly specialized writing in the composition anthologies. The literary essay, which appeals to the general reader as well as the specialist, does a better job of winning and keeping an academic audience. See his *Public Discourse and Academic Inquiry* (New York: Garland, 1996), especially pp. 66-72.

4. Is thinking a passive state? Might not an appreciation of good writing be a crucial factor in learning to write? The desire to imitate, answer, and write variations upon certain types of writing would seem to be enhanced by an admiration of the best qualities of those types, particularly when the encounter with literature is linked with appropriate exercises and assignments.

5. Why should critical theory be more important than the encounter with literature? The productive combination of composition and literature does not seem to need sophisticated theories for its success in the classroom.

6. Is it accurate to characterize the study of literature as an exclusion of ethical and political ideas and concerns? On the other hand, can we claim to teach writing well if we do not cultivate the literary imagination?

7. Students will not learn to write if they do not write, or if their writing finds no careful reader who can help spur them on. But are we right, then, to deny those students access to literature as a means toward that end of learning to write—especially if, as many believe, carefully chosen literary texts can help their efforts more than anything else? The question is how we organize and teach classes in which students learn to be better writers with the help of literature.

Paths Toward Reform

To recombine composition and literature for the sake of improving the teaching of composition, faculty and administrators have a number of options. The paths of various reforms may join and diverge as new initiatives proceed. Some reforms may be philosophically preferable to others, or more practicable, or both. Some may require the action of faculty senates and the cooperation of deans; others might need only departmental or personal effort. It is worth recalling that our survey of faculty attitudes indicated widespread interest in using literature in the composition class, but not in a wholesale conversion of composition into the study of literature.

There must be a renewal of discussions of curriculum that do not depend upon a complete resolution of the ancient quarrel between composition and literature. The stakes are too high, and the opportunity to benefit millions of students too great, to countenance delay. None of the following proposals depends upon or presupposes the abolition of the composition course; all of them are ways to change the status quo. They expand the current conception of literature to include powerful and lasting nonfiction, and include ideas to strengthen the teaching of writing in literature classes.

Recommendations:

1. It is time to rediscover literature's power to contribute to the teaching of composition, not only as a stimulus for ideas but also as a model and point of departure for the organization and presentation of those ideas. Literature should inform the study of invention, organization, syntax, and style—the matter and form of articulate thought.

2. Judiciously chosen literary texts, including admirable non-fiction, should serve as models for emulative and creative imitation, from the composing of sentences to the crafting of entire arguments, descriptions, narratives, and analyses. Upon this basis, such texts can stimulate the development of a literate voice, and the practical appreciation of the kinds of writing by which that voice can find expression, reach understanding, and secure assent.

3. To pursue these goals, the selection of literary works now used in composition should be enlarged in terms of literary period, level of difficulty, and depth of appeal—with particular attention to works that have stood the test of generations.

4. Graduate training should consider literature's contribution to the effective teaching of writing.

5. Where common core courses or freshman seminars take the place of conventional composition, assigned writings should be substantial, and students should be given access to assistance from faculty, discussion leaders, and writing centers.

6. English departments should prepare their students, by force of example, for teaching composition and literature together in the secondary schools.

7. A review of previous generations of textbooks, as well as current works that feature mimetic and creative approaches to literary models, should help guide the creation of new curricula.[15]

At stake, whatever reforms are pursued, is the prospect for effective instruction in composition. An incipient and correctable deafness to the written and printed page increasingly limits many of our students' prospects. Yet literature, as we have defined it here, offers them what is probably the most powerful guide to literate expression. The composition curriculum cannot in itself supply the literary education these students need, but it can incorporate carefully chosen literary works, particular lines, sentences, and excerpted passages that repay students' attention, helping them—in ways that other readings cannot do so well—become independent writers.

Wayne Booth may well have been right when he wrote, "As a stimulus for thinking and writing, as a source of subject matter, and as a model for style and grammar, imaginative literature is, as the students say, the best thing with which they can come in contact."[16] We are obliged to act, again and again, upon the idea that literature, properly combined with composition, offers our students an indispensable means of getting an education. For without the life-blood of literature, the teaching of composition becomes a form of rule-driven linguistic engineering.[17]

---

[15] Old textbooks, as this report has noted, frequently draw from literary materials. The power and flexibility of the mimetic approach at the sentence level is amply evident in Robert Miles, Marc Bertonasco, and William Karns, *Prose Style: A Contemporary Guide* (Englewood Cliffs: Prentice-Hall, 1991); P. J. Corbett and Robert J. Connors, *Style and Statement* (New York: Oxford University Press, 1999); Richard Lanham, *Style: An Anti-Textbook* (New Haven and London: Yale University Press, 1974); Joseph M. Williams, *Style: Ten Lessons in Clarity and Grace* (New York: Harper Collins, 1994).

[16] Booth, "Imaginative Literature Is Indispensable," 35.

[17] The research for this study was facilitated by a modest grant from the Association of Literary Scholars and Critics, with the condition that the study be under my supervision. For their help in gathering and ordering materials, I would like to thank Richard Hishmeh, Dean Papas, John Stamp, and Sharon Tyler.

Discussion Questions

1. Discuss the explanation for the statement included in the selection from John Briggs's "Professional Literature: The Disappearance of Literary Reading" that "unskilled writers are frequently poor readers." Do you believe it is possible to be excellent at writing but poor at reading? Explain.

2. For each of Erika Lindemann's seven assumptions that help support her position against the use of literature in the composition classroom, Gary Tate et al. provide a rebuttal. Consider all of the statements on both sides of the issue, and then choose what you think is the weakest point from each side. Explain your reason for finding each of them to be unconvincing.

3. Among Briggs's recommendations is more use of literary texts that have "stood the test of generations." Compile a list of five books you believe would be included on a syllabus designed with this principle in mind. Explain why you think reading these books would or would not help you to improve your own writing.

Does Great Literature Make Us Better People?

Essay

GREGORY CURRIE

Gregory Currie was educated at the London School of Economics and the University of California, Berkeley. Until 2013, he was Professor of Philosophy and Director of Research in the Humanities at the University of Nottingham. He is currently an editor of Mind and Language.

You agree with me, I expect, that exposure to challenging works of literary fiction is good for us. That's one reason we deplore the dumbing-down of the school curriculum and the rise of the Internet and its hyperlink culture. Perhaps we don't all read very much that we would count as great literature, but we're apt to feel guilty about not doing so, seeing it as one of the ways we fall short of excellence. Wouldn't reading about Anna Karenina, the good folk of Middlemarch, and Marcel and his friends expand our imaginations and refine our moral and social sensibilities?

If someone now asks you for evidence for this view, I expect you will have one or both of the following reactions. First, why would anyone need evidence for something so obviously right? Second, what kind of evidence would he or she want? Answering the first question is easy: if there's no evidence—even indirect evidence—for the civilizing value of literary fiction, we ought not to assume that it does civilize. Perhaps you think there are questions we can sensibly settle in ways other than by appeal to evidence: by faith, for instance. But even if there are such questions, surely no one thinks this is one of them.

What sort of evidence could we present? Well, we can point to specific examples of our fellows who have become more caring, wiser people through encounters with literature. Indeed, we are such people ourselves, aren't we?

I hope no one is going to push this line very hard. Everything we know about our understanding of ourselves suggests that we are not very good at knowing how we got to be the kind of people we are.

In fact we don't really know, very often, what sorts of people we are. We regularly attribute our own failures to circumstance and the failures of others to bad character. But we can't all be exceptions to the rule (supposing it is a rule) that people do bad things because they are bad people.

We are poor at knowing why we make the choices we do, and we fail to recognize the tiny changes in circumstances that can shift us from one choice to another. When it comes to other people, can you be confident that your intelligent, socially attuned, and generous friend who reads Proust got that way partly because of the reading? Might it not be the other way around: that bright, socially competent and empathic people are more likely than others to find pleasure in the complex representations of human interaction we find in literature?

There's an argument we often hear on the other side, illustrated earlier this year by a piece on the *New Yorker*'s Web site. Reminding us of all those cultured Nazis, Teju Cole notes the willingness of a president who reads novels and poetry to sign weekly drone strike permissions. What, he asks, became of "literature's vaunted power to inspire empathy?" I find this a hard argument to like, and not merely because I am not yet persuaded by the moral case against drones. No one should be claiming that exposure to literature protects one against moral temptation absolutely, or that it can reform the truly evil among us. We measure the effectiveness of drugs and other medical interventions by thin margins of success that would not be visible without sophisticated statistical techniques; why assume that literature's effectiveness should be any different?

We need to go beyond the appeal to common experience and into the territory of psychological research, which is sophisticated enough these days to make a start in testing our proposition. Psychologists have started to do some work in this area, and we have learned a few things so far. We know that if you get people to read a short, lowering story about a child murder they will afterward report feeling worse about the world than they otherwise would. Such changes, which are likely to be very short-term, show that fictions press our buttons; they don't show that they refine us emotionally or in any other way.

We have learned that people are apt to pick up (purportedly) factual information stated or implied as part of a fictional story's background. Oddly, people are more prone to do that when the story is set away from home: in a study conducted by Deborah Prentice and colleagues and published in 1997, Princeton undergraduates retained more from a story when it was set at Yale than when it was set on their own campus (don't worry Princetonians, Yalies are just as bad when you do the test the other way around). Television, with its serial programming, is good for certain kinds of learning; according to a study from 2001 undertaken for the Kaiser Foundation, people who regularly watched the show *E.R.* picked up a good bit of medical information on which they sometimes acted. What we don't have is compelling evidence that suggests that people are morally or socially better for reading Tolstoy.

Not nearly enough research has been conducted; nor, I think, is the relevant psychological evidence just around the corner. Most of the studies undertaken so far don't draw on serious literature but on short snatches of fiction devised especially for experimental purposes. Very few of them address questions about the effects of literature on moral and social development, far too few for us to conclude that literature either does or doesn't have positive moral effects. There is a puzzling mismatch between the strength of opinion on this topic and the state of the evidence. In fact I suspect it is worse than that; advocates of the view that literature educates and civilizes don't over-rate the evidence—they don't even think that evidence comes into it. While the value of literature ought not to be a matter of faith, it looks as if, for many of us, that is exactly what it is.

Now, philosophers are careful folk, trained in the ways of argument and, you would hope, above these failings. It's odd, then, that some of them write so confidently and passionately about the kinds of learning we get from literature, and about the features of literature that make it a particularly apt teacher of moral psychology. In her influential book *Love's Knowledge*, Martha Nussbaum argues that the narrative form gives literary fiction a peculiar power to generate moral insight; in the hands of a literary master like Henry James, fiction is able to give us scenarios that make vivid the details of a moral issue, while allowing us to think them through without the distortions wrought by personal interest. I'm not inclined to write off such speculations; it is always good to have in mind a stock of ideas about ways literature might enhance our thought and action. But it would be refreshing to have some acknowledgment that suggestions about how literature might aid our learning don't show us that it does in fact aid it. (Suppose a school inspector reported on the efficacy of our education system by listing ways that teachers might be helping students to learn; the inspector would be out of a job pretty soon.)

I'm confident we can look forward to better evidence. I'm less optimistic about what the evidence will show. Here, quickly, is a reason we already have for thinking that the idea of moral and social learning from literature may be misguided. One reason people like Martha Nussbaum have argued for the benefits of literature is that literature, or fictional narrative of real quality, deals in complexity. Literature turns us away from the simple moral rules that so often prove unhelpful when we are confronted with messy real-life decision making, and gets us ready for the stormy voyage through the social world that sensitive, discriminating moral agents are supposed to undertake. Literature helps us, in other words, to be, or to come closer to being, moral "experts." The problem with this argument is that there's long been evidence that much of what we take for expertise in complex and unpredictable domains—of which morality is surely one—is bogus. Beginning fifty years ago with work by the psychologist Paul Meehl, study after study has shown that following simple rules—rules that take account of many fewer factors than an expert would bother to consider—does at least as well as and generally better than relying on an expert's judgment. (Not that rules do particularly well either; but they do better than expert judgment.) Some of the evidence for this view is convincingly presented in Daniel Kahneman's recent book *Thinking Fast and Slow*: spectacular failures of expertise include predictions of the future value of wine, the performance of baseball players, the health of newborn babies, and a couple's prospects for marital stability.

But why, I hear you say, do you complain about people's neglect of evidence when you yourself have no direct evidence that moral expertise fails? After all, no one has done tests in this area. Well, yes, I grant that in the end, the evidence could go in favor of the idea that literature can make moral experts of us. I also grant that moral thinking is probably not a single domain, but something that goes on in bewilderingly different ways in different circumstances. Perhaps we can find kinds of moral reasoning whereby experts trained partly by exposure to the fictional literature of complex moral choice do better than those who rely on simple moral rules of thumb. I haven't, then, in any way refuted the claim that moral expertise is a quality we should aspire to. But I do think we have identified a challenge that needs to be met by anyone who seriously wants to press the case for moral expertise.

Everything depends in the end on whether we can find direct, causal evidence: We need to show that exposure to literature itself makes some sort of positive difference to the people we end up being. That will take a lot of careful and insightful psychological research (try designing an experiment to test the effects of reading *War and Peace*, for example). Meanwhile, most of us will probably soldier on with a positive view of the improving effects of literature, supported by nothing more than an airy bed of sentiment.

I have never been persuaded by arguments purporting to show that literature is an arbitrary category that functions merely as a badge of membership in an elite. There is such a thing as aesthetic merit, or more likely, aesthetic merits, complicated as they may be to articulate or impute to any given work. But it's hard to avoid the thought that there is something in the anti-elitist's worry. Many who enjoy the hard-won pleasures of literature are not content to reap aesthetic rewards from their reading; they want to insist that the effort makes them more morally enlightened as well. And that's just what we don't know yet.

Discussion Questions

1. Discuss the value that people generally attribute to the reading of good literature. Where or when have you encountered this argument? How did you react to it (try to read more, feel guilty or stupid, treat with skepticism)? Explain your response to Gregory Currie's challenge of the assumption that reading "is good for us."

2. In terms of evidence for the effectiveness of literature, what research has been done, and what research will or should be done? If you were given the task of constructing an experiment testing the effectiveness of reading, describe the design your experiment would take. Consider such details as materials used, participants selected, length of time involved, and other conditions.

3. Draft a hypothetical response to Currie that either Dana Gioia or John Briggs might post.

4. Relate an example from your own observations or experiences in which having read a particular book or article seems to have resulted in a change of behavior. The effect might be something easily visible, such as wearing a particular style of item of apparel, or something internal, such as a change in religious or political beliefs.

Is Reading Really at Risk?
It Depends on What the Meaning of Reading Is

JOSEPH EPSTEIN

Joseph Epstein is a writer of books, essays, and short stories, and a contributing editor to the Weekly Standard. *He earned a BA from the University of Chicago and lectured at Northwestern University. In 2003, he was awarded a National Humanities Medal by the National Endowment for the Humanities. For many years, he was a controversial editor of the* American Scholar, *and was ultimately let go because of his nonpolitically correct views. Epstein's body of work is known for its examination of popular culture, read widely in books such as* Fabulous Small Jews *(2003) and* Envy *(2003). The essay below appeared in the* Weekly Standard *in 2004.*

"Reading at Risk" is one of those hardy perennials, a government survey telling us that in some vital area—obesity, pollution, fuel depletion, quality of education, domestic relations—things are even worse than we thought. In the category of literacy, the old surveys seemed always to be some variant of "Why Johnny Can't Read." "Reading at Risk"— the most recent survey, carried out under the auspices of the National Endowment for the Arts as part of its larger Survey of Public Participation in the Arts, the whole conducted by the US Census Bureau—doesn't for a moment suggest that Johnny Can't Read. The problem is that, now grown, Johnny (though a little less Jane) doesn't much care to read a lot in the way of imaginative writing—fiction, poems, plays—also known to the survey as literature. For the first time in our history, apparently, less than half the population bothers to read any literature (so defined) at all.

"Reading at Risk" reports that there has been a decline in the reading of novels, poems, and plays of roughly 10 percentage points for all age cohorts between 1982 and 2002, with actual numbers of readers having gained only slightly despite a large growth (of 40 million people) in the overall population. More women than men continue to participate in what the survey also calls literary reading—in his trip to the United States in 1905, based on attendance at his lectures, Henry James noted that culture belonged chiefly to women—though even among women the rate is slipping. Nor are things better among the so-called educated; while they do read more than the less educated, the decline in literary reading is also found among them. But the rate of decline is greatest among young adults 18 to 24 years old, and the survey quotes yet another study, this one made by the National Institute for Literacy, showing that things are not looking any better for kids between 13 and 17, but are even a little worse.

Although the general decline in literary reading is not attributed to any single cause in "Reading at Risk," the problem, it is hinted, may be the distractions of electronic culture. To quote an item from the survey's executive summary: "A 1999 study showed that the average American child lives in a household with 2.9 televisions, 1.8 VCRs, 3.1 radios, 2.1 CD players, 1.4 video game players, and 1 computer." By 2002, to quote from the same summary, "electronic spending had soared to 24 percent [of total recreational spending by Americans], while spending on books declined . . . to 5.6 percent." Up against all this easily accessible and endlessly varied fare—from Palm Pilots to iPods—the reading of stories, poems, and plays is having a tough time competing.

"Reading at Risk" does provide a few not exactly surprises but slight jars to one's expectations. For me, one is that "people in managerial, professional, and technical occupations are more likely to read literature than those in other occupation groups." I would myself have expected that these were all jobs in which one worked more than an eight-hour day and then took work home, which, consequently, would allow a good deal less time for reading things not in some way related to one's work. The survey also claims that readers are "highly social people," more active in their communities and participating more in sports. I should have thought that lots of reading might make one introspective, slightly detached, a touch reclusive, even, but, according to the survey, not so. "People who live in the suburbs," the survey states, "are more likely to be readers than either those who live in the city or the country." Perhaps this is owing in good part to suburbs' being generally more affluent than cities; and, too, to book clubs, in which neighbors meet to discuss recent bestsellers and sometimes classics, and which tend to be suburban institutions.

The one area in which "Reading at Risk" is (honorably) shaky is in its conclusions on the subject of television, which is the standard fall-guy in almost all surveys having to do with education. Only among people who watch more than four hours of television daily does the extent of reading drop off, according to the survey, while watching no television whatsoever makes it more likely one will be a more frequent reader. On the other hand, the presence of writers on television—on C-SPAN and talk shows—may, the survey concedes, encourage people to buy books. No mention is made of those people, myself among them, who are able to read with a television set, usually playing a sports event, humming away in the background. In the end, "Reading at Risk" concludes that "it is not clear from [its] data how much influence TV watching has on literary reading." The survey does suggest that surfing the Internet may have made a dent in reading: "During the time period when the literature participation rates declined, home Internet use soared." But it does not take things further than that. My own speculation is that our speeded-up culture—with its FedEx, fax, e-mail, channel surfing, cell-phoning, fast-action movies, and other elements in its relentless race against boredom—has ended in a shortened national attention span. The quickened rhythms of new technology are not rhythms congenial to the slow and time-consuming and solitary act of reading. Sustained reading, sitting quietly and enjoying the aesthetic pleasure that words elegantly deployed on the page can give, contemplating careful formulations of complex thoughts—these do not seem likely to be acts strongly characteristic of an already jumpy new century.

Like all surveys, "Reading at Risk" is an example of the style of statistical thinking dominant in our time. It's far from sure that statistics are very helpful in capturing so idiosyncratic an act as reading, except in a bulky and coarse way. That the Swedes read more novels, poems, and plays than Americans and the Portuguese read fewer than we do is a statistical fact, but I'm not sure what you do with it, especially when you don't know the quality of the material being read in the three countries. The statistical style of thinking has currently taken over medicine, where it may have some role to play: I am, for example, taking a pill because a study has shown that 68 percent of the people who take this pill and have a certain condition live 33 percent longer than those who don't. Dopey though this is, I play the odds—the pill costs $1 a day—and go along. But I'm not sure that statistics have much to tell us about a cultural activity so private as reading books.

Read any amount of serious imaginative literature with care, and you will be highly skeptical of the statistical style of thinking. You will quickly grasp that, in a standard statistical report such as "Reading at Risk," serious reading, always a minority interest, isn't at stake here. Nothing more is going on, really, than the *crise du jour*, soon to be replaced by the report on eating disorders, the harmfulness of aspirin, or the drop in high-school math scores.

Discussion Questions

1. How useful, according to Epstein, is the information provided by the "Reading at Risk" survey, and what conclusions does he draw from it?

2 Do you agree with his evaluation of this survey? Be sure to support your answer with examples. These examples can come from your own observations and readings.

The Future of Books

Kathryn Keeton

Kathryn Keeton was a magazine publisher and author. She founded the magazines Viva *(1972),* OMNI *(1979), and* Longevity *(1989), and published two nonfiction books,* Woman of Tomorrow *(1985) and* Longevity: The Science of Staying Young *(1992). She served as president and chief operating officer of General Media Communications Inc. She also established the Kathy Keeton Cancer Research Foundation to promote research in alternative cancer therapies.*

For most of us, our first visit to another world comes not through the wonder of television or the joy of travel, but through the simple pleasure of a book. Books have served, and will continue to serve, as time machines capable of transporting us back to the past and far into the future.

While television and movies may grab our attention, books require that we join hands with the author and create our own view of characters and places. No one reads a book like Edgar Rice Burroughs's *Tarzan* without bringing to that classic his or her own special vision of the ape-man. The appearance of a movie doesn't replace the need or desire to read; indeed, many people are inspired to read a novel after seeing the film.

In the realm of education, textbooks will continue to be essential to the learning process. So much of the information basic to the area of science and mathematics, for example, is best imparted through textbooks, which are the work of not one or two teachers, but dozens of experts in a particular field. Access to books by these professionals gives children access to the minds of these individuals.

Through books, we gain admittance to the parlors of the greatest thinkers of all time, from Aristotle to Elie Wiesel. Each time a new strain of intellectual thought enters society, or an observance is made by the psychological community, a series of books ensues, as witnessed by the plethora of books on everything from selecting a mate to coping with death. Books become our therapists, our inspiration, our friends.

Talking books, and video books, will become part of the common fare of reading. Sales for talking books for both adults and children are skyrocketing; in fact, the lost art of storytelling is found again through this medium. Futurists predict that the twenty-first century will bring us increasing amounts of leisure time and I believe, with it, the freedom to pursue what has been and will remain a favorite pastime, reading.

Discussion Questions

1. According to Keeton, how do most of us experience other times and places? Do you think there are more popular ways of mentally traveling to other worlds? If so, what are they?

2. Do you think more people read a book after seeing the movie, or do you think people are more likely to go to a movie if they have read and liked the book?

3. Discuss the importance of textbooks to your education.

4. What are some of the roles Keeton claims books play in our lives? What role do they most often play in yours?

5. Do you think that reading in the twenty-first century will ultimately increase or decrease? Why?

Assignment #2

"Why We Take Pictures"

This assignment requires you to write a response to the central argument in Susan Sontag's reading selection "Why We Take Pictures." Sontag explores the motives behind our growing use of cameras. While she acknowledges the traditional way in which cameras function to capture family events and history, she also argues in an interesting and unexpected way about some less-recognized motives that may be generating our picture-taking. See if you agree.

Be sure to read the essay carefully and think about its ideas as you complete the supporting activities that follow it. Some of the exercises repeat the strategies you used in the first unit on "Reading and Thought," but don't let that deter you from using these strategies again for this assignment. Also, carefully read the background readings in the "Extending the Discussion" section to see what others have to say about photography and its place in our lives. After you have read critically and done the prewriting activities in this section, you will be ready to develop your own essay in response to the writing topic that follows Sontag's reading selection.

Why We Take Pictures

SUSAN SONTAG

Susan Sontag received her BA from the College of the University of Chicago and did graduate work in philosophy, literature, and theology at Harvard University and Saint Anne's College, Oxford. She was an American writer, teacher, and human rights activist. Her stories and essays have appeared in newspapers, magazines, and literary publications all over the world, and her books have been translated into thirty-two languages. The following essay comes from one of her best-known works, On Photography *(1978).*

The age when taking photographs required a cumbersome and expensive contraption—the toy of the clever, the wealthy, and the obsessed—seems remote indeed from the era of sleek pocket cameras that invite anyone to take pictures. The first cameras, made in France and England in the early 1840s, had only inventors and buffs to operate them, and taking photographs had no clear social use. Recently, photography has become almost as widely practiced an amusement as sex and dancing. For most people, photography is mainly a social rite, but it can also be a defense against anxiety and a tool of power.

Memorializing the achievements of individuals considered as members of families, as well as of other groups, is the earliest popular use of photography. For at least a century, the wedding photograph has been as much a part of the ceremony as the prescribed verbal formulas. Cameras go with family life. According to a sociological study done in France, most households have a camera, but a household with children is twice as likely to have at least one camera as a household in which there are no children. Not to take pictures of one's children, particularly when they're small, is a sign of parental indifference, just as not turning up for one's graduation picture is a gesture of adolescent rebellion.

Through photographs, each family constructs a portrait-chronicle of itself—a portable kit of images that bears witness to its connectedness. It hardly matters what activities are photographed so long as photographs get taken and are cherished. Photography became a rite of family life just when, in the industrializing countries of Europe and America, the very institution of the family started undergoing radical surgery. As that claustrophobic unit—the nuclear family—was being carved out of a much larger family aggregate, photography came along to memorialize, to restate symbolically, the imperiled continuity and vanishing extendedness of family life. Those ghostly traces, photographs, supply the token presence of the dispersed relatives. A family's photograph album is generally about the extended family—and, often, is all that remains of it.

As photographs give people an imaginary possession of a past that is unreal, they also help people to take possession of space in which they are insecure. Thus, photography develops in tandem with one of the most characteristic of modern activities: tourism. For the first time in history, large numbers of people regularly travel out of their habitual environments for short periods of time. It seems to them positively unnatural to travel for pleasure without taking a camera along: Their photographs will offer indisputable evidence that the trip was made, that the program was carried out, that fun was had. Photographs document sequences of consumption carried on outside of the view of family, friends, and neighbors. The camera makes real what one is experiencing, and the compulsion to use it doesn't fade when people travel more. Taking photographs fills the same need for the cosmopolitans accumulating photograph-trophies of their boat trip up the Nile or their fourteen days in China as it does for less-traveled vacationers taking snapshots of Disneyland or Niagara Falls.

Besides being a way of certifying experience, taking photographs is also a way of refusing it—by limiting experience to a search for the photogenic, by converting experience into an image, a souvenir. Travel becomes a strategy for accumulating photographs. The very activity of taking pictures is soothing, and assuages general feelings of disorientation that are likely to be exacerbated by travel. Most tourists feel compelled to put the camera between themselves and whatever is remarkable that they encounter. Unsure of other responses, they take a picture. This gives shape to their experience: They stop, take a photograph, and move on. This activity especially appeals to Americans and other people handicapped by a ruthless work ethic. Using a camera appeases the anxiety that work-driven people feel about not working when they are on vacation and supposed to be having fun. They have something to do that is a friendly imitation of work: They can take pictures.

Writing Topic

According to Sontag, in what ways can taking pictures be a defense against anxiety, and sometimes even a tool of power? Do you agree with her analysis? Be sure to support your argument with specific examples; these examples can be taken from your own experience and observations or anything you have read, especially the readings from this course.

Vocabulary Check

To deepen your comprehension of any reading selection, you need to understand the selection's key vocabulary terms and the way the writer uses them. Words can have a variety of meanings, or they can have specialized meanings in certain contexts. Look up the definitions of the following words from "Why We Take Pictures." Choose the meaning that you think Sontag intended when she selected that particular word. Then, explain the way the meaning or concept behind the definition is key to understanding her argument.

1. *cumbersome*

   definition: _____

   _____

   explanation: _____

   _____

   _____

   _____

2. *contraption*

   definition: _____

   _____

   explanation: _____

   _____

   _____

   _____

3. *rite*

   definition: _____

   _____

explanation: _____

_____

_____

_____

4. *anxiety*

definition: _____

_____

explanation: _____

_____

_____

_____

5. *claustrophobic*

definition: _____

_____

explanation: _____

_____

_____

_____

6. *aggregate*

definition: _____

_____

explanation: _____

_____

_____

_____

7. *imperil*

definition: _____

_____

explanation: _____

_____

_____

_____

8. *token*

definition: _____

_____

explanation: _____

_____

_____

_____

9. *tandem*

definition: _____

_____

explanation: _____

_____

_____

_____

10. *indisputable*

    definition: _____

    _____

    explanation: _____

    _____

    _____

    _____

11. *consumption*

    definition: _____

    _____

    explanation: _____

    _____

    _____

    _____

12. *compulsion*

    definition: _____

    _____

    explanation: _____

    _____

    _____

    _____

13. *cosmopolitan (noun).*

    definition: _____

    _____

    explanation: _____

    _____

    _____

    _____

14. *assuage*

    definition: _____

    _____

    explanation: _____

    _____

    _____

    _____

15. *exacerbate*

    definition: _____

    _____

    explanation: _____

    _____

    _____

    _____

Questions to Guide Your Reading

Answer the following questions so you can gain a thorough understanding of "Why We Take Pictures."

Paragraphs 1-2

How have the cameras themselves, their users, and their use changed since the early 1840s?

Paragraph 3

How did pictures become important to families as industrialization developed?

Paragraphs 4-5

According to Sontag, what are the two ways that taking photographs is a response to the experience of traveling?

Prewriting for a Directed Summary

The first part of the writing topic that follows "Why We Take Pictures" asks you about a central idea from Sontag's essay. To answer this part of the writing topic, you will want to write a *directed* summary, meaning one that responds specifically to the writing topic's first question.

first part of the writing topic:

According to Sontag, in what ways can taking pictures be a defense against anxiety, and sometimes even a tool of power?

 Hint

Don't forget to look back to Part 1's "Guidelines for Writing a Directed Summary."

Focus Questions

1. According to Sontag, what are the underlying anxieties of modern life that can be associated with travel?

2. Explain Sontag's idea that taking pictures can relieve these anxieties.

3. How can taking a picture provide some sense of control over an unfamiliar environment?

4. What do you think Sontag means when she says that sometimes photography can become a powerful weapon?

Developing an Opinion and Working Thesis Statement

The second question in the writing topic for "Why We Take Pictures" asks you to take a position of your own. Your response to this part of the writing topic will become the thesis statement of your essay, so it is important to spend some time ensuring that it reflects the position you want to take. Do you think that taking pictures stems from more than simply a way to record our family's memories for posterity?

The framework below will help you develop your working thesis. But keep an open mind as you complete the prewriting pages that follow this one and read the positions other writers take in the essays in the "Extending the Discussion" section of this chapter. You may find that, after giving more thought to the issue, you want to modify your position.

writing topic's second part:

Do you agree with her analysis?

Do you agree with Sontag that sometimes we take pictures to relieve stress, to comfort ourselves when we are faced with new experiences, and perhaps to gain a sense of power over our experiences? As you think about the position you want to take in your working thesis statement, keep in mind Sontag's ideas, the ideas of some of the writers in the "Extending the Discussion" section of this unit, and your own experiences.

1. Use the following thesis frame to identify the basic elements of your working thesis statement:

   a. What is the issue of "Why We Take Pictures" that the writing topic's first question asks you to consider?

   _____

   b. What is Sontag's position on that issue?

   _____

   c. Will your position be that her analysis applies, or doesn't apply, to people today?

   _____

   _____

   _____

2. Now use the elements you isolated in the thesis frame to write a thesis statement. You may have to revise it several times until it captures your ideas clearly.

_____

_____

Prewriting to Find Support for Your Thesis Statement

The last part of the writing topic asks you to support the position you put forward in your thesis statement. Well-developed ideas are crucial when you are making an argument because you will have to be clear, logical, and thorough if you are to be convincing. As you work through the exercises below, you will generate much of the 4Cs material you will need when you draft your essay's body paragraphs.

writing topic's last part:

Be sure to support your argument with specific examples; these examples can be taken from your own experience and observations or anything you have read, especially the readings from this course.

Complete each section of this prewriting activity; your responses will become the material you will use in the next stage—planning and writing the essay.

1. As you begin to develop your own examples, think about how you and the people you know use photography. In what situations are you and they likely to pull out a camera? List the things that you—and those you were with—chose to photograph in the past year. What kinds of moments were photographed? Did any of them seem connected to defending against anxiety or a way to gain a feeling of power? How important are these moments to you now? For what reasons would you keep most or all of the photos you have?

    Sontag recognizes that families use cameras as a "social rite," but she is also interested in how cameras can become a crutch at times. Can you recall any times when, by taking pictures, you avoided boredom, embarrassment, or nervousness? Do any friends or family members appear to use a camera in this way? Would you say that the act of picture-taking gives a sense of power to the camera's user? How might this be true? List as many ideas as you can, and freewrite about the significance of each. Then, look at what you have written in response to the above questions and see whether your experiences and ideas support or challenge Sontag's analysis.

Once you have listed your specific examples and done some speculative free-writing about the meaning or significance of each, carefully look over all that you have written. Try to group your ideas into categories. Then, give each category a label. In other words, cluster ideas that seem to have something in common and, for each cluster, identify that shared quality by giving it a title.

2. What views on photography do the essays in this unit's "Extending the Discussion" take? Review each author's arguments and supporting evidence, and compare them to Sontag's argument. Are any of them especially convincing for you? If so, list them here. (If you refer to any of their ideas in your essay, be sure to cite them.) List and/or freewrite about all the relevant ideas from these reading selections that you can think of, even those about which you are hesitant.

Once you've written down your ideas, look them over carefully. Try to group your ideas into categories. Then, give each category a label. In other words, cluster ideas that seem to have something in common and, for each cluster, identify that shared quality by giving the group of ideas a title.

3. Now that you've developed categories, look through them and select two or three to develop in your essay. Make sure they are relevant to your thesis and are important enough to persuade your readers. Then, in the space below, briefly summarize each item in your categories and explain how it supports your thesis statement.

The information and ideas you develop in this exercise will become useful when you turn to planning and drafting your essay.

Revising Your Thesis Statement

Now that you have spent some time working out your ideas more systematically and developing some supporting evidence for the position you want to take, look again at the working thesis statement you crafted earlier and see if it is still accurate. As your first step, look again at the writing topic, and then write your original working thesis on the lines that follow it.

Writing Topic:

According to Sontag, in what ways can taking pictures be a defense against anxiety, and sometimes even a tool of power? Do you agree with her analysis? Be sure to support your argument with specific examples; these examples can be taken from your own experience and observations or anything you have read, especially the readings from this course.

Working Thesis Statement:

_____

_____

_____

Remember that your thesis statement must address the second part of the writing topic, but also take into consideration the writing topic as a whole. The first part of the writing topic identifies the issue that is up for debate, and the last part reminds you that, whatever position you take on the issue, you must be able to support it with specific examples.

Take some time now to revise your thesis statement. Consider whether you should change it significantly because it no longer represents your position, or whether only a word or phrase should be added or deleted to make it clearer.

Now, check it one more time by asking yourself the following questions:

a. Does the thesis statement directly identify Sontag's argument?

b. Does your thesis state your position on the issue?

c. Is your thesis well punctuated, grammatically correct, and precisely worded?

Add any missing elements, correct the grammar errors, and refine the wording. Then, write your polished thesis on the lines below. Try to look at it from your readers' perspective. Is it strong and interesting?

_____

_____

Planning and Drafting Your Essay

You may not be in the habit of outlining or planning your essay before you begin drafting it, and some of you may avoid outlining altogether. If you haven't been using an outline as you move through the writing process, try using it this time. Creating an outline will give you a clear and coherent structure for incorporating all of the ideas you have developed in the preceding pages. It will also show you where you may have gone off track, left logical holes in your reasoning, or failed to develop one or more of your paragraphs.

Your outline doesn't have to use Roman numerals or be highly detailed. Just use an outline form that suits your style and shows you a bird's-eye view of your argument. Below is a form that we think you will find useful. Consult the academic essay diagram in Part 1 of this book, too, to remind yourself of the conventional form of a college essay and its basic parts.

I. Introductory Paragraph

    A. An opening sentence that gives the reading selection's title and author and begins to answer the first part of the writing topic:

        _____

        _____

        _____

    B. Main points to include in the directed summary:

        1.

        2.

        3.

        4.

    C. Write out your thesis statement. (Look back to "Revising Your Thesis Statement," where you reexamined and refined your working thesis statement.) It should clearly state whether Sontag's claim about the connection between picture-taking, anxiety, and power is true.

        _____

        _____

II. Body Paragraphs

    A. The paragraph's one main point that supports the thesis statement:

        _____

1. Controlling idea sentence:

   _____

   _____

2. Corroborating details:

   _____

   _____

   _____

   _____

3. Careful explanation of why the details are relevant:

   _____

   _____

   _____

   _____

   _____

4. Connection to the thesis statement:

   _____

   _____

   _____

B. The paragraph's one main point that supports the thesis statement:

   _____

   1. Controlling idea sentence:

      _____

      _____

2. **C**orroborating details:

_____

_____

_____

_____

3. **C**areful explanation of why the details are relevant:

_____

_____

_____

_____

_____

4. **C**onnection to the thesis statement:

_____

_____

_____

C. The paragraph's one main point that supports the thesis statement:

_____

1. **C**ontrolling idea sentence:

_____

_____

2. **C**orroborating details:

_____

_____

_____

_____

3. **C**areful explanation of why the details are relevant:

_____

_____

_____

_____

_____

4. **C**onnection to the thesis statement:

_____

_____

_____

D. The paragraph's one main point that supports the thesis statement:

_____

1. **C**ontrolling idea sentence:

_____

_____

2. **C**orroborating details:

_____

_____

_____

_____

3. **C**areful explanation of why the details are relevant:

_____

_____

_____

_____

_____

4. **C**onnection to the thesis statement:

_____

_____

_____

Repeat this form for any remaining body paragraphs.

III. Conclusion (For help, see "Conclusions" in Part 1.)

A. Type of conclusion to be used:

_____

B. Key words or phrases to include:

_____

Getting Feedback on Your Draft

Use the following guidelines to give a classmate feedback on his or her draft. Read the draft through first, and then answer each of the items below as specifically as you can.

Name of draft's author: _____

Name of draft's reader: _____

The Introduction

1. Within the opening sentences:
   a. Sontag's first and last names are given.   yes   no
   b. The reading selection's title is given and
      placed within quotation marks.   yes   no

2. The opening contains a summary that:
   a. presents Sontag's claim that taking pictures can be
      a defense against anxiety and a tool of power.   yes   no
   b. explains how she connects taking pictures
      to anxiety and power.   yes   no

3. The opening provides a thesis that makes clear
   the draft writer's opinion regarding Sontag's claim.   yes   no

If you circled yes in #3 above, state the thesis below as it is written. If you circled no, explain to the draft writer what information is needed to make the thesis complete.

_____

_____

_____

The Body

1. How many paragraphs are in the body of this essay? _____

2. To support the thesis, this number is   sufficient   not enough

3. Do body paragraphs contain the 4Cs?

   Paragraph 1   Controlling idea sentence   yes   no
                  Corroborating details   yes   no
                  Careful explanation of why
                  the details are relevant   yes   no
                  Connection to the thesis statement   yes   no

Paragraph 2	Controlling idea sentence	yes	no
	Corroborating details	yes	no
	Careful explanation of why the details are relevant	yes	no
	Connection to the thesis statement	yes	no
Paragraph 3	Controlling idea sentence	yes	no
	Corroborating details	yes	no
	Careful explanation of why the details are relevant	yes	no
	Connection to the thesis statement	yes	no
Paragraph 4	Controlling idea sentence	yes	no
	Corroborating details	yes	no
	Careful explanation of why the details are relevant	yes	no
	Connection to the thesis statement	yes	no
Paragraph 5	Controlling idea sentence	yes	no
	Corroborating details	yes	no
	Careful explanation of why the details are relevant	yes	no
	Connection to the thesis statement	yes	no

(Continue as needed.)

4. Identify any of the body paragraphs that are underdeveloped (too short).

   _____

5. Identify any of the body paragraphs that fail to support the thesis.

   _____

6. Identify any of the body paragraphs that are redundant or repetitive.

   _____

7. Suggest any ideas for additional body paragraphs that might improve this essay.

   _____

   _____

   _____

The Conclusion

1. Does the final paragraph avoid introducing new ideas
   and examples that really belong in the body of the essay?   yes   no

2. Does the conclusion provide closure (let readers know
   that the end of the essay has been reached)?   yes   no

3. Does the conclusion leave readers with an
   understanding of the significance of the argument?   yes   no

   State in your own words what the draft writer considers to be important about his or her argument.

   _____

   _____

   _____

4. Identify the type of conclusion used (see the guidelines for conclusions in Part 1).

   _____

Editing

1. During the editing process, the writer should pay attention to the following problems in sentence structure, punctuation, and mechanics:

   fragments
   misplaced and dangling modifiers
   fused (run-on) sentences
   comma splices
   misplaced, missing, and unnecessary commas
   misplaced, missing, and unnecessary apostrophes
   incorrect quotation mark use
   capitalization errors
   spelling errors

2. While editing, the writer should pay attention to the following areas of grammar:

   verb tense
   subject-verb agreement
   irregular verbs
   pronoun type
   pronoun reference
   pronoun agreement
   noun plurals
   prepositions

Final Draft Checklist

Content:

- My essay has an appropriate title.
- I provide an accurate summary of Sontag's analysis of photography as presented in "Why We Take Pictures."
- My thesis states a clear position that can be supported by evidence.
- I have enough paragraphs and argument points to support my thesis.
- Each body paragraph is relevant to my thesis.
- Each body paragraph contains the 4Cs.
- I use transitions whenever necessary to connect ideas.
- The final paragraph of my essay (the conclusion) provides readers with a sense of closure.

Grammar, Punctuation, and Mechanics:

- I use the present tense to discuss Sontag's argument and examples.
- I use verb tenses correctly to show the chronology of events.
- I have verb tense consistency throughout my sentences and paragraphs.
- I have checked for subject-verb agreement in all of my sentences.
- I have revised all fragments and mixed or garbled sentences.
- I have repaired all fused (run-on) sentences and comma splices.
- I have placed a comma after introductory elements (transitions and phrases) and all dependent clauses that open a sentence.
- If I present items in a series (nouns, verbs, prepositional phrases), they are parallel in form.
- If I include material spoken or written by someone other than myself, I have correctly punctuated it with quotation marks, using the MLA style guide's rules for citation.
- If I include material spoken or written by someone other than myself, I have included a works cited list that follows the MLA style guide's rules for citation.

Reviewing Your Graded Essay

After your instructor has returned your essay, you may have the opportunity to revise your paper and raise your grade. Many students, especially those whose essays receive nonpassing grades, feel that their instructors should be less "picky" about grammar and should pass the work on content alone. However, most students at this level have not yet acquired the ability to recognize quality writing, and they do not realize that content and writing actually cannot be separated in this way. Experienced instructors know that errors in sentence structure, grammar, punctuation, and word choice either interfere with content or distract readers so much that they lose track of content. In short, good ideas badly presented are no longer good ideas; to pass, an essay must have passable writing. So even if you are not submitting a revised version of this essay to your instructor, it is important that you review your work carefully in order to understand its strengths and weaknesses. This sheet will guide you through the evaluation process.

You will want to continue to use the techniques that worked well for you and to find strategies to overcome the problems that you identify in this sample of your writing. To recognize areas that might have been problematic for you, look back at the scoring rubric in this book. Match the numerical/verbal/letter grade received on your essay to the appropriate category. Study the explanation given on the rubric for your grade.

Write a few sentences below in which you identify your problems in each of the following areas. Then, suggest specific changes you could make that would improve your paper. Don't forget to use your handbook as a resource.

1. **Grammar/punctuation/mechanics**
    My problem:

    My strategy for change:

2. **Thesis/response to assignment**
    My problem:

    My strategy for change:

3. Organization
My problem:

My strategy for change:

4. Paragraph development/examples/reasoning
My problem:

My strategy for change:

5. Assessment
In the space below, assign a grade to your paper using the rubric in Part 1 of this book. If your instructor assigned your essay a grade of *High Fail*, you might give it the letter grade you now feel the paper warrants. If your instructor used the traditional letter grade to evaluate the essay, choose a category from the rubric in this book, or any other grading scale that you are familiar with, to show your evaluation of your work. Then, write a short narrative explaining your evaluation of the essay and the reasons it received the grade you gave it.

Grade: _____

Narrative: _____

_____

_____

_____

_____

Extending the Discussion: Considering Other Viewpoints

Reading Selections

"Every Portrait Tells a Lie" by Debra Brehmer

"Photographs of My Mother" by Maxine Hong Kingston

"Experience and Image: The Essential Connection" by Jim Richardson

"The Walking Photograph" by Geoff Nicholson

"Art at Arm's Length: A History of the Selfie" by Jerry Saltz

"What Your Selfies Say about You" by Peggy Drexler

"A Thousand Pictures for a Million Words" by Lash Keith Vance

Every Portrait Tells a Lie

DEBRA BREHMER

Debra Brehmer is an art historian who runs a contemporary art gallery in Milwaukee, Wisconsin, called Portrait Society. She is interested in the cultural role of the portrait, from the ancient world to the selfie. She is also an adjunct professor of art history and writing at the Milwaukee School of Art and Design and writes about art regularly for the national online art review Hyperallergic.

Every portrait tells a story, and that story usually involves some kind of lie.

Here's one: I am lined up in a tiny faded snapshot from the 1960s in front of a Christmas tree with my brother. Side by side in our pajamas, he is smiling and I am squinting into the lens. The tree looms large and promising behind us. I remember those picture moments so well—the feeling of being posed and staged, of being complicit in the making of a mostly false vignette. My brother was mean to me, and I didn't like standing by him and smiling. Seconds before the shutter clicked, he probably said or did something nasty. The father who stood framing the picture was a stern, remote presence in our lives. This interaction between kids, dad, and camera was as close as anything came to family intimacy, and I knew, even at a young age, that we were participating in a history that was manufactured.

With portraiture, we can never mistake the picture for the thing itself. But we forget. Now if the staging and shaping of reality, or the "lie" as I call it, were the only subtext of portraiture, it wouldn't be that interesting an art form. But it's deeper than that. Within that moment of control, when the photographer or artist imposes his or her reality on the picture, there is a more tender concern. The fact that my father even desired to frame a happy family in front of the Christmas tree was evidence of a hopeful vision. This was the reality he must have desired and wanted to believe in even if daily life didn't support it. The attempt to create an idealized image contains the imprint of not who we are but who we hope to be. Perhaps every time we try to capture the likeness of a person we are essentially attempting to make contact. Portraiture is the only art form that exists out of a dependency on human exchange and that models the struggles and pleasures of human relationships as a subtext to its surface desire to represent.

"Portraiture is a sad art," the great photographer Richard Avedon once said. "It's gone but it remains." He really got it, didn't he? I might add that portraiture is also a tender art. It tries to hold onto what can't be contained, which is life itself and a clear view of it. What we learn from portraiture is that our view of any person, including ourselves, is often subjective and contingent. The portrait, in the choices the artist makes, alludes to the fact that who we are involves selection, interpretation, and chance.

One of the most interesting portrait stories in history is the tale of Picasso's attempt to paint a commissioned likeness of the writer and art patron Gertrude Stein. Picasso wasn't the kind of artist who routinely doubted himself or labored over the creative process. But this portrait got the best of him. He couldn't get it right. The year was 1905, and he made Stein pose for him ninety times, month after month, for over a year. What was he after? Picasso said that the more he looked at Gertrude Stein, the more he lost sight of her. He finally gave up, smeared out the face, and retreated to his native Spain for an extended holiday. When he returned to Paris, he confronted the canvas again and abruptly painted her face from memory and declared the picture complete. The resulting face is asymmetrical, distorted, and masklike, less Gertrude Stein than the Iberian, African, and Roman artifacts to which he had recently been exposed. Picasso's dilemma with the painting may have stemmed from the weightiness of the task he had shouldered: He knew he had to take the age-old art form, steeped in the conventions of a dusty work ethic, and revitalize it for a changing culture. Picasso's portrait of Gertrude Stein both embraces tradition and steps out of it. Only by distorting her face could he express a greater truth about Gertrude Stein: the slippery truth of the subjective which he grounds within the larger truth of the universal.

Every portrait that isn't a hackneyed commercial product illustrates this tug of war between the objective and subjective or between likeness and interpretation. The greatest portraits ever made were in the Baroque period in the Netherlands where Frans Hals and Rembrandt plied their trade. It has been said that Hals painted when he was drunk. His expressive brush was so loosely held and forcefully applied that his paintings look like the wind blew the pigments into place. Hals didn't want his portraits to look frozen or dead like so many others of the period. He found a way to keep life on the canvas. Rembrandt was another story. His genius was to allude to the layering of experience and the accretion of identity by building his images up into thick, tactile skins. His portraits make us remember that the years have assembled somewhere inside us and still live there.

Without portraiture, we wouldn't really know what we thought of ourselves at different stages in history. Portraits are maps of what we privilege and long for in both the material and spiritual worlds. Within their seeming simplicity and directness of purpose are innumerable signifiers of culture's sneaky hand shaping image and identity without our even realizing it.

Avedon is right: A portrait is always a deceased moment. It's gone, but remains. A portrait is evidence of our decimation at the same time that it is proof of our need to stop and value as many moments as possible. Picasso did get it right with Gertrude Stein. His painting is not a picture of her likeness; it is a picture of her weight, form, and mass as an artist. Her large, dark form leans slightly out of the picture plane, toward us, but not enough to interact or interrupt our in-time space. Picasso places her just on the other side of human time. Her space is reflective, contained, and forever. Her image alludes to her material, weighty presence on earth without the burden and superficiality of fleeting likeness.

When looking at portraits, think of this: Every portrait exposes a truth that rides on the inherent lies. Our existence is transitional and subjective, and this is the condition that portraiture tries to absolve. Every portrait, then, is a fight or, you could say, a prayer that calls out from the most troubled condition of our humanity, our temporality. Portraiture wants what cannot be had: life to stop without being dead. It's an art with a built-in condition of failure. And that's why it is so interesting.

Discussion Questions

1. Discuss the difference between a posed picture and reality. Why does Debra Brehmer call every portrait a "lie"? How are the subjects "manufacturing" history? Describe one of your family photos, and explain why it is or is not a lie.

2. Why does Brehmer think Richard Avedon is right to call portraiture a "sad art"? Do you think Brehmer's and Avedon's reasons for believing it is "sad" are the same? Why or why not?

3. Why was Picasso, the great artist, unable at first to paint a portrait of Gertrude Stein? What does his later result say about Stein, about Picasso himself, and about art?

4. Explain Avedon's contradictory conclusion about truth and lies in relation to portraits.

5. Look back at your graduation photo. What truths and lies does it present?

Photographs of My Mother

Essay

Maxine Hong Kingston

Maxine Hong Kingston is a Chinese American author and Professor Emerita at the University of California, Berkeley. She has written books—fiction and nonfiction—about the experiences of Chinese immigrants in the United States. Some of her best-known work is autobiographical. Kingston won the National Book Critics Circle Award for nonfiction in 1976 for her autobiography The Woman Warrior: Memoirs of a Childhood among Ghosts. *The following is an excerpt from that work.*

Once in a long while, four times so far for me, my mother brings out the metal tube that holds her medical diploma. On the tube are gold circles crossed with seven red lines each, "joy" ideographs in abstract. There are also little flowers that look like gears for a gold machine. According to the scraps of labels with Chinese and American addresses, stamps, and postmarks, the family airmailed the can from Hong Kong in 1950. It got crushed in the middle, and whoever tried to peel the labels off stopped because the red and gold paint came off too, leaving silver scratches that rust. Somebody tried to pry the end off before discovering that the tube pulls apart. When I open it, the smell of China flies out, a thousand-year-old bat flying heavyheaded out of the Chinese caverns where bats are as white as dust, a smell that comes from long ago, far back in the brain. Crates from Canton, Hong Kong, Singapore, and Taiwan have that smell too, only stronger because they are more recently come from the Chinese.

Inside the can are three scrolls, one inside another. The largest says that in the twenty-third year of the National Republic, the To Keung School of Midwifery, where she has had two years of instruction and Hospital Practice, awards its diploma to my mother, who has shown through oral and written examination her Proficiency in Midwifery, Pediatrics, Gynecology, "Medecine," "Surgary," Therapeutics, Ophthalmology, Bacteriology,

Dermatology, Nursing, and Bandage. This document has eight stamps on it: one, the school's English and Chinese names embossed together in a circle; one, as the Chinese enumerate, a stork and a big baby in lavender ink; one, the school's Chinese seal; one, an orangish paper stamp pasted in the border design; one, the red seal of Dr. Wu Pak-liang, MD, Lyon, Berlin, president and "*Ex-assistant étranger à la clinique chirugicale et d'accouchement de-l'université de Lyon*"; one, the red seal of Dean Woo Yin-kam, MD; one, my mother's seal, her chop mark larger than the president's and the dean's; and one, the number 1279 on the back. Dean Woo's signature is followed by "(Hackett)." I read in a history book that Hackett Medical College for Women at Canton was founded in the nineteenth century by European women doctors. The school seal has been pressed over a photograph of my mother at the age of thirty-seven.

The diploma gives her age as twenty-seven. She looks younger than I do; her eyebrows are thicker, her lips fuller. Her naturally curly hair is parted on the left, one wavy wisp tendrilling off to the right. She wears a scholar's white gown, and she is not thinking about her appearance. She stares straight ahead as if she can see me and past me to her grandchildren and grandchildren's grandchildren. She has spacy eyes, as all people recently from Asia have. Her eyes do not focus on the camera. My mother is not smiling; Chinese do not smile for photographs. Their faces command relatives in foreign lands, "Send money," and posterity forever, "Put food in front of this picture." My mother does not understand Chinese-American snapshots. "What are you laughing at?" she asks.

The second scroll is a long, narrow photograph of the graduating class with the school officials seated in front. I picked out my mother immediately. Her face is exactly her own, though forty years younger. She is so familiar, I can only tell whether or not she is pretty or happy or smart by comparing her to the other women. For this formal group picture, she straightened her hair with oil to make a chin-length bob like the others'. On the other women, strangers, I can recognize a curled lip, a sidelong glance, pinched shoulders. My mother is not soft; the girl with the small nose and dimpled underlip is soft. My mother is not humorous, not like the girl at the end who lifts her mocking chin to pose like Girl Graduate. My mother does not have smiling eyes; the old woman teacher (Dean Woo?) in front crinkles happily, and the one faculty member in the Western suit smiles Westernly. Most of the graduates are girls whose faces have not yet formed; my mother's face will not change anymore, except to age. She is intelligent, alert, pretty. I can't tell if she's happy.

The graduates seem to have been looking elsewhere when they pinned the rose, zinnia, or chrysanthemum on their precise black dresses. One thin girl wears hers in the middle of her chest. A few have a flower over a left or right nipple. My mother put hers, a chrysanthemum, below her left breast. Chinese dresses at that time were dartless, cut as if women did not have breasts; these young doctors, unaccustomed to decorations, may have seen their chests as black expanses with no reference points for flowers. Perhaps they couldn't shorten that far gaze that lasts only a few years after a Chinese emigrates. In this picture, too, my mother's eyes are big with what they held—reaches of oceans beyond China, land beyond oceans. Most emigrants learn the barbarians' directness—how to gather themselves and stare rudely into talking faces as if trying to catch lies. In America, my mother has eyes as strong as boulders, never once skittering off a face, but she has not learned to place decorations and phonograph needles, nor has she stopped seeing land on the other side of the oceans. Now her eyes include the relatives in China, as they once included my father smiling and smiling in his many Western outfits, a different one for each photograph that he sent from America.

He and his friends took pictures of one another in bathing suits at Coney Island beach, the salt wind from the Atlantic blowing their hair. He's the one in the middle with his arms about the necks of his buddies. They pose in the cockpit of a biplane, on a motorcycle, and on a lawn beside the "Keep Off the Grass" sign. They are always laughing. My father, white shirt sleeves rolled up, smiles in front of a wall of clean laundry. In the spring, he wears a new straw hat, cocked at a Fred Astaire angle. He steps out, dancing down the stairs, one foot forward, one back, a hand in his pocket. He wrote to her about the American custom of stomping on straw hats come fall. "If you want to save your hat for next year," he said, "you have to put it away early, or else when you're riding the subway or walking along Fifth Avenue, any stranger can snatch it off your head and put his foot through it. That's the way they celebrate the change of seasons here." In the winter, he wears a gray felt hat with his gray overcoat. He is sitting on a rock in Central

Park. In one snapshot, he is not smiling; someone took it when he was studying, blurred in the glare of the desk lamp.

There are no snapshots of my mother. In two small portraits, however, there is a black thumbprint on her forehead, as if someone had inked in bangs, as if someone had marked her. "Mother, did bangs come into fashion after you had the picture taken?" One time, she said yes. Another time when I asked, "Why do you have fingerprints on your forehead?" she said, "Your First Uncle did that." I disliked the unsureness in her voice.

The last scroll has columns of Chinese words. The only English is "Department of Health, Canton," imprinted on my mother's face, the same photograph as on the diploma. I keep looking to see whether she was afraid. Year after year, my father did not come home or send for her. Their two children had been dead for ten years. If he did not return soon, there would be no more children. ("They were three and two years old, a boy and a girl. They could talk already.") My father did send money regularly, though, and she had nobody to spend it on but herself. She bought good clothes and shoes. Then she decided to use the money for becoming a doctor. She did not leave for Canton immediately after the children died. In China, there was time to complete feelings. As my father had done, my mother left the village by ship. There was a sea bird painted on the ship to protect it against shipwreck and winds. She was in luck. The following ship was boarded by river pirates, who kidnapped every passenger, even old ladies. "Sixty dollars for an old lady" was what the bandits used to say. "I sailed alone," she says, "to the capital of the entire province." She took a brown leather suitcase and a sea-bag stuffed with two quilts.

Discussion Questions

1. What things does Maxine Hong Kingston learn about her mother from the photographs? Do you think some of Kingston's observations are as much about Kingston herself as they are about her mother? Explain. What conclusions about Kingston's relationship with her mother have you formed after reading this essay?

2. What pictures does Kingston have of her father's early life? What do these photos show about the kind of person he was and the life he was living? Do you think that his wife, Kingston's mother, would have been in these pictures if she had been with him in America at that time? Why or why not?

3. What "truths" would Debra Brehmer in "Every Portrait Tells a Lie" say are revealed by the portraits of Kingston's mother? What truths do you think are revealed in the essay about these portraits?

4. Discuss Kingston's essay in terms of Sontag's analysis. Is there a way to connect Kingston's thoughts about these pictures to the anxiety that Sontag discusses? Explain your answer.

Experience and Image: The Essential Connection

JIM RICHARDSON

Jim Richardson is a photojournalist known for his depictions of small-town life. His photos appear frequently in National Geographic *magazine.*

Recently, I came across a picture I had taken in British Columbia. A father and his children were down on the dock, admiring the sunset together. It was a nice moment for them, though I suppose my image might be a bit maudlin. Somehow, it connected me again with another place and time, which resulted in a powerful image, but not of the photographic kind. On that day, I hadn't taken any pictures at all.

That image is still fresh in my mind, even all these years later. Strange how some sights get burned into our brains and come to stand for so much. It was late afternoon in Bryce Canyon National Park. The sun was just below the rim of the canyon, casting the valley floor into cool shadows. Light reflected from the sandstone walls, bringing a bit of warmth to families enjoying their precious shared summer moments of memory-making.

Suddenly, a car scooted down the road, with husband driving and wife standing high on the seat, emerging from the sunroof like a turtle sticking its head out of its shell. Soon enough, the video camera was visible in her hands. Determination was in his eyes. Without blinking or slowing down, they made the loop at the end of the canyon, the video camera panning all the while. Then they were gone, the wife retracting her head inside as the car sped away with their canyon images safely digitized. Maybe the scenes would be enjoyed in some dark room back home, I suppose—or maybe never.

A collective silence gathered over all of us left in the canyon, our jaws still gaping open like barn doors. We glanced around at one another, our eyes conveying the same message: Did you just see what I saw? Soon enough, the gentle sounds of the canyon were mingling with the happy laughter of children.

The incident occurred more than two decades ago, but the image never left me. My conclusion remains firm, as well. The images they captured had no meaning. That is because the images represent only what the camera "saw." Divorced from any real human experience of the place, the images became mute. The linkage is broken between seeing and feeling. However technically sufficient the images may have been, they don't actually mean anything to anyone. The images are worse than bad: They are a waste of time.

How different they were, I thought—these fleeting images of opportunity lost—compared with the simple snapshots I saw families taking all around me. Some may have been blurred or a little crooked; maybe some heads got cut off. But these images were precious and full of life, replete with meaning and tender moments and just the plain ordinary great stuff of life.

Perhaps I should have forgotten all about this by now. But the image flashes into my brain at every castle in Europe and every monument in America. I am seeing more of us adopting a new posture when we travel. Arms are cocked to hold the camera. Chins are tipped high to ogle the screen. Eyes dart and brains are not quite in the moment as we make the world small and slightly late.

Meanwhile, everyone else around us is made to duck and weave their way out of our line of sight, lest our pictures be ruined by real life actually happening. The spectacle is as sad as it is comical. I don't know whether to laugh or cry. What I actually want to do is to say, "Put the camera down." (Of course I don't. I am, after all, from the Midwest, where suffering in silence is an art form.)

Photographic technology has not progressed so far that we can tell when the photographer could "smell the roses." But we can almost always tell when the photographer slowed down and actually experienced a bit of the world.

Discussion Questions

1. Why does Jim Richardson believe that the photographic images of Bryce Canyon taken by the couple in the car have no meaning? How do you think the couple would respond to his assertion?

2. What are the reasons for the author's attitude about the less-than-perfect pictures taken by the other families visiting that national park? Would you rather spend an evening watching the couple's video or looking at the family photos taken that day? Explain your answer.

3. What observation and analysis does Richardson offer about travel photography? How do his thoughts compare or contrast with those of Sontag?

The Walking Photograph

Essay

GEOFF NICHOLSON

Geoff Nicholson is a British novelist and nonfiction writer. He was educated at the Universities of Cambridge and Essex. His novels are best known for their interweaving storylines and treatment of subcultures, done with an overlay of dark humor. Some of his most recent novels include The Hollywood Dodo *(2004),* Gravity's Volkswagen *(2009), and* The City under the Skin *(2014). The following selection is an excerpt from one of his works of nonfiction, titled* The Lost Art of Walking *(2008).*

Garry Winogrand walked on the crowded streets of New York in the 1970s, carrying a Leica M4 with a 28mm lens, the leather strap wound tightly round his hand, the camera being constantly raised and lowered to and from his eye, turning his head, refocusing his gaze, looking for visual triggers, for subjects, endlessly, relentlessly pressing the shutter, shooting pictures, sometimes just shooting.

Winogrand walks, but not at the same pace as the pedestrians around him, and sometimes he stops completely so that the flow of people splits and eddies past, and sometimes he sees something on the other side of the street, and pushes through the crowd, dashes over there, dodging traffic or forcing the traffic to dodge him. Then he continues taking photographs. You'd think that New York's angry, purposeful walkers would knock him out of the way, walk all over him; but he's found a way to avoid that.

Sometimes he smiles and nods at the people he's photographing, offers a word or two, chats, and in the main nobody minds. It's a technique he's developed, a way of presenting himself as just another eccentric on the streets of New York, crazy, self-absorbed, obsessive but essentially harmless—which is not a complete misrepresentation of Winogrand. And then somebody perceives him as something else. A woman, irate, offended, full of righteous indignation, believes that in photographing her, Winogrand has stolen something from her. "Hey, you took my picture!" she protests, and Winogrand, in his rough, tough, amused New York voice, says "Honey, it's *my* picture now." It's an old story, and another one that I very much want to be true.

Garry Winogrand (1928-1984) was from the Bronx. He told Tod Papageorge that when he was about ten years old, he walked the streets of his neighborhood until midnight to avoid going home to the family apartment, because "his parents did not put a high priority on privacy." The idea that the streets offer more privacy than the family home is one that needs no explaining.

Winogrand was a street photographer, by most reckonings the ultimate street photographer. The term is a porous one; even the most studio-bound of photographers occasionally takes a photograph on the street. And paparazzi are certainly street photographers of a sort, along with their modern mutations, the stalkerazzi and the snapperazzi members of the public who happen to see a celeb in the street and take their picture.

You might also think it's a term that doesn't require much definition; if you take a photograph in the street, you're a street photographer. Well, not quite. Eddie Adams was certainly in the street in Saigon in 1968 when he photographed the Vietnamese chief of police, Nguyen Ngoc Loan, walking up to a suspected Vietcong collaborator and shooting him in the head, but he wasn't quite a street photographer in the way that Winogrand was. A street photographer, as we generally conceive it, is someone who finds subject matter not in exotic locales or war zones, but in quotidian settings in the city. If, in the process, he or she manages to make that setting look like an exotic locale or a war zone, then so much the better. There was a time when these photographers were often referred to as "candids," but nobody seems to use that word anymore. Perhaps candidness is no longer considered something that a photograph can offer us.

All my favorite photographers are, in some sense or another, at least some of the time, street photographers: Henri Cartier-Bresson, Robert Frank, William Klein, Diane Arbus, Stephen Shore, William Eggleston, Martin Parr, Bruce Gilden, as well as Winogrand. Some of these people view the world with a comparatively benign eye; others are downright brutal in their gaze. In either case, the streets offer them the kinds of subjects they're looking for, that they and their art need.

There are ways in which street photography might seem very straightforward. There's no need for props, lights, assistants, paid models, stylists, or any of the other detritus that some photographers carry with them. You simply go out with your camera and take pictures of what's there. There may be some premeditation, but in the end, it's an improvised form with an unpredictable outcome, a sort of visual free jazz. Much of street life is quite banal. Even in a city as full of grotesques as New York, for every character there are thousands of ordinary Joes. People come and go rapidly, without arranging themselves into attractive or dramatic tableaux. Conflict and awkwardness may be part of the deal; nevertheless, the best street photographers do demonstrate something that looks like ease. They're at home in their environment; they're able to operate confidently in public, among people. Street photographers share a space with their subjects, are on equal footing, in the same place at the same time.

What makes a great street photographer is the amount of walking he or she does. Street photographers inevitably take a lot of photographs of people walking. Just as inevitably, they themselves spend a lot of time walking as they look for subjects. They are walkers who photograph other walkers. Luck plays an enormous part in street photography, and the cliché remains true that the more work you put in, the luckier you get. There are times when Winogrand seems to have had the luck of the devil. Every time he walked down the street, dwarves, identical twins, and people cuddling monkeys would appear and pose themselves for his delight.

In 1978, Winogrand moved to Los Angeles. Some of the work he did there is wonderful. One of my favorite photographs—I have a poster of it in my office—was taken at LAX airport and shows two women in stylish 1960s dresses, heels, and hairdos, backs to the camera, walking toward the futuristic Theme Building. However, the move to L.A. coincided with Winogrand's going shutter-crazy. In the eight or so years he was there, he took more than a third of a million pictures, or at least that's how often he pressed his camera's shutter. But this was not picture-making or photography as most of us understand it. The vast majority of the film he exposed was left unprocessed. Some rolls were developed but never printed. Even when contact sheets were made, he gave them only the slightest attention, never engaging with them long enough or seriously enough to do anything resembling editing.

Some of these contact sheets have been displayed in exhibitions and published in magazines, and although no photographer should be judged by the quality of his contact sheets, it appears from these that Winogrand had not only lost his luck, he had lost his eye, too. Apparently, he also lost some of his basic technical competence when it came to exposure, processing, and camera shake. Most significant, a lot of them are taken from a moving car. Often, in his L.A. period, Winogrand sat in the passenger seat and was driven around the city by various friends and associates while he shot relentlessly through the windshield or the open side window. He had always done this to some extent—quite a few of the photographs of the road trip depicted in his book *1964* are taken from a car, but by no means most. Maybe he thought this *modus operandi* was appropriate to Los Angeles. All the same, there's something dispiriting about it.

Of course, a photographer can do whatever he wants, use any method that occurs to him; but for Winogrand, this method of working seemed to mark a profound dislocation and separation. The pictures have a perfunctory, stolen look. Once he had been a fellow walker, a fellow traveler, sharing the same street, the same sidewalk, as his subjects; now he was doing drive-bys. He still photographed people, including people walking, but he also endlessly pointed his camera at parked cars, empty intersections, and blank streets. John Szarkowski has written, "Many of the last frames seem to have cut themselves free from the familiar claims of art," which is a thrillingly elegant and charitable way of saying that a lot of these photographs seem to be of nothing in particular, though not quite of nothing at all.

I once went to see Martin Parr at his London office, just a stone's throw from Bunhill Fields. He was the only street photographer I happened to know at the time. Parr accepted my basic premise that being a street photographer involves doing a lot of walking. "Yes. Basically you keep walking and you think, 'God, this is boring, it's going nowhere,' and suddenly something will happen. So really all you do is keep walking, because you know that sooner or later you're going to get something. You'll become a hunter, if you like, a hunter-gatherer. The thing you've got to remember is, most of the time there's nothing happening and suddenly it *will* happen, but you can't have the time when it happens without having all the dull time, so even though you're not taking good pictures, you're in the rhythm. You know, you have to take some bad pictures, because if you only saved yourself for one good one you'd never take one at all, and suddenly you're onto something, and you might take two or three frames of the same shot." In fact, this describes my own experience of walking without a camera. A walk is never equally fascinating for its whole length.

Certain stretches may seem dull or mundane, and then suddenly you see a number of amazing things that make it all worthwhile.

I wondered if Martin Parr had developed a sense for loitering in certain places that were likely to produce the shots he was looking for. Did he ever simply lurk rather than walk? "Sure. You're looking for a place where you know things might reveal themselves, but generally on the street you don't get much background, people take up most of the action, but I certainly know in the case of Bruce Gilden, he returns to the same place, he knows exactly where, the time of the day, the traffic flow in terms of people, and he'll keep going back to those places. You can almost recognize people, you know. You [the photographer] become almost part of the street furniture." I asked what reaction he got from people he photographed on the street. "It varies," he said. "Occasionally, people say 'Hi. What on earth are you doing?' I'm not as aggressive as Bruce Gilden. He's aggressive. If you appear guilty, then people are going to get cross with you. If you appear confident in what you're doing, it helps enormously. That's why Gilden gets away with it. He thinks it's his absolute right to be on the street photographing, and he's absolutely correct, of course. Therefore, there is no problem, there is no issue, whereas I get people who write to me or I meet people who say, 'How can you do that, photograph strangers walking on the street?'"

DiCorcia was the photographer who set up cinematic lighting rigs on the street, waited for people to walk into the frame where they were perfectly lit, and then pressed the shutter. He got into a whole lot of trouble for it, too. He was sued by a Jewish Orthodox priest, of eye-catching appearance, named Emo Nussenzweig, under New York's right-to-privacy laws that forbid the use of a person's likeness for commercial purposes without the person's permission. The case went to the Manhattan State Supreme Court, where it came down to a definition of commerce, or more properly, of art. Even though diCorcia made money from the photographs, it was declared they were first and foremost art, and therefore he was protected under the First Amendment. This is something else Garry Winogrand might have said to the woman who protested his taking her picture. It's good to know that street photography is a form of free speech, but having to go to the Manhattan Supreme Court to prove it is the kind of thing that must deter newcomers to the field.

Equally, this law may make pedestrians feel especially vulnerable. They are protected from commerce but not from art. It's illegal for a company, or its advertising agency, to take a picture of you in the street and print it with a headline that says, "This Man Eats Hamburgers" or "This Man Needs Life Insurance." But, if there's no headline, or if there's a caption indicating that this is a piece of street photography taken by a serious street photographer, then you have no recourse. Personally, on balance, I think it is as it should be, but then nobody's made a ton of money by taking my photograph while I was walking on the street.

Discussion Questions

1. What is the difference between street photography and the pictures people today take on the streets with their cell phones? Could the cell phone photos ever be seen as art? Why or why not?

2. What changes in method and result occurred when Garry Winogrand relocated from New York to Los Angeles? What is Geoff Nicholson's assessment of the work he produced after the move? Assuming that Nicholson is correct, consider boredom, location, and decline of talent as possible explanations for the differences.

3. Explain the distinction made by the Supreme Court regarding the taking of a person's picture without permission. How does this legal position correspond with your own opinion regarding the right to privacy and/or the photographic prohibitions of some cultures and religions?

4. Discuss Sontag's ideas about photography as a tool of power and a defense against anxiety in relation to the production and appreciation of street photography.

Art at Arm's Length: A History of the Selfie

Essay

Jerry Saltz

Jerry Saltz is an American art critic and a columnist for New York *magazine. He is a visiting critic at a number of academic institutions, including Columbia University, Yale University, and the Art Institute of Chicago. He is also the author of two books on art,* Seeing Out Loud: The Village Voice Art Columns, 1998-2003 *(2003) and* Seeing Out Louder *(2009).*

We live in the age of the selfie. A fast self-portrait, made with a smartphone's camera and immediately distributed and inscribed into a network, is an instant visual communication of where we are, what we're doing, who we think we are, and who we think is watching. Selfies have changed aspects of social interaction, body language, self-awareness, privacy, and humor, altering temporality, irony, and public behavior. It's become a new visual genre—a type of self-portraiture formally distinct from all others in history. Selfies have their own structural autonomy. This is a very big deal for art.

Genres arise relatively rarely. Portraiture is a genre. So are still-life, landscape, animal painting, history painting. (They overlap, too: A portrait might be in a seascape.) A genre possesses its own formal logic, with tropes and structural wisdom, and lasts a long time, until all the problems it was invented to address have been fully addressed. (Genres are distinct from styles, which come and go: There are Expressionist portraits, Cubist portraits, Impressionist portraits, Norman Rockwell portraits. Style is the endless variation within genre.)

These are not like the self-portraits we are used to. Setting aside the formal dissimilarities between these two forms—of framing, of technique—traditional photographic self-portraiture is far less spontaneous and casual than a selfie is. This new genre isn't dominated by artists. When made by amateurs, traditional photographic self-portraiture didn't become a distinct thing, didn't have a codified look or transform into social dialogue and conversation. These pictures were not usually disseminated to strangers and were never made in such numbers by so many people. It's possible that the selfie is the most prevalent popular genre ever.

Let's stipulate that most selfies are silly, typical, boring. Guys flexing muscles, girls making pouty lips ("duckface"), people mugging in bars or throwing gang signs or posing with monuments or someone famous. Still, the new genre has its earmarks. Excluding those taken in mirrors—a distinct subset of this universe—selfies are nearly always taken from within an arm's length of the subject. For this reason, the cropping and composition of selfies are very different from those of all preceding self-portraiture. There is the near-constant visual presence of one of the photographer's arms, typically the one holding the camera. Bad camera angles predominate, as the subject is nearly always off-center. The wide-angle lens on most cell-phone cameras exaggerates the depth of noses and chins, and the arm holding the camera often looks huge. (Over time, this distortion has become less noticeable. Recall, however, the skewed look of the early cell-phone snap.) If both your hands are in the picture and it's not a mirror shot, technically, it's not a selfie—it's a portrait.

Selfies are usually casual, improvised, fast; their primary purpose is to be seen here, now, by other people, most of them unknown, in social networks. They are never accidental: Whether carefully staged or completely casual, any selfie that you see had to be approved by the sender before being embedded into a network. This implies control as well as the presence of performing, self-criticality, and irony. The distributor of a selfie made it to be looked at by us, right now, and when we look at it, we know that. (And the maker knows we know that.) The critic Alicia Eler notes that they're "where we become our own biggest fans and private paparazzi," and that they are "ways for celebrities to pretend they're just like regular people, making themselves their own controlled PR machines."

When it is not just PR, though, it is a powerful, instantaneous ironic interaction that has intensity, intimacy, and strangeness. In some way, selfies reach back to the Greek theatrical idea of methexis—a group sharing wherein the speaker addresses the audience directly, much like when comic actors look at the TV camera and make a face. Finally, fascinatingly, the genre wasn't created by artists. Selfies come from all of us; they are a folk art that is already expanding the language and lexicon of photography. Selfies are a photography of modern life—not that academics or curators are paying much attention to them. They will, though: In a hundred years, the mass of selfies will be an incredible record of the fine details of everyday life. Imagine what we could see if we had millions of these from the streets of imperial Rome.

I've taken them. (I used to take self-shots with old-fashioned cameras and send the film off to be developed, then wait by the mailbox, antsy that my parents would open the Kodak envelope and find the dicey ones. These, unlike selfies, were not for public view.) You've taken them. So has almost everyone you know. Selfies are front-page news, subject to intense, widespread public and private scrutiny, shaming, revelation. President Obama caught hell for taking selfies with world leaders. Kim Kardashian takes them of her nude body parts. The pope takes them. So did Anthony Weiner; so did that woman on the New York Post's front page who, perhaps inadvertently, posted pics of herself with a would-be suicide on the Brooklyn Bridge in the background. James Franco has been called "the selfie king." A Texas customer-service rep named Benny Winfield Jr. has declared himself "King of the Selfie Movement." Many fret that this explosion of selfies proves that ours is an unusually narcissistic age.

Discussing one selfie, the *Post* trotted out a tired line about "the greater global calamity of Western decline." C'mon: The moral sky isn't falling. Marina Galperina, who with fellow curator Kyle Chayka presented the National #Selfie Portrait Gallery, rightly says, "It's less about narcissism—narcissism is so lonely!—and it's more about being your own digital avatar." Chayka adds, "Smartphone selfies come out of the same impulse as Rembrandt's . . . to make yourself look awesome." Franco says selfies "are tools of communication more than marks of vanity . . . Mini-Mes that we send out to give others a sense of who we are." Selfies are our letters to the world. They are little visual diaries that magnify, reduce, dramatize—that say, "I'm here; look at me."

Unlike traditional portraiture, selfies don't make pretentious claims. They go in the other direction—or no direction at all. Although theorists such as Susan Sontag and Roland Barthes saw melancholy and signs of death in every photograph, selfies aren't for the ages. They're like the cartoon dog who, when asked what time it is, always says, "Now! Now! Now!"

We might ask what art-historical and visual DNA form the selfie's roots and structures. There are old photos of people holding cameras out to take their own pictures. (Often, people did this to knock off the last frame in a roll of film, so it could be rewound and sent to be processed.) Still, the genre remained unclear, nebulous, and uncodified. Looking back for trace elements, I discern strong selfie echoes in Van Gogh's amazing self-portraits—some of the same intensity, immediacy, and need to reveal something inner to the outside world in the most vivid way possible. Warhol, of course, comes to mind with his love of the present, performative persona and his wild Day-Glo color. But he took his own instant photos of other subjects, or had his subjects shoot themselves in a photo booth—both devices with far more objective lenses than a smartphone, as well as different formats and depths of field. Many will point to Cindy Sherman. But none of her pictures is taken in any selfie way. Moreover, her photographs show us the characters and selves that exist in her unbridled pictorial imagination. She's not there.

Maybe the first significant twentieth-century pre-selfie is M. C. Escher's 1935 lithograph *Hand With Reflecting Sphere*. Its strange compositional structure is dominated by the artist's distorted face, reflected in a convex mirror held in his hand and showing his weirdly foreshortened arm. It echoes the closeness, shallow depth, and odd cropping of modern selfies. In another image, which might be called an allegory of a selfie, Escher rendered a hand drawing another hand drawing the first hand. It almost says, "What comes first, the self or the selfie?" My favorite proto-selfie is Parmigianino's 1523–24 *Self-Portrait in a Convex Mirror*. All the attributes of the selfie are here: the subject's face from a bizarre angle, the elongated arm, foreshortening, compositional distortion, the close-in intimacy. As the poet John Ashbery wrote of this painting (and seemingly all good selfies), "The right hand / Bigger than the head, thrust at the viewer / And swerving easily away, as though to protect what it advertises."

Everyone has his or her own idea of what makes a good selfie. I like the ones that metamorphose into what might be called selfies-plus—pictures that begin to speak in unintended tongues, that carry surpluses of meaning that the maker may not have known were there. Barthes wrote that such images produce what he called "a third meaning," which passes "from language to significance" (1.2.2).

I'm not talking about cute contradictions, unintended parody, nip slips, moose knuckles. Everyone's subject to these unveilings. No, I'm talking about more unstable, obstinate meanings that come to the fore: fictions, paranoia, fantasies, voyeurism, exhibitionism, confessions—things that take us to a place where we become the author of another story. That's thrilling. And something like art. Take, for example, a photo posted last July by John Quirke. The picture itself is nothing; a strapping twentysomething, shot from below in what looks like a basement. His mouth is agape, his eyes wide open. He wears headphones. The impact of the picture comes in Quirke's tag:

"Selfie from the gas chamber in Auschwitz." The picture exceeds itself, vaults outside meaning, becoming what Barthes described as "locatable but not describable." Image and text merge in ways that add more oomph. There are similar pictures of people at Chernobyl, in front of car wrecks, with a suicide taking place over one's shoulder. Another selfie is captioned "The photos are of me at Treblinka. . . ."

We can't merely dismiss these as violations of sanctified spaces or lapses of judgment. Atget photographed crime scenes. War correspondents catch images of people being blown to bits. Many of us have taken pictures of homeless people, Dealey Plaza in Dallas, an electric chair, the hole left by the World Trade Center. I photographed the second tower falling. The new twist of the selfie is that we're *in* these pictures. (I didn't include myself in that one.) Many are in bad taste, and some indulge in shock value for shock value's sake, but they are, nevertheless, reactions to death, fear, confusion, terror, annihilation.

They can, at times, evince our need to unsee things. On the pickup site Grindr, people use as their avatars selfies taken in Berlin's Holocaust memorial. Captions include "Aussie on holidays :-) Lets [sic] have some fun" and "How many times did you jerk off." We know our sex drives are with us always, but so is something just as archaic: taboo. After making an idiotic knock-knock joke in court, George Zimmerman's defense lawyer, Don West, took a selfie in a car with his daughters eating ice-cream cones. The chilling caption is by his daughter Molly: "We beat stupidity celebration cones," followed by emoticons of a ringing bell, a grinning face, and the hashtag "#dadkilledit." The world grows dark before our eyes in selfies like these.

The bizarre side of the mirror is Kim Kardashian's now-famous picture of her unclothed. The pose is utterly banal; she's like millions of others admiring themselves in mirrors, trying to show some part of their body to best advantage. Kardashian goes a step further. As she gets everything to show just right while admiring her own image in the phone, the third meaning that pops out is not her body. It's how weirdly stage-managed the scene is. Her body is blatantly visible while her décor is carefully blocked off by Japanese screens. Kim has even authored four rules for the perfect selfie: "Hold your phone high [as you shoot]; know your angle; know your lighting; and no duckface!" Equally idiotic winds of third meaning blow through other recent celebrity selfies. Seventy-year-old Geraldo Rivera's selfie shows him gazing at his own stomach muscles in a bathroom mirror, naked but for a low-slung towel. Unlike third meanings that tell us something new, selfies like this confirm what we already know. (Here, that Geraldo is a self-involved publicity-loving hound dog.) It's no different from those celebrity porn films that are self-released accidentally-on-purpose, either to remake images or out of simple sociopathology.

Then there's the subcategory of what I call the Selfie Sublime: an extraordinary moment, photographed to incorporate the shooter's own astonishment. We see it in astronaut Aki Hoshide's selfie hovering in space, his silver helmet showing none of his features, the sun behind him, the Earth reflected in his visor. In its counterpart, the Selfie Terrible Sublime, we see not beauty but agony. On December 11, Ferdinand Puentes photographed himself in the beautiful blue ocean off the shore of Molokai, in Hawaii, seconds after his small passenger plane crashed and began to sink. The look on his face is spectral, terrified, ecstatic, eerie, vertiginous. This is someone photographing himself lost and imperiled, recording and sending off what he knows might be his final moments. After being rescued, Puentes said that when they heard sirens and bells going off in the plane and the water coming up fast, "Everyone knew what was going on." While looking at the selfie, he repeated, "It hurts." We know this from his selfie. Soon, from somewhere in the digital universe, came comparisons to Puentes's with selfies taken by gamer avatars in *Grand Theft Auto 5* that depict themselves with catastrophes. Here, people have created fictional figures that mimic what we do, and amazingly enough, the genre's earmarks are often present in their avatars' self-shots: the telltale raised shoulder, the close-in view, the bad camera angle, and the stare.

Back on Earth, the most famous selfie of 2013 has never actually been seen. When President Obama, British Prime Minister David Cameron, and Danish Prime Minister Helle Thorning-Schmidt took a group selfie at Nelson Mandela's memorial service, we saw only Roberto Schmidt's photograph of them doing so. This was a kind of Las Meninas selfie—akin to Velázquez's astonishing royal-portrait-plus-self-portrait, which ricochets among the subjects, switching up who's seeing whom from where. Many bellowed about the Obama selfie's gall and pomposity. Its third meaning, however, is far more pedestrian and human: It's the invisible thought balloon over the subjects. "It is totally incomprehensible, even to us, to be us," they are saying, "or to be us, being here." It pictures three famous people engaged in what Hegel called "picture-thinking." Or selfie-thinking.

Prank selfies abound; most are banal, fun *Jackass*-type pictures. However, there are oddities here as well, like the guy who quietly crawled atop a bathroom stall and photographed himself with the unaware person sitting on a toilet below. There are antic photos of, say, someone doing a headstand with his head in a fishbowl or break-dancing on a sink. A lot of quasi-performance-art selfies are better than a lot of so-called real art: People throwing computers timed to do something—light up, blow up, whatever—in midair and then photographing themselves as the event unfolds, or holding a giant copy machine up to a mirror. There's a selfie-plus of a guy and his dog taken by—wait for it—the dog! Of course, there are also selfies of people performing oral sex. My predilections lean toward Balzacian selfies, pictures with strange stuff visible in the background—the ones where we see the books on the coffee table, items on the shelves, posters on the walls, leftovers in the kitchen. All these things let me think I'm getting some peek into the person's unseen life. The less publicity-driven (non-Kardashian) celebrity Instagram and Twitter feeds are good for this, because those lives are usually closed off to us, and the small details seem extra-revelatory. How much they have been staged, of course, we will never know.

I'm far from the first to say the selfie is something significant. Way back in 2010, the artist-critic David Colman wrote in the *New York Times* that the selfie "is so common that it is changing photography itself." Colman in turn quoted the art historian Geoffrey Batchen saying that selfies represent "the shift of the photograph [from] memorial function to a communication device." What I love about selfies is that we then do a second thing after making them: We make them public, which is, again, something like art.

Whatever the selfie represents, it's safe to say it's in its Neolithic phase. In fact, the genre has already mutated at least once. Artist John Monteith has saved thousands of anonymous images from the selfie's early digital era, what Monteith calls the "Wild West days" of selfies. These are self-portraits taken with crude early webcams, showing weird coloration, hot spots, bizarre resolution. Posted online starting around 1999, they have mostly evaporated into the ethersphere. The "aesthetic" of these early selfie calling cards and come-ons is noticeably different from today's, because the cameras were deskbound. Settings are more private, poses more furtive, sexual. Tics crop up: women showing new tongue piercings, shirtless men with *nunchaku*. They seem as ancient as photographs of nineteenth-century Paris.

It's easy to project that, with only small changes in technology and other platforms, we will one day see amazing masters of the form. We'll see selfies of ordeal, adventure, family history, sickness, and death. There will be full-size lifelike animated holographic self-ies (can't wait to see what porn does with that!), pedagogical and short-story selfies. There could be a selfie-Kafka. We will likely make great selfies—but not until we get rid of the stupid-sounding, juvenile, treacly name. It rankles and grates every time one reads, hears, or even thinks it. We can't have a Rembrandt of selfies with a word like *selfie*.

Works Cited

Ashbery, John. "Self Portrait in a Convex Mirror." Poemhunter.com

http://www.poemhunter.com/poem/self-portrait-in-a-convex-mirror.

Barthes, John. *Elements of Semiology*. Hill and Wang: New York, 1968. Print.

Eler, Alicia. "Keeping Up With the Selfies." *Hyperallergic*, April, 2014.

http://hyperallergic.com/122640/keeping-up-with-your-selfies/

Galperina, Marina and Kyla Chayka. "Beyond the Selfie." Haiku Deck. Nov. 18, 2015.

https://www.haikudeck.com/beyond-the-selfie—self-as-art—making-and-responding-education-presentation-Q9HdBFATwS

Discussion Questions

1. How are selfies as a genre different from photographic self-portraiture?

2. Explain your response to the concern that selfies show that we have become a narcissistic society.

3. Discuss the use of selfies as a means of gaining the power and control that Sontag claims amateur photography provides in today's world.

4. Jerry Saltz believes that the name "selfie" limits the future of the genre. Propose and explain your alternative to the term.

What Your Selfies Say About You

PEGGY DREXLER

Essay

Peggy Drexler, PhD, is a research psychologist; Assistant Professor of Psychology at Weill Medical College, Cornell University; and author of two books about modern families and the children they produce.

Earlier this week, a Texas mother of four, Kimberly Hall, made national headlines with her online manifesto to teenage girls prone to taking and posting self-portraits on social media. "Who are you trying to reach?" the mom asked. "What are you trying to say?" Girls who keep this sort of thing up, the mom went on to write, will be blocked in her household, because "Did you know that once a male sees you in a state of undress, he can't ever un-see it? You don't want the Hall boys to only think of you in this sexual way, do you? Neither do we." [1]

Though her post is rife with sexism—the post runs beneath a photograph of her own three boys shirtless on the beach and includes no mention of the responsibility of the viewer, or her sons, in how he, or she, or they respond to such images—Hall makes a valid point. Ever since smartphones came equipped with cameras that face not just outward but also backward at the user, the self-portrait—dubbed the "selfie"—has taken over social media, particularly Instagram. (It's popular on dating sites, as well.) Because of the selfie's close-up nature, it's far more intimate than, say, the portrait your sister took of you standing in front of the Grand Canyon. Many selfies carry sexual undertones, especially since the majority of selfies are, obviously, user-approved, and designed to leave a positive impression or elicit a positive response. But it's not just technology that has driven the selfie—and it's not only teenage girls and singles using it to take control of how they present themselves to the world.

Sarabeth, a forty-year-old, married chief operating officer of a digital media company, routinely wove into her Instagram feed magazine-worthy photographs of herself lounging seductively on the beach, laughing by candlelight, and snuggling with her kids. They weren't all posed, though all were flawless, and served to project a certain image, that of money, power, and love of what, by all visual

---

[1]http://jezebel.com/concerned-mom-slutty-girls-selfies-are-tempting-my-pe-1251831479

accounts, was her amazingly fun-filled life. "I don't put much thought into what I post other than if it's a nice photograph of a meaningful moment, I like to share it," she told me. "But no, if I look god-awful, that's not a photo that will see the light of day."

On the surface, the trend is sort of affirming, if undeniably self-absorbed: Women, whether rich and powerful like Sarabeth or otherwise, increasingly have a healthy image of themselves. That's a good thing. *Girls* creator Lena Dunham is a big fan of the selfie, both on social media and through her show—which shares with selfies a confessional quality. On TV, Dunham's character often appears naked or in various states of undress; in real life, her Instagram selfies aren't necessarily flattering by typical standards. They challenge the "Hollywood ideal" and that, too, is a good thing, especially when size 0 celebrities dominate so much of the modern day visual barrage. The more we see a range of body types, the better.

And yet selfies are also a manifestation of society's obsession with looks and its ever-narcissistic embrace. There's a sense that selfie subjects feel as though they're starring in their own reality shows, with an inflated sense of self that allows them to believe that their friends or followers are interested in seeing them lying in bed, lips pursed, in a real world headshot. It's like looking in the mirror all day long, and letting others see you do it. And that can have real and serious implications. Excessive narcissism, studies have found, can have adverse effects on marriage and relationships[2], parenting[3], and the workplace. One study found a link between excessive narcissism and violence.[4]

What's more, a recent study out of the UK found that the selfie phenomenon may be damaging to real world relationships, concluding that both excessive photo sharing and sharing photos of a certain type—including self-portraits—make people less likeable.[5] The same study found that increased frequency of sharing self-portraits is related to a decrease in intimacy with others. For one thing, putting so much emphasis on your own looks can make others feel self-conscious about theirs in your presence. The pressure to

---

[2]http://psp.sagepub.com/content/28/4/484.short
[3]http://persweb.wabash.edu/facstaff/hortonr/pubs/horton%20et%20al.%20%282006%29.pdf
[4]http://ocean.otr.usm.edu/~w535680/Bushman%20%26%20Baumeister%20%281998%29.pdf
[5]http://www.hw.ac.uk/news/sharing-photographs-facebook-could-damage-13069.htm

be "camera-ready" can also heighten self-esteem issues and increase feelings of competition among friends.

The trick with selfies may be to look at why you're taking them—and what they do for you. Posting affirming selfies can be empowering. They can help readjust the industry standard of the beauty ideal. But they can also help reinforce the idea that what matters most in this world is how things, and people, look. For Sarabeth, the problem she noticed first, before she even noticed her increasing fixation with her own appearance and that of her family, was the fact that she was so busy controlling her image that she'd often miss the moment in real life. Capturing something on camera took priority over reacting to something in person. "Documenting the experience took precedence over living it," she said. "And finally I realized, well, how can I expect others to pay attention to what's happening in my life when I can't even say the same for myself?"

Discussion Questions

1. How, according to Peggy Drexler, is the selfie more intimate than other forms of photography? Do you agree that this is always true? Explain.

2. In what way does the author see the selfie as both a positive and a negative thing? Why do you think the good outweighs the bad or vice versa?

3. Discuss the issues that Drexler raises about selfies. Do the issues she raises correspond to concerns raised in some of the other readings in this unit? Do you think that any of the issues will influence the way you take pictures in the future? Explain your thinking.

A Thousand Pictures for a Million Words

Essay

Lash Keith Vance

Lash Keith Vance is a faculty member in the University Writing Program at the University of California, Riverside. He has published Compass: Paths to Effective Reading, *and* Compass: Guidebook to English Grammar

Experts estimate that this year people will click one trillion photos, many of them selfies. That's one trillion distinct moments in time where everything is paused for the sake of the shutter. Ultimately, such emphasis on capturing that "Kodak" moment degrades the experience, for once we take out the cell phone or the camera to snap a shot, we disrupt the flow of the event: We change—in essence—how we experience it. If we are at a concert, for example, transported by the music to somewhere else, the photographic apparatus shocks us back to the now when we try to capture the moment. We degrade the experience—at least a little—the second we interrupt it. This may not have been much of an issue in 1960 or 1980 when there were no digital photos and developing actual film cost real money. People weren't snapping pictures all the time. But when taking a thousand or ten thousand photos costs nothing, then we end up chronicling every single experience in our lives, whether important or mundane, even at the cost of the experience itself.

The lens of a camera creates an artificial barrier between the person and the event. Instead of living the moment, the person moves from being a participant to an observer. Take, for instance, a recent concert by Andrea Bocelli held at the Hollywood Bowl. The grand outdoor auditorium was filled to capacity, but many of the audience members were not listening to the soaring rendition of "Time to Say Goodbye." They were busy fiddling with their cell phones, taking pictures, maneuvering for selfies. There were so many people shuffling about that the auditorium was illuminated from the cell phone screens, like thousands of fireflies flickering at dusk.

One couple nearby took at least sixty selfies in order to get "the best view" of the stage, the lights, and the close-up. They were prepared, after all, for they even had a "selfie stick" to mount their phone on, to snap as many pictures as they wanted, and to avoid interacting with anyone in that process.

This "best" view is another symptom of the problem. Besides the time wasted in messing with their cell phone, adjusting light input, turning off the flash, and manipulating the focus, they were convinced that a "best" shot could be had. This very desire epitomizes the notion that there is one "best" moment that can or should be preserved, and the skilled photographer enhances the moment to preserve it forever through the ambered glass of forgetfulness. Forget the real experience; preserve only the idealized one.

The idealized Bocelli concert photos were immediately uploaded to Facebook as proof of people's presence at the concert. But were they really there at all? From what I could see, they spent almost all of their time fussing with the camera, taking selfies, and posting on Facebook; they were performing "how great a time they were having" for all their friends instead of listening or experiencing, and absorbing "Nessun Dorma."

The age of nearly free digital photography has joined forces with Facebook to create a dead zone of social landmines. The couple with their selfie and Facebook infatuation, though vacuous, may have suffered only the loss of any semblance of a real experience the music provided, but other picture posts are far less complimentary. Everyone knows someone who has stayed up too late, consumed too much alcohol, broken up with a boyfriend/girlfriend, gotten angry at a coworker or boss, or generally erupted at life's "slings and arrows." These unfortunate moments are far too often immortalized in digital pictures and posted to Facebook, sent via text, or uploaded in some way to the Cloud. Heated by righteous anger, foolish by virtue of age, or inebriated by some form of substance, these people post moments that may cause problems years afterwards, for, once the upload button is pressed, there is a loss of control over the image. How these images are handled, where they are stored, or to whom they are sent are all out of the person's jurisdiction. With every posting or text, the digital control is forfeited.

The danger to one's future is clear. One CBS news report offers this sage advice to job seekers: double-check Facebook settings, sanitize social media profiles, review Google+ posts, and, above all, check for untoward online pictures that can harm your chances at landing the "dream job." Indeed, job seekers have to manage their online presence as part of their résumé-building process, but this becomes more and more difficult, for once foolish photos are uploaded, they tend to remain on the Net. They can be saved or reposted by anyone else. This is more common than not, as the sexting scandals from high school students in Colorado and New York show. In these cases, hundreds of students participated, and these explicit photos were not kept private by the individuals they were originally sent to. They were shared among a vast community of people. How would a naked or provocative picture look to a corporation you are applying to for a job?

Once digital photos are uploaded or sent, they cease to be the property of the one who took them. There often is no possibility for contextualizing the photo because control over the photo has been surrendered. The problem here is that technology has erased the cooling-off period for stupidity. Before Kodak created the first digital camera, if a teenager took an explicit photo or took pictures while sneaking booze from his parents, the pictures would have to be developed at a local store. There were restrictions on what could and could not be developed, which already created barriers to the dissemination of inappropriate content. If they did somehow develop questionable photos, they would, at least, have both the picture and the negative. So while in a better frame of mind, they could decide to destroy the pictures or at least not distribute them. Now, people, especially young people, can make detrimental decisions about their future with the click of a button. Is 3 AM at a party the best time to be updating the status on Facebook with a picture or sending an explicit text?

Besides the foolish decisions people make with their photos, smartphones are dumbing us down—literally. This goes well beyond what other neuroscientists and authors such as Nicholas Carr (*The Shallows*) have been testifying to: that extensive use of the internet has off-loaded much of our executive brain function and caused significant changes in the distribution and number of dendrites within nerve cells. In other words, we have shifted the burden of developing extensive memory, and thus a vast array of connections within the brain have never been developed to service the need for memory. Instead, information is now securely housed on the Internet, and we don't need to put in the effort to collect knowledge. This ties into what scientists have long known to be true: Participants in research studies are much less likely to remember information if they know they can Google it later or if they have been told that it is unimportant.

It turns out that extensive use of photography may be doing the same thing: obfuscating memory instead of clarifying it. One psychologist, Linda Henkel, has shown in research published in *Psychological Science* that participants who snapped photos of an event in a museum had an impairment of subsequent recall, recognition, and detail memory. For Henkel, the cognitive processes engaged in participating in an event versus documenting it via photograph are quite different (i.e., fiddling with the camera as a task versus being fully immersed in the experience). Henkel's research is not alone. Indeed, she expands on the science of the so-called "directed forgetting effect" in which study participants routinely forget unimportant information or simply misremember. For instance, if subjects are told in advance of a museum tour that information about the mummy exhibit will be available in full after the tour or will not be tested, participants have a much higher chance of forgetting that entire section of the museum.

According to Henkel, photographs work in the same way. If we click the moment into ones and zeroes, then our brain perceives the event in a different way. Drawing on cognitive load theory, she explains that our brains perceive the moment as something it is not required to remember, so it won't. Like a finely tuned machine, the brain often takes shortcuts to conserve mental processing power, and a photograph is precisely that: a shortcut. So, imagine for a second how many photographs are taken per day of special or mundane events. How easy is it for the brain to elide portions of that experience since it would be available for processing or review later on?

Technology has made photography so easy that it takes real willpower and concentration to put away the digital camera or smartphone. There is a constant gravitational pull from the device, an urge to document what is happening or to upload our status to Facebook. This is no accident since the brain acclimates to certain stimuli as receptors prepare for the neural impulse. While in most cases this is short of actual addiction, it could be called a significant neural habit. In the same way, we have trained ourselves not to be immersed in events, but to constantly interrupt them by taking photos to document them on social media. In our desire for the perfect moment, the best shot, the need to preserve or share the moment, we end up losing more than we gain.

Discussion Questions

1. Explain Lash Keith Vance's assertion that taking a picture alters both the event and the person taking the picture of it. Describe an experience of your own where this alteration did or did not happen.

2. What is the difference between the way Vance and Sontag discuss the issue of "control" in relation to photography? Which one of these discussions is most likely to create a change in your behavior or attitude? Explain.

3. What are the consequences to the brain of repeated picture-taking? What possible results do you think might result from these consequences?

Assignment #3

"In Defense of Masks"

This unit asks you to focus on your idea of yourself and others as individuals, and on how the way we see ourselves as individuals affects our lives. In order to write a successful essay, you will have to understand what Kenneth Gergen, the author of the lead essay, means by "masks" and the way we make use of them as we interact with others. He presents an interesting argument about the importance of masks, and he questions the idea that we successfully achieve mental health by maintaining one coherent and fixed identity. Be sure to spend some time thinking about and discussing some of the key terms in Gergen's essay. You must understand his use of psychological concepts such as "masks" and a "coherent sense of identity" before you can respond to his argument and be able to support it with compelling, concrete evidence.

Don't neglect the stages of the writing process as you work through his ideas and yours. We hope that by now you realize the value in doing extensive prewriting as you work on an essay, and we suggest that you make systematic use of the pages that follow "In Defense of Masks" to guide you. Instructors have told us that they can always tell which students are using these pages because their essays are consistently more successful than the essays of those students who skip them or rush through them just to get course credit. With that said, feel free to use these supporting exercises in ways that suit your own thinking and writing style.

In Defense of Masks

Essay

KENNETH GERGEN

Kenneth Gergen is an eminent psychologist. He has spent a large part of his career as a professor at Swarthmore College. Through his research and publications, he has made many groundbreaking contributions to the field of experimental psychology. He is known primarily for his work in the study of social constructionism. The following passage is adapted from an article he published in 1977.

In Shakespeare's *Hamlet*, Polonius advises his son Laertes, "To thine own self be true, / And it must follow, as the night the day, / Thou canst not then be false to any man." Polonius undoubtedly had good intentions; his counsel to his son seems entirely reasonable, and fits our religious and moral values. But it is poor psychology. I think we are not apt to find a single basic self to which we can be true.

Writers from poet Alexander Pope to sociologist Erving Goffman have been alternately impressed and irritated by the use of masks in social life. Psychologists like Erik Erikson speak of self-alienation, a depressed feeling of estrangement from the masks of identity that society forces on the individual. Such critics and psychologists have been working on two assumptions: that it is normal for a person to develop a firm and coherent sense of identity, and that it is good and healthy to do so and pathological not to. My research over the past few years has led me to question both of these assumptions very seriously. I doubt that people normally develop a coherent sense of identity, and I believe that, to the extent that they do, they may experience severe emotional distress.

My colleagues and I designed a series of studies to explore the shifting masks of identity, hoping to document the shifts in an empirically reliable way. We wanted to find the factors that influence the individual's choice of masks; we were interested in both outward appearances and inward feelings of personal identity. For instance, in one experiment, a woman whom we identified as a clinical trainee interviewed eighteen female college students. She asked each student a variety of questions about the student's background, then sixty questions about how the student saw herself. Every time that the student gave a self-evaluation that was more positive than the norm, the interviewer showed subtle signs of approval: She nodded her head, smiled, occasionally spoke agreement. Conversely, she would disapprove of the student's negative self-evaluations: She would shake her head, frown, or speak disagreement. It became clear to the student that the trainee took a very positive view of her. As a result of this procedure, the students' self-evaluations became progressively more positive. This increase was significantly greater than the minimal change that occurred in the control condition, a parallel series of interviews in which eighteen other students received no feedback from the trainee.

This finding demonstrates that it is easy to modify the mask of identity, but it says little about underlying feelings. Did the young women think they were misleading the interviewer—telling her one thing while they secretly believed something else? After the interview, to check on their private evaluations of themselves, we asked the students to undertake honest self-ratings that were not to be seen by the interviewer. Comparing these self-ratings to those taken in other circumstances a month earlier, we found significant increases in the self-esteem of students who had received the positive feedback; we found no such increases in the control condition. One student in the experimental group told me later: "You know, it's very strange; I spent the rest of the day whistling and singing. Something about that interview really made me happy."

We also studied the relationship between masks and motives in several experiments, most of them based on approval-seeking. Carl Rogers pointed out that the warm regard of others is vital to feelings of self-regard and hence to feelings of personal worth. So we asked: How do individuals present themselves when they want to gain the approval of others? In experiments designed to answer this question, we varied the characteristics of the other in systematic ways. The other person might be senior to the subject in authority, or junior; open and revealing, or closed and remote; a stern task-master or an easy-going boss. When an individual seeks approval from this diverse range of personalities, he or she adopts wholly different masks or public identities. When people are not seeking approval, their self-presentations are much different in character. Taken together, our experiments document the remarkable flexibility of the self. We are made of soft plastic, and molded by social circumstances. But we should not conclude that all of our relationships are fake: Subjects in our studies generally believed in the masks they wore. Once donned, the mask becomes reality.

I believe we must abandon the assumption that normal development equips the individual with a coherent sense of identity. In the richness of human relations, a person receives varied messages about who he is. Parents, friends, lovers, teachers, kin, counselors, acquaintances all behave differently toward us; in each relationship, we learn something new about ourselves, and, as the relations change, so do the messages. The lessons are seldom connected, and they are often inconsistent. In this light, the value that society places on a coherent identity is unwarranted and possibly detrimental. It means that the vegetarian must worry about cravings for bacon, the commune dweller about cravings for a ride in a Mercedes-Benz, the husband or wife about fantasies of infidelity. All of us are burdened by the code of coherence, which demands that we ask: *How can I be X if I am already Y, its opposite?* We should ask instead: *What is causing me to be X at this time?* We may be justifiably concerned with tendencies that disrupt our preferred modes of living and loving, but we should not be anxious, depressed, or disgusted when we find a multitude of interests, potentials, and selves.

The mask may be not the symbol of superficiality that we have thought it was, but the means of realizing our potential. Walt Whitman wrote: "Do I contradict myself? / Very well then I contradict myself. / (I am large, I contain multitudes.)"

Writing Topic

What is Gergen's thesis regarding the idea of "a coherent sense of identity" versus the idea of multiple identities represented by masks? Do you agree with his position? Be sure to support your position with concrete examples; these examples may come from your personal experience and observations, or from things you have read, including the reading material from this course.

Vocabulary Check

You will want to know the definitions of the vocabulary terms in "Masks," and, by looking them up in a dictionary, you will be able to better understand the way they are used by the writer. Words can have a variety of meanings, or they can have specialized meanings in certain contexts. Look up the definitions of the following words from the reading. Choose the meaning that you think Gergen intended when he selected that particular word. Then, explain the way the meaning or concept behind the definition is key to understanding his argument.

1. *apt*

   definition: _____

   _____

   explanation: _____

   _____

   _____

   _____

2. *pathological*

   definition: _____

   _____

   explanation: _____

   _____

   _____

   _____

3. *empirical*

    definition: _____

    _____

    explanation: _____

    _____

    _____

    _____

4. *modify*

    definition: _____

    _____

    explanation: _____

    _____

    _____

    _____

5. *stern*

    definition: _____

    _____

    explanation: _____

    _____

    _____

    _____

6. *don*

definition: _____

_____

explanation: _____

_____

_____

_____

7. *unwarranted*

definition: _____

_____

explanation: _____

_____

_____

_____

8. *detrimental*

definition: _____

_____

explanation: _____

_____

_____

_____

9. *superficiality*

definition: _____

_____

explanation: _____

_____

_____

_____

Questions to Guide Your Reading

Answer the following questions so you can gain a thorough understanding of "In Defense of Masks."

Paragraph 1

What problem does the author have with Polonius's advice to his son?

Paragraph 2

According to Gergen, what are two false assumptions that most psychologists make in their understanding of mental health?

Paragraphs 3–4

Describe the experiment devised to explore "shifting masks of identity" and the findings from the experiment.

Paragraph 5

What relationship between masks and the seeking of approval did other experiments reveal?

Paragraphs 6–7

What does Gergen conclude about normal identity development and an individual's self-presentation using a variety of masks?

Prewriting for a Directed Summary

The first part of the writing topic that follows "In Defense of Masks" asks you about a central idea from Gergen's essay. To answer this part of the writing topic, you will want to write a *directed* summary, meaning one that responds specifically to the writing topic's first question.

first part of the writing topic:

What is Gergen's thesis regarding the idea of "a coherent sense of identity" versus the idea of multiple identities represented by masks?

Hint

Don't forget to look back to Part 1's "Guidelines for Writing a Directed Summary."

Focus Questions

1. What do psychologists mean by a "coherent sense of identity," and how do they generally feel about its role in maintaining mental health? Does Gergen agree with them?

2. What is Gergen's idea concerning the use of multiple masks?

3. What reasons does Gergen give to support this idea?

Developing an Opinion and Working Thesis Statement

To fully answer the writing assignment that follows "In Defense of Masks" you will have to take a position of your own on the issue Gergen addresses.

writing topic's second part:

Do you agree with his position?

Do you agree with his claim that people have continually shifting identities rather than one fixed and coherent one? In order to make your position clear to readers, state it clearly early in your essay, preferably at the end of your introductory paragraph. A clear thesis statement, one that takes a position on the importance of what Gergen calls "masks" and their importance to mental health and human potential, will unify your essay and give it a clear purpose.

It is likely that you aren't yet sure what position you want to take in your essay. If this is the case, you can explore your ideas on a blank page of this book, or go on to the next section and work on developing your ideas through specific evidence drawn from your experience. Then, you can come back to this page and work on developing a thesis statement based on the discoveries you made when you explored your ideas more systematically.

1. Use the following thesis frame to identify the basic elements of your working thesis statement:

   a. What is the issue of "In Defense of Masks" that the writing topic's first question asks you to consider? In other words, what is the main topic the essay is about?

   _____

   b. What is Gergen's opinion about that issue?

   _____

   c. What is your opinion about the issue, and will you agree or disagree with Gergen's opinion that we don't have a single identity but instead adopt different identities in different social situations?

   _____

   _____

   _____

2. Now use the elements you isolated in the thesis frame to write a thesis statement. You may have to revise it several times until it captures your ideas clearly.

_____

_____

Prewriting to Find Support for Your Thesis Statement

The last part of the writing topic asks you to support the position you put forward in your thesis statement. Well-developed ideas are crucial when you are making an argument because you will have to be clear, logical, and thorough if you are to be convincing. As you work through the exercises below, you will generate much of the 4Cs material you will need when you draft your essay's body paragraphs.

writing topic's last part:

Be sure to support your position with concrete examples; these examples may come from your personal experience and observations, or from things you have read, including the reading material from this course.

Complete each section of this prewriting activity; your responses will become the material you will use in the next stage—planning and writing the essay.

1. As you begin to develop your own examples, think about your own self-image.

   • Make a list of characteristics you think best represent you.

   • Now choose another person in your life and create the list of characteristics you think they would choose to describe you. Would their list of characteristics match yours? Choose a few others in your life, people you meet with in different ways, and try to create the lists they might create. Would they all characterize you in the same way?

   • Now do some exploratory writing to speculate about any differences in these lists and the way they represent you.

   • What accounts for these differences, if any? Do you think you play a part in creating the different impressions of you that others may have? Do you see this as a kind of dishonesty on your part, or do you have another explanation?

   • If you could, would you prefer that the lists would be virtually alike? Would that be possible?

- Now think about Gergen's challenge to the idea that we should all work towards having one coherent sense of self. Will you agree with him that wearing masks and experiencing multiple identities are actually healthier?

Once you've explored your ideas, look them over carefully. Try to group your ideas into categories. Then, give each category a label. In other words, cluster ideas that seem to have something in common and, for each cluster, identify that shared quality by giving it a name.

2. Now broaden your focus; choose two or three people in your life, and create a list for each that identifies them. Then, imagine what the lists might look like if each of these people created his or her own list. Speculate on any significant differences. Do your findings support those that you developed in #1 above? If not, try to account for the differences. If your findings agree, determine the overarching conclusion you might draw now that you've worked through your ideas and perhaps read some of the reading selections at the end of this unit.

   Look over the categories you created above for #1 and add them to the categories, or create new ones and give them a name.

3. Once you've created topics by clustering your ideas into categories, go through them and pick two or three specific ones to develop in your essay. Make sure they are relevant to your thesis and that they have enough substance to be compelling to your reader. Then, in the space below, briefly summarize each item.

Hint

Once you've decided which items or categories on your lists you will use in your essay, take some time to explain below how each category and its items connect to your thesis statement. You will use these details for the next stage.

Revising Your Thesis Statement

Now that you have spent some time working out your ideas more systematically and developing some supporting evidence for the position you want to take, look again at the working thesis statement you crafted earlier and see if it is still accurate. As your first step, look again at the writing topic, and then write your original working thesis on the lines that follow it.

> **writing topic:**
>
> *What is Gergen's thesis regarding the idea of "a coherent sense of identity" versus the idea of multiple identities represented by masks? Do you agree with his position? Be sure to support your position with concrete examples; these examples may come from your personal experience and observations, or from things you have read, including the reading material from this course.*

Working Thesis Statement:

_____

_____

_____

Remember that your thesis statement must address the second part of the writing topic, but also take into consideration the writing topic as a whole. The first part of the writing topic identifies the issue that is up for debate, and the last part of the topic reminds you that, whatever position you take on the issue, you must be able to support it with specific evidence.

Take some time now to see if you want to revise your thesis statement. Often, after extensive prewriting and focused thought, you will find that the working thesis statement is no longer an accurate reflection of what you plan to say in your essay. You may need to add or change a word or phrase in the subject or the claim. Or, you may decide that the thesis statement must be completely rewritten so that it takes a very different position on the issue.

After examining your working thesis statement and completing any necessary revisions, check it one more time by asking yourself the following questions:

a. Does the thesis include an accurate depiction of Gergen's position on maintaining a coherent sense of identity versus having multiple identities represented by masks?

b. Do you make clear your position on the issue?

c. Is your thesis well punctuated, grammatically correct, and precisely worded?

Add any missing elements, correct the grammar errors, and refine the wording. Then, write your polished thesis on the lines below. Try to look at it from your readers' perspective. Is it strong and interesting?

_____

_____

Planning and Drafting Your Essay

Now that you have examined Gergen's argument and thought at length about your own views, draft an essay that responds to all parts of the writing topic question. Use the material you developed in this section to compose your draft, and then exchange drafts with a classmate and use the peer review activity to revise your draft.

Getting started on the draft is often the hardest part of the writing process because this is where you move from exploring and planning to getting your ideas down in a unified, coherent shape. Creating an outline will give you a basic structure for incorporating all the ideas you have developed in the preceding pages. An outline will also give you a bird's-eye view of your essay and help you spot problems in development or logic. Consult the academic essay diagram in Part 1 of this book, too, to remind yourself of the conventional form of a college essay and its basic parts.

Hint

This outline doesn't have to contain polished writing. You may want to fill in only the basic ideas in phrases or terms.

I. Introductory Paragraph

    A. An opening sentence that gives the reading selection's title and author and begins to answer the first part of the writing topic:

        _____

        _____

        _____

    B. Main points to include in the directed summary:

        1.

        2.

        3.

        4.

C. Write out your thesis statement. (Look back to "Revising Your Thesis Statement," where you reexamined and refined your working thesis statement.) It should clearly state whether Gergen's claim that we all have multiple identities or "masks" is true.

_____

_____

II. Body Paragraphs

A. The paragraph's one main point that supports the thesis statement:

_____

1. **C**ontrolling idea sentence:

_____

_____

2. **C**orroborating details:

_____

_____

_____

_____

3. **C**areful explanation of why the details are relevant:

_____

_____

_____

_____

_____

4. **C**onnection to the thesis statement:

_____

_____

_____

B. The paragraph's one main point that supports the thesis statement:

_____

1. **C**ontrolling idea sentence:

_____

_____

2. **C**orroborating details:

_____

_____

_____

_____

3. **C**areful explanation of why the details are relevant:

_____

_____

_____

_____

4. **C**onnection to the thesis statement:

_____

_____

_____

C. The paragraph's one main point that supports the thesis statement:

_____

1. **C**ontrolling idea sentence:

_____

_____

2. Corroborating details:

_____

_____

_____

_____

3. Careful explanation of why the details are relevant:

_____

_____

_____

_____

_____

4. Connection to the thesis statement:

_____

_____

_____

D. The paragraph's one main point that supports the thesis statement:

_____

1. Controlling idea sentence:

_____

_____

2. Corroborating details:

_____

_____

_____

_____

3. Careful explanation of why the details are relevant:

_____

_____

_____

_____

_____

4. Connection to the thesis statement:

_____

_____

_____

Repeat this form for any remaining body paragraphs.

III. Conclusion (For help, see "Conclusions" in Part 1.)

A. Type of conclusion to be used:

_____

B. Key words or phrases to include:

_____

Getting Feedback on Your Draft

Use the following guidelines to give a classmate feedback on his or her draft. Read the draft through first, and then answer each of the items below as specifically as you can.

Name of draft's author: _____

Name of draft's reader: _____

Discuss this draft's thesis statement. *Does it provide a clear answer to the writing topic? Is it appropriate? complete? prominently placed?*

Discuss the content of this draft. *Is each of the supporting ideas relevant and convincing enough to make a credible argument?*

Discuss the development of this draft. *Is each argument fully defended with the use of concrete examples and further explanations?*

Discuss the organization of this draft. *Could the paragraphs be ordered in a more reasonable way? Does the essay seem to develop in a logical manner?*

Discuss the sentence-level fluency of this draft. *Are there problems with basic grammar? Do idiom and word choice errors interfere with the reader's comprehension? Does the writer correctly use punctuation marks to identify clause and sentence boundaries?*

Final Draft Checklist

Content:

- My essay has an appropriate title.
- I provide an accurate summary of Gergen's position on the issue presented in "In Defense of Masks."
- My thesis states a clear position that can be supported by evidence.
- I have enough paragraphs and argument points to support my thesis.
- Each body paragraph is relevant to my thesis.
- Each body paragraph contains the 4Cs.
- I use transitions whenever necessary to connect ideas.
- The final paragraph of my essay (the conclusion) provides readers with a sense of closure.

Grammar, Punctuation, and Mechanics:

- I use the present tense to discuss Gergen's argument and examples.
- I use verb tenses correctly to show the chronology of events.
- I have verb tense consistency throughout my sentences and paragraphs.
- I have checked for subject-verb agreement in all of my sentences.
- I have revised all fragments and mixed or garbled sentences.
- I have repaired all fused (run-on) sentences and comma splices.
- I have placed a comma after introductory elements (transitions and phrases) and all dependent clauses that open a sentence.
- If I present items in a series (nouns, verbs, prepositional phrases), they are parallel in form.
- If I include material spoken or written by someone other than myself, I have correctly punctuated it with quotation marks, using the MLA style guide's rules for citation.
- If I include material spoken or written by someone other than myself, I have included a works cited list that follows the MLA style guide's rules for citation.

Reviewing Your Graded Essay

After your instructor has returned your essay, you may have the opportunity to revise your paper and raise your grade. Many students, especially those whose essays receive nonpassing grades, feel that their instructors should be less "picky" about grammar and should pass the work on content alone. However, most students at this level have not yet acquired the ability to recognize quality writing, and they do not realize that content and writing actually cannot be separated in this way. Experienced instructors know that errors in sentence structure, grammar, punctuation, and word choice either interfere with content or distract readers so much that they lose track of content. In short, good ideas badly presented are no longer good ideas; to pass, an essay must have passable writing. So even if you are not submitting a revised version of this essay to your instructor, it is important that you review your work carefully in order to understand its strengths and weaknesses. This sheet will guide you through the evaluation process.

You will want to continue to use the techniques that worked well for you and to find strategies to overcome the problems that you identify in this sample of your writing. To recognize areas that might have been problematic for you, look back at the scoring rubric in this book. Match the numerical/verbal/letter grade received on your essay to the appropriate category. Study the explanation given on the rubric for your grade.

Write a few sentences below in which you identify your problems in each of the following areas. Then, suggest specific changes you could make that would improve your paper. Don't forget to use your handbook as a resource.

1. **Grammar/punctuation/mechanics**

   My problem:

   My strategy for change:

2. **Thesis/response to assignment**

   My problem:

   My strategy for change:

3. Organization

My problem:

My strategy for change:

4. Paragraph development/examples/reasoning

My problem:

My strategy for change:

5. Assessment

In the space below, assign a grade to your paper using a rubric other than the one used by your instructor. In other words, if your instructor assigned your essay a grade of *High Fail*, you might give it the letter grade you now feel the paper warrants. If your instructor used the traditional letter grade to evaluate the essay, choose a category from the rubric in this book, or any other grading scale that you are familiar with, to show your evaluation of your work. Then, write a short narrative explaining your evaluation of the essay and the reasons it received the grade you gave it.

Grade: _____

Narrative: _____

_____

_____

_____

_____

Extending the Discussion: Considering Other Viewpoints

Reading Selections

"Appearance Equals Identity" by Ted Polhemus

"Metaperceptions: How Do You See Yourself?" by Carlin Flora

"The Truth about Beauty" by Amy Alkon

"The Beauty Myth" by Naomi Wolf

"Differentiating the Hijab from the Headscarf" by Rawan AbuShaban

"The Style Imperative" by Hara Estroff

"The Importance of Getting Your Appearance in Order" by Chris MacLeod

Appearance Equals Identity

Essay

TED POLHEMUS

Ted Polhemus is an American anthropologist, writer, and photographer. His work focuses on fashion, identity, and the importance of personal expression in style. He has written or edited more than a dozen books. One of his most popular books is Streetstyle: From Sidewalk to Catwalk *(1994), which he originally wrote as the book for his exhibition at the Victoria & Albert Museum in London. In* Streetstyle, *Polhemus examines street fashion from 1940 to the present day. The following selection is an excerpt from the introduction of his book* Style Surfing: What to Wear in the 3rd Millennium.

Human beings have always used their appearance as personal advertising—a calling card signaling who we are and where we are. As our world grows ever more complex and fragmented, the importance of appearance grows ever greater, our visible differences and similarities facilitating interaction and relationships.

Throughout human history, the most seemingly illogical of adornment and dress styles have served eminently practical purposes. Far from being frivolous and absurd, style is functional in the true sense of the word. Central to any such argument is the idea that our dress, hairstyle, footwear, make-up and so forth—what the sociologist Irving Goffman collectively termed our "presentation of self"—functions as a medium of expression. And, moreover, that such visual communication can "say" certain things—or, at the very least, express them—more immediately and powerfully than verbal language ever can. (To appreciate this, try composing a brief, written description of yourself for a "personal ad." Now get out a prized photo of yourself dressed in a favorite set of clothes. Which medium communicates "you" more effectively and fully?)

Our lives are made up of innumerable micro moments of often trivial but sometimes enormously important visual interaction. Imagine that you are walking down a city street late at night. No one is around. And then, in the distance, a solitary figure approaches on the same side of the road. As you and this alien "other" come closer and closer—with each step more and more visual clues are discernible—you scrutinize and "check out" each other.

All the visual data are cross-indexed against an enormous data bank of previous experience to arrive at a tentative conclusion (dangerous or peculiar, but not threatening, boring, interesting, or desirable), out of which emerges a behavioral strategy—you run in the opposite direction; you cross cautiously, nonchalantly, to the other side of the road; you more or less ignore this person as irrelevant; or, perhaps, you try to catch his or her eye. Skills in "checking people out" and, alternatively, in the "presentation of self" are fundamental to our lives—in particular, in avoiding those who might cause us harm and, just as importantly, in finding people who are "on our wavelength."

In an ever more heterogeneous, complex world, finding "people like us" is no easy matter. While once it might have been sufficient to categorize people according to easily discernible and identifiable labels—white, middle class, conservative, respectable—such categories increasingly have little real meaning or value. To evaluate effectively where someone is "at" today, you need other kinds of (often extremely complex) information—information which, more often than not, is difficult or impossible to put into words. As the hipper people in marketing have come to realize, "people like us" are now identifiable only by extremely subtle differences of personal philosophy as expressed in "lifestyle" and "taste."

Accordingly, it is the careful, subtle manipulation of our own appearance to send precisely the right signals, coupled with a sensitive, sharp "reading" of others' appearance, that is most likely to make the identification of "our kind of people" possible. Verbal descriptions ("left-wing," "feminist," "old-fashioned," "fun-loving") have failed us; it is only differences of style that are capable of expressing the complex—yet increasingly significant—differences of personal "wavelength" which really matter in today's world.

Discussion Questions

1. Do you think that Ted Polhemus is correct in saying that physical appearance has become even more important in today's world than it was in the past? Why or why not?

2. What are some of the things that visual communication can say "more immediately and more powerfully" than words can? How do you think users of Facebook would respond to his position?

3. In what ways could style become the kind of mask that Kenneth Gergen defends?

Metaperceptions: How Do You See Yourself?

CARLIN FLORA

Carlin Flora earned degrees from the University of Michigan and the Columbia University School of Journalism. She has been an editor of Psychology Today *magazine and has contributed a number of articles, such as "Just Say It," "How Luck Works," and "Six Ways You Are Healthier Than You Think," to several leading magazines, such as* Discover *and* Women's Health. *She is well known for her book* Friendfluence: The Surprising Ways Friends Make Us Who We Are *(2013), a well-researched and insightful look at the influence of friendship.*

I gave a toast at my best friend's wedding last summer, a speech I had carefully crafted and practiced delivering. And it went well: The bride and groom beamed; the guests paid attention and reacted in the right spots; a waiter gave me a thumbs-up. I was relieved and pleased with myself, until months later—when I saw the cold, hard video documentation of the event. As I watched myself getting ready to make the toast, a funny thing happened. I got butterflies in my stomach all over again. I was nervous for myself, even though I knew that the outcome would be just fine. Except maybe the jitters were warranted. The triumph of that speech in my mind's eye morphed into the duller reality unfolding on the TV screen. My body language was awkward, my voice was grating, my facial expressions, odd. My timing was not quite right. Is this how people saw me? It's a terrifying thought: What if I possess a glaring flaw that everyone notices but me? Or, fears aside, what if there are a few curious chasms between how I view myself and how others view me? What if I think I'm efficient but I'm seen as disorganized? What if I think I am critical, but I'm perceived as accepting?

While many profess not to care what others think, we are, in the end, creatures who want and need to fit into a social universe. Humans are psychologically suited to interdependence. Social anxiety is really just an innate response to the threat of exclusion; feeling that we're not accepted by a group leaves us agitated and depressed. The ability to intuit how people see us is what enables us to connect authentically to others and to reap the deep satisfaction that comes with those ties.

We can never be a fly on the wall to our own personality dissections, watching as people pick us apart after meeting us. Hence, we are left to rely on the accuracy of what psychologists call our "metaperceptions"—the ideas we have about others' ideas about us.

Your ideas about what others think of you hinge on your self-concept—your own beliefs about who you are. Our self-concept is fundamentally shaped by one person in particular: Mama. How our mother (or primary caregiver) responded to our first cries and gestures heavily influences how we expect to be seen by others. "Children behave in ways that perpetuate what they have experienced," says Martha Farrell Erickson, senior fellow with the Children, Youth and Family Consortium at the University of Minnesota. "A child who had an unresponsive mother will act obnoxious or withdrawn so that people will want to keep their distance. Those with consistently responsive mothers are confident and connect well with their peers." As an infant scans his mother's face, he absorbs clues to who he is; as adults, we continue to search for our reflections in others' eyes. While the parent-child bond is not necessarily destiny, it does take quite a bit to alter self-concepts—good or bad—that are forged in childhood. People rely on others' impressions to nurture their views about themselves, says William Swann, professor of psychology at the University of Texas, Austin. His research shows that people with negative self-concepts goad others to evaluate them harshly, especially if they suspect that the other person likes them—they would rather be right than be admired.

You probably do know what people think of you, but it's likely you don't know any one person's assessment. "We have a fairly stable view of ourselves," says Bella DePaulo, visiting professor of psychology at the University of California at Santa Barbara. "We expect other people to see that same view immediately." And they do. On average, there is consensus about how you come off. But you can't apply that knowledge to any one individual, for a variety of reasons. For starters, each person has an idiosyncratic way of sizing up others that (like metaperceptions themselves) is governed by his or her own self-concept. The people you meet will assess you through their own unique lens, which lends consistency to their views on others. Some people, for example, are "likers" who perceive nearly everyone as good-natured and smart. Furthermore, if a particular person doesn't care for you, it won't always be apparent. "People are generally not direct in everyday interactions," says DePaulo. Classic work by psychologist Paul Ekman has shown that most people can't tell when others are faking expressions.

Who knows how many interactions you've walked away from thinking you were a hit while your new friend was actually faking agreeability? There's just a whole lot going on when you meet someone. You're talking, listening, and planning what you're going to say next, as well as adjusting your nonverbal behavior and unconsciously responding to the other person's. DePaulo calls it "cognitive busyness." Because of all we have to contend with, she says, we are unable to effectively interpret someone else's reactions. "We take things at face value and don't really have the means to infer others' judgments." That is, until afterward, of course, when you mull over the interaction, mining your memory for clues.

The context is key. While our personalities (and self-concepts) are fairly consistent across time and place, some situations, by their very structure, can change or even altogether wipe out our personality. You might feel like the same old you wherever you are, but the setting and role you happen to be playing affect what people think of you. Suppose you describe yourself as lighthearted and talkative. Well, no one could possibly agree if they meet you at your brother's funeral.

What type of person can handle feedback? Are you open to experience? Are you, say, perennially taking up new musical instruments or scouting out-of-the-way neighborhoods? If so, your curiosity will drive you to learn new things about the world and yourself. You'll be inclined to ask people how you're doing as you embark on new challenges, and you will gather a clearer idea of how you come off to others, says David Funder, professor of psychology at the University of California at Riverside. People endowed with the trait of physical awareness have a keen sense of how they present themselves. If you are concerned with the observable parts of personality—voice, posture, clothes, and walk—as an actor would be, says Funder, "you will control the impression you give, and your self-perception will be more accurate." If, for example, you slouch but don't know it, your droopy posture registers in the minds of those you meet and enters into how they see you—unbeknownst to you. If you are someone who craves approval, you will tend to think you make a positive impression on other people. And generally, you will, says DePaulo.

People who have learned to regulate their emotions are in a much better position to know what others think of them, says Carroll Izard, professor of psychology at the University of Delaware: "They are able to detect emotions on others' faces and to feel empathy." If you are either overwhelmed with feelings or unable to express them at all, it becomes difficult to interpret someone else's response to you. Learning to give concrete expression to your feelings and to calm yourself in highly charged moments will give you a much better grip on your own and others' internal states. Those with personalities that feed the accuracy of their metaperceptions are handsomely rewarded. "The more accurate you are about how others perceive you, the better you fare socially," says Leary. "Think of a person who thinks he's really funny but isn't. He interprets polite laughter as genuine laughter, but everyone is onto him and annoyed by him."

What kind of person rejects feedback? There are people who behave in ways that prevent them from getting direct feedback from others, which renders them less able to know how they come off. Maybe you're a boss who is prickly and hostile in the face of criticism, or a student who bursts into tears over a bad evaluation. Either way, coworkers and teachers will start leaving you in the dark to fumble over your own missteps. Such a demeanor may even encourage others to lie to you, says DePaulo. You may project a fragility that makes others afraid they will break you by offering honest criticism.

Narcissism also blocks metaperception. Instead of wincing, as "normal" subjects do, when forced to see themselves onscreen, narcissists become even more self-biased, finds Oliver John, professor of psychology at the University of California at Berkeley. When he and his team videotaped people diagnosed as pathological narcissists, a group absorbed with themselves, their subjects loved watching the footage and uniformly thought they came off beautifully! The finding underscores how fiercely we defend our self-concepts, even if they reflect psychological instability.

Discussion Questions

1. Explain the primary origin, identified by Carlin Flora, of a person's self concept. How can a person's self concept be changed? Give an example from your own experience or observation of an identity-altering moment in someone's life.

2. Describe the behavior Bella DePaulo calls "cognitive busyness." Explain the possible connection between this process and the concept of "masks" that Gergen discusses. Explain the psychologically deviant group, identified by Flora, who might not experience "cognitive busyness."

3. How could an understanding of the concept of metaperceptions influence the external factors of appearance and style discussed by other authors in this unit? Do a mini self analysis of the way you see yourself (your self-concept) and the way you think others see you (metaperception). Identify any outward changes you could make so that the type of person you believe yourself to be is the same as the one you think others believe you to be. If the two are already identical, describe the specific factors of appearance, style, and behavior that achieve this result.

The Truth about Beauty

Essay

Amy Alkon

Amy Alkon is a syndicated advice columnist, journalist, author, and blogger. She is also known as the Advice Goddess and writes a weekly advice column, "Ask the Advice Goddess," which is published in over one hundred newspapers within North America.

It would be so nice if inner beauty triumphed over outer appearance. But men are designed to care about packaging. It's time to accept the not-so-pretty facts about looks.

There are certain practical realities of existence that most of us accept. If you want to catch a bear, you don't load the trap with a copy of *Catch-22*—not unless you rub it with a considerable quantity of raw hamburger. If you want to snag a fish, you can't just slap the water with your hand and yell, "Jump on my hook, already!" Yet if you're a woman who wants to land a man, there's this notion that you should be able to go around looking like Ernest Borgnine: If you're "beautiful on the inside," that's all that should count. Right. And I should have a flying car and a mansion in Bel Air with servants and a moat.

Welcome to Uglytopia—the world reimagined as a place where it's the content of a woman's character, not her pushup bra, that puts her on the cover of *Maxim*. It just doesn't seem fair to us that some people come into life with certain advantages—whether it's a movie-star chin or a multimillion-dollar shipbuilding inheritance. Maybe we need affirmative action for ugly people; make George Clooney rotate in some homely women between all his gorgeous girlfriends. While we wish things were different, we'd best accept the ugly reality: No man will turn his head to ogle a woman because she looks like the type to buy a turkey sandwich for a homeless man or read to the blind.

There is a vast body of evidence indicating that men and women are biologically and psychologically different, and that what heterosexual men and women want in partners directly corresponds to these differences. The features men evolved to go for in women—youth, clear skin, a symmetrical face and body, feminine facial features, an hourglass figure—are those indicating that a woman would be a healthy, fertile candidate to pass on a man's genes.

These preferences span borders, cultures, and generations, meaning that, yes, there really are universal standards of beauty. And while Western women do struggle to be slim, the truth is, women in all cultures eat (or don't) to appeal to "the male gaze." The body size that's idealized in a particular culture appears to correspond to the availability of food. In cultures such as ours, where you can't go five miles without passing a 7-Eleven and food is sold by the pallet-load at warehouse grocery stores, thin women are in. In cultures where food is scarce (such as in Sahara-adjacent hoods), blubber is beautiful, and women appeal to men by stuffing themselves until they're slim like Jabba the Hutt.

Men's looks matter to heterosexual women only somewhat. Most women prefer men who are taller than they are, with symmetrical features (a sign that a potential partner is healthy and parasite-free). But women across cultures are intent on finding male partners with high status, power, and access to resources—which means a really short man can add maybe a foot to his height with a private jet. And, just like women who aren't very attractive, men who make very little money or are chronically out of work tend to have a really hard time finding partners. There is some male grumbling about this. Yet while feminist journalists deforest North America publishing articles urging women to bow out of the beauty arms race and "Learn to love that woman in the mirror!", nobody gets into the ridiculous position of advising men to "Learn to love that unemployed guy sprawled on the couch!"

Now, before you brand me a traitor to my gender, let me say that I'm all for women's having the vote, and I think a woman with a mustache should make the same money as a man with a mustache. But you don't help that woman by advising her, "No need to wax that lip fringe or work off that beer belly!" (Because the road to female empowerment is . . . looking just like a hairy old man?) But take *The Beauty Myth* author Naomi Wolf: She contends that standards of beauty are a plot to keep women politically, economically, and sexually subjugated to men—apparently by keeping them too busy curling their eyelashes to have time for political action and too weak from dieting to stand up for what they want in bed. Wolf and her feminist sob sisters bleat about the horror of women's being pushed to conform to "Western standards of beauty"—as if eyebrow plucking and getting highlights are the real hardships compared to the walk in the park of footbinding and clitoridectomy. Most insultingly, Wolf paints women who look after their looks as the dim, passive dupes of Madison Avenue and magazine editors. Apparently, women need only open a page of *Vogue* and they're under its spell—they sleepwalk to Sephora to load up on anti-wrinkle potions, then go on harsh diets, eating only carrots fertilized with butterfly poo.

It turns out that the real beauty myth is the damaging one Wolf and other feminists are perpetuating—the absurd notion that it serves women to thumb their noses at standards of beauty. Of course, looks aren't *all* that matter (as I'm lectured by female readers of my newspaper column when I point out that male lust seems to have a weight limit). But looks matter a great deal. The more attractive the woman is, the wider her pool of romantic partners and range of opportunities in her work and day-to-day life. We all know this, and numerous studies confirm it—it's just heresy to say so.

We consider it admirable when people strive to better themselves intellectually; we don't say, "Hey, you weren't born a genius, so why ever bother reading a book?" Why should we treat physical appearance any differently? For example, research shows that men prefer women with full lips, smaller chins, and large eyes—indicators of higher levels of estrogen. Some lucky women have big eyes; others just seem to, thanks to the clever application of eyeshadow. As the classic commercial says, "Maybe she's born with it. Maybe it's Maybelline." (If it increases her options, who cares which it is?)

Unfortunately, because Americans are so conflicted and dishonest about the power of beauty, we approach it like novices. At one end of the spectrum are the "Love me as I am!" types, such as the woman who asked me why she was having such a terrible time meeting men . . . while dressed in a way that advertised not "I want a boyfriend" but "I'm just the girl to clean out your sewer line!" At the other extreme are women who go around resembling porn-ready painted dolls. Note to the menopausal painted doll: Troweled-on makeup doesn't make you look younger; it makes you look like an aging caricature.

Once women start seeing wrinkles and crow's feet, the desperation to look like they were born yesterday often makes them act like it, too. Women want to believe there's such a thing as "hope in a jar"—and there is: hope from the CEO selling the jars that you and millions of others will buy him a new yacht and a chateau in the south of France. There actually is hope to be found in a plastic bottle—of sunblock, the kind that protects against both UVA and UVB rays (the skin-aging ones). But the Beauty Brains, a group of blogging cosmetic scientists, write, "The sad truth is that creams that claim to be anti-aging are not much more effective than standard moisturizing lotions."

French women, too, buy into the idea that there's some fountain of youth at the Clarins counter. But, perhaps because feminism never seeped into mainstream culture in France like it did here, they generally have a healthier and more realistic relationship with beauty, accepting it as the conduit to love, sex, relationships, and increased opportunities. They take pleasure in cultivating their appearance and in accentuating their physical differences from men. They don't give up on looking after their looks as they age, nor do they tart themselves up like sexy schoolgirls at fifty. They simply take pride in their appearance and try to look like sensual older women.

To understand what it takes to be beautiful, we need to be very clear about what being beautiful means—being sexually appealing to men. And then, instead of snarling that male sexuality is evil, we need to accept that it's just different—far more visually-driven than female sexuality. To focus our efforts, we can turn to an increasing number of studies by evolutionary psychologists on what most men seem to want. For example, the University of Texas's Devendra Singh discovered that men, across cultures, are drawn to a woman with an hourglass figure. Men like to see a woman's waist—even on the larger ladies—so burn those muumuus, which only reveal your girlish figure in a Category 5 hurricane; and if you don't have much of a waist, do your best to give yourself one with the cut of your clothes or a belt.

Too many women try to get away with a bait-and-switch approach to appearance upkeep. If you spend three hours a day in the gym while you're dating a man, don't think that you can walk down the aisle and say "I do . . . and, guess what . . . now I don't anymore!" A woman needs to come up with a workable routine for maintaining her looks throughout her lifetime and avoid rationalizing slacking off—while she's seeking a man and after she has one. Yeah, you might have to put five or ten extra minutes into prettying up just to hang around the house. And, sure, you might be more "comfortable" in big sloppy sweats, but how "comfortable" will you be if he leaves you for a woman who cares enough to look hot for him?

Like French women, we, too, need to understand that a healthy approach to beauty is neither pretending it's unnecessary or unimportant nor making it important beyond all else. By being honest about it, we help women make informed decisions about how much effort to put into their appearance—or accept the opportunity costs of going ungroomed. The truth is, like knowledge, beauty is power. So, ladies, read lots of books, develop your mind and your character, exercise the rights that the heroes of the women's movement fought for us to have, and strive to become somebody who makes a difference in the world. And, pssst . . . while you're doing all of that, don't forget to wear lip gloss.

Discussion Questions

1. Explain the concept of "universal standards of beauty." What does Amy Alkon suggest about the relationship between body size, food availability, and this standard? Evaluate her claim on the limited basis of your own experience.

2. What is Alkon's response to Naomi Wolf's clarification of "the beauty myth"? Which claim about "the beauty myth" seems to have more validity from your perspective? Share the reasons for your choice.

3. What does the author say "being beautiful" means? Tell why you do or do not accept her approach to outward appearance. How do you think Gergen would respond to her claim?

The Beauty Myth

Essay

Naomi Wolf

Naomi Wolf received a BA in English literature from Yale University and then became a Rhodes Scholar at New College, Oxford. She is an American author and a spokesperson for what has come to be known as the third wave of the feminist movement. The following is an excerpt from her first book, The Beauty Myth *(1991), which became an international best seller.*

At last, after a long silence, women took to the streets. In the two decades of radical action that followed the rebirth of feminism in the early 1970s, Western women gained legal and reproductive rights, pursued higher education, entered the trades and the professions, and overturned ancient and revered beliefs about their social role. A generation on, do women feel free?

The affluent, educated, liberated women of the First World, who can enjoy freedoms unavailable to any women ever before, do not feel as free as they want to. And they can no longer restrict to the subconscious their sense that this lack of freedom has something to do with apparently frivolous issues, things that really should not matter. Many are ashamed to admit that such trivial concerns—to do with physical appearance, bodies, faces, hair, clothes—matter so much. But in spite of shame, guilt, and denial, more and more women are wondering if it isn't that they are entirely neurotic and alone but rather that something important is indeed at stake that has to do with the relationship between female liberation and female beauty.

The more legal and material hindrances women have broken through, the more strictly and heavily and cruelly images of female beauty have come to weigh upon us. Many women sense that women's collective progress has stalled; compared with the heady momentum of earlier days, there is a dispiriting climate of confusion, division, cynicism, and above all, exhaustion. After years of much struggle and little recognition, many older women feel burned out; after years of taking its light for granted, many younger women show little interest in touching new fire to the torch.

During the past decade, women breached the power structure; meanwhile, eating disorders rose exponentially, and cosmetic surgery became the fastest-growing medical specialty. During the past five years, consumer spending doubled; pornography became the main media category, ahead of legitimate films and records combined; and 33,000 American women told researchers that they would rather lose ten to fifteen pounds than achieve any other goal. More women have more money and power and scope and legal recognition than we have ever had before; but in terms of how we feel about ourselves *physically*, we may actually be worse off than our unliberated grandmothers. Recent research consistently shows that inside the majority of the West's controlled, attractive, successful working women, there is a secret "underlife" poisoning our freedom; infused with notions of beauty, it is a dark vein of self-hatred, physical obsessions, terror of aging, and dread of lost control.

It is no accident that so many potentially powerful women feel this way. We are in the midst of a violent backlash against feminism that uses images of female beauty as a political weapon against women's advancement: the beauty myth. It is the modern version of a social reflex that has been in force since the Industrial Revolution. As women released themselves from the feminine mystique of domesticity, the beauty myth took over its lost ground, expanding as it waned to carry on its work of social control.

The contemporary backlash is so violent because the ideology of beauty is the last one remaining of the old feminine ideologies that still has the power to control those women whom second-wave feminism would have otherwise made relatively uncontrollable: It has grown stronger to take over the work of social coercion that myths about motherhood, domesticity, chastity, and passivity no longer can manage. It is seeking right now to undo psychologically and covertly all the good things that feminism did for women materially and overtly.

This counterforce is operating to checkmate the inheritance of feminism on every level in the lives of Western women. Feminism gave us laws against job discrimination based on gender; immediately, case law evolved in Britain and the United States that institutionalized job discrimination based on women's appearances. Patriarchal religion declined; new religious dogma, using some of the mindaltering techniques of older cults and sects, arose around age and weight to functionally supplant traditional ritual. Feminists, inspired by Betty Friedan, broke the stranglehold on the women's popular press of advertisers for household products, who were promoting the feminine mystique; at once, the diet and skin care industries became the new cultural censors of women's intellectual space, and because of their pressure, the gaunt, youthful model supplanted the happy housewife as the arbiter of successful womanhood. The sexual revolution promoted the discovery of female sexuality; "beauty pornography"—which for the first time in women's history artificially linked a commodified "beauty" directly and explicitly to sexuality—invaded the mainstream to undermine women's new and vulnerable sense of sexual self-worth. Reproductive rights gave Western women control over our own bodies; the weight of fashion models plummeted to twenty-three percent below that of ordinary women, eating disorders rose exponentially, and a mass neurosis was promoted that used food and weight to strip women of that sense of control. Women insisted on politicizing health; new technologies of invasive, potentially deadly "cosmetic" surgeries developed apace to re-exert old forms of medical control of women.

Every generation since about 1830 has had to fight its version of the beauty myth. "It is very little to me," said the suffragist Lucy Stone in 1855, "to have the right to vote, to own property, etcetera, if I may not keep my body, and its uses, in my absolute right" (Stone and Blackwell 186). Eighty years later, after women had won the vote, and the first wave of the organized women's movement had subsided, Virginia Woolf wrote that it would still be decades before women could tell the truth about their bodies (288). In 1962, Betty Friedan quoted a young woman trapped in the Feminine Mystique: "Lately, I look in the mirror, and I'm so afraid I'm going to look like my mother" (74). Eight years after that, heralding the cataclysmic second wave of feminism, Germaine Greer described "the Stereotype": "To her belongs all that is beautiful, even the very word beauty itself. . . . she is a doll. . . . I'm sick of the masquerade" (47, 52, 53). In spite of the great revolution of the second wave, we are not exempt. Now we can look out over ruined barricades: A revolution has come upon us and changed everything in its path; enough time has passed since then for babies to have grown into women, but there still remains a final right not fully claimed.

The beauty myth tells a story: The quality called "beauty" objectively and universally exists. Women must want to embody it, and men must want to possess women who embody it. This embodiment is an imperative for women and not for men, which situation is necessary and natural because it is biological, sexual, and evolutionary:

Strong men battle for beautiful women, and beautiful women are more reproductively successful. Women's beauty must correlate to their fertility, and since this system is based on sexual selection, it is inevitable and changeless.

None of this is true. "Beauty" is a currency system like the gold standard. Like any economy, it is determined by politics; and in the modern age in the West, it is the last, best belief system that keeps male dominance intact. In assigning value to women in a vertical hierarchy according to a culturally imposed physical standard, it is an expression of power relations in which women must unnaturally compete for resources that men have appropriated for themselves.

"Beauty" is not universal or changeless, though the West pretends that all ideals of female beauty stem from one Platonic Ideal Woman; the Maori admire a fat vulva, and the Padung, droopy breasts. Nor is "beauty" a function of evolution: Its ideals change at a pace far more rapid than that of the evolution of species, and Charles Darwin was himself unconvinced by his own explanation that "beauty" resulted from a "sexual selection" that deviated from the rule of natural selection; for women to compete with women through "beauty" is a reversal of the way in which natural selection affects all other mammals (597). Anthropology has overturned the notion that females must be "beautiful" to be selected to mate: Evelyn Reed, Elaine Morgan, and others have dismissed sociobiological assertions of innate male polygamy and female monogamy. Female higher primates are the sexual initiators; not only do they seek out and enjoy sex with many partners, but "every nonpregnant female takes her turn at being the most desirable of all her troop. And that cycle keeps turning as long as she lives" (Morgan 250). The inflamed pink sexual organs of primates are often cited by male sociobiologists as analogous to human arrangements relating to female "beauty," when in fact that is a universal, nonhierarchical female primate characteristic.

Nor has the beauty myth always been this way. Though the pairing of the older rich men with young, "beautiful" women is taken to be somehow inevitable, in the matriarchal Goddess religions that dominated the Mediterranean from about 25,000 BCE to about 700 BCE, the situation was reversed. Nor is it something only women do and only men watch: Among the Nigerian Wodaabe, the women hold economic power, and the tribe is obsessed with male beauty; Wodaabe men spend hours together in elaborate makeup sessions, and compete—provocatively painted and dressed, with swaying hips and seductive expressions—in beauty contests judged by women. There is no legitimate historical or biological justification for the beauty myth; what it is doing to women today is a result of nothing more exalted than the need of today's power structure, economy, and culture to mount a counteroffensive against women.

If the beauty myth is not based on evolution, sex, gender, aesthetics, or God, on what is it based? It claims to be about intimacy and sex and life, a celebration of women. It is actually composed of emotional distance, politics, finance, and sexual repression. The beauty myth is not about women at all. It is about men's institutions and institutional power. The qualities that a given period calls beautiful in women are merely symbols of the female behavior that that period considers desirable: *The beauty myth is always actually prescribing behavior and not appearance.* Competition between women has been made part of the myth so that women will be divided from one another. Youth and (until recently) virginity have been "beautiful" in women since they stand for experiential and sexual ignorance. Aging in women is "unbeautiful" since women grow more powerful with time and since the links between generations of women must always be newly broken: Older women fear young ones, young women fear old, and the beauty myth truncates for all the female life span. Most urgently, women's identity must be premised upon our "beauty" so that we will remain vulnerable to outside approval, carrying the vital sensitive organ of self-esteem exposed to the air.

Though there has, of course, been a beauty myth in some form for as long as there has been patriarchy, the beauty myth in its modern form is a fairly recent invention. The myth flourishes when material constraints on women are dangerously loosened. Before the Industrial Revolution, the average woman could not have had the same feelings about "beauty" that modern women do who experience the myth as continual comparison to a mass-disseminated physical ideal. Before the development of technologies of mass production—daguerrotypes, photographs, etc.—an ordinary woman was exposed to few such images outside the Church. Since the family was a productive unit and women's work complemented men's, the value of women who were not aristocrats or prostitutes lay in their work skills, economic shrewdness, physical strength, and fertility. Physical attraction, obviously, played its part; but "beauty" as we understand it was not, for ordinary women, a serious issue in the marriage marketplace. The beauty myth in its modern form gained ground after the upheavals of industrialization, as the work unit of the family was destroyed, and urbanization and the emerging factory system demanded what social engineers of the time termed the "separate sphere" of domesticity, which supported the new labor category of the "breadwinner" who left home for the workplace during the day. The middle class expanded, the standards of living and of literacy rose, the size of families shrank; a new class of literate, idle women developed, on whose submission to enforced domesticity the evolving system of industrial capitalism depended. Most of our assumptions about the way women have always thought about "beauty" date from no earlier than the 1830s, when the cult of domesticity was first consolidated and the beauty index invented.

For the first time, new technologies could reproduce—in fashion plates, daguerreotypes, tintypes, and rotogravures—images of how women should look. In the 1840s, the first nude photographs of prostitutes were taken; advertisements using images of "beautiful" women first appeared in mid-century. Copies of classical artworks, postcards of society beauties and royal mistresses, Currier and Ives prints, and porcelain figurines flooded the separate sphere to which middle-class women were confined.

Since the Industrial Revolution, middle-class Western women have been controlled by ideals and stereotypes as much as by material constraints. This situation, unique to this group, means that analyses that trace "cultural conspiracies" are uniquely plausible in relation to them. The rise of the beauty myth was just one of several emerging social fictions that masqueraded as natural components of the feminine sphere, the better to enclose those women inside it. Other such fictions arose contemporaneously: a version of childhood that required continual maternal supervision; a concept of female biology that required middle-class women to act out the roles of hysterics and hypochondriacs; a conviction that respectable women were sexually anesthetic; and a definition of women's work that occupied them with repetitive, time-consuming, and painstaking tasks such as needlepoint and lacemaking. All such Victorian inventions as these served a double function—that is, though they were encouraged as a means to expend female energy and intelligence in harmless ways, women often used them to express genuine creativity and passion. But in spite of middle-class women's creativity with fashion and embroidery and child rearing, and, a century later, with the role of the suburban housewife that devolved from these social fictions, the fictions' main purpose was served: During a century and a half of unprecedented feminist agitation, they effectively counteracted middle-class women's dangerous new leisure, literacy, and relative freedom from material constraints.

Though these time- and mind-consuming fictions about women's natural role adapted themselves to resurface in the post-war Feminine Mystique, when the second wave of the women's movement took apart what women's magazines had portrayed as the "romance," "science," and "adventure" of homemaking and suburban family life, they temporarily failed. The cloying domestic fiction of "togetherness" lost its meaning, and middle-class women walked out of their front doors in masses. So the fictions simply transformed themselves once more: Since the women's movement had successfully taken apart most other necessary fictions of femininity, all the work of social control once spread out over the whole network of these fictions had to be reassigned to the only strand left intact, which action consequently strengthened it a hundredfold.

This reimposed onto liberated women's faces and bodies all the limitations, taboos, and punishments of the repressive laws, religious injunctions, and reproductive enslavement that no longer carried sufficient force. Inexhaustible but ephemeral beauty work took over from inexhaustible but ephemeral housework. As the economy, law, religion, sexual mores, education, and culture were forcibly opened up to include women more fairly, a private reality colonized female consciousness. By using ideas about "beauty," it reconstructed an alternative female world with its own laws, economy, religion, sexuality, education, and culture, each element as repressive as any that had gone before. Since middle-class Western women can best be weakened psychologically now that we are stronger materially, the beauty myth, as it has resurfaced in the last generation, has had to draw on more technological sophistication and reactionary fervor than ever before.

The modern arsenal of the myth is a dissemination of millions of images of the current ideal; although this barrage is generally seen as a collective sexual fantasy, there is in fact little that is sexual about it. It is summoned out of political fear on the part of male-dominated institutions threatened by women's freedom, and it exploits female guilt and apprehension about our own liberation—latent fears that we might be going too far. This frantic aggregation of imagery is a collective reactionary hallucination willed into being by both men and women stunned and disoriented by the rapidity with which gender relations have been transformed: a bulwark of reassurance against the flood of change. The mass depiction of the modern woman as a "beauty" is a contradiction: Where modern women are growing, moving, and expressing their individuality, as the myth has it, "beauty" is by definition inert, timeless, and generic. That this hallucination is necessary and deliberate is evident in the way "beauty" so directly contradicts women's real situation.

And the unconscious hallucination grows ever more influential and pervasive because of what is now conscious market manipulation: Powerful industries—the $33-billion-a-year diet industry, the $20-billion cosmetics industry, the $300-million cosmetic surgery industry, and the $7-billion pornography industry—have arisen from the capital made out of unconscious anxieties, and are in turn able, through their influence on mass culture, to use, stimulate, and reinforce the hallucination in a rising economic spiral.

This is not a conspiracy theory; it doesn't have to be. Societies tell themselves necessary fictions in the same way that individuals and families do. Psychologist Daniel Goleman describes them working the same way on the social level that they do within families: "The collusion is maintained by directing attention away from the fearsome fact, or by repackaging its meaning in an acceptable format" (17). The costs of these social blind spots, he writes, are destructive communal illusions. Possibilities for women have become so open-ended that they threaten to destabilize the institutions on which a male-dominated culture has depended, and a collective panic reaction on the part of both sexes has forced a demand for counterimages.

The resulting hallucination materializes, for women, as something all too real. No longer just an idea, it becomes three-dimensional, incorporating within itself how women live and how they do not live: It becomes the Iron Maiden. The original Iron Maiden was a medieval German instrument of torture, a body-shaped casket painted with the limbs and features of a lovely, smiling young woman. The unlucky victim was slowly enclosed inside her; the lid fell shut to immobilize the victim, who died either of starvation or, less cruelly, of the metal spikes embedded in her interior. The modern hallucination in which women are trapped or trap themselves is similarly rigid, cruel, and euphemistically painted. Contemporary culture directs attention to imagery of the Iron Maiden, while censoring real women's faces and bodies. Why does the social order feel the need to defend itself by evading the fact of real women, our faces and voices and bodies, and reducing the meaning of women to these formulaic and endlessly reproduced "beautiful" images? Though unconscious personal anxieties can be a powerful force in the creation of a vital lie, economic necessity practically guarantees it. An economy that depends on slavery needs to promote images of slaves that "justify" the institution of slavery. Western economies are absolutely dependent now on the continued underpayment of women. An ideology that makes women feel "worth less" was urgently needed to counteract the way feminism had begun to make us feel worth more. This does not require a conspiracy, merely an atmosphere.

The myth is undermining—slowly, imperceptibly, without our being aware of the real forces of erosion—the ground that women have gained through long, hard, honorable struggle. The beauty myth of the present is more insidious than any mystique of femininity yet: A century ago, Nora slammed the door of the doll's house; a generation ago, women turned their backs on the consumer heaven of the isolated multiapplianced home; but where women are trapped today, there is no door to slam. The contemporary ravages of the beauty backlash are destroying women physically and depleting us psychologically. If we are to free ourselves from the dead weight that has once again been made out of femaleness, it is not ballots or lobbyists or placards that women will need first; it is a new way to see.

Works Cited

Darwin, Charles. *The Descent of Man, and Selection in Relation to Sex.* 2nd ed. New York: Appleton, 1896. Print.

Friedan, Betty. *The Feminine Mystique.* New York: Norton, 1963. Print.

Goleman, Daniel. *Vital Lies, Simple Truths: The Psychology of Self-Deception.* New York: Simon & Schuster, 1985. Print.

Greer, Germaine. *The Female Eunuch.* New York: McGraw-Hill, 1971. Print.

Stone, Lucy, and Henry B. Blackwell. *Loving Warriors: Selected Letters of Lucy Stone and Henry B. Blackwell, 1853 to 1893.* Ed. Leslie Wheeler. New York: Dial, 1981. Print.

Woolf, Virginia. "Professions for Women." *Collected Essays.* Vol. 2. London: Hogarth, 1966. 284–89. Print.

Discussion Questions

1. What does Naomi Wolf mean by her use of the term "the beauty myth"? How, according to Wolf, has the "beauty myth" been commodified and industrialized? Give some examples you have observed recently of the general understanding of a physical ideal.

2. How, according to Wolf, does "the beauty myth" change the way women feel about themselves and about other women? Besides belonging to the patriarchy by virtue of their gender, discuss ways you think this myth might influence men as individuals. How do you think Gergen would respond to Wolf's argument?

3. How do you think Wolf would respond to Amy Alkon's assertion that Wolf is wrong because she fails to consider the fact that female beauty presents opportunities for women in many areas? Explain which of their arguments you find to be more persuasive.

Differentiating the Hijab from the Headscarf

Essay

RAWAN ABUSHABAN

Hijab has been the topic of longstanding debates in both Western and mainstream Islamic discourses alike. However, how productive are these arguments, based on the observations that stimulate them, if the focal point is consistently the outward appearance of hijab? By focusing merely on a faith's visual aspect, we exclude much of the significance and spirituality that the component contains. In a way, we appropriate the visual aspects of a faith to suit our arguments and comprehension of the world.

Much like how a millennial might appropriate the visual aspects of Hinduism by wearing a bindi to Coachella, many debate hijab without ever studying or realizing the meaning of what it is that they see, and how much of it cannot be seen. In the contexts of these arguments, hijab has been reduced to only one of its visual elements, which is commonly understood as a scarf upon a woman's head. Even in many Muslim societies, "hijab" is used colloquially to describe a head-cover. However, hijab is not a term that is synonymous with the headscarf; it is a term that encompasses much more than an article of clothing.

Hijab refers to one's behavior, speech, countenance, and dress. It is a habitual practice that is applicable to both men and women: not engaging in obnoxious or boisterous behavior; resisting flirtations, prolonged staring, and idleness with the opposite sex; and wearing clothes that conceal one's figure, and preserve one's beauty. Hijab isn't something one *wears*; it is how one *is*. A person's hijab is one's modesty in its entirety. It is an Islamic code of conduct, respect for oneself and for one another.

When an integral part of the Islamic faith is reduced to only its appearance, it shuts the doors that lead to understanding, sophisticated dialogue, and—eventually—acceptance. Far too often, one will observe a woman, raise one's eyes to the scarf wrapped around her head and neck, and assume that someone else put it there. Whether it's part of a niqab or the *dernier cri* of Islamic fashion, the headscarf appears to be backwards, the symbol of a retrograde culture. The headscarf, and these assumptions, becomes the definition of hijab, and "modesty in Islam" cannot be stripped from thoughts of coercion, compulsion, and punishment.

Unfortunately, many Muslims, and especially women who identify as "hijabi," fuel these shallow-minded debates on the necessity and importance of hijab and the headscarf. By neglecting to open the discussion to the broader elements of hijab and Islamic practices, too many of the responses made by the Muslim community have given an equally narrow view of the hijab, and miss the point of providing a counterargument.

Muslim fashion blogs often seem to perpetuate the reliance on a graphic, material identity to those unfamiliar with Islamic theology and tradition. Other Muslim women promote their headscarves as a political statement. Others frame their whole identities around the piece of fabric. By attributing our political views, personalities, and what otherwise may be construed as flaws or ultra-subjective qualities to the headscarf as a means of seeking validation, we fail to increase awareness of the greater meaning of hijab, and subjugate participants of hijab to more scrutiny by association.

Furthermore, defining hijab as only a headscarf alienates Muslim women who follow other modest practices outlined in hijab. Compromising hijab to conform to Western ideals often leads to the general belief that other modest practices in Islam are unessential—societal ailments—and are then looked upon negatively by Muslims and non-Muslims alike. By supporting the idea that the headscarf is the single facet of hijab, one actively disenfranchises Muslim men and women who are critical about their lifestyles and aim to live by the standards of modesty as outlined by the Qur'an and the ways of the Prophet ("peace be upon him"). While one's way of participating in hijab and wearing the headscarf are completely subjective and unique to that person, these anecdotal experiences should not be used to describe the genesis of hijab in Islamic tradition, or why it continues to be so important to the faith.

This poor understanding and miscommunication of hijab make it easier to justify discriminating against or banning the headscarf in some areas of the world. Deprived of its spirituality, intent, and divine service, the headscarf is nothing more than a gilded towel on someone's head. Without these crucial elements, the headscarf becomes inconsequential—a target for removal.

As long as hijab is debated and derided on the basis of its immediate visual traits without understanding or explanation, then those who engage in these shallow discussions denigrate the meaning of the Muslim woman's appearance, disregard her intentions, and shut down the possibility of constructive conversations.

Discussion Questions

1. How does Rawan AbuShaban explain the difference between hijab as appearance and as a representative of identity? What impact do you think education of non-Muslims about the hijab would have in today's world?

2. What connection can you make between Polhemus's assertion that appearance equals identity and AbuShaban's assertion that a lack of understanding of hijab makes discrimination easier? Do you think that Muslim women who do not wear a headscarf are less likely to experience discrimination? Why or why not?

3. Discuss the conflict some Muslim women may feel about the job application process or other social situations if they should read such articles as "The Importance of Getting Your Appearance in Order"? What advice would you offer these women?

The Style Imperative

Essay

Hara Estroff

Hara Estroff is an author and a journalist. For more than a dozen years, she has worked as an editor of Psychology Today, *and she contributes to that publication a regular advice column titled "Unconventional Wisdom." Her articles have appeared in publications such as the* New York Times *and* Smithsonian. *She has done groundbreaking work in identifying depression and other psychological disorders on American college campuses. She has written three books that explore the issues and challenges in raising children, her most recent titled* A Nation of Wimps: The High Cost of Invasive Parenting *(2008) .*

"Do designers dictate hemlines?" the late style doyenne Diana Vreeland was once asked. "Only if you take dictation," she replied. With that remark, she exposed a rift the fashion world seldom flaunts. There is a vast gap between fashion and style. Fashion is about clothes and their relationship to the moment. Style is about you and your relationship to yourself. Fashion is in the clothes. Style is in the wearer. The distinction could not be more revealing.

Despite the proliferation of fashion, style has been out of style for decades. As the economy expanded, America embarked on a collective shopping spree. In place of style, we have honored merchandise, clothes. Style, on the other hand, doesn't demand a credit card. It prospers on courage and creativity. Style goes way beyond fashion; it is an individually distinctive way of putting ourselves together. It is a unique blend of spirit and substance—personal identity imposed on, and created through, the world of things. It is a way of capturing something vibrant, making a statement about ourselves in clothes. It is what people really want when they aspire to be fashionable (if they aren't just adorning themselves in status symbols).

In some quarters, it's fashionable, as it were, to trivialize style. It's true that style doesn't have life-or-death impact, but it isn't devoid of substance, either. "Clothes are separated from all other objects by being inseparable from the self," Anne Hollander writes in her classic

Seeing through Clothes. "They give a visual aspect to consciousness itself." Through clothes, we reinvent ourselves every time we get dressed. Our wardrobe is our visual vocabulary. Style is our distinctive pattern of speech, our individual poetry.

Fashion is the least of it. Style is, for starters, one part identity: self-awareness and self-knowledge. You can't have style until you have articulated a self. And style requires security—feeling at home in one's body, physically and mentally. Of course, like all knowledge, self-knowledge must be updated as you grow and evolve; style takes ongoing self-assessment.

Style is also one part personality: spirit, verve, attitude, wit, inventiveness. It demands the desire and confidence to express whatever mood one wishes. Such variability is not only necessary but a reflection of a person's unique complexity as a human being. People want to be themselves and to be seen as themselves. In order to work, style must reflect the *real* self, the character and personality of the individual; anything less appears to be a costume.

Lastly, style is one part fashion. It's possible to have lots of clothes and not an ounce of style. But it's also possible to have very few clothes and lots of style. Yes, fashion is the means through which we express style, but it takes less in the way of clothes to be stylish than you might imagine. That's why generations of women have coveted the little black dress, a garment so unassuming in line and perfect in proportion that it is the finest foil for excursions into self-expression.

It's tempting to think that style is a new invention, open to us only now because we particularly value self-expression and because an extraordinary range of possibilities for doing so is available to us. But Joan DeJean, a professor of French language and culture at the University of Pennsylvania, contends that style has its well-shod feet firmly planted in the seventeenth century; it was the deliberate creation of Louis XIV of France, the Sun King. He was, she says in *The Essence of Style* (2005), history's greatest exemplar of it. DeJean sums up the style that Louis created in a word—*sparkle* (p. 174). Louis bedecked himself in diamonds for their sheer dazzling impact, his vision of power and prosperity reflecting on the state itself. He greeted visiting royalty and other heads of state in a black velvet suit encrusted with virtually every diamond in the possession of the crown. Louis didn't just impose his grand sense of self on his clothes and his court. He transformed Versailles from a hunting lodge to the resplendent palace we recognize today. He made Paris glitter at night, literally creating the City of Light. He used his power to create the fashion industry.

For all his legitimate and illegitimate progeny, Louis had only one true aesthetic heir—Gabrielle "Coco" Chanel. She revolutionized style, too, but in the opposite direction. She stripped it down to what we recognize today. In giving clothes simplicity, clarity of line, functionality, emotional directness—inventing sportswear and that blank slate known as the little black dress—she allowed clothes to be animated by the wearer. Driving gloves, sunglasses, safari jackets—these are a few of the things that defy the laws of fashion. They seem to always be in style. All suggest movement, action, excitement, a life spent not standing still. They embody the essence of the modern. Coco Chanel didn't invent them, but she paved the way for them. What she did invent was the "Chanel jacket," a fashion classic now nearing the century mark. It covers the body sparely, without encumbering it, so as to permit action. The "decoration" (contrast borders, gold buttons) is really an intrinsic part of the garment. The jacket exemplifies how much an ounce of invention—"finishing" an edge by letting the fabric unravel to a natural fringe—can electrify the most uncomplicated design. It represents the emergence of line over embellishment as the soul of attraction. And it has pockets—something Madame believed took the ultimate step into style by conferring confidence on a woman. Style, of course, is not exclusive to women. Coco Chanel today breathes through Karl Lagerfeld, whose aristocratic attire, with its slightly sadistic starched collars, submits to a funky white ponytail and dark glasses. And that is the style of style—one bold and unexpected gesture against a perfectly proportioned backdrop.

Whatever else it is, style is optimism made visible. Style presumes that you are a person of interest, that the world is a place of interest, that life is worth making the effort for. True style, in addition to being irrevocably social, is even morally responsible. Consumption isn't promiscuous or random, at the whim of the marketplace or the urging of marketers. Rather, it is focused on what is personally suitable and expressive.

Style is psychologically subversive; it exposes the American ambivalence over good looks. It always demonstrates that appearances do count. Deep down we suspect this, since we ourselves make judgments about others from how they look. No one should be penalized for not having style, of course, but those who have it are distinctive and thus more memorable. In the end, style is fundamentally democratic. It assumes every person has the potential to create a unique identity and express it through grooming and a few well-chosen clothes. Yet style is also aristocratic. It sets apart those who have it from those whose dress is merely utilitarian. It announces to the world that the wearer has assumed command of herself.

As the speed of all our transactions increases, we need fast ways of transmitting information about ourselves *without losing authenticity*; we have less and less time to make our mark in other, more leisurely ways of knowing. Style, like a perfectly fitting book jacket, evokes the substance within by way of the surface. It makes an authentic visual impression, is a memorable mark of identity in a world that otherwise strips people of identity. There was a time when style was a luxury. Today it is a necessity.

Works Cited

DeJean, Joan. *The Essence of Style: How the French Invented High Fashion, Fine Food, Chic Cafés, Style, Sophistication, and Glamour.* New York: Free Press, 2005. Print.

Hollander, Anne. *Seeing through Clothes*. New York: Viking, 1978. Print.

Discussion Questions

1. Explain the difference to Hara Estroff between fashion and style. How much attention did you pay to fashion or trends when selecting most items in your closet? What is your particular "visual vocabulary" saying about you?

2. Discuss Gergen's ideas about masks in relation to Estroff's understandings of fashion and style. How might he find her distinction between them relevant? Do you think he would consider attention paid to style and/or fashion to be healthy? Explain.

3. Why does Estroff find style to be both optimistic and subversive? How do these concepts support the ideas presented in the reading "The Importance of Getting Your Appearance in Order"?

The Importance of Getting Your Appearance in Order

CHRIS MACLEOD

Chris MacLeod, a Canadian, earned a BA with honors in psychology and an MSW (Masters in Social Work) with a focus on counseling. In 2006, he launched his social skills site SucceedSocially.com, *which formed the basis for his 2016 book,* The Social Skills Guidebook.

Putting more thought into your appearance is one of the easiest ways to improve your social prospects and the way people see you. It falls under the broader category of nonverbal communication. Unless you're really likable as a person, a lot of people will have a hard time looking past a sloppy exterior. And why not live up to your appearance's full potential?

Most people are pretty superficial and mentally lazy when they size others up. If you look like you have your act together, they can't help but assume you really do. The opposite is true, too, if you don't look all that great, people will attribute all kinds of negative traits to you. But clean up your look, and suddenly you don't seem so bad, and everyone's more willing to give you a chance, even though you're the same person deep down.

This article is referring to the kinds of good grooming and dressing that cut across all social groups and identities. Sometimes, certain ways of dressing or styling yourself are central to a niche you belong to. I'm not saying everyone has to adopt a standardized "fashionable" uniform. I'm more talking about just looking decent, whatever your scene is, and not selling yourself short.

For some people, improving their appearance can have a drastic effect on their social lives. As an example, several times I've heard anecdotes from people regarding the impact of losing a lot of weight. Rightly or wrongly, when they got in better shape everyone started treating them much, much better. They realized:

For years, I couldn't seem to get anywhere with people, even though I considered myself someone who made an effort to be personable and friendly. I got pretty depressed and wondered what was wrong with me. Then I lost the weight, and it became clear that my only problem in the past was that I was fat, and people weren't giving me a chance because of it. Now they suddenly think I'm likable and worth knowing, even though I'm the same person.

I won't lie, stories like that can make you lose faith in your fellow man, but it does drive home how much outward appearances play a role in social situations.

The Two Levels of Improving Your Look

When I talk about looking better, there are two degrees of this. The first is to just get yourself looking half-decent and eliminate any blatant appearance-related mistakes. I'd have a hard time arguing that someone shouldn't at least do this. There aren't any downsides at all to it.

The second level would be to put the effort into becoming more fashionable than average. There are benefits to doing this, but it takes more work. You have to learn about clothes and style, devote time to shopping, and possibly spend more money.

You don't *have* to take this extra step to have a good social life. As long as you're reasonably well put together, your clothes won't be a big influence on your social results. Outside of a few fashion-obsessed types, most people don't devote a lot of mental energy to their friends' clothing choices (unless their buddies are wearing something blatantly unstylish).

This article is about the importance of looking half-decent, but that doesn't automatically mean you need to change anything. It's possible your current style is absolutely fine, and any worries you have about it are just insecurities. It's also possible you think you look presentable, but you've got some blind spots in your grooming and fashion sense. The best way to know where you stand is to get an outside opinion on how you present yourself. You could ask a supportive friend or family member for feedback. There are also fashion-related forums where can post photos of yourself and get a critique.

A Few Basic Tips for Men on Looking Better

Below, I'll list some basic tips and things to avoid (geared towards men, since that's all I know), but really, this almost isn't necessary.

Once you start devoting even a little thought to how you look, you'll very quickly notice and correct all these yourself:

Basic Grooming

It feels condescending to write these out, but I suppose I should anyway:

- Groom your facial hair: Avoid the patchy beard, long black mustache hairs, or chin pube goatee. Pluck your unibrow. Tame your eyebrows if they're really thick and bushy.
- Brush and floss your teeth regularly.
- Always be conscious of your breath.
- Wash your hair regularly enough that it doesn't look super greasy.
- Take care of your skin.
- Trim your fingernails and toenails on a regular basis.
- Always wear deodorant.
- Shower or bathe at least once a day.
- Pay attention to little details such as keeping your ears clean, or your nose hair trimmed, or not having a mole with a single distracting long hair growing out of it.

Basic Dressing

Again, a list of stereotypical mistakes:

- Don't wear the same outfit two days or more in a row.
- Don't wear a similar, uninspired outfit every day (i.e., a dull black t-shirt with jeans).
- Don't keep wearing your clothes after they've become ratty or faded.
- Don't wear clothes that are overly wrinkled.
- Don't keep wearing an item if you've dirtied or stained it.
- Don't wear shirts that are too big and baggy, or too small and tight.
- Don't wear white socks with dark shoes, and vice versa.
- Don't wear socks with sandals.

Basic Appearance

- Find the best-looking haircut for your face. That might involve growing it out or cutting it much shorter. Good-looking hair can be the cornerstone of an attractive appearance.

- If you have glasses, consider getting contacts. They're not as expensive or high-maintenance as you may think. At the very least, if you do wear glasses, make sure to get some frames that look stylish on you. Glasses suit some people, but just as many would be better off without them.

- If you don't have great teeth, see what you can do about getting them whitened or straightened. Of course, I realize this isn't something anyone can cheaply do in five minutes.

- Get in shape, but don't feel you absolutely have to get huge, shredded muscles. If someone is fit for his natural frame, people subconsciously pick up on it and think he looks better. Subtle differences in things like the size of your chest muscles, the width of your shoulders, or the V-shape in your torso show through. Don't think your only options are lifting weights or running on a treadmill, either. You can do tons of activities that will make you fitter. Take up rock climbing, kick boxing, dancing, or Ultimate Frisbee. Pick something you enjoy doing and that isn't an unnecessary hassle to take part in. If you truly don't like doing something, or it's just a pain to do it, you'll quit before long.

- Tanning is controversial because of the increased risk of skin cancer, so it's your call whether you want to do it. I think the idea here is more about not looking so pale that you glow in the dark, rather than trying to turn your skin a deep brown.

Some Advice on Getting Better Clothes

Having decent clothes is one of the biggest factors in looking better. It's also a bit more complicated than vowing to take good care of your skin. This site's readers are too diverse for me to try to recommend any specific styles, stores, or labels. I'm not enough of a fashion maven to get away with doing that, anyway. Here are just some more general pointers:

- For many people who are only semi-motivated, the hardest part about getting new clothes is getting themselves out the door and to the store. After they've picked up some nice new outfits, they're usually happy about it, but it seemed like such a hassle beforehand to take a few hours to go shopping.

- You may think you don't know much about fashion, but you likely have an idea deep down about what looks good. A rigid self-image can make it hard to admit to yourself that you can wear these attractive clothes yourself.

- Go to a store that sells good clothes and start trying items on. You can use the staff's knowledge and style to your advantage by asking them to help pick out some good outfits for you (of course, trust your gut and don't let them push or falsely flatter you into buying something you're not keen about).

- Don't judge anything until you try it on and see if it looks good on you. Many clothes look a lot better than you'd think from just seeing them hanging on the rack or sitting folded up on a table.

- Your self-image or a sense of discomfort with change may pop up here and make you think things like, "That's not me, I'm not the type of person who wears this stuff" in response to styles that truly would look good on you. Try to ignore these thoughts and push out of your comfort zone. You may be surprised at how comfortable you are in outfits that you initially dismissed as "not me".

- You may have some emotional baggage associated with certain styles, even though you think deep down that they look good. If you don't like the people (e.g., jocks, preps, hipsters) who wear certain styles, the idea of dressing like one of "them" may seem traitorous to you.

There are two broad paths you can take when it comes to getting better clothes. One is to just dress like your peers (the ones who look good, that is). This is cheaper and easier. Okay, you're not being a one-of-a-kind trailblazer, but you'll still come out looking a lot better than you did before. The problem is that your clothes will go out of style sooner rather than later and you'll have to get new ones.

The second option is to go to hip, higher-end stores and buy some slightly more unique items. This is more expensive, and there's a higher risk that you'll accidentally buy something that isn't a good fit for your personality. On the upside, these clothes tend to just look better and attract more positive attention. They also exist outside of the short-lived trends more mainstream styles are subjected to, so it takes much longer before they're blatantly out of fashion.

- Like anything, there's a learning curve involved in picking out your own clothes. You get better at it with practice. As such, I'd recommend not blowing too much money your first few times out.

- Some people don't have a problem with paying more for what they feel are good clothes. However, it's totally understandable if that's not your thing. It's possible to look good and not kill your bank account. Some well-dressed men take pride in the fact that all their shirts cost less than $15.

- If in doubt, lean toward (relatively) plain and conservative clothes over flashier ones. If you don't pull them off properly, flashy clothes can backfire and make you look gaudy and like you're trying too hard.

- Don't forget about accessories such as a fun pair of sunglasses, a stylish watch, or a necklace. None of them have to be disgustingly expensive. As a general rule, though, you want to lean towards wearing fewer accessories rather than overdoing it.

- Get some nice shoes. The standard advice for dressier shoes is to have a good pair each of black and brown ones.

Your external looks are influenced by your internal state. If you took two outwardly identical men, but one was insecure and had a lot of other issues, and the other was self-assured, happy and confident, they would come across as quite different from each other. They would carry themselves differently and wear different expressions on their faces. One would literally be better looking than the other. As you invest in the inner you, your outer appearance will benefit.

Discussion Questions

1. Comment on the two levels of "improving your look." Do they both seem equally valid? Are there any items on the list that you think could or should be eliminated? Explain your response to each of them.

2. By the second page of this article, the author addresses his advice specifically to men. Do you think a similar type of article written for women would resemble this one? What differences would you expect to find in an article directed to women? Explain. Do you think any of these differences could be tied to Wolf's "beauty myth"?

3. This article suggests working on outward appearance as a means to more successful social interactions. What do you think of this idea? What suggestions do you have in this regard? How do your suggestions relate to personal identity and Gergen's idea of masks?

4. Skim the reading selection again and notice how often the author uses the word "you." By now, you have learned to avoid the use of the second person in formal writing, but in this somewhat informal blog the author chooses to use it throughout. Discuss the tone of the selection and especially the way the frequent use of "you" contributes to that tone. If you were his editor, would you advise him to revise to avoid the use of "you"? Why or why not?

Assignment #4

"Walking and the Suburbanized Psyche"

This unit asks you to think about walking, about why and how much you walk. Most of us probably take walking for granted, or think of it primarily in regard to losing weight or keeping in shape, but in this unit you will be asked to think of it as a subject for analysis that extends beyond walking's calorie-burning potential. The lead essay, written by Rebecca Solnit, examines the shrinking presence of walking in our society, and she presents an argument about the value of walking and the cost of its displacement in our lives. In order to write a successful essay in response to her argument, you will have to understand what she means by walking as a cultural activity that has an integral connection to our bodies, minds, and spirits, and how that connection is threatened by what she calls the "suburbanization of the American mind."

Remember to make full use of the stages of the writing process as you work through Solnit's ideas and your own. If you make full use of the writing activities in this unit, we believe that you will have a new awareness of the subject of walking, and will be prepared to offer an interesting, well-developed, and coherent argument about walking in the context that Solnit addresses. Use the activity pages as guides, and their questions and directions as catalysts for doing a thorough exploration and for developing insightful ideas.

Walking and the Suburbanized Psyche

REBECCA SOLNIT

Rebecca Solnit is an art critic and a writer. Her work reflects her interest in the history of the American West, and in environmental issues that threaten our environment and fail to foster communal, artistic, and personal life. The following is from her book Wanderlust: A History of Walking *(2000).*

Freedom to walk is not of much use without someplace to go. There is a sort of golden age of walking that began late in the eighteenth century and, I fear, expired some decades ago, a flawed age more golden for some than others, but still impressive for its creation of places in which to walk and its valuation of recreational walking. This age peaked around the turn of the twentieth century, when North Americans and Europeans were as likely to make a date for a walk as for a drink or meal. Walking was a sort of sacrament and a routine recreation, and walking clubs flourished. At that time, nineteenth-century urban innovations such as sidewalks and sewers were improving cities not yet menaced by twentieth-century speedups, and rural developments such as national parks and mountaineering were in first bloom. Perhaps 1970, when the US Census showed that the majority of Americans were—for the first time in the history of any nation—suburban, is a good date for this golden age's tombstone. Suburbs are bereft of the natural glories and civic pleasures of those older spaces, and suburbanization has radically changed the scale and texture of everyday life, usually in ways inimical to getting about on foot. This transformation has happened in the mind as well as on the ground. Ordinary Americans now perceive, value, and use time, space, and their own bodies in radically different ways than they did before. Walking still covers the ground between cars and buildings and the short distances within the latter, but walking as a cultural activity, as a pleasure, as travel, as a way of getting around, is fading, and with it goes an ancient and profound relationship between body, world, and imagination.

The history of the suburbs is the history of fragmentation. The twentieth-century American suburb reached a new level of fragmentation when cars made it possible to place people's homes ever farther from work, stores, public transit, schools, and social life. To illustrate how suburbs designed with curving streets and cul-de-sacs vastly expand distances, Philip Langdon gives the example of an Irvine, California, subdivision where, in order to reach a destination only a quarter mile away as the crow flies, the traveler must walk or drive more than a mile. These American suburbs are built with a diffuseness that the unenhanced human body is inadequate to cope with. Suburbanization has radically changed the scale and texture of everyday life, usually in ways inimical to getting about on foot. There are many reasons suburban sprawls generally make dull places to walk, and a large subdivision can become numbingly repetitious at three miles an hour instead of thirty or sixty.

But this transformation has happened in the mind as well as on the ground. The suburbanization of the American mind has made walking increasingly rare even when it is effective. Walking can become a sign of powerlessness or low status, and new urban and suburban design disdains the walker. Walking is no longer, so to speak, how many people think. Even in San Francisco, which is very much a "walking city," people have brought this suburbanized consciousness to their local travel, or so my observations seem to indicate. I routinely see people drive and take the bus for remarkably short distances, often distances that could be covered more quickly by foot. During one of my city's public transit crises, a commuter declared he could *walk* downtown in the time it took the streetcar, as though walking was some kind of damning comparison—but he had apparently been traveling from a destination so near downtown that he could've walked every day in less than half an hour. Once, I made my friend Maria—a surfer, biker, and world traveler—walk the half mile from her house to the shops and restaurants on Sixteenth Street, and she was pleased to realize how startlingly close they were. It had never occurred to her before that they were accessible by foot. Last Christmas season, the parking lot of the hip outdoor equipment store in Berkeley was full of drivers idling their engines and waiting for a parking space, while the streets around were full of such spaces. Apparently, shoppers weren't willing to walk two blocks to buy their outdoor gear. People have a kind of mental radius of how far they are willing to go on foot, a radius that seems to be shrinking. In defining neighborhoods and shopping districts, planners say this walking distance is about a quarter mile, the distance that can be walked in five minutes. But sometimes it hardly seems to be fifty yards.

More recent developments have been more radical in their retreat from communal space: We are in a new era of walls, guards, and security systems, and of architecture, design, and technology intended to eliminate or nullify public space. Urbanity and automobiles are antithetical in many ways, for a city of drivers is only a dysfunctional suburb of people shuttling from private interior to private interior. Cars have encouraged the diffusion and privatization of space, as shopping malls replace shopping streets, public buildings become islands in a sea of asphalt, civic design lapses into traffic engineering, and people mingle far less freely and frequently. Jane Holtz Kay, in her book on the impact of cars, *Asphalt Nation*, writes of a study that compared the lives of ten-year-olds in a walkable Vermont small town and an unwalkable southern California suburb. The California children watched four times as much television because the outdoor world offered them few adventures and destinations. And a recent study of the effects of television on Baltimore adults concluded that the more local news television, with its massive emphasis on sensational crime stories, local people watched, the more fearful they were, and the more discouraged they were from going out. These developments have made it less necessary to go out into the world, and have accommodated the deterioration of public space and social conditions.

Nature's occasional inconveniences resulting from biological and meteorological factors are now seen as drawbacks. Progress consists of the transcendence of time, space, and nature by the train and later the car, airplane, and electronic communications. But eating, resting, moving, experiencing the weather, are primary experiences of being embodied. To view them as negative is to condemn biology and the life of the senses, and severs human perception, expectation, and action from the organic world in which our bodies exist. Alienation from nature can be seen as an estrangement from natural spaces. Musing takes place in a kind of meadowlands of the imagination, a part of the imagination that has not yet been plowed, developed, or put to any immediately practical use. Time spent there is not work time, and without that time the mind becomes sterile, dull, domesticated. The fight for free space—for wilderness and for public space—must be accompanied by a fight for free time to spend wandering in that space. Otherwise, the individual imagination will be bulldozed over for the chain-store outlets of consumer appetite, true-crime titillations, and celebrity crises.

Walking has been one of the constellations in the starry sky of human culture, a constellation whose three stars are the body, the imagination, and the wide-open world. This constellation called walking has a history, the history trod out by all those poets and philosophers and insurrectionaries, by jaywalkers, streetwalkers, pilgrims, tourists, hikers, mountaineers, but whether it has a future depends on whether those connecting paths are traveled still.

Works Cited

Kay, Jane Holtz. *Asphalt Nation: How the Automobile Took Over America and How We Can Take It Back*. New York: Crown Press Publishers, 1997. Print.

Langdon, Philip. *Within Walking Distance: Creating Livable Communities for All*. Washington, D.C.: Island Press, 2016. Print.

Writing Topic

What, according to Solnit, will be lost if walking continues to be devalued by our society? Do you agree with her? Be sure to support your position with specific evidence. This evidence may come from your experience, your observations, or your reading, especially the reading from this course.

Vocabulary Check

Once again, be sure to use the following activity to ensure that you comprehend the key vocabulary terms in "Walking and the Suburbanized Psyche," and the way Solnit uses them. Words can have a variety of meanings, or they can have specialized meanings in certain contexts. Look up the definitions of the following words from the reading. Choose the meaning that you think Solnit intended when she selected that particular word. Then, explain the way the meaning or concept behind the definition is key to understanding her argument.

1. *suburbanize*

   definition: _____

   _____

   explanation: _____

   _____

   _____

   _____

2. *psyche*

   definition: _____

   _____

   explanation: _____

   _____

   _____

   _____

3. *expire*

   definition: _____

_____

explanation: _____

_____

_____

_____

4. *flourish (verb)*

   definition: _____

_____

   explanation: _____

_____

_____

_____

5. *profound*

   definition: _____

_____

   explanation: _____

_____

_____

_____

6. *diffuseness*

   definition: _____

_____

explanation: _____

_____

_____

_____

7. *unenhanced*

definition: _____

_____

explanation: _____

_____

_____

_____

8. *accessible*

definition: _____

_____

explanation: _____

_____

_____

_____

9. *muse* (verb)

definition: _____

_____

explanation: _____

_____

_____

_____

10. *titillation*

definition: _____

_____

explanation: _____

_____

_____

_____

11. *insurrectionary*

definition: _____

_____

explanation: _____

_____

_____

_____

Questions to Guide Your Reading

Answer the following questions so you can gain a thorough understanding of "Walking and the Suburbanized Psyche."

Paragraph 1

Why does Rebecca Solnit consider the period beginning in the late eighteenth century and ending just a few decades ago the "golden age of walking"?

Paragraph 2

What does Solnit claim is the connection between suburbs and the end of that "golden age"?

Paragraphs 3–4

According to Solnit, why should the decline of walking be viewed as a mental as well as a geographical transformation? List some of the examples she gives to illustrate this new attitude toward walking.

Paragraph 5

What is the relationship between natural spaces and imagination, according to Solnit?

Paragraph 6

How does Solnit use metaphor in her conclusion to show her concern about the future of walking?

Prewriting for a Directed Summary

The first part of the writing topic that follows "Walking and the Suburbanized Psyche" asks you about a central idea from Solnit's essay. To answer this part of the writing topic, you will want to write a *directed* summary, meaning one that responds specifically to the writing topic's first question.

first part of the writing topic:

What, according to Solnit, will be lost if walking continues to be devalued by our society?

Hint

Don't forget to look back to Part 1's "Guidelines for Writing a Directed Summary."

Focus Questions

1. How does Solnit explain the physical relationship between cars, the suburbs, and the decline of walking?

2. What does she think is the current attitude toward walking?

3. What is one measurable negative effect that Solnit believes can be attributed to the decline of walking?

4. What mental and physical activities take place in open spaces, according to Solnit?

5. What does Solnit believe happens to a mind deprived of the opportunity to experience free space?

Developing an Opinion and Working Thesis Statement

To fully answer the writing assignment that follows "Walking and the Suburbanized Psyche," you will have to take a position of your own on the issue Solnit addresses.

writing topic's second part:

Do you agree with her?

Do you agree with Solnit that walking is vital to the health of our bodies, minds, and imaginations? State your position clearly so that it will unify your essay and give it a clear purpose.

It is likely that you aren't yet sure what position you want to take in your essay. If this is the case, you can explore your ideas on a blank page of this book, or go on to the next section and work on developing your ideas through specific evidence drawn from your experience. Then, you can come back to this page and work on developing a thesis statement based on the discoveries you made when you explored your ideas more systematically.

1. Use the following thesis frame to identify the basic elements of your working thesis statement:

    a. What is the issue that the writing topic asks you to consider? In other words, what is the main topic the essay is about?

    _____

    b. What is Solnit's opinion about that issue?

    _____

    c. What is your opinion about the issue, and will you agree or disagree with Solnit's opinion?

    _____

    _____

    _____

2. Now use the elements you isolated in the thesis frame to write a thesis statement. You may have to revise it several times until it captures your ideas clearly.

    _____

    _____

Prewriting to Find Support for Your Thesis Statement

The last part of the writing topic asks you to support the position you put forward in your thesis statement. Well-developed ideas are crucial when you are making an argument because you will have to be clear, logical, and thorough if you are to be convincing. As you work through the exercises below, you will generate much of the 4Cs material you will need when you draft your essay's body paragraphs.

writing topic's third part:

Be sure to support your position with specific evidence. This evidence may come from your experience, your observations, or your reading, especially the reading from this course.

Hint

Complete each section of this prewriting activity; your responses will become the material you will use in the next stage—planning and writing the essay.

1. As you begin to develop some evidence as a basis for the position you decide to take, think about your own attitude toward walking. Use the following to guide your thinking:

   • How many times have you walked, even short distances, in the past week? List as many instances as you can recall. For each, include a brief description of the distance and the purpose, and try to recall how you felt about the walk. List as many instances as you can think of, both patterns (such as walking from one class to another two or three times a week) and specific occasions. (If you are not ambulatory, skip to #2.)

   • Examine the instances you have listed and see if you can group them somehow. You might cluster them under titles such as, say, "necessary walking," "voluntary walking," "voluntary walking with a purpose," or "voluntary walking for recreation and with no particular purpose other than enjoyment." You might also take into account the places where you walked, since Solnit's argument includes a discussion of spaces such as public, open, and urban environments and how they influence us. Create titles for your clusters that make sense, given the kind of walking you do in your life.

- If the examples on your list are all of the same type, speculate on what that demonstrates about the part that walking plays in your life. If you had to sum up in one sentence how important walking is to you, what would it be?

- If you are able to cluster the kinds of walking you do into two or more types, do some exploratory writing about any differences in these types and the way they represent you.

Look over the categories you've created and the examples in each category, and see if you can sum up in one sentence a statement about your walking. If you were going to represent—say, to a friend or family member—when, how, and why you walk, what would you say? Write your representative statement below.

2. Now broaden your focus; choose two or three people in your life and create a list for each that identifies—based on your observations and knowledge—when, where, how, and why they walk. Do your findings support those that you developed about yourself in #1 above? If not, try to account for the differences. If your findings agree, determine the overarching conclusion you might draw now that you've worked through your ideas. If the lists you've created differ significantly, which set of characteristics do you think is predominant for our society as a whole?

Speculate below on the results of your thinking at this point, and see if you can draw a conclusion based on your findings and insights.

3. If you have read and discussed any of the readings at the end of this unit, list the title of each, and then write just a couple of sentences that capture each reading's perspective on walking. Look over your list and determine whether one or more of them will influence your own view and the argument you want to make. Do some freewriting to explore your ideas.

Now you are ready to think about Solnit's argument and to revisit your working thesis statement to see if it still represents your thinking.

Revising Your Thesis Statement

Now that you have spent some time working out your ideas more systematically and developing some supporting evidence for the position you want to take, look again at the working thesis statement you crafted earlier and see if it is still accurate. As your first step, look again at the writing topic, and then write your original working thesis on the lines that follow it.

writing topic:

What, according to Solnit, will be lost if walking continues to be devalued by our society? Do you agree with her? Be sure to support your position with specific evidence. This evidence may come from your experience, your observations, or your reading, especially the reading from this course.

Working Thesis Statement:

_____

_____

_____

Remember that your thesis statement must address the second part of the writing topic, but also take into consideration the writing topic as a whole. The first part of the writing topic identifies the issue that is up for debate, and the last part of the topic reminds you that, whatever position you take on the issue, you must be able to support it with specific evidence.

Take some time now to see if you want to revise your thesis statement. Often, after extensive prewriting and focused thought, you will find that the working thesis statement is no longer an accurate reflection of what you plan to say in your essay. Sometimes only a word or phrase must be added or deleted; other times, the thesis statement must be significantly rewritten, as either the subject section or the claim portion or both are inaccurate.

After examining your working thesis statement and completing any necessary revisions, check it one more time by asking yourself the following questions:

a. Does the thesis include an accurate depiction of Solnit's position on the connection walking has to our body, mind, and imagination?

b. Do you make clear your position on the issue?

c. Is your thesis well punctuated, grammatically correct, and precisely worded?

Add any missing elements, correct the grammar errors, and refine the wording. Then, write your polished thesis on the lines below. Try to look at it from your readers' perspective. Is it strong and interesting?

_____

_____

Planning and Drafting Your Essay

Now that you have examined Solnit's argument and thought at length about your own views, draft an essay that responds to all parts of the writing topic question. Use the material you developed in this section to compose your draft, and then exchange drafts with a classmate and use the peer review activity to revise your draft.

Getting started on the draft is often the hardest part of the writing process because this is where you move from exploring and planning to getting your ideas down in a unified, coherent shape. Creating an outline will give you a basic structure for incorporating all the ideas you have developed in the preceding pages. An outline will also give you a bird's-eye view of your essay and help you spot problems in development or logic. Consult the academic essay diagram in Part 1 of this book, too, to remind yourself of the conventional form of a college essay and its basic parts.

Hint

This outline doesn't have to contain polished writing. You may want to fill in only the basic ideas in phrases or terms.

I. Introductory Paragraph

    A. An opening sentence that gives the reading selection's title and author and begins to answer the first part of the writing topic:

        _____

        _____

        _____

    B. Main points to include in the directed summary:

        1.

        2.

        3.

        4.

C. Write out your thesis statement. (Look back to "Revising Your Thesis Statement," where you reexamined and refined your working thesis statement.)
It should clearly state whether Solnit's claim about the connection between
walking and a healthy body, mind, and imagination is true.

_____

_____

II. Body Paragraphs

A. The paragraph's one main point that supports the thesis statement:

_____

1. Controlling idea sentence:

_____

_____

2. Corroborating details:

_____

_____

_____

_____

3. Careful explanation of why the details are relevant:

_____

_____

_____

_____

_____

4. <u>C</u>onnection to the thesis statement:

_____

_____

_____

B. The paragraph's one main point that supports the thesis statement:

_____

1. <u>C</u>ontrolling idea sentence:

_____

_____

2. <u>C</u>orroborating details:

_____

_____

_____

_____

3. <u>C</u>areful explanation of why the details are relevant:

_____

_____

_____

_____

4. <u>C</u>onnection to the thesis statement:

_____

_____

_____

C. The paragraph's one main point that supports the thesis statement:

_____

1. Controlling idea sentence:

_____

_____

2. Corroborating details:

_____

_____

_____

_____

3. Careful explanation of why the details are relevant:

_____

_____

_____

_____

4. Connection to the thesis statement:

_____

_____

_____

D. The paragraph's one main point that supports the thesis statement:

_____

1. Controlling idea sentence:

_____

_____

2. **C**orroborating details:

_____

_____

_____

_____

3. **C**areful explanation of why the details are relevant:

_____

_____

_____

_____

_____

4. **C**onnection to the thesis statement:

_____

_____

_____

Repeat this form for any remaining body paragraphs.

III. Conclusion (For help, see "Conclusions" in Part 1.)

A. Type of conclusion to be used:

_____

B. Key words or phrases to include:

_____

Getting Feedback on Your Draft

Use the following guidelines to give a classmate feedback on his or her draft. Read the draft through first, and then answer each of the items below as specifically as you can.

Name of draft's author: _____

Name of draft's reader: _____

Discuss the success of the thesis of this draft. *Does it provide a clear answer to the writing topic? Is it appropriate? complete? prominently placed?*

Discuss the content of this draft. *Is each of the supporting ideas relevant and convincing enough to make a credible argument?*

Discuss the development of this draft. *Is each argument fully defended with the use of concrete examples and further explanations?*

Discuss the organization of this draft. *Could the paragraphs be ordered in a more reasonable way? Does the essay seem to develop in a logical manner?*

Discuss the sentence-level fluency of this draft. *Are there problems with basic grammar? Do idiom and word choice errors interfere with the reader's comprehension? Does the writer correctly use punctuation marks to identify clause and sentence boundaries?*

Final Draft Checklist

Content:

- My essay has an appropriate title.
- I provide an accurate summary of Solnit's position on the issue presented in "Walking and the Suburbanized Psyche."
- My thesis states a clear position that can be supported by evidence.
- I have enough paragraphs and argument points to support my thesis.
- Each body paragraph is relevant to my thesis.
- Each body paragraph contains the 4Cs.
- I use transitions whenever necessary to connect ideas.
- The final paragraph of my essay (the conclusion) provides readers with a sense of closure.

Grammar, Punctuation, and Mechanics:

- I use the present tense to discuss Solnit's argument and examples.
- I use verb tenses correctly to show the chronology of events.
- I have verb tense consistency throughout my sentences and paragraphs.
- I have checked for subject-verb agreement in all of my sentences.
- I have revised all fragments and mixed or garbled sentences.
- I have repaired all fused (run-on) sentences and comma splices.
- I have placed a comma after introductory elements (transitions and phrases) and all dependent clauses that open a sentence.
- If I present items in a series (nouns, verbs, prepositional phrases), they are parallel in form.
- If I include material spoken or written by someone other than myself, I have correctly punctuated it with quotation marks, using the MLA style guide's rules for citation.
- If I include material spoken or written by someone other than myself, I have included a works cited list that follows the MLA style guide's rules for citation.

Reviewing Your Graded Essay

After your instructor has returned your essay, you may have the opportunity to revise your paper and raise your grade. Many students, especially those whose essays receive nonpassing grades, feel that their instructors should be less "picky" about grammar and should pass the work on content alone. However, most students at this level have not yet acquired the ability to recognize quality writing, and they do not realize that content and writing actually cannot be separated in this way. Experienced instructors know that errors in sentence structure, grammar, punctuation, and word choice either interfere with content or distract readers so much that they lose track of content. In short, good ideas badly presented are no longer good ideas; to pass, an essay must have passable writing. So even if you are not submitting a revised version of this essay to your instructor, it is important that you review your work carefully in order to understand its strengths and weaknesses. This sheet will guide you through the evaluation process.

You will want to continue to use the techniques that worked well for you and to find strategies to overcome the problems that you identify in this sample of your writing. To recognize areas that might have been problematic for you, look back at the scoring rubric in this book. Match the numerical/verbal/letter grade received on your essay to the appropriate category. Study the explanation given on the rubric for your grade.

Write a few sentences below in which you identify your problems in each of the following areas. Then, suggest specific changes you could make that would improve your paper. Don't forget to use your handbook as a resource.

1. **Grammar/punctuation/mechanics**

   My problem:

   My strategy for change:

2. **Thesis/response to assignment**

   My problem:

   My strategy for change:

3. **Organization**

   My problem:

   My strategy for change:

4. **Paragraph development/examples/reasoning**

   My problem:

   My strategy for change:

5. **Assessment**

   In the space below, assign a grade to your paper using the rubric in Part 1 of this book. If your instructor assigned your essay a grade of *High Fail*, you might give it the letter grade you now feel the paper warrants. If your instructor used the traditional letter grade to evaluate the essay, choose a category from the rubric in this book, or any other grading scale that you are familiar with, to show your evaluation of your work. Then, write a short narrative explaining your evaluation of the essay and the reasons it received the grade you gave it.

Grade: _____

Narrative: _____

_____

_____

_____

_____

Extending the Discussion: Considering Other Viewpoints

Reading Selections

Walking

HENRY DAVID THOREAU

Henry David Thoreau was an American philosopher, poet, author, and naturalist. Thoreau was one of the leading nineteenth-century transcendentalist poets of New England, and he is probably best known for his works Walden *(1854) and* Civil Disobedience *(1849).* Walden *is an account of the two years that Thoreau spent living off the land— and by his own ingenuity— at Walden Pond. Thoreau earned a degree from Harvard, became an outspoken abolitionist, and, throughout his relatively short life, occupied a number of odd jobs, supporting himself simply and devoting most of his time to writing. The essay below is an excerpt from a longer essay of the same name, and was developed out of his journal entries from the mid-1850s. "Walking" was published in 1862 just after his death.*

I wish to speak a word for Nature, for absolute freedom and wildness, as contrasted with a freedom and culture merely civil—to regard man as an inhabitant, or a part and parcel of Nature, rather than a member of society. I wish to make an extreme statement, if so I may make an emphatic one, for there are enough champions of civilization: the minister and the school committee and every one of you will take care of that. . . .

I think that I cannot preserve my health and spirits, unless I spend four hours a day at least—and it is commonly more than that—sauntering through the woods and over the hills and fields, absolutely free from all worldly engagements. You may safely say, a penny for your thoughts, or a thousand pounds. When sometimes I am reminded that the mechanics and shopkeepers stay in their shops not only all the forenoon, but all the afternoon too, sitting with crossed legs, so many of them—as if the legs were made to sit upon, and not to stand or walk upon—I think that they deserve some credit for not having all committed suicide long ago.

I, who cannot stay in my chamber for a single day without acquiring some rust, and when sometimes I have stolen forth for a walk at the eleventh hour, or four o'clock in the afternoon, too late to redeem the day, when the shades of night were already beginning to be mingled with the daylight, have felt as if I had committed some

"Walking" by Henry David Thoreau, 1861

sin to be atoned for—I confess that I am astonished at the power of endurance, to say nothing of the moral insensibility, of my neighbors who confine themselves to shops and offices the whole day for weeks and months, aye, and years almost together. I know not what manner of stuff they are of, sitting there now at three o'clock in the afternoon, as if it were three o'clock in the morning. . . .

How womankind, who are confined to the house still more than men, stand it I do not know; but I have ground to suspect that most of them do not *stand* it at all. When, early in a summer afternoon, we have been shaking the dust of the village from the skirts of our garments, making haste past those houses with purely Doric or Gothic fronts, which have such an air of repose about them, my companion whispers that probably about these times their occupants are all gone to bed. Then it is that I appreciate the beauty and the glory of architecture, which itself never turns in, but forever stands out and erect, keeping watch over the slumberers.

No doubt temperament, and, above all, age, have a good deal to do with it. As a man grows older, his ability to sit still and follow indoor occupations increases. He grows vespertinal in his habits as the evening of life approaches, till at last he comes forth only just before sundown, and gets all the walk that he requires in half an hour.

But the walking of which I speak has nothing in it akin to taking exercise, as it is called, as the sick take medicine at stated hours—as the swinging of dumbbells or chairs; but is itself the enterprise and adventure of the day. If you would get exercise, go in search of the springs of life. Think of a man's swinging dumbbells for his health, when those springs are bubbling up in far-off pastures unsought by him!

Moreover, you must walk like a camel, which is said to be the only beast which ruminates when walking. When a traveler asked Wordsworth's servant to show him her master's study, she answered, "Here is his library, but his study is out of doors."

Living much out of doors, in the sun and wind, will no doubt produce a certain roughness of character—will cause a thicker cuticle to grow over some of the finer qualities of our nature, as on the face and hands, or as severe manual labor robs the hands of some of their delicacy of touch. So staying in the house, on the other hand, may produce a softness and smoothness, not to say thinness of skin, accompanied by an increased sensibility to certain impressions. Perhaps we should be more susceptible to some influences important to our intellectual and moral growth, if the sun had shone and the wind blown on us a little less; and no doubt it is a nice matter to proportion rightly the thick and thin skin. But methinks that is a scurf that will fall off fast enough—that the natural remedy is to be found in the proportion which the night bears to the day, the winter to the summer, thought to experience. There will be so much the more air and sunshine in our thoughts. The callous palms of the laborer are conversant with finer tissues of self-respect and heroism, whose touch thrills the heart, than the languid fingers of idleness. That is mere sentimentality that lies abed by day and thinks itself white, far from the tan and callus of experience.

When we walk, we naturally go to the fields and woods: What would become of us, if we walked only in a garden or a mall? Even some sects of philosophers have felt the necessity of importing the woods to themselves, since they did not go to the woods. "They planted groves and walks of Platanes," where they took *subdiales ambulationes* in porticos open to the air. Of course it is of no use to direct our steps to the woods, if they do not carry us thither. I am alarmed when it happens that I have walked a mile into the woods bodily, without getting there in spirit. In my afternoon walk I would fain forget all my morning occupations and my obligations to Society. But it sometimes happens that I cannot easily shake off the village. The thought of some work will run in my head and I am not where my body is—I am out of my senses. In my walks I would fain return to my senses. What business have I in the woods, if I am thinking of something out of the woods? I suspect myself, and cannot help a shudder when I find myself so implicated even in what are called good works—for this may sometimes happen.

My vicinity affords many good walks; and though for so many years I have walked almost every day, and sometimes for several days together, I have not yet exhausted them. An absolutely new prospect is a great happiness, and I can still get this any afternoon. Two or three hours' walking will carry me to as strange a country as I expect ever to see. A single farmhouse which I had not seen before is sometimes as good as the dominions of the King of Dahomey. There is in fact a sort of harmony discoverable between the capabilities of the landscape within a circle of ten miles' radius, or the limits of an afternoon walk, and the threescore years and ten of human life. It will never become quite familiar to you.

Nowadays almost all man's improvements, so called, as the building of houses and the cutting down of the forest and of all large trees, simply deform the landscape, and make it more and more tame and cheap. A people who would begin by burning the fences and let the forest stand! I saw the fences half consumed, their ends lost in the

middle of the prairie, and some worldly miser with a surveyor looking after his bounds, while heaven had taken place around him, and
he did not see the angels going to and fro, but was looking for an old
post-hole in the midst of paradise. I looked again, and saw him standing in the middle of a boggy Stygian fen, surrounded by devils, and
he had found his bounds without a doubt, three little stones, where
a stake had been driven, and looking nearer, I saw that the Prince of
Darkness was his surveyor.

I can easily walk ten, fifteen, twenty, any number of miles, com-
mencing at my own door, without going by any house, without crossing a road except where the fox and the mink do: first along by the
river, and then the brook, and then the meadow and the woodside.
There are square miles in my vicinity which have no inhabitant.
From many a hill I can see civilization and the abodes of man afar.
The farmers and their works are scarcely more obvious than wood-
chucks and their burrows. Man and his affairs, church and state and
school, trade and commerce, and manufactures and agriculture, even
politics, the most alarming of them all—I am pleased to see how little space they occupy in the landscape. Politics is but a narrow field,
and that still narrower highway yonder leads to it. I sometimes direct
the traveler thither. If you would go to the political world, follow the
great road, follow that market-man, keep his dust in your eyes, and it
will lead you straight to it; for it, too, has its place merely, and does
not occupy all space. I pass from it as from a bean field into the forest, and it is forgotten. In one half-hour I can walk off to some portion of the earth's surface where a man does not stand from one year's
end to another, and there, consequently, politics are not, for they are
but as the cigar-smoke of a man.

The village is the place to which the roads tend, a sort of expansion of the highway, as a lake of a river. It is the body of which roads
are the arms and legs—a trivial or quadrivial place, the thoroughfare
and ordinary of travelers. The word is from the Latin *villa* which
together with *via*, a way, or more anciently *ved* and *vella*, *varro* derives
from *veho*, to carry, because the villa is the place to and from which
things are carried. They who got their living by teaming were said
vellaturam facere. Hence, too, the Latin word *vilis* and our vile, also
villain. This suggests what kind of degeneracy villagers are liable to.
They are wayworn by the travel that goes by and over them, without
traveling themselves.

Some do not walk at all; others walk in the highways; a few walk
across lots. Roads are made for horses and men of business. I do not

travel in them much, comparatively, because I am not in a hurry to get to any tavern or grocery or livery-stable or depot to which they lead. I am a good horse to travel, but not from choice a roadster. The landscape-painter uses the figures of men to mark a road. He would not make that use of my figure. I walk out into a nature such as the old prophets and poets, Menu, Moses, Homer, Chaucer, walked in. You may name it America, but it is not America; neither Americus Vespucius, nor Columbus, nor the rest were the discoverers of it. There is a truer amount of it in mythology than in any history of America, so called, that I have seen. . . .

At present, in this vicinity, the best part of the land is not private property; the landscape is not owned, and the walker enjoys comparative freedom. But possibly the day will come when it will be partitioned off into so-called pleasure-grounds, in which a few will take a narrow and exclusive pleasure only—when fences shall be multiplied, and man-traps and other engines invented to confine men to the public road, and walking over the surface of God's earth shall be construed to mean trespassing on some gentleman's grounds. To enjoy a thing exclusively is commonly to exclude yourself from the true enjoyment of it. Let us improve our opportunities, then, before the evil days come.

What is it that makes it so hard sometimes to determine whither we will walk? I believe that there is a subtle magnetism in Nature, which, if we unconsciously yield to it, will direct us aright. It is not indifferent to us which way we walk. There is a right way; but we are very liable from heedlessness and stupidity to take the wrong one. We would fain take that walk, never yet taken by us through this actual world, which is perfectly symbolical of the path which we love to travel in the interior and ideal world; and sometimes, no doubt, we find it difficult to choose our direction, because it does not yet exist distinctly in our idea.

When I go out of the house for a walk, uncertain as yet whither I will bend my steps, and submit myself to my instinct to decide for me, I find, strange and whimsical as it may seem, that I finally and inevitably settle southwest, toward some particular wood or meadow or deserted pasture or hill in that direction. My needle is slow to settle, varies a few degrees, and does not always point due southwest, it is true, and it has good authority for this variation, but it always settles between west and south-southwest. The future lies that way to me, and the earth seems more unexhausted and richer on that side.

The outline which would bound my walks would be, not a circle, but a parabola, or rather like one of those cometary orbits which have been thought to be non-returning curves, in this case opening westward, in which my house occupies the place of the sun. I turn round and round irresolute sometimes for a quarter of an hour, until I decide, for a thousandth time, that I will walk into the southwest or west. Eastward I go only by force; but westward I go free. Thither no business leads me. It is hard for me to believe that I shall find fair landscapes or sufficient wildness and freedom behind the eastern horizon. I am not excited by the prospect of a walk thither; but I believe that the forest which I see in the western horizon stretches uninterruptedly toward the setting sun, and there are no towns nor cities in it of enough consequence to disturb me. Let me live where I will, on this side is the city, on that the wilderness, and ever I am leaving the city more and more, and withdrawing into the wilderness. I should not lay so much stress on this fact, if I did not believe that something like this is the prevailing tendency of my countrymen. I must walk toward Oregon, and not toward Europe. And that way the nation is moving, and I may say that mankind progresses from east to west. Within a few years we have witnessed the phenomenon of a southeastward migration, in the settlement of Australia; but this affects us as a retrograde movement, and, judging from the moral and physical character of the first generation of Australians, has not yet proved a successful experiment. The eastern Tartars think that there is nothing west beyond Tibet. "The world ends there," say they; "beyond there is nothing but a shoreless sea." It is unmitigated East where they live.

We go eastward to realize history and study the works of art and literature, retracing the steps of the race; we go westward as into the future, with a spirit of enterprise and adventure. The Atlantic is a Lethean stream, in our passage over which we have had an opportunity to forget the Old World and its institutions. If we do not succeed this time, there is perhaps one more chance for the race left before it arrives on the banks of the Styx; and that is in the Lethe of the Pacific, which is three times as wide. . . .

We had a remarkable sunset one day last November. I was walking in a meadow, the source of a small brook, when the sun at last, just before setting, after a cold, gray day, reached a clear stratum in the horizon, and the softest, brightest morning sunlight fell on the dry grass and on the stems of the trees in the opposite horizon and on the leaves of the shrub oaks on the hillside, while our shadows stretched long over the meadow east-ward, as if we were the only motes in its beams. It was such a light as we could not have imagined a moment before, and the air also was so warm and serene that nothing was wanting to make a paradise of that meadow. When we reflected that this was not a solitary phenomenon, never to happen again, but that it would happen forever and ever, an infinite number of evenings, and cheer and reassure the latest child that walked there, it was more glorious still.

The sun sets on some retired meadow, where no house is visible, with all the glory and splendor that it lavishes on cities, and perchance as it has never set before—where there is but a solitary marsh hawk to have his wings gilded by it, or only a musquash looks out from his cabin, and there is some little black-veined brook in the midst of the marsh, just beginning to meander, winding slowly round a decaying stump. We walked in so pure and bright a light, gilding the withered grass and leaves, so softly and serenely bright, I thought I had never bathed in such a golden flood, without a ripple or a murmur to it. The west side of every wood and rising ground gleamed like the boundary of Elysium, and the sun on our backs seemed like a gentle herdsman driving us home at evening.

So we saunter toward the Holy Land, till one day the sun shall shine more brightly than ever he has done, shall perchance shine into our minds and hearts, and light up our whole lives with a great awakening light, as warm and serene and golden as on a bankside in autumn.

Discussion Questions

1. Discuss the distinction Thoreau makes between the right and wrong way of walking. Do you agree that one kind of walk is better than another? Does the amount of time Thoreau requires for a good walk seem reasonable to you? What besides length and time can prevent a walk from offering a beneficial experience? Do you think Solnit is concerned with the same benefits of walking as Thoreau?

2. Describe the geography of Thoreau's habitat as you imagine it from reading this experience. Now, do some research and find the location of Thoreau's cabin. Does the environment of your imagination match the actuality? How are the details in this passage responsible for your accuracy or inaccuracy?

3. What are the factors both physical and intellectual that cause Thoreau to walk in a westerly direction? Why are these factors relevant or irrelevant today?

4. Consider the metaphor Thoreau uses in the final paragraph of this selection. Where is he going? When is he going? How does he feel about going there?

Street Haunting: A London Adventure

VIRGINIA WOOLF

Virginia Woolf was a modern British writer of the early twentieth century. Woolf was educated at home by her intellectually well-connected parents, and in the course of her life wrote a number of novels and essays. She is probably best known for her experimental and innovative use of stream of consciousness writing, found in her novels such as To the Lighthouse *and* Mrs. Dalloway. *In her famous essay "A Room of One's Own" (1929), Woolf puts forward the thesis that "a woman must have money and a room of her own if she is to write fiction," and the essay challenges the gender imbalance that denied the women of her time a formal education. The essay is still widely known and read, and many consider it to be one of the most important works of feminist literary criticism. The following is an excerpt from an essay of the same title that was published in 1927.*

No one perhaps has ever felt passionately towards a lead pencil. But there are circumstances in which it can become supremely desirable to possess one, moments when we are set upon having an object, an excuse for walking half across London between tea and dinner. As the foxhunter hunts in order to preserve the breed of foxes, and the golfer plays in order that open spaces may be preserved from the builders, so when the desire comes upon us to go street rambling the pencil does for a pretext, and getting up we say: "Really I must buy a pencil," as if under cover of this excuse we could indulge safely in the greatest pleasure of town life in winter—rambling the streets of London.

The hour should be the evening and the season winter, for in winter the champagne brightness of the air and the sociability of the streets are grateful. We are not then taunted as in the summer by the longing for shade and solitude and sweet airs from the hayfields. The evening hour, too, gives us the irresponsibility which darkness and lamplight bestow. We are no longer quite ourselves. As we step out of the house on a fine evening between four and six, we shed the self our friends know us by and become part of that vast republican army of anonymous trampers, whose society is so agreeable after the solitude of one's own room. For there we sit surrounded by objects which perpetually express the oddity of our own temperaments and enforce the memories of our own experience. That bowl on the mantelpiece, for instance, was bought at Mantua on a windy day. We were leaving the shop when the sinister old woman plucked at our skirts and said she would find herself starving one of these days, but, "Take it!" she cried, and thrust the blue and white china bowl into our hands as if she never wanted to be reminded of her quixotic generosity. So, guiltily, but suspecting nevertheless how badly we had been fleeced, we carried it back to the little hotel where, in the middle of the night, the innkeeper quarreled so violently with his wife that we all leaned out into the courtyard to look, and saw the vines laced about among the pillars and the stars white in the sky. The moment was stabilized, stamped like a coin indelibly among a million that slipped by imperceptibly. There, too, was the melancholy Englishman, who rose among the coffee cups and the little iron tables and revealed the secrets of his soul—as travelers do. All this—Italy, the windy morning, the vines laced about the pillars, the Englishman and the secrets of his soul—rise up in a cloud from the china bowl on the mantelpiece. And there, as our eyes fall to the floor, is that brown stain on the carpet. Mr. Lloyd George made that. "The man's a devil!" said Mr. Cummings, putting the kettle down with which he was about to fill the teapot so that it burnt a brown ring on the carpet.

But when the door shuts on us, all that vanishes. The shell–like covering which our souls have excreted to house themselves, to make for themselves a shape distinct from others, is broken, and there is left of all these wrinkles and roughnesses a central oyster of perceptiveness, an enormous eye. How beautiful a street is in winter! It is at once revealed and obscured. Here vaguely one can trace symmetrical straight avenues of doors and windows; here under the lamps are floating islands of pale light through which pass quickly bright men and women, who, for all their poverty and shabbiness, wear a certain look of unreality, an air of triumph, as if they had given life the slip, so that life, deceived of her prey, blunders on without them. But, after all, we are only gliding smoothly on the surface. The eye is not a miner, not a diver, not a seeker after buried treasure. It floats us smoothly down a stream; resting, pausing, the brain sleeps perhaps as it looks.

How beautiful a London street is then, with its islands of light, and its long groves of darkness, and on one side of it perhaps some tree–sprinkled, grass–grown space where night is folding herself to sleep naturally and, as one passes the iron railing, one hears those little cracklings and stirrings of leaf and twig which seem to suppose the silence of fields all round them, an owl hooting, and far away the rattle of a train in the valley. But this is London, we are reminded; high among the bare trees are hung oblong frames of reddish yellow light—windows; there are points of brilliance burning steadily like low stars—lamps; this empty ground, which holds the country in it and its peace, is only a London square, set about by offices and houses where at this hour fierce lights burn over maps, over documents, over desks where clerks sit turning with wetted forefinger the files of endless correspondences; or more suffusedly the firelight wavers and the lamplight falls upon the privacy of some drawing-room, its easy chairs, its papers, its china, its inlaid table, and the figure of a woman, accurately measuring out the precise number of spoons of tea which—She looks at the door as if she heard a ring downstairs and somebody asking, is she in?

But here we must stop peremptorily. We are in danger of digging deeper than the eye approves; we are impeding our passage down the smooth stream by catching at some branch or root. At any moment, the sleeping army may stir itself and wake in us a thousand violins and trumpets in response; the army of human beings may rouse itself and assert all its oddities and sufferings and sordidities. Let us dally a little longer, be content still with surfaces only—the glossy brilliance of the motor omnibuses; the carnal splendor of the butchers' shops with their yellow flanks and purple steaks; the blue and red bunches of flowers burning so bravely through the plate glass of the florists' windows.

For the eye has this strange property: it rests only on beauty; like a butterfly it seeks color and basks in warmth. On a winter's night like this, when nature has been at pains to polish and preen herself, it brings back the prettiest trophies, breaks off little lumps of emerald and coral as if the whole earth were made of precious stone. . . .

Passing, glimpsing, everything seems accidentally but miraculously sprinkled with beauty, as if the tide of trade which deposits its burden so punctually and prosaically upon the shores of Oxford Street had this night cast up nothing but treasure. With no thought of buying, the eye is sportive and generous; it creates; it adorns; it enhances.

Standing out in the street, one may build up all the chambers of an imaginary house and furnish them at one's will with sofa, table, carpet. That rug will do for the hall. That alabaster bowl shall stand on a carved table in the window. Our merrymaking shall be reflected in that thick round mirror. But, having built and furnished the house, one is happily under no obligation to possess it; one can dismantle it in the twinkling of an eye, and build and furnish another house with other chairs and other glasses. Or let us indulge ourselves at the antique jewelers, among the trays of rings and the hanging necklaces. Let us choose those pearls, for example, and then imagine how, if we put them on, life would be changed. It becomes instantly between two and three in the morning; the lamps are burning very white in the deserted streets of Mayfair. Only motor–cars are abroad at this hour, and one has a sense of emptiness, of airiness, of secluded gaiety. Wearing pearls, wearing silk, one steps out on to a balcony which overlooks the gardens of sleeping Mayfair. There are a few lights in the bedrooms of great peers returned from Court, of silk–stockinged footmen, of dowagers who have pressed the hands of statesmen. A cat creeps along the garden wall. Love–making is going on sibilantly, seductively in the darker places of the room behind thick green curtains. Strolling sedately as if he were promenading a terrace beneath which the shires and counties of England lie sun–bathed, the aged Prime Minister recounts to Lady So–and–So with the curls and the emeralds the true history of some great crisis in the affairs of the land. We seem to be riding on the top of the highest mast of the tallest ship; and yet at the same time we know that nothing of this sort matters; love is not proved thus, nor great achievements completed thus; so that we sport with the moment and preen our feathers in it lightly, as we stand on the balcony watching the moonlit cat creep along Princess Mary's garden wall.

But what could be more absurd? It is, in fact, on the stroke of six; it is a winter's evening; we are walking to the Strand to buy a pencil. How, then, are we also on a balcony, wearing pearls in June? What could be more absurd? Yet it is nature's folly, not ours. When she set about her chief masterpiece, the making of man, she should have thought of one thing only. Instead, turning her head, looking over her shoulder, into each one of us she let creep instincts and desires which are utterly at variance with his main being, so that we are streaked, variegated, all of a mixture; the colors have run. Is the true self this which stands on the pavement in January, or that which bends over the balcony in June? Am I here, or am I there? Or is the true self neither this nor that, neither here nor there, but something so varied and wandering that it is only when we give the rein to its wishes and let it take its way unimpeded that we are indeed ourselves?

Circumstances compel unity; for convenience's sake a man must be a whole. The good citizen when he opens his door in the evening must be banker, golfer, husband, father; not a nomad wandering the desert, a mystic staring at the sky, a debauchee in the slums of San Francisco, a soldier heading a revolution, a pariah howling with skepticism and solitude. When he opens his door, he must run his fingers through his hair and put his umbrella in the stand like the rest. . . .

But we are come to the Strand now, and as we hesitate on the curb, a little rod about the length of one's finger begins to lay its bar across the velocity and abundance of life. "Really I must—really I must"—that is it. Without investigating the demand, the mind cringes to the accustomed tyrant. One must, one always must, do something or other; it is not allowed one simply to enjoy oneself. Was it not for this reason that, some time ago, we fabricated the excuse, and invented the necessity of buying something? But what was it? Ah, we remember, it was a pencil. Let us go then and buy this pencil. But just as we are turning to obey the command, another self disputes the right of the tyrant to insist. The usual conflict comes about. Spread out behind the rod of duty we see the whole breadth of the river Thames—wide, mournful, peaceful. And we see it through the eyes of somebody who is leaning over the Embankment on a summer evening, without a care in the world. Let us put off buying the pencil; let us go in search of this person—and soon it becomes apparent that this person is ourselves. For if we could stand there where we stood six months ago, should we not be again as we were then—calm, aloof, content? Let us try then. But the river is rougher and greyer than we remembered. The tide is running out to sea. It brings down with it a tug and two barges, whose load of straw is tightly bound down beneath tarpaulin covers. There is, too, close by us, a couple leaning over the balustrade with the curious lack of self–consciousness lovers have, as if the importance of the affair they are engaged on claims without question the indulgence of the human race. The sights we see and the sounds we hear now have none of the quality of the past; nor have we any share in the serenity of the person who, six months ago, stood precisely were we stand now. His is the happiness of death; ours the insecurity of life. He has no future; the future is even now invading our peace. It is only when we look at the past and take from it the element of uncertainty that we can enjoy perfect peace. As it is, we must turn, we must cross the Strand again, we must find a shop where, even at this hour, they will be ready to sell us a pencil.

It is always an adventure to enter a new room, for the lives and characters of its owners have distilled their atmosphere into it, and directly we enter it we breast some new wave of emotion. Here, without a doubt, in the stationer's shop, people had been quarrelling. Their anger shot through the air. They both stopped; the old woman—they were husband and wife evidently—retired to a back room; the old man whose rounded forehead and globular eyes would have looked well on the frontispiece of some Elizabethan folio, stayed to serve us. "A pencil, a pencil," he repeated, "certainly, certainly." He spoke with the distraction yet effusiveness of one whose emotions have been roused and checked in full flood. He began opening box after box and shutting them again. He said that it was very difficult to find things when they kept so many different articles. He launched into a story about some legal gentleman who had got into deep waters owing to the conduct of his wife. He had known him for years; he had been connected with the Temple for half a century, he said, as if he wished his wife in the back room to overhear him. He upset a box of rubber bands. At last, exasperated by his incompetence, he pushed the swing door open and called out roughly: "Where d'you keep the pencils?" as if his wife had hidden them. The old lady came in. Looking at nobody, she put her hand with a fine air of righteous severity upon the right box. There were pencils. How then could he do without her? Was she not indispensable to him? In order to keep them there, standing side by side in forced neutrality, one had to be particular in one's choice of pencils; this was too soft, that too hard. They stood silently looking on. The longer they stood there, the calmer they grew; their heat was going down, their anger disappearing. Now, without a word said on either side, the quarrel was made up. The old man, who would not have disgraced Ben Jonson's title–page, reached the box back to its proper place, bowed profoundly his good–night to us, and they disappeared. She would get out her sewing; he would read his newspaper; the canary would scatter them impartially with seed. The quarrel was over.

In these minutes in which a ghost has been sought for, a quarrel composed, and a pencil bought, the streets had become completely empty. Life had withdrawn to the top floor, and lamps were lit. The pavement was dry and hard; the road was of hammered silver. Walking home through the desolation, one could tell oneself the story of the dwarf, of the blind men, of the party in the Mayfair mansion, of the quarrel in the stationer's shop. Into each of these lives one could penetrate a little way, far enough to give oneself the illusion that one is not tethered to a single mind, but can put on briefly for a few minutes the bodies and minds of others. One could become a wash-erwoman, a publican, a street singer. And what greater delight and wonder can there be than to leave the straight lines of personality and deviate into those footpaths that lead beneath brambles and thick tree trunks into the heart of the forest where live those wild beasts, our fellow men? That is true: To escape is the greatest of pleasures; street haunting in winter the greatest of adventures. Still as we approach our own doorstep again, it is comforting to feel the old possessions, the old prejudices, fold us round; and the self, which has been blown about at so many street corners, which has battered like a moth at the flame of so many inaccessible lanterns, sheltered and enclosed. Here again is the usual door; here the chair turned as we left it and the china bowl and the brown ring on the carpet. And here—let us examine it tenderly, let us touch it with reverence—is the only spoil we have retrieved from all the treasures of the city, a lead pencil.

Discussion Questions

1. Discuss the way an object can be for Virginia Woolf a means to an end or a reminder of the past. Choose an object in your house or room and tell how that object functions, as either a means to an end or a memento.

2. How do you suppose Woolf's musings as she walked the streets of London helped her become a great novelist? Consider especially her discussions of beauty, time, and imagination in this passage. You may want to do a little research on the plots and ideas in her novels, especially *Mrs. Dalloway* and *To the Lighthouse*.

3. Consider where Woolf was walking and her purpose(s) for walking, and explain in what ways her walk conforms to the kinds of walking advocated by Thoreau and Solnit. Are the criteria for their approval of Woolf's walk the same?

The Chair

Essay

DAVE DAWSON

David Dawson was born and raised in a small town in California's central valley. After serving in the Army and undergoing rehabilitation for his combat injuries, he attended college, earning a BA in psychology and an MA in social work. He has spent his career working for an organization that assists disabled veterans with their reintegration into society and educates possible enlistees about the realities of military service.

I enlisted in the Army the week after my eighteenth birthday. At the time, I was 6' 3½" tall, looking down upon everybody else in Basic Training. The Drill Instructor for my platoon constantly singled me out for put-downs, extra "volunteer" assignments and any opportunity to, as he said, toughen me up. Only later did I discover that he and my dad were in cahoots, grooming me for Special Forces, what everyone knows as the Green Berets.

The Green Beret training was varied and intensive, different from anything I had expected. It gave me a whole new perspective on life, war, and what it means to occupy a country. For one thing, instead of a combat mission, after training I was sent to the hills of northwest Vietnam; I found myself working with and among the local people, villagers, families. I became fluent in Vietnamese and Cambodian, and learned a little Chinese as well. As a "Beret," I got to see a very different Vietnam from that of the typical Army or Marine grunt.

I was one of a dozen Special Forces assigned to a camp with about 450 South Vietnamese soldiers and their families. Despite the fact the camp felt like a small town on the inside—having a school, clinic, rec center, and coffee shop—the perimeter sported over a dozen machine guns, layers of barbed wire in the brush, and hidden trip-wire alarms. Our purpose there was to train the local troops, as well as to protect the local villages and scout the local trails for Viet Cong. Because of my height, the locals gave me the nickname John Wayne. After a time, I not only got used to the name but started to see myself in that role. I walked tall and proud through camps and jungle.

The phased drawdown of our troops from Vietnam began in the summer of 1968. This just meant replacements would not match the numbers going home. I was coming up on the end of my second tour, ready to go back to "the world," but was stuck for however many days remained to be colored in on my short-timer's calendar. February 1969. I was leading a patrol through a field of white and pink flowers. A thick wooded area bordered one side of the field, making it difficult to see any movement there. However, we had "secured" the area long ago and traversed this field many times before. I always marveled at the beauty of flowered fields such as this in the middle of a war zone. A sudden searing pain in my back dropped me flat to ground level, only the stems of the flowers visible to my blurring vision.

Dust-off flattened a large circular area in the flower field from the force of the rotor blades. First stop, Camp Eagle's Nest, I Corps for stabilization. Three days later, a C-17 flying CSU headed stateside, to the world, with me on it. I was short, with barely two weeks to go in my tour. This was not the ticket home I had looked for or expected.

All the doctors and nurses kept telling me how lucky I was. Yes, I had gotten shot, but many VC guns were antiquated and did not use high velocity rounds like the NVA's weapons. Otherwise, I likely would be dead. Furthermore, removal of wounded soldiers from the battlefield had progressed by giant steps over the centuries from hand-carried litters to the Bell UH-1 Huey helo that medevacked me. There was a time, too, when only those of noble birth were considered worthy of saving on the battlefield.

Yea, I thought, lucky me.

My family looked down upon me lying in the hospital bed. My mom kept dabbing the corners of her eyes and her cheeks with tissues, making her mascara look a mess. My younger brother, after saying things like, "Hey, Dude, how's it goin'?" just hung in the back of the room. From the look in his eyes, I was pretty sure I knew what was going on in his head. It was my dad, however, who got me to change my attitude about being paraplegic.

Dad had fought in both WWII and the Korean War, leaving the service as a decorated Sergeant First Class. His awards included two Purple Hearts. He was considered a hero in our home town, where he was always in demand as a speaker at various clubs and to walk in

Memorial Day and Fourth of July parades. For several years running, he was president of the local VFW chapter.

I grew up wanting to be just like my dad. When I played war games with the other kids, I was always the one charging the machine gun nest, lobbing grenades every which direction—either that or taking down a couple of enemy soldiers with a commando fighting knife. As a Boy Scout, I always volunteered for the color guard and having all eyes upon me and our nation's flag. I couldn't wait until I was eighteen to enlist in the Army, where I would get my chance to follow in my dad's footsteps.

The thing was, despite dad's pep talk at my bedside—telling me I'd be "up and at 'em" in no time, that they'd probably want me to go back to the Zone before I knew it—I had had a lot of time flat on my back, thinking about the old story that had practically been my daily bread. Not to mention almost making the flowers in that field my funeral wreath.

I thought about the story of who the men in our family truly were. It was the story told over and over again in the movies and the government newsreels. It was the John Wayne story. Very likely, it is the same story that Hector would have taught his son had Achilles not brought him low before the gates of Troy. My father's trumpet call to arms at my hospital bedside hit me like another bullet. Bang! Suddenly, I knew that this epic tale of hero-ism not only could never be my story again, but maybe never was. I will say this for my dad. More than anything, his faith in the story got him through two wars pretty much in one piece. But my father's faith in that story motivated me to use the rest of my life to create a different story.

Now it's my turn to speak before school assemblies and club meet-ings, but also at Congressional hearings and in television interviews. Sometimes I even get to roll my wheelchair in parades. It took me awhile to become comfortable with public speaking. It was every bit as scary as coming under enemy fire. But I soon learned that it was not my words alone that made a strong impression on people. It was also my chair. When I wheel the chair onto a stage to speak or down an aisle to give testimony—all eyes upon me once again—without fail, a hush falls upon the room. And once again, I come to a different per-spective—on life, on myself, on those who now tower over me. And on those flowered fields.

Discussion Questions

1. How does the incident while he is walking along a trail alter Dave Dawson's body and his beliefs about himself, his family, and his country? How does your understanding of the chair in the title of the essay change after reading the essay?

2. Considering his history, why do you think Dawson originally experiences fear when he is called upon to speak in public? What do you think might be the message of his presentations?

3. Think about Solnit's point, when she writes of walking, that "whether it has a future depends on whether those connecting paths are traveled still," and compare her interpretation of these words with the way you think Dawson would understand them. How might his reaction differ from that of Thoreau or Woolf?

Wild

CHERYL STRAYED

Cheryl Strayed was born in Pennsylvania but later moved to Minnesota. Her abusive father abandoned the family when she was six years old. Her financially challenged but loving mother struggled to provide a home for Strayed and her siblings. During Strayed's senior year of college, her mother died of cancer. Unable to accept her mother's death, she became depressed and engaged in self-destructive behaviors. A chance encounter with a book on the Pacific Crest Trail motivated Strayed, an inexperienced hiker, to make her journey, a solo walk from the Mojave Desert of California to Portland, Oregon. This walk through both desert and mountain wilderness, detailed in her memoir Wild: From Lost to Found on The Pacific Crest Trail *(2012), profoundly affected Strayed's perspectives on life, nature, love, and her own identity.*

But walking along a path I carved myself—one I hoped was the PCT—was the opposite of using heroin. The trigger I'd pulled in stepping into the snow made me more alive to my senses than ever. Uncertain as I was as I pushed forward, I felt right in my pushing, as if the effort itself meant something: that perhaps being amidst the undesecrated beauty of the wilderness meant I too could be undesecrated, regardless of what I'd lost or what had been taken from me, regardless of the regrettable things I'd done to others or myself or the regrettable things that had been done to me. Of all the things I'd been skeptical about, I didn't feel skeptical about this: The wilderness had a clarity that included me.

Somber and elated, I walked in the cool air, the sun glimmering through the trees, bright against the snow, even though I had my sunglasses on. As omnipresent as the snow was, I also sensed its waning, its melting imperceptibly by the minute all around me. It seemed as alive in its dying as a hive of bees was in its life. Sometimes I passed by places where I heard a gurgling, as if a stream ran beneath the snow, impossible to see. Other times it fell in great wet heaps from the branches of the trees.

On my third day out from Sierra City, as I sat hunched near the open door of my tent and doctoring my blistered feet, I realized the day before had been the Fourth of July. The fact that I could so clearly imagine what not only my friends but also a good portion of the residents of the United States had done without me made me feel all the more far away. No doubt they'd had parties and parades, acquired sunburns and lit firecrackers, while I was here, alone in the cold. In a flash, I could see myself from far above, a speck on the great mass of green and white, no more or less significant than a single one of the nameless birds in the trees. Here it could be the fourth of July or the tenth of December. These mountains didn't count the days.

The next morning, I walked through the snow for hours until I came to a clearing where there was a large fallen tree, its trunk bare of both snow and branches. I took my pack off and climbed up on top of it, its bark rough beneath me. I pulled a few strips of beef jerky out of my pack and sat eating it and swigging my water. Soon I saw a streak of red to my right: a fox walking into the clearing, his paws landing soundlessly on top of the snow. He gazed straight ahead without looking at me, not even seeming to know I was there, though that seemed impossible. When the fox was directly in front of me, perhaps ten feet away, he stopped and turned his head and looked peaceably in my direction, his eyes not exactly going to mine as he sniffed. He looked part feline, part canine, his facial features sharp and compact, his body alert.

My heart raced, but I sat perfectly still, fighting the urge to scramble to my feet and leap behind the tree for protection. I didn't know what the fox would do next. I didn't think he would harm me, but I couldn't help but fear that he would. He was barely knee-high, though his strength was irrefutable, his beauty dazzling, his superiority to me apparent down to his every pristine hair. He could be on me in a flash. This was his world. He was as certain as the sky.

"Fox," I whispered in the gentlest possible voice I could, as if by naming him I could both defend myself against him and also draw him nearer. He raised his fine-boned red head, but remained standing as he'd been and studied me for several seconds more before turning away without alarm to continue walking across the clearing and into the trees.

"Come back," I called lightly, and then suddenly shouted, "MOM! MOM! MOM! MOM!" I didn't know the word was going to come out of my mouth until it did, and then, just as suddenly, I went silent, spent.

I thought about the fox. I wondered if he'd returned to the fallen tree and wondered about me. I remembered the moment after he'd disappeared into the woods and I'd called out for my mother. It had been so silent in the wake of that commotion, a kind of potent silence that seemed to contain everything—the songs of the birds and the creak of the tree, the dying snow and the unseen gurgling water, the glimmering sun, the certain sky, the gun that didn't have a bullet in its chamber. And the mother. Always the mother. The one who would never come to me.

As difficult and maddening as the trail could be, there was hardly a day that passed that didn't offer up some form of what was called trail magic in the PCT vernacular—the unexpected and sweet happenings that stand out in stark relief to the challenges of the trail. Before I stood to put Monster [the name refers to her backpack] on, I heard footsteps and turned. There was a deer walking toward me on the trail, seemingly unaware of my presence. I made a small sound, so as not to startle her, but instead of bolting away she only stopped and looked at me, sniffing in my direction before slowly continuing toward me. With each step, she paused to assess whether she should continue forward and each time she did, coming closer and closer until she was only two feet away. Her face was calm and curious, her nose extending as far as it dared in my direction. I sat still watching her, not feeling even a little bit afraid, as I'd been weeks before when the fox had stood to study me in the snow.

"It's okay," I whispered to the deer, not knowing what I was going to say until I said it: "You're safe in this world."

When I spoke, it was as if a spell had been broken. The deer lost all interest in me, though she still didn't run. She only lifted her head and stepped away, picking through the azaleas with her delicate hooves, nibbling on plants as she went.

I hiked alone the next few days, up and down and up again, over Etna Summit and into the Marble Mountains on the long hot slog to Seiad Valley, past lakes where I was compelled by mosquitoes to slather myself in DEET for the first time on my trip and into the paths of day hikers who gave me reports about the wildfires that were raging to the west, though still not encroaching on the PCT.

One night, I made camp in a grassy spot from which I could see the evidence of those fires: a hazy scrim of smoke blanketing the westward view. I sat in my chair for an hour, looking out across the land as the dawn faded into the smoke. I'd seen a lot of breathtaking sunsets in my evenings on the PCT, but this one was more spectacular than any in a while, the light made indistinct, melting into a thousand shades of yellow, pink, orange, and purple over the waves of green land. I could've been reading *Dubliners* or falling off to sleep in the cocoon of my sleeping bag, but on this night, the sky was too mesmerizing to leave. As I watched it, I realized I'd passed the midpoint of my hike. I'd been out on the trail for fifty-some days. If all went as planned, in another fifty days I'd be done with the PCT. Whatever was going to happen to me out here would have happened.

"Oh remember the Red River Valley and the cowboy who loved you so true . . . ,'" I sang, my voice trailing off, not knowing the rest of the words. Images of the child and mother I had met the day before came to me, of Kyle's little face and hands, reverberations of his flawless voice. I wondered if I would ever be a mother and what kind of "horrible situation" Kyle's mother was in, where his father might be and where mine was. *What is he doing right this minute"* I'd thought occasionally throughout my life, but I was never able to imagine it. I didn't know my own father's life. He was there, but invisible, a shadow beast in the woods, a fire so far away it's nothing but smoke.

That was my father: the man who hadn't fathered me. It amazed me every time, again and again, and again. Of all the wild things, his failure to love me the way he should have had always been the wildest thing of all. But on that night, as I gazed out over the darkening land fifty-some nights out on the PCT, it occurred to me that I didn't have to be amazed by him anymore. There were so many other amazing things in this world.

They opened up inside of me like a river. Like I didn't know I could take a breath and then I breathed. I laughed with the joy of it, and the next moment I was crying my first tears on the PCT. I cried and I cried and I cried. I wasn't crying because I was happy. I wasn't crying because I was sad. I wasn't crying because of my mother or my father or my brother Paul. I was crying because I was full, of those fifty-some hard days on the trail and of the 9, 760 days that had come before them, too.

I was entering. I was leaving. California streamed behind me like a long silk veil. I didn't feel like a big fat idiot anymore. And I didn't feel like a hard-ass Amazonian queen. I felt fierce and humble and gathered up inside, like I was safe in this world, too.

. . . .

Down, down, down I went on that last full day of hiking, descending four thousand feet in just over sixteen miles, the creeks and streams and trailside seeps I crossed and paralleled going down and down, too. I could feel the river pulling me like a great magnet below and to the north. I could feel myself coming to the end of things. I stopped to spend the night on the banks of Eagle Creek. It was five o'clock, and I was only six miles away from Cascade Locks. I could have been in town by dark, but I didn't want to finish my trip that way. I wanted to take my time, to see the river and the Bridge of the Gods in the bright light of day.

That evening, I sat next to Eagle Creek, watching the water rush over the rocks. My feet were killing me from the long descent. Even after all this way, with my body now stronger than it had ever been and would likely ever be, hiking on the PCT still hurt. New blisters had formed on my toes in places that had gone soft from the relatively few extreme descents throughout Oregon. I put my fingers delicately to them, soothing them with my touch. Another toenail looked like it was finally going to come off. I gave it a gentle tug and it was in my hand, my sixth. I had only four intact toenails left. The PCT and I weren't tied anymore. The score was 4–6, advantage trail.

I slept on my tarp, not wanting to shelter myself on that last night, and woke before dawn to watch the sun rise over Mount Hood. It was really over, I thought. There was no way to go back, to make it stay. There was never that. I sat for a long while, letting the light fill the sky, letting it expand and reach down into the trees. I closed my eyes and listened hard to Eagle Creek. I was running to the Columbia River, like I was.

I seemed to float the four miles to the little parking area near the head of the Eagle Creek Trail, buoyed by a pure, unadulterated emotion that can only be described as joy. I strolled through the mostly empty parking lot and passed the restrooms, then followed another trail that would take me the two miles into Cascade Locks. The trail turned sharply to the right, and before me was the Columbia River, visible through the chain-link fence that bordered the trail to set it off from Interstate 84, just below. I stopped and grasped the fence and stared. It seemed like a miracle that I finally had the river in my sights, as if a newborn baby had just slipped finally into my palms after a long labor. That glimmering dark water was more beautiful than anything I'd imagined during all those miles I'd hiked to reach it.

I walked east along a lush, green corridor, the roadbed of the long-abandoned Columbia River Highway, which had been made into a trail. I could see patches of concrete in places, but the road had mostly been reclaimed by the moss that grew along the rocks at the road's edge, the trees that hung heavy and low over it, the spiders who'd spun webs that crossed its expanse. I walked through the spider webs, feeling them like magic on my face, pulling them out of my hair. I could hear but not see the rush of automobiles on the interstate to my left, which ran between the river and me, the ordinary sound of them, a great whooshing whine and hum.

When I emerged from the forest, I was in Cascade Locks, which unlike so many towns on the trail was an actual town, with a population of a little more than a thousand. It was Friday morning and I could feel the Friday morningness emanating from the houses I passed. I walked beneath the freeway and wended my way along the streets with my ski pole clicking against the pavement, my heart racing when the bridge came into view. It's an elegant steel truss cantilever, named for a natural bridge that was formed by a major landslide approximately three hundred years ago that had temporarily dammed the Columbia River. The local Native Americans had called it the Bridge of the Gods. The human-made structure that took its name spans the Columbia for a little more than a third of a mile, connecting Oregon to Washington, the towns of Cascade Locks and Stevenson on either side. There's a tollbooth on the Oregon side, and when I reached it, the woman who worked inside told me I could cross the bridge, no charge.

"I'm not crossing," I said. "I only want to touch it." I walked along the shoulder of the road until I reached the concrete stanchion of the bridge, put my hand on it, and looked down at the Columbia River flowing beneath me. It's the largest river in the Pacific Northwest and the fourth largest in the nation. Native Americans have lived on the river for thousands of years, sustained by its once-bountiful salmon for most of them. Meriwether Lewis and William Clark had paddled down the Columbia in dugout canoes on their famous expedition in 1805. One hundred and ninety years later, two days before my twenty-seventh birthday, here I was.

I had arrived. I'd done it. It seemed like such a small thing and such a tremendous thing at once, like a secret I'd always tell myself, though I didn't know the meaning of it just yet. I stood there for several minutes, cars and trucks going past me, feeling like I'd cry, though I didn't. I sat on that white bench on the day I finished my hike. Everything except the fact that I didn't have to know. That it was enough to trust that what I'd done was true. To understand its meaning without yet being able to say precisely what it was, like all those lines from Adrienne Rich's *The Dream of a Common Language* that had run through my nights and days. To believe that I didn't need to reach with my bare hands anymore, to know that seeing the fish beneath the surface of the water was enough—that it was everything. It was my life—like all lives, mysterious and irrevocable and sacred, so very close, so very present, so very belonging to me.

How wild it was, to let it be.

Discussion Questions

1. What does the wilderness have to offer Cheryl Strayed? (Hint: Her last name is one she chose after her divorce.)

2. Describe her reaction to her encounter with the fox. Why do you think that her meeting with the woodland creature is either a positive or negative indication that her journey is accomplishing its purpose? Compare that meeting with her later response to the deer. How do you account for the difference?

3. Discuss the way Cheryl Strayed's "walk" is different from or similar to the walking explored by the other authors you have read in this unit.

Making Great Strides

Essay

N. J. GLEASON

N. J. Gleason is a community college English professor with interests in science writing, creative writing, and autobiography.

As a child, I often had peculiar ideas about many things. Walking, for instance: Boys, I felt, strode decisively in a single-minded bid to get where they were going; girls, on the other hand, were slower and more deliberate. Nothing illustrated this perception better than a trip to London when I was nine.

My family used various forms of locomotion while assiduously avoiding everything that was peculiarly English. To my lifelong regret, we never used the Underground, not once. I remember being fascinated by the double-decker buses and terribly disappointed when we finally mounted one but *stayed in the lower level*. What was the point? And, of course, we took taxis. But much of the time, we walked, for London is famous for being a walkable city.

I have a clear memory of moving purposefully down a rather quaint London street: My father, my teenage brother, and I marched along in an inconsiderate pack, while my mother lagged far behind, being, well, a girl. I never considered that perhaps she saw walking in a foreign city not as a method of transportation but as a way to relax and soak up the ambience. I never thought that on vacation, a person might be less concerned about *getting* somewhere and more interested in *being* somewhere. My father and brother outpaced her because they were tall and had long legs; I kept up with them because it was very important for me to be one of the men, and I took great pride in my ability to cover ground with greater success than my mother did. But I was so caught up in staying with the pack that I have unclear memories of that street. It wasn't like the streets at home, but what made it different? Did it have shops? Perhaps. Cobblestones? Surely they were only the stuff of movies. No, it had row houses. Or perhaps not.

Later in the trip, we visited Hyde Park, ambling because of the high density of foot traffic and because we were rather lost in the huge green expanse that, along with the contiguous Kensington Gardens, covers nearly a square mile. Being in unfamiliar territory is a boon to the casual walker. We appreciated the vibrant grass, shrubs, and trees; passed Speakers' Corner without quite realizing its significance; crossed the picturesque Serpentine Bridge; and marveled at the large tribes of colorfully uniformed schoolchildren on outings. However, I thought of this ramble as belonging to my mother, the slow one. If we had known where we were going, *we men* would have far outstripped her. The sheer rudeness of it all never occurred to me, nor did I ever stop to think that a woman isolated is a woman vulnerable.

For despite such literary luminaries as Little Red Riding Hood and Tess d'Urberville—both of whom met their fates in the country—I see the urban landscape as a potentially dangerous proposition for anyone, but especially women. In today's cities, why walk when you don't have to?

Even the suburbs seem much safer; on many evening walks in my old suburban neighborhood, I aroused no obvious alarm even from unknown women who were walking alone. But in the city, where I have recently relocated, I am seen as a potential predator. One woman, noticing me behind her, whipped out her cell phone and reached her party in record time, far faster than she could possibly have speed-dialed and actually connected. She knew that she was safer if I thought she was talking to someone. Another yanked her child nearer to her as I approached. Other women have simply been startled or fearful, their apprehension all too plain even in the dim glow of streetlights.

An experience of my own a couple of years ago drives home the danger of walking alone at night in the city. After an evening social event, my friends and I visited a convenient coffeehouse and lounged on the patio, watching the pedestrians go by. One man, moving slowly down the sidewalk with a male companion, gave me a shiver as I saw the expression—or lack of it—in his eyes: not the faraway mien of a man in thought, not the glazed or swimmy look of a man under the influence, but a chilling deadness that made me glad that he would be long gone after I had finished my decaf.

I was wrong. After I took leave of my friends, I crossed the street and headed home on foot, declining a ride because I wanted the exercise. Unemployed at that time, I had left my own car at home to save on gas and justify my cup of coffee. I passed the church, the attorney, and the dentist, becoming aware that two men were pacing me on the opposite side of the street. As I approached the intersection where I would normally turn right, the two men split up. One, whom

I recognized as the man with the dead eyes, strode diagonally across the street as if to cut me off. His companion split off and crossed the street as if to flank me. I was in trouble.

I had moments to think. Turning around, obviously, was not an option. I couldn't go left, of course, since I would be thrown into the path of my would-be attackers. But if I turned right at the looming intersection, I would be on a residential street with spotty street-light coverage, where the men could converge upon me. Similarly, if I stopped at the menacing red DON'T WALK signal and waited politely on the curb to go straight, they would be on me in seconds. If I ran, I would tip them off.

I saw only one alternative to reach a well-lighted and busy inter-section only minutes away. Still walking, I quickened my pace, practi-cally bolted through the ominous crossing signal, and forged ahead of the dead-eyed man, who (despite his long diagonal trajectory) had nearly crossed the multi-lane street by this time. Glancing behind me, I saw that his friend had already crossed but was well behind me, thanks to my swift stride. They could catch me only if they started running, but then I would start to run and likely reach safety ahead of them. I continued my trek to the major intersection, and they fell away harmlessly, perhaps to await some other hapless victim. I had made myself more trouble than I was worth.

I still don't know for sure that those men intended me harm, but I believe that they did. I feel that I was safe because I was a strong walker, as I had demonstrated as a child on a London thoroughfare many years before. I sometimes imagine how ill-equipped my mother would have been in such a situation. A well-off woman with a hus-band to protect her wouldn't be out alone in the city at ten o'clock at night, of course, but many women—and men as well—have fewer options and are often hamstrung by odd working hours, financial straits, and the lack of a vehicle. They run a higher risk of being tar-geted by predators.

In my new neighborhood, I no longer walk for any reason after dark—not for transportation, nor for pleasure, nor for exercise as I used to do in my old neighborhood in the suburbs. The city is a place to be watchful. Ever since my close shave, I see the evening stroll as a suburban luxury that many people simply do not have.

Discussion Questions

1. Why does the London experienced by the author's mother and Virginia Woolf differ from that of Gleason, his father, and brother? How does he suggest that cultural conditioning contributes to this difference? When you travel with your family or friends, what is the usual pace and method of your sightseeing? Why do you believe that you are or are not fully enjoying the experience?

2. What danger is Gleason most concerned about when walking in the city? What are some of the other risks of city walking that he fails to consider? Discuss the hazard that would most influence your decision on whether to walk, or use some alternative means of getting from one point to another in the city.

3. Gleason refers to fictional characters who experience danger while walking in the country, not the city. Based on your readings in this unit, compare the benefits and drawbacks of country and city walking. Explain which type of walking holds the most appeal for you.

Nightwalking: A Subversive Stroll through the City Streets

Essay

Matthew Beaumont

Matthew Beaumont is a British novelist and Senior Lecturer in the Department of English at University College London. He has written Utopia Ltd.: Ideologies of Social Dreaming in England, 1870–1900 *(2005), and coauthored, with Terry Eagleton,* The Task of the Critic: Terry Eagleton in Dialogue *(2009). The following reading selection is an excerpt from his most recent book,* Nightwalking: A Nocturnal History of London, Chaucer to Dickens *(2015).*

In the dead of night, in spite of the electric lights, London seems an alien city, especially if you are walking through it alone. In the more sequestered streets—once the pubs are closed, and at a distance from the twenty-four-hour convenience stores—the sodium gleam of the street lamps, or the flickering striplight from a sleepy minicab stand, offers little consolation. There are alleys and street corners and shop entrances where the darkness appears to collect in a solid mass. There are secluded squares where, to take a haunting line from the poem *Alastor; or, The Spirit of Solitude*, by Shelley, night makes "a weird sound of its own stillness" (30). There are buildings, monuments, and statues that, at a distance, and in the absence of people, pulsate mysteriously in the sepulchral light. There are foxes that slope and trot across the road as you interrupt their attempts to pillage scraps from upended bins. And, from time to time, there are the faintly sinister silhouettes of other solitary individuals—as threatened by your presence, no doubt, as you are by theirs. "However efficiently artificial light annihilates the difference between night and day," Al Alvarez has remarked, "it never wholly eliminates the primitive suspicion that night people are up to no good" (p. xiii).

It is easy to feel disoriented in the city at the dead of night, especially if you are tired from roaming its distances, dreamily or desperately somnambulant. For in the darkness, above all perhaps in familiar or routine places, everything acquires a subtly different form or volume. Ford Madox Ford, in *The Soul of London*, lamented a century ago that, "little by little, the Londoner comes to forget that his London is built upon real earth: he forgets that under the pavements there are hills, forgotten water courses, springs, and marshlands" (v). It is not quite the same at night. At two a.m., in the empty streets, no longer fighting against the traffic of cars and commuters, the solitary pedestrian's feet begin to recall the "real earth." In the abstracted, monochromatic conditions of the nighttime, it becomes more apparent that a sloping road curves over the sleeping form of a hill and tracks the course of an underground stream. The city is at its most earthly and unearthly at night. A prehistoric landscape comes to seem more palpable beneath the pavements of the city. And in this half-familiar environment, it is difficult to eliminate entirely the archaic conviction that, as for our ancestors, the night itself remains ominous, threatening. Residues of a primal fear of the dark begin to trouble you.

The nighttime city is another city. Rhapsodizing the public parks of the French metropolis in *Paris Peasant* (1926), the surrealist Louis Aragon comments that "night gives these absurd places a sense of not knowing their own identity" (32). It is a point that applies to all aspects of the city's architecture or terrain. The nighttime self, moreover, is another self. It, too, is less certain of its own identity.

Who walks *alone* in the streets at night except the sad, the mad, the bad, the lost, the lonely, the sleepless, the homeless—all the city's internal exiles. The night has always been the time for daylight's dispossessed—the dissident, the different. Walking alone at night in the city by both men and women has, since time immemorial, been interpreted as a sign of moral, social, or spiritual dereliction. Solitary women, because of a long history of discrimination and patriarchal oppression, have been especially susceptible to this sort of suspicion. If women appear on the streets of the city at night alone, they are commonly portrayed as either predators, in the form of prostitutes, or predated— the potential victims of sexual assault. In both cases, they are denied a right to the city at night.

The historian Joachim Schlör has pointed out that, in terms of the freedom to inhabit the nocturnal city, "Women's needs and wishes are not fundamentally different from men's" since for both it is a case of entering it and circulating inside it freely and independently— "through the whole city, during the whole night, and not just in certain spatial and temporal reserves" (104). But he has rightly insisted that, historically, "Men's freedom of movement has [had] a real restrictive effect on that of women" (Schlör 106). If solitary men on the streets at night have exercised a right to the city denied to solitary women, then they too have often been identified or represented as pariahs. People who walk about at night with no obvious reason to do so, whether male or female, have attracted suspicion, opprobrium, and legal recrimination from patriarchs, politicians, priests, and others in authority, including the police, for thousands of years. In 1285, Edward I introduced a specific "nightwalker statute" in order to police the movement of plebeian people—especially migrants, vagrants and prostitutes—after the nine p.m. curfew. But long after this statute became impossible to implement because of the rise of "nightlife," the authorities continued to construe nightwalking as deviant.

Today, more than ever, solitary walking at night in the streets of the city does not necessarily mean deviant movement. It may well be perfectly legitimate, purposeful. Contemporary capitalist society requires what Jonathan Crary has identified as the despoliation of sleep in the interests of maximizing the individual's potential—both as a producer and a consumer—for generating profit (10). The political economy of the night, in this dispensation, means that plenty of people have to commute after dark, sometimes on foot, sometimes across considerable distances. This is the daily, or nightly, reality of post-circadian capitalism, as it might be called. For the city's army of nocturnal workers, many of whom are recent immigrants forced to perform the least popular forms of labor, traveling at night is in effect travailing at night. Sex workers and the police have, for their part, always had to patrol pavements at night for professional reasons. So have streetcleaners and others employed to collect and dispose of the city's waste.

Not all walking at night, then, is nightwalking. But most forms of solitary walking at night are nonetheless tainted, sometimes faintly, with dubious moral or social associations. Indeed, even apparently purposeful walking in the city at night is not exempt from the assumption that it is suspicious. To be alone in the streets, even if one walks rapidly, determinedly, is to invite the impression that one is on the run, either from oneself or from another. The late Chilean novelist Roberto Bolaño alludes to these conditions of being in the night—those of the haunted and the hunted—in a reference to the life, or half-life, of the city "at an hour when the only people out walking [are] two opposite types: those running out of time and those with time to burn" (180). In fact, these types are not really opposite: Many people who are running out of time or resources, paradoxically, have time to burn. This contradictory state, of idling and hastening at once, is a comparatively common experience. It is even more potent on the streets at night.

To use a Dickensian phrase, nightwalking is a matter of "going astray" in the streets of the city after dark. Dickens is the great heroic and neurotic nightwalker of the nineteenth century. In 1860, in the guise of the Uncommercial Traveller, he made a crucial distinction between two kinds of walking: one that is "straight on end to a definite goal at a round pace"; another that is "objectless, loitering, [and] purely vagabond" (qtd. in Shore 51). If the point of the first kind of walking is to travel from one point to another, the point of the second is that there is no point at all. Its purpose is its purposelessness. Nightwalking, according to this logic, is pointless. It is uncommercial.

In an economy in which time, including nighttime, is money, wandering the streets after dark—when most people are sleeping in order to prepare themselves for the next day's labor—is in symbolic terms subversive. In the aberrant and deviant form celebrated by Dickens in the nineteenth century, and surreptitiously practiced by innumerable others before and since, nightwalking is quintessentially objectless, loitering, and vagabond.

Works Cited

Alvarez, A. *Night: An Exploration of Night Life, Night Language, Sleep and Dreams*. 1994. New York: Norton, 1995. Print.

Aragon, Louis. *Paris Peasant*. Trans. Simon Watson Taylor. 1926. New York: Exact Change Publishing, 2004. Print.

Bolaño, Roberto. *2666: A Novel*. Trans. Natasha Wimmer. New York: Farrar, Straus, and Giroux, 2008. Print.

Crary, Jonathan. *24/7: Late Capitalism and the Ends of Sleep*. New York: Verso, 2013. Print.

Ford, Ford Madox. *The Soul of London: A Survey of a Modern City*. 1905. London: Read Books, Ltd., 2011. Print.

Schlör, Joachim. *Nights In the Big City: Paris, Berlin, London 1840–1930*. Trans. Pierre Imhoff. London: Reaktion Books, 1998. Print.

Shelley, Percy Bysshe. *Alastor; or, The Spirit of Solitude*. London: BiblioLife, 2009. Print.

Shore, William Teignmouth. *Bell's Miniature Series of Great Writers: Dickens*. London: George Bell & Sons, 1904. Print.

Discussion Questions

1. How can the city, according to Matthew Beaumont, be both "earthly" and "unearthly" at night? (Hint: think about the image created by such words as "dead," "alone," "mysteriously," "threatened," "suspicion.")

2. Discuss the general attitude toward nightwalkers. How does the perception of men who walk at night differ from that of women? What is the history behind these ideas? Do you see evidence in any of the other readings in this unit that the authors share this view of nightwalking?

3. Beaumont discusses the two kinds of walking Dickens identifies. What kinds of nightwalkers fall into each category? How do Dickens's comments about night walking compare with the ideas about walking in the selections by the other authors in this unit? How do you think present-day economics and lifestyles might complicate or change attitudes and definitions of nightwalking?

The Walking Photograph

Essay

GEOFF NICHOLSON

Geoff Nicholson is a British novelist and nonfiction writer. He was educated at the Universities of Cambridge and Essex. His novels are best known for their interweaving storylines and treatment of subcultures, done with an overlay of dark humor. Some of his most recent novels include The Hollywood Dodo *(2004),* Gravity's Volkswagen *(2009), and* The City under the Skin *(2014). The following selection is an excerpt from one of his works of nonfiction, titled* The Lost Art of Walking *(2008).*

Garry Winogrand walked on the crowded streets of New York in the 1970s, carrying a Leica M4 with a 28mm lens, the leather strap wound tightly round his hand, the camera being constantly raised and lowered to and from his eye, turning his head, refocusing his gaze, looking for visual triggers, for subjects, endlessly, relentlessly pressing the shutter, shooting pictures, sometimes just shooting.

Winogrand walks, but not at the same pace as the pedestrians around him, and sometimes he stops completely so that the flow of people splits and eddies past, and sometimes he sees something on the other side of the street, and pushes through the crowd, dashes over there, dodging traffic or forcing the traffic to dodge him. Then he continues taking photographs. You'd think that New York's angry, purposeful walkers would knock him out of the way, walk all over him; but he's found a way to avoid that.

Sometimes he smiles and nods at the people he's photographing, offers a word or two, chats, and in the main nobody minds. It's a technique he's developed, a way of presenting himself as just another eccentric on the streets of New York, crazy, self-absorbed, obsessive but essentially harmless-which is not a complete misrepresentation of Winogrand. And then somebody perceives him as something else. A woman, irate, offended, full of righteous indignation, believes that in photographing her, Winogrand has stolen something from her. "Hey, you took my picture!" she protests, and Winogrand, in his rough, tough, amused New York voice, says, "Honey, it's *my* picture now." It's an old story, and another one that I very much want to be true.

Garry Winogrand (1928–1984) was from the Bronx. He told Tod Papageorge that when he was about ten years old, he walked the streets of his neighborhood until midnight to avoid going home to the family apartment, because "his parents did not put a high priority on privacy." The idea that the streets offer more privacy than the family home is one that needs no explaining.

Winogrand was a street photographer, by most reckonings the ultimate street photographer. The term is a porous one; even the most studio-bound of photographers occasionally takes a photograph on the street. And paparazzi are certainly street photographers of a sort, along with their modern mutations, the stalkerazzi and the snapperazzi members of the public who happen to see a celeb in the street and take their picture.

You might also think it's a term that doesn't require much definition, if you take a photograph in the street, you're a street photographer. Well, not quite. Eddie Adams was certainly in the street in Saigon in 1968 when he photographed the Vietnamese chief of police, Nguyen Ngoc Loan, walking up to a suspected Vietcong collaborator and shooting him in the head, but he wasn't quite a street photographer in the way that Winogrand was. A street photographer, as we generally conceive it, is someone one finds subject matter not in exotic locales or war zones, but in quotidian settings in the city. If, in the process, he or she manages to make that setting look like an exotic locale or a war zone, then so much the better. It was a time when these photographers were often referred to as "candids," but nobody seems to use that word anymore. Perhaps candidness is no longer considered something that a photograph can offer us.

All my favorite photographers are, in some sense or another, at least some of the time, street photographers, Henri Cartier-Bresson, Robert Frant, William Klein, Diane Arbus, Stephen Shore, William Eggleston, Martin Parr, Bruce Gilden, as well as Winogrand. Some of these people view the world with a comparatively benign eye; others are downright brutal in their gaze. In either case, the streets offer them the kind of subjects they're looking for, that they and their art need.

There are ways in which street photography might seem very straightforward. There's no need for props, lights, assistants, paid models, stylists, or any of the other detritus that some photographers carry with them. You simply go out with your camera and take pictures of what's there. There may be some premeditation, but in the end it's an improvised form with an unpredictable outcome, a sort of visual free jazz. Much of street life is quite banal. Even in a city as full of grotesques as New York, for every character there are thousands of ordinary Joes. People come and go rapidly, without arranging themselves into attractive or dramatic tableaux. Conflict and awkwardness may be part of the deal; nevertheless, the best street photographers do demonstrate something that looks like ease. They're at home in their environment, they're able to operate confidently in public, among people. Street photographers share a space with their subjects, are on equal footing, in the same place at the same time.

What makes a great street photographer is the amount of walking he or she does. Street photographers inevitably take a lot of photographs of people walking. Just as inevitably, they themselves spend a lot of time walking as they look for subjects. They are walkers who photograph other walkers. Luck plays an enormous part in street photography, and the cliché remains true that the more work you put in, the luckier you get. There are times when Winogrand seems to have had the luck of the devil. Every time he walked down the street, dwarves, identical twins, and people cuddling monkeys would appear and pose themselves for his delight.

In 1978, Winogrand moved to Los Angeles. Some of the work he did there is wonderful. One of my favorite photographs–I have a poster of it in my office–was taken at LAX airport and shows two women in stylish 1960s dresses, heels, and hairdos, backs to the camera, walking toward the futuristic Theme Building. However, the move to L.A. coincided with Winogrand's going shutter-crazy. In the eight or so years he was there he took more than a third of a million pictures, or at least that's how often he pressed his camera's shutter. But this was not picture making or photography as most of us understand it. The vast majority of the film he exposed was left unprocessed. Some rolls were developed but never printed. Even when contact sheets were made, he gave them only the slightest attention, never engaging with them long enough or seriously enough to do anything resembling editing.

Some of these contact sheets have been displayed in exhibitions and published in magazines, and although no photographer should not be judged by the quality of his contact sheets, it appears from these that Winogrand had not only lost his luck, he had lost his eye, too. Apparently, he also lost some of his basic technical competence when it came to exposure, processing, and camera shake. Most significant, a lot of them are taken from a moving car. Often in his L.A. period Winogrand, sat in the passenger seat and was driven around the city by various friends and associates while he shot relentlessly through the windshield or the open side window. He had always done this to some extent–quite a few of the photographs of the road trip depicted in his book 1964 are taken from a car, but by no means most. Maybe he thought this *modus operandi* was appropriate to Los Angeles. All the same, there's something dispiriting about it.

Of course a photographer can do whatever he wants, use any method that occurs to him; but for Winogrand, this method of working seemed to mark a profound dislocation and separation. The pictures have a perfunctory, stolen look. Once he had been a fellow walker, a fellow traveler, sharing the same street, the same sidewalk, as his subjects; now he was doing drive-bys. He still photographed people, including people walking, but he also endlessly pointed his camera at parked cars, empty intersections, and blank streets. John Szarkowski has written, "Many of the last frames seem to have cut themselves free from the familiar claims of art," which is a thrillingly elegant and charitable way of saying that a lot of these photographs seem to be of nothing in particular, though not quite of nothing at all.

I once went to see Martin Parr at his London office, just a stone's throw from Bunhill Fields. He was the only street photographer I happened to know at the time. Parr accepted my basic premise that being a street photographer involves doing a lot of walking. "Yes. Basically you keep walking and you think, 'God, this is boring, it's going nowhere,' and suddenly something will happen. So really all you do is keep walking, because you know that sooner or later you're going to get something. You'll become a hunter, if you like, a hunter-gatherer. The thing you've got to remember is, most of the time there's nothing happening and suddenly it *will* happen, but you can't have the time when it happens without having all the dull time, so even though you're not taking good pictures, you're in the rhythm. You know, you have to take some bad pictures, because if you only saved yourself for one good one you'd never take one at all, and suddenly you're onto something, and you might take two or three frames of the same shot." In fact, this describes my own experience of walking without a camera. A walk is never equally fascinating for its whole length. Certain stretches may seem dull or mundane, and then suddenly you see a number of amazing things that make it all worthwhile.

I wondered if Martin Parr had developed a sense for loitering in certain places that were likely to produce the shots he was looking for. Did he ever simply lurk rather than walk? "Sure. You're looking for a place where you know things might reveal themselves, but generally on the street you don't get much background, people take up most of the action, but I certainly know in the case of Bruce Gilden, he returns to the same place, he knows exactly where, the time of the day, the traffic flow in terms of people, and he'll keep going back to those places. You can almost recognize people, you know. You [the photographer] become almost part of the street furniture." I asked what reaction he got from people he photographed on the street. "It varies," he said. "Occasionally, people say 'Hi. What on earth are you doing?' I'm not as aggressive as Bruce Gilden. He's aggressive. If you appear guilty, then people are going to get cross with you. If you appear confident in what you're doing, it helps enormously. That's why Gilden gets away with it. He thinks it's his absolute right to be on the street photographing, and he's absolutely correct, of course. Therefore, there is no problem, there is no issue, whereas I get people who write to me or I meet people who say, 'How can you do that, photograph strangers walking on the street?'"

DiCorcia was the photographer who set up cinematic lighting rigs on the street, waited for people to walk into the frame where they were perfectly lit, and then pressed the shutter. He got into a whole lot of trouble for it, too. He was sued by a Jewish Orthodox priest, of eye-catching appearance, named Emo Nussenzweig, under New York's right-to-privacy laws that forbid the use of a person's likeness for commercial purposes without the person's permission. The case went to the Manhattan State Supreme Court, where it came down to a definition of commerce, or more properly, of art. Even though diCorcia made money from the photographs, it was declared they were first and foremost art, and therefore he was protected under the First Amendment. This is something else Garry Winogrand might have said to the woman who protested his taking her picture. It's good to know that street photography is a form of free speech, but having to go to the Manhattan Supreme Court to prove it is the kind of thing that must deter newcomers to the field.

Equally, this law may make pedestrians feel especially vulnerable. They are protected from commerce but not from art. It's illegal for a company, or its advertising agency, to take a picture of you in the street and print it with a headline that says, "This Man Eats Hamburgers" or "This Man Needs Life Insurance." But, if there's no headline, or if there's a caption indicating that this is a piece of street photography taken by a serious street photographer, then you have no recourse. Personally, on balance, I think it is as it should be, but then nobody's made a ton of money by taking my photograph while I was walking on the street.

Discussion Questions

1. Consider Gary Winogrand's initial formation of the habit of walking the city streets. How do his motives at that time for walking compare with the reasons other authors you have read, such as Cheryl Strayed, had for beginning to walk?

2. Explain the relationship between Winogrand's art and his habit of walking the city streets. Why do you or do you not think that he would have become a photographer if his childhood home had been more welcoming?

3. Discuss the effects that Winogrand's relocation to Los Angeles had on his art and his habit of walking.

Learning Responsibility on City Sidewalks

JANE JACOBS

Architectural and social critic Jane Jacobs opposed the conventional wisdom of most architects and city planners in the 1950s and 1960s by championing the value of human interaction on "lively" city streets, streets like those of Jacobs's own New York City neighborhood of Greenwich Village. The following passage, adapted from Jacobs's influential book The Death and Life of Great American Cities *(1961), presents one important aspect of her argument.*

On a recent walk home, I passed a block of Puerto Rican families. Twenty-eight children of all ages were playing on the sidewalk without any event more serious than a squabble over a bag of candy. They were under the casual surveillance of adults, who were primarily visiting in public with each other. Their surveillance was only seemingly casual, however, as was proved when the candy squabble broke out and peace and justice were quickly reestablished. The identities of the adults kept changing because some kept putting their heads out the windows, others kept coming in and going on errands, and others passed by and lingered a little. But the number of adults stayed fairly constant, between eight and eleven, during the evening I watched. Arriving home, I noticed a similar scene at our end of our block: In front of the tailor's, our apartment-house, the laundry, the pizza place, and the fruit man's store, twelve children were playing on the sidewalk in sight of fourteen adults.

Lively sidewalks have positive aspects for city children's play, and these are at least as important as safety and protection. The people of cities can, and on lively diversified sidewalks they do, supervise the incidental play of children and assimilate the children into city society. They do it in the course of carrying on their other pursuits. To waste the normal presence of adults on lively sidewalks and to bank instead (however idealistically) on hiring substitutes for them, is frivolous in the extreme. It is frivolous not only socially but also economically because cities have desperate shortages of money and of personnel for more interesting uses of the outdoors than playgrounds. City planners do not seem to realize how high a ratio of adults is needed to rear children. Nor do they seem to understand that parks and recreational equipment do not rear children. These can be useful adjuncts, but only people can rear children and assimilate them into civilized society. It is folly to build cities in a way that wastes this normal, casual manpower for child rearing and either leaves this essential job too much undone—with terrible consequences—or makes it necessary to hire substitutes such as playground monitors. The myth that playgrounds and grass and hired guards or supervisors are innately wholesome for children and that city streets, filled with ordinary people, are innately evil for children, boils down to a deep contempt for ordinary people.

In real life, only from the ordinary adults on city sidewalks do children learn—if they learn at all—the first fundamental of successful city life: People must take a modicum of public responsibility for each other, even if they have no ties of kinship or friendship. This is a lesson nobody learns by being told. It is learned from the experience of having other people without ties of kinship or close friendship take a modicum of public responsibility for you. When Mr. Lacey, the locksmith, bawls out one of my sons for running into the street, and then later reports the transgression to my husband as he passes the locksmith shop, my son gets more than an overt lesson in safety. He also gets, indirectly, the lesson that Mr. Lacey, with whom we have no ties other than street propinquity, feels responsible for him to a degree. The boy who goes unrescued in the elevator of a high-rise housing project learns the opposite lesson from his experience. So do the children in housing projects who squirt water into house windows and on passersby, and go unrebuked because they are anonymous children in anonymous grounds.

The lesson that city dwellers have to take responsibility for what goes on in the city streets is taught again and again to children on the sidewalks that enjoy a local public life. They can absorb it astonishingly early. They show they have absorbed it by taking it for granted that they, too, are part of the management. They volunteer—before they're asked—directions to people who are lost; they tell a man he will get a ticket if he parks where he thinks he is going to park; they offer unsolicited advice to the building superintendent to use rock salt instead of a chopper to attack the ice on the sidewalk. The presence or absence of this kind of street bossiness in city children is a fairly good tip-off to the presence or absence of responsible adult behavior toward the sidewalk and the children who use it. The children are imitating adult attitudes. This has nothing to do with income. Some of the poorest parts of cities do the best by their children in this respect. And some do the worst.

This is instruction in civic responsibility that people hired to look after children cannot teach, because the essence of this responsibility is that you do it without being hired. It is a lesson that parents, by themselves, are powerless to teach. If parents take minor public responsibility for strangers or neighbors in a society where nobody else does, this simply means that the parents are embarrassingly different and meddlesome, not that this is the proper way to behave. Such instruction must come from society itself, and in cities, if it comes, it comes almost entirely during the time children spend at incidental play on the sidewalks.

Discussion Questions

1. Discuss the positive effects Jane Jacobs claims result from children playing on the sidewalks of the city with only casual adult supervision. Do you agree with her that the benefits gained from this activity are at least as important as safety and protection? Explain your answer. If you were raising children in that environment, what would their playtime look like?

2. How would you respond to Jacobs's assertion that parks and recreational equipment show a lack of respect for ordinary people? What do you think Solnit would say about Jacobs's idea?

3. What kinds of behaviors of the city children does Jacobs cite to support her point of view? How do you think children in the suburbs or rural communities learn such behaviors? Give some examples from your own experiences or observations.

4. Would you be embarrassed and think your parents were "being meddlesome" in a situation in which they showed some form of public responsibility for other people's children? Explain.

Traffic Safety Facts by U.S. Department of Transportation: National Highway Traffic Safety Administration

DDT HS 811 888   APRIL 2014

Pedestrians

In 2012, 4,743 pedestrians were killed and an estimated 76,000 were injured in traffic crashes in the United States (Tables 1 and 3). On average, a pedestrian was killed every 2 hours and injured every 7 minutes in traffic crashes.

A pedestrian, as defined for the purpose of this Traffic Safety Fact Sheet, is any person on foot, walking, running, jogging, hiking, sitting or lying down who is involved in a motor vehicle traffic crash. Also, a traffic crash is defined as an incident that involves one or more vehicles where at least one vehicle is in transport and the crash originates on a public trafficway. Crashes that occurred exclusively on private property, including parking lots and driveways, were excluded.

> *In 2012, 4,743 pedestrians died in traffic crashes—a 6-percent increase from the number reported in 2011.*

The 4,743 pedestrian fatalities in 2012 represented an increase of 6 percent from 2011 and were the highest number of fatalities in the last 5 years. In 2012, pedestrian deaths accounted for 14 percent of all traffic fatalities (Table 1), and made up 3 percent of all the people injured in traffic crashes (Table 3).

Table 1

Total Fatalities and Pedestrian Fatalities in Traffic Crashes, 2003–2012

Year	Total Fatalities	Pedestrian Fatalities	Percent of Total Fatalities
2003	42,884	4,774	11%
2004	42,836	4,675	11%
2005	43,510	4,892	11%
2006	42,708	4,795	11%
2007	41,259	4,699	11%
2008	37,423	4,414	12%

From *Traffic Safety Facts–2012 Data, April 2014, DOT HS 811 888* by the U.S. Department of Transportation, National Highway Traffic Safety Administration.

Year	Total Fatalities	Pedestrian Fatalities	Percent of Total Fatalities
2009	33,883	4,109	12%
2010	32,999	4,302	13%
2011	32,479	4,457	14%
2012	33,561	4,743	14%

In 2012, almost three-fourths (73%) of pedestrian fatalities occurred in an urban setting versus a rural setting. Over two-thirds (70%) of pedestrian fatalities occurred at non-intersections versus at intersections. Eighty-nine percent of pedestrian fatalities occurred during normal weather conditions (clear/cloudy), compared to rain, snow and foggy conditions. A majority of the pedestrian fatalities, 70 percent, occurred during the nighttime (6 p.m.–5:59 a.m). Between 2011 and 2012 all these percentages stayed relatively level (Table 2).

In 2012, pedestrian deaths accounted for 14 percent of all traffic fatalities in motor vehicle traffic crashes.

> In 2012, more than one-fifth of the children ages 10 to 15 killed in traffic crashes were pedestrians.

Table 2

Percentage of Pedestrian Fatalities in Relation to Land Use, Non-Motorist Location, Weather, and Time of Day

Pedestrians Killed	Percentage of Pedestrians Killed	
	2011	2012
Land Use		
Rural	26%	26%
Urban	73%	73%
Non-Motorist Location		
Intersection	20%	20%
Non-Intersection	70%	70%
Other	10%	10%
Weather		
Clear/Cloudy	88%	89%
Rain	8%	8%
Snow	1%	1%
Fog	1%	1%
Time of Day*		
Daytime	30%	30%
Nighttime	69%	70%

Note: Percentage of unknown values are not displayed. * Daytime: 6 a.m.-5:59 p.m.
Nighttime: 6 p.m.-5:59 a.m.

Age

Older pedestrians (age 65+) accounted for 20 percent (935) of all pedestrian fatalities and an estimated 9 percent (7,000) of all pedestrians injured in 2012. The fatality rate for older pedestrians (age 65+) was 2.17 per 100,000 population–higher than the rate for all the other ages under 65 (Tables 3 and 4). Starting at age 45 the fatality rates are generally higher than they are in the younger age groups. In 2012, people 65 and older made up only 14 percent of the country's population.

In 2012, the average age of pedestrians killed in traffic crashes was 46 and the average age of those injured was 35. Over the past 10 years the average age of those killed has remained almost unchanged, while the age of those injured has steadily increased. The highest three pedestrian injury rates by age group were 21–24, 16–20 and 10–15 (Table 4).

In 2012, more than one-fifth (22%) of the children ages 5 to 15 who were killed in traffic crashes were pedestrians (Table 3). Children age 15 and younger accounted for 6 percent of the pedestrian fatalities in 2012 and 18 percent of all pedestrians injured in traffic crashes.

Table 3

Motor Vehicle Traffic Crash Fatalities and Injuries and Pedestrians Killed or Injured, by Age Group, 2012

Age Group (Years)	Total Killed	Pedestrians Killed	Percentage of Total Killed
<5	405	85	21%
5–9	345	75	22%
10–15	613	132	22%
16–20	3,224	265	8%
21–24	3,436	355	10%
25–29	3,265	335	10%
30–34	2,637	338	13%
35–39	2,205	259	12%
40–44	2,329	321	14%
45–49	2,447	401	16%
50–54	2,737	494	18%
55–59	2,366	405	17%
60–64	1,931	319	17%
65–69	1,481	236	16%
70–74	1,211	203	17%
75–79	979	184	19%
80+	1,889	312	17%
Total*	33,561	4,743	14%

Age Group (Years)	Total Injured	Pedestrians Injured	Percentage of Total Injured
<5	41,000	2,000	4%
5–9	61,000	4,000	7%
10–15	85,000	8,000	9%
16–20	299,000	8,000	3%
21–24	256,000	7,000	3%
25–29	241,000	7,000	3%
30–34	212,000	6,000	3%
35–39	167,000	6,000	3%
40–44	187,000	6,000	3%
45–49	180,000	5,000	3%
50–54	166,000	5,000	3%
55–59	139,000	5,000	4%
60–64	114,000	3,000	2%
65–69	83,000	3,000	4%
70–74	46,000	1,000	3%
75–79	34,000	1,000	4%
80+	50,000	1,000	3%
Total	2,362,000	76,000	3%

*Total includes 61 overall fatalities and 24 pedestrian fatalities of unknown age. Note: Totals may not equal sum of components due to independent rounding.

Gender

In 2012, more than two-thirds (69%) of the pedestrians killed were males, and the male pedestrian fatality rate per 100,000 population was 2.13—more than double the rate for females (0.91 per 100,000 population). The male pedestrian injury rate per 100,000 population was 27, compared with 21 for females (Table 4).

Table 4

Pedestrians Killed and Injured and Fatality and Injury Rates by Age and Sex, 2012

Age (Years)	Male			Female			Total		
	Killed	Population (thousands)	Fatality Rate*	Killed	Population (thousands)	Fatality Rate*	Killed	Population (thousands)	Fatality Rate*
<5	53	10,216	0.52	32	9,783	0.33	85	19,999	0.43
5–9	43	10,459	0.41	32	10,016	0.32	75	20,476	0.37
10–15	75	12,686	0.59	57	12,128	0.47	132	24,813	0.53
16–20	191	11,179	1.71	74	10,581	0.70	265	21,760	1.22
21–24	250	9,214	2.71	105	8,825	1.19	355	18,039	1.97
25–34	483	21,339	2.26	190	20,971	0.91	673	42,309	1.59
35–44	414	20,174	2.05	166	20,343	0.82	580	40,516	1.43
45–54	654	21,807	3.00	241	22,462	1.07	895	44,269	2.02
55–64	514	18,603	2.76	210	19,983	1.05	724	38,586	1.88
65–74	300	11,203	2.68	138	12,783	1.08	439	23,985	1.83
75–84	211	5,648	3.74	146	7,624	1.91	358	13,273	2.70
85 +	79	1,964	4.02	59	3,923	1.50	138	5,887	2.34
Total1	3,285	154,492	2.13	1,454	159,422	0.91	4,743	313,914	1.51

Age (Years)	Male			Female			Total		
	Injured	Population (thousands)	Injury Rate*	Injured	Population (thousands)	Injury Rate*	Injured	Population (thousands)	Injury Rate*
<5	1,000	10,216	12	**	9,783	**	2,000	19,999	9
5–9	2,000	10,459	22	2,000	10,016	19	4,000	20,476	20
10–15	4,000	12,686	34	3,000	12,128	27	8,000	24,813	31
16–20	4,000	11,179	34	4,000	10,581	36	8,000	21,760	35
21–24	2,000	9,214	26	4,000	8,825	49	7,000	18,039	37
25–34	7,000	21,339	33	5,000	20,971	24	12,000	42,309	29
35–44	8,000	20,174	37	4,000	20,343	20	12,000	40,516	29
45–54	6,000	21,807	27	4,000	22,462	18	10,000	44,269	23
55–64	4,000	18,603	23	4,000	19,983	18	8,000	38,586	20
65–74	2,000	11,203	20	2,000	12,783	15	4,000	23,985	17
75–84	1,000	5,648	18	1,000	7,624	9	2,000	13,273	13
85 +	**	1,964	**	**	3,923	**	1,000	5,887	14
Total2	42,000	154,492	27	34,000	159,422	21	76,000	313,914	24

* Rate per 100,000 population.
** Less than 500 injured, injury rate not shown.
[1]Total killed includes 24 of unknown age.
[2]Totals may not equal sum of components due to independent rounding.
Source: Fatalities—Fatality Analysis Reporting System, NHTSA. Injured—General Estimates System, NHTSA. Population—Bureau of the Census.

Time of Day and Day of Week

Thirty-two percent of the pedestrian fatalities occurred in crashes between 8 p.m. and 11:59 p.m. The highest percentage of weekday and weekend fatalities also occurred between

8 p.m. and 11:59 p.m. (28% and 37%, respectively). The lowest 8 a.m. and 11:59 a.m. (9% and 4%, respectively; Figure 1).

Figure 1

Percentage of Pedestrian Fatalities by Time of Day and Day of Week, 2012

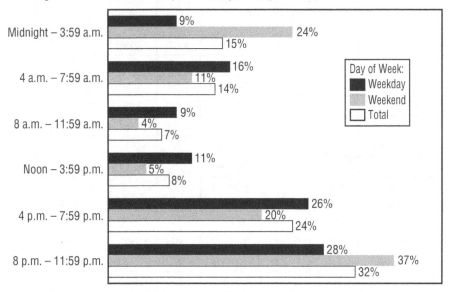

Alcohol Involvement in Pedestrian Crashes

Alcohol involvement—either for the driver or for the pedestrian—was reported in 48 percent of the traffic crashes that resulted in pedestrian fatalities. Of the pedestrians involved in fatal crashes, 34 percent had a blood alcohol concentration (BAC) of .08 grams per deciliter (g/dL) or higher. Of the drivers involved in these fatal crashes, only 14 percent had a BAC of .08 g/dL or higher (Table 5).

Table 5

Alcohol Involvement in Crashes That Resulted in Pedestrian Fatalities, 2012

	No Driver Alcohol Involvement		Driver Alcohol Involvement, BAC .01-.07 g/dL		Driver Alcohol Involvement, BAC .08 g/dL or Greater		Total	
	Number	Percent	Number	Percent	Number	Percent	Number	Percent
No Pedestrian Alcohol Involvement	2,417	52%	75	2%	361	8%	2,852	61%
Pedestrian Alcohol Involvement, BAC .01-.07 g/dL	161	3%	10	<1%	41	1%	212	5%
Pedestrian Alcohol Involvement, BAC .08 g/dL or Greater	1,271	27%	61	1%	262	6%	1,593	34%
Total	3,849	83%	145	3%	663	14%	4,657	100%

Note: The alcohol levels in this table are determined using the alcohol levels of the pedestrians killed and the involved drivers (killed and other).

Alcohol Involvement for Pedestrians Killed

Of the pedestrians who were killed in fatal crashes, 36 percent had a BAC of .08 g/dL or higher. Pedestrians ages 45–54 who were killed had the highest percentage of alcohol impairment at 49 percent (Table 6).

Table 6

Alcohol Involvement for Pedestrians Killed in Fatal Crashes by Age, 2003 and 2012

Age (Years)	2003					2012				
	Number of Fatalities	% With BAC=.00	% With BAC=.01-.07	% With BAC=.08+	% With BAC=.01+	Number of Fatalities	% With BAC=.00	% With BAC=.01-.07	% With BAC=.08+	% With BAC=.01+
16–20	302	66%	4%	30%	34%	265	72%	3%	25%	28%
21–24	266	41%	7%	52%	59%	355	49%	6%	46%	51%
25–34	564	49%	4%	47%	51%	673	47%	6%	47%	53%
35–14	852	42%	5%	53%	58%	580	49%	5%	46%	51%
45–54	780	50%	5%	45%	50%	895	46%	5%	49%	54%
55–64	553	65%	5%	30%	35%	724	62%	4%	33%	38%
65–74	394	78%	5%	17%	22%	439	81%	4%	15%	19%
75–84	424	92%	2%	6%	8%	358	89%	3%	8%	11%
85 +	163	94%	1%	5%	6%	138	95%	1%	4%	5%
Total*	4,298	59%	4%	36%	41%	4,427	59%	5%	36%	41%

*Excludes pedestrians under 16 years old and pedestrians of unknown age.

For more information:

Information on traffic fatalities is available from the National Center for Statistics and Analysis (NCSA), NVS-424, 1200 New Jersey Avenue SE, Washington, DC 20590. NCSA can be contacted at 800-934-8517 or via the following e-mail address: ncsaweb@dot.gov. General information on highway traffic safety can be accessed by Internet users at www.nhtsa.gov/NCSA. To report a safety-related problem or to inquire about motor vehicle safety information, contact the Vehicle Safety Hotline at 888-327-4236.

Other fact sheets available from the National Center for Statistics and Analysis are Alcohol-Impaired Driving, Bicyclists and Other Cyclists, Children, Large Trucks, Motorcycles, Occupant Protection, Older Population, Overview, Passenger Vehicles, Race and Ethnicity, Rural/Urban Comparisons, School Transportation-Related Crashes, Speeding, State Alcohol Estimates, State Traffic Data, and Young Drivers. Detailed data on motor vehicle traffic crashes are published annually in *Traffic Safety Facts: A Compilation of Motor Vehicle Crash Data from the Fatality Analysis Reporting System and the General Estimates System.* The fact sheets and annual Traffic Safety Facts report can be accessed online at www-nrd.nhtsa.dot.gov/CATS/index.aspx.

Motor Vehicles

In 2012, 90 percent of the pedestrians were killed in motor vehicle traffic crashes that involved a single vehicle.

In 2012, 90 percent of the pedestrians were killed in motor vehicle traffic crashes that involved a single vehicle. In those single-vehicle crashes, 86 percent of the time the pedestrian was struck by the front of the vehicle. Passenger cars, SUV's, pickups and vans had the highest percentage of front impacts with a pedestrian who was killed (90%, 89%, 90%, and 89%, respectively). Large trucks had the highest percentage of right side and rear impacts with a pedestrian who was killed (8% and 7%, respectively; Table 7). Of the 4,743 pedestrians killed in 2012, 884 (19%) were involved in hit-and-run crashes.

Fatalities by State

Nearly one-fifth of the pedestrians killed in 2012 were involved in hit-and-run crashes.

Among all States, the total motor vehicle traffic fatalities in 2012 ranged from 3,398 (highest) to 15 (lowest). Pedestrian fatalities were highest in California (612), followed by Texas (478) and Florida (476). The individual State percentage of pedestrian fatalities by total traffic fatalities ranged from a high of 46.7 percent (District of Columbia) to a low of 1.5 percent (South Dakota). The highest pedestrian fatality rate per 100,000 population was in Delaware (2.94), followed by New Mexico (2.92) (Table 9). The pedestrian fatality rate of major cities are often much higher than the national average. Of cities with populations higher than 500,000, Detroit has the highest pedestrian fatality rate, followed by Oklahoma City and Albuquerque (3.99, 3.34, and 3.24 respectively; Table 8).

Table 7

Pedestrians Killed in Single-Vehicle Crashes, by Vehicle Type Involved, 2012

Vehicle Type	Initial Point of Impact on Vehicle											Total	
	Front		Right Side		Left Side		Rear		Other/Unknown				
	Number	Percent	Number	Percent	Number	Percent	Number	Percent	Number	Percent		Number	Percent
Passenger Car	1,692	90.4%	47	2.5%	31	1.7%	18	1.0%	83	4.4%		1,871	100.0%
Light Truck*	1,530	88.9%	38	2.2%	35	2.0%	38	2.2%	81	4.7%		1,722	100.0%
-SUV	636	88.5%	11	1.5%	18	2.5%	21	2.9%	33	4.6%		719	100.0%
-Pickup	637	89.6%	14	2.0%	13	1.8%	11	1.5%	36	5.1%		711	100.0%
-Van	249	88.6%	12	4.3%	4	1.4%	6	2.1%	10	3.6%		281	100.0%
Large Truck	175	72.3%	20	8.3%	6	2.5%	17	7.0%	24	9.9%		242	100.0%
Bus	47	69.1%	5	7.4%	3	4.4%	2	2.9%	11	16.2%		68	100.0%
Other/Unknown Vehicle	208	56.5%	4	1.1%	2	0.5%	-	-	154	41.8%		368	100.0%
Total	3,652	85.5%	114	2.7%	77	1.8%	75	1.8%	353	8.3%		4,271	100.0%

*Includes other/unknown light trucks.

Note: Totals may not equal the sum of components due to independent rounding.

Important Safety Reminders

For Pedestrians:

- Walk on a sidewalk or path whenever one is available.
- If there is no sidewalk or path available, walk facing traffic (on the left side of the road) on the shoulder, as far away from traffic as possible. Keep alert at all times; don't be distracted by electronic devices, including radios, smart phones, and other devices that take your eyes (and ears) off the road environment.
- Be cautious night and day when sharing the road with vehicles. Never assume a driver sees you (he or she could be distracted, under the influence of alcohol and/or drugs, or just not seeing you). Try to make eye contact with drivers as they approach you to make sure you are seen.
- Be predictable as a pedestrian. Cross streets at crosswalks or intersections whenever possible. This is where drivers expect pedestrians.
- If a crosswalk or intersection is not available, locate a well-lit area, wait for a gap in traffic that allows you enough time to cross safely, and continue to watch for traffic as you cross.
- Stay off of freeways, restricted-access highways, and other pedestrian-prohibited roadways.
- Be visible at all times. Wear bright clothing during the day, and wear reflective materials or use a flash light at night.
- Avoid alcohol and drugs when walking; they impair your abilities and judgment too.

For Drivers:

- Look out for pedestrians everywhere, at all times. Very often, pedestrians are not walking where they should be.
- Be especially vigilant for pedestrians in hard-to-see conditions, such as night-time or in bad weather.
- Slow down and be prepared to stop when turning or otherwise entering a crosswalk.
- Always stop for pedestrians in crosswalks and stop well back from the crosswalk to give other vehicles an opportunity to see the crossing pedestrians so they can stop too.
- Never pass vehicles stopped at a crosswalk. They are stopped to allow pedestrians to cross the street.
- Never drive under the influence of alcohol and/or drugs.
- Follow the speed limit, especially around pedestrians.
- Follow slower speed limits in school zones and in neighborhoods where there are children present.

    — NHTSA's Safety Countermeasures Division

Table 8

Persons Killed, Pedestrians Killed, Population, and Fatality Rates in Cities With a Population of 500,000 or Greater, 2012

City	Total Killed	Fatalities — Pedestrians Killed — Number	Fatalities — Pedestrians Killed — Percent of Total Killed	Population	Fatality Rate per 100,000 Population — Total	Fatality Rate per 100,000 Population — Pedestrian
New York, NY	268	127	47%	8,336,697	3.21	1.52
Los Angeles, CA	242	99	41%	3,857,799	6.27	2.57
Chicago, IL	145	47	32%	2,714,856	5.34	1.73
Houston, TX	196	46	23%	2,160,821	9.07	2.13
Philadelphia, PA	107	31	29%	1,547,607	6.91	2.00
Phoenix, AZ	151	39	26%	1,488,750	10.14	2.62
San Antonio, TX	132	37	28%	1,382,951	9.54	2.68
San Diego, CA	70	22	31%	1,338,348	5.23	1.64
Dallas, TX	136	40	29%	1,241,162	10.96	3.22
San Jose, CA	42	12	29%	982,765	4.27	1.22
Austin, TX	76	25	33%	842,592	9.02	2.97
Jacksonville, FL	113	27	24%	836,507	13.51	3.23
Indianapolis, IN	77	15	19%	834,852	9.22	1.80
San Francisco, CA	29	14	48%	825,863	3.51	1.70
Columbus, OH	58	8	14%	809,798	7.16	0.99
Fort Worth, TX	59	20	34%	777,992	7.58	2.57
Charlotte, NC	61	22	36%	775,202	7.87	2.84
Detroit, MI	102	28	27%	701,475	14.54	3.99
El Paso, TX	54	21	39%	672,538	8.03	3.12
Memphis, TN	78	11	14%	655,155	11.91	1.68
Boston, MA	23	5	22%	636,479	3.61	0.79
Seattle, WA	27	9	33%	634,535	4.26	1.42
Denver, CO	36	18	50%	634,265	5.68	2.84
Washington, DC	15	7	47%	632,323	2.37	1.11
Nashville-Davidson, TN	56	14	25%	624,496	8.97	2.24
Baltimore City, MD	27	6	22%	621,342	4.35	0.97
Louisville/Jefferson, KY	59	6	10%	605,110	9.75	0.99
Portland, OR	32	14	44%	603,106	5.31	2.32

Oklahoma City, OK	83	20	24%	599,199	13.85	3.34
Milwaukee, WI	42	11	26%	598,916	7.01	1.84
Las Vegas, NV	59	15	25%	596,424	9.89	2.51
Albuquerque, NM	50	18	36%	555,417	9.00	3.24
Tucson, AZ	55	11	20%	524,295	10.49	2.10
Fresno, CA	29	14	48%	505,882	5.73	2.77

Sources: Population—Bureau of the Census.

Table 9

Motor Vehicle Traffic Crash Fatalities, Pedestrian Traffic Fatalities, and Fatality Rates by State, 2012

State	Total Traffic Fatalities	Resident Population (thousands)	Pedestrian Fatalities	Percent of Total	Pedestrian Fatalities per 100,000 Population
Alabama	865	4,822,023	77	8.9%	1.60
Alaska	59	731,449	8	13.6%	1.09
Arizona	825	6,553,255	122	14.8%	1.86
Arkansas	552	2,949,131	44	8.0%	1.49
California	2,857	38,041,430	612	21.4%	1.61
Colorado	472	5,187,582	76	16.1%	1.47
Connecticut	236	3,590,347	36	15.3%	1.00
Delaware	114	917,092	27	23.7%	2.94
Dist of Columbia	15	632,323	7	46.7%	1.11
Florida	2,424	19,317,568	476	19.6%	2.46
Georgia	1,192	9,919,945	167	14.0%	1.68
Hawaii	126	1,392,313	26	20.6%	1.87
Idaho	184	1,595,728	13	7.1%	0.81
Illinois	956	12,875,255	138	14.4%	1.07
Indiana	779	6,537,334	59	7.6%	0.90
Iowa	365	3,074,186	20	5.5%	0.65
Kansas	405	2,885,905	26	6.4%	0.90
Kentucky	746	4,380,415	49	6.6%	1.12
Louisiana	722	4,601,893	118	16.3%	2.56
Maine	164	1,329,192	9	5.5%	0.68
Maryland	505	5,884,563	96	19.0%	1.63
Massachusetts	349	6,646,144	72	20.6%	1.08
Michigan	938	9,883,360	129	13.8%	1.31

Minnesota	395	5,379,139	38	9.6%	0.71
Mississippi	582	2,984,926	48	8.2%	1.61
Missouri	826	6,021,988	84	10.2%	1.39
Montana	205	1,005,141	8	3.9%	0.80
Nebraska	212	1,855,525	15	7.1%	0.81
Nevada	258	2,758,931	54	20.9%	1.96
New Hampshire	108	1,320,718	8	7.4%	0.61
New Jersey	589	8,864,590	156	26.5%	1.76
New Mexico	365	2,085,538	61	16.7%	2.92
New York	1,168	19,570,261	297	25.4%	1.52
North Carolina	1,292	9,752,073	197	15.2%	2.02
North Dakota	170	699,628	7	4.1%	1.00
Ohio	1,123	11,544,225	115	10.2%	1.00
Oklahoma	708	3,814,820	65	9.2%	1.70
Oregon	336	3,899,353	55	16.4%	1.41
Pennsylvania	1,310	12,763,536	163	12.4%	1.28
Rhode Island	64	1,050,292	5	7.8%	0.48
South Carolina	863	4,723,723	123	14.3%	2.60
South Dakota	133	833,354	2	1.5%	0.24
Tennessee	1,014	6,456,243	67	6.6%	1.04
Texas	3,398	26,059,203	478	14.1%	1.83
Utah	217	2,855,287	28	12.9%	0.98
Vermont	77	626,011	10	13.0%	1.60
Virginia	777	8,185,867	98	12.6%	1.20
Washington	444	6,897,012	72	16.2%	1.04
West Virginia	339	1,855,413	31	9.1%	1.67
Wisconsin	615	5,726,398	45	7.3%	0.79
Wyoming	123	576,412	6	4.9%	1.04
U.S. Total	33,561	313,914,040	4,743	14.1%	1.51
Puerto Rico	347	3,667,084	110	31.7%	3.00

Note: Totals may not equal sum of components due to independent rounding.

Sources: Fatalities—Fatality Analysis Reporting System, NHTSA. Population—Bureau of the Census.

Discussion Questions

1. What facts/statistics in this report surprised you? What facts/statistics confirmed what you already suspected? How does this report change your view of walking in the city, around campus, or at home?

2. What do you think might account for the fact that California, Texas, and Florida are the states that have the highest rate of pedestrian fatalities? What are the cities that have the highest fatality rates? What cities would you have expected to top the list? Explain the reasons behind your expectations. These statistics are national, specific to the United States; however, after reading this report, could you recommend a walking experience in New York similar to Virginia Woolf's in London? Why or why not? How do you think the other writer, Matthew Beaumont, who discusses night walking in London, could accommodate the issue of pedestrian fatality in his article?

3. How could you use this report to respond to ideas in Rebecca Solnit's "Walking and the Suburbanized Psyche"? Before answering this question, be sure to consider such concerns as use of space, physical health, and mental well being, as well as safety. After thinking about these issues, what new topics, emphases, or adjustments might Solnit wish to include in her essay?

4. This selection is a government report. A report is an objective presentation of facts and statistics. It offers no opinion or interpretation of the information it gives. After reading this report, however, you must have formed some opinion about pedestrian safety. If you were to write an argumentative essay on this topic, what would your thesis be?

Assignment #5

"Practicing Medicine Can Be Grimm Work"

The following reading selection is written by Valerie Gribben and presents and supports a thesis statement about fairy tales and their influence on us. The reading is followed by a writing topic that you will use as the basis for the essay you will write. In order to respond successfully to that writing topic, you will have to present, develop, and support your own position on whether you think that fairy tales can offer us a way to make sense of our experiences.

To help prepare you to respond in a thoughtful and insightful way, the "Extending the Discussion" section includes several fairy tales that will give you an opportunity to test Gribben's ideas. The section also includes a group of readings that develop their own arguments about fairy tales. We hope that they will give you some additional ways to think about fairy tales and to test Gribben's claim regarding their impact on us. Again, in this assignment unit, make full use of all of the prewriting and drafting activities as you consider how you want to respond to Gribben's argument. The more time and thought you put into these supporting activities, the more prepared you will be to formulate your essay's thesis statement and develop your ideas so that your essay is insightful, persuasive, and coherent.

Practicing Medicine Can Be Grimm Work

Essay

VALERIE GRIBBEN

Valerie Gribben wrote the following essay when she was a fourth-year medical student at the University of Alabama at Birmingham. She is also the author of The Fairytale Trilogy.

Today, after four arduous years of examinations, graduating medical doctors will report to their residency programs. Armed with stethoscopes and scalpels, they're preparing to lead the charge against disease in its ravaging, chimerical forms. They carry with them the classic tomes: Harrison's *Principles of Internal Medicine* and *Gray's Anatomy*. But I have an unlikely addition for their mental rucksacks: *Grimm's Fairy Tales*. Fairy tales have always fascinated me: fishermen and talking flounder, siblings wending their way through a shadowy forest, seven brothers transformed into ravens. Although I always wanted to be a doctor and took the requisite courses to be admitted to medical school, in my undergraduate years I majored in English and studied Victorian fairy tales. Immersing myself in period documents, I saw tenuous connections between the worlds of fantasy and medicine, between fairy dust and consumption.

But when I started medical school, I packed up my youthful literary indiscretions. I reordered my bookshelf, moving my well-thumbed but now irrelevant Brothers Grimm stories behind a biochemistry textbook. Within weeks, my desk was crammed with printouts on fractures of the humerus and the intermediates of oxidative phosphorylation. I was thinking in terms of proximal and distal instead of hither and thither.

Then, I started my third year of medical school, when students rotate through the different specialties, crisp white coats venturing into the grime of clinical medicine. I felt I was prepared with my color-coded pharmacology flashcards and issues of the *New England Journal of Medicine*. But soon, I came across an elderly woman with hyponatremia, a sodium deficiency. I knew what treatment she needed. But my textbooks and articles let me down. They couldn't tell me why her adult children had been neglecting her and denying her food. They gave no answers to the mysteries behind the physical symptoms or how to process them.

In pediatrics, my team discovered long, thin scratches on a child's back—made by metal coat hangers that someone had dug into her skin and pulled. In physical medicine and rehabilitation, we supervised occupational therapy for a ten-year-old who'd shot himself in the head. He shrugged when we asked why: "I dunno." In neurology, a stroke patient went off life support on his daughter's birthday, and the sound of her convulsive weeping went up and down the hallways, knocking against other patients' doors.

In internal medicine, I cared for a woman who had been so badly beaten by her late husband that her eyes pointed in different directions. She came in for trouble swallowing, and I had to hold her down during an endoscopy to see if esophageal cancer was the cause. In surgery, a handsome young man was being eaten alive by cancer. From above the operating table, I could peer inside him and see tumors wrapping themselves around his vital organs. In psychiatry, a waifish princess look-alike—mascara dripping down her porcelain cheekbones—was committed to our ward for hearing voices not of this world. The practice of medicine bestows the sacred privilege to ask about the unmentionable. But what happens when the door to Bluebeard's horror chamber opens, and the bloody secrets spill onto your aseptic field of study? How do you process the pain of your patients?

I found my way back to stories. The Grimm fairy tales once seemed as if they had taken place in lands far, far away, but I see them now in my everyday hospital rotations. I've met the eternal cast of characters. I've taken down their histories (the abandoned prince, the barren couple) or seen their handiwork (the evil stepmother, the lecherous king). Fairy tales are, at their core, heightened portrayals of human nature, revealing, as the glare of injury and illness does, the underbelly of mankind. Both fairy tales and medical charts chronicle the bizarre, the unfair, the tragic. And the terrifying things that go bump in the night are what doctors treat at 3 a.m. in emergency rooms.

So I now find comfort in fairy tales. They remind me that happy endings are possible. With a few days of rest and proper medication, the bewildered princess left relaxed and smiling, with a set of goals and a new job in sight. The endoscopy on my cross-eyed confidante showed she was cancer-free. Fairy tales also remind me that what I'm seeing now has come before. Child endangerment is not an invention of the Facebook age. Elder neglect didn't arrive with Gen X. And discharge summaries are not always happy; "Cinderella" originally ended with a blinding, and Death, in his tattered shroud, waits at the end of many journeys. Healing, I'm learning, begins with kindness, and most fairy tales teach us to show kindness wherever we can, to the stooped little beggar and the highest nobleman. In another year, I'll be among the new doctors reporting to residency training. And the Brothers Grimm will be with me.

Writing Topic

How have fairy tales influenced Valerie Gribben, especially as she learned to be a doctor? Do you share her belief in the power of fairy tales to help us deal with the experiences in our lives? Write an essay in which you develop your own position; you may use your own experiences, observations, and examples from readings, including "Practicing Medicine Can Be Grimm Work."

Vocabulary Check

You will want to be sure that you understand the key vocabulary terms below and the way they are used by Gribben in "Practicing Medicine Can Be Grimm Work." Look up the definitions of the following words. Look at all of the possible meanings given, and then choose the meaning that you think Gribben intended when she selected that particular word. Explain the way the meaning or concept behind the definition is key to understanding her argument.

1. *chimerical*

    definition: _____

    _____

    explanation: _____

    _____

    _____

    _____

2. *rucksack*

    definition: _____

    _____

    explanation: _____

    _____

    _____

    _____

3. *tenuous*

   definition: _____

   _____

   explanation: _____

   _____

   _____

   _____

4. *waifish*

   definition: _____

   _____

   explanation: _____

   _____

   _____

   _____

5. *bestow*

   definition: _____

   _____

   explanation: _____

   _____

   _____

   _____

6. *aseptic*

definition: _____

_____

explanation: _____

_____

_____

_____

7. *abandon*

definition: _____

_____

explanation: _____

_____

_____

_____

8. *barren*

definition: _____

_____

explanation: _____

_____

_____

_____

9. *lecherous*

   definition: _____

   _____

   explanation: _____

   _____

   _____

   _____

10. *bewildered*

   definition: _____

   _____

   explanation: _____

   _____

   _____

   _____

11. *tattered*

   definition: _____

   _____

   explanation: _____

   _____

   _____

   _____

12. *shroud*

definition: _____

_____

explanation: _____

_____

_____

_____

13. *stooped*

definition: _____

_____

explanation: _____

_____

_____

_____

Questions to Guide Your Reading

Answer the following questions so you can gain a thorough understanding of "Practicing Medicine Can Be Grimm Work."

Paragraph 1

What will Valerie Gribben's future profession be, and what was her undergraduate course of study?

Paragraph 2

What changes occurred in her environment and in her mental state when she began medical school?

Paragraphs 3–5

When did she discover that her medical studies were insufficient preparation for the reality of addressing patients' problems? What examples does she give of patients whose physical symptoms were troubling for her as a doctor and as a human being?

Paragraphs 6–7

How have fairy tales helped her in her practice of medicine?

Prewriting for a Directed Summary

The first part of the writing topic that follows "Practicing Medicine Can Be Grimm Work" asks you about a central idea from Gribben's essay. To answer this part of the writing topic, you will want to write a *directed* summary, meaning one that responds specifically to the writing topic's first question.

first part of the writing topic:

How have fairy tales influenced Valerie Gribben, especially as she learned to be a doctor?

Hint

Don't forget to look back to Part 1's "Guidelines for Writing a Directed Summary."

Focus Questions

1. In what way did Valerie Gribben's medical training "let her down"?

2. According to Gribben, what emotional skill necessary to practice medicine is not adequately covered by the medical school curriculum?

3. Explain the similarities Gribben sees between characters in fairy tales and the patients she treats.

4. How does Gribben draw comfort from fairy tales as she does her daily work?

5. What important lesson about healing can be learned from fairy tales, according to Gribben?

Developing an Opinion and Working Thesis Statement

The second part of the writing topic for "Practicing Medicine Can Be Grimm Work" asks you to take a position of your own on the issue Gribben addresses. Your response to this part of the writing topic will become the thesis statement of your essay, so it is important to spend some time ensuring that it reflects the position you want to take. Do you think that fairy tales offer us strategies for dealing with our experiences?

> writing topic's second part:
>
> *Do you share her belief in the power of fairy tales to help us deal with the experiences in our lives?*

Do you think Gribben is convincing? That is, do you think fairy tales reflect many of our human experiences and therefore offer us a way to understand and cope with those experiences? In order to make your position clear to readers, state it early in your essay, preferably at the end of your introductory paragraph. A clear thesis statement, one that takes a position on the power of fairy tales, will unify your essay and allow it to effectively communicate with readers.

It is likely that you aren't yet sure what position you want to take in your essay. If this is the case, go on to the next section and work on developing your ideas through specific evidence drawn from your experience. Then, you will be asked to reexamine the working thesis statement you write here to see if you want to revise it based on the discoveries you made when you explored your ideas more systematically.

1. Use the following thesis frame to identify the basic elements of your working thesis statement:

   a. What is the issue of "Practicing Medicine Can Be Grimm Work" that the writing topic asks you to consider?

   _____

   b. What is Gribben's opinion about that issue?

   _____

   c. What is your opinion about the issue, and will you agree or disagree with Gribben?

   _____

   _____

   _____

2. Now use the elements you isolated in the thesis frame to write a thesis statement. You may have to revise it several times until it captures your ideas clearly.

_____

_____

Prewriting to Find Support for Your Thesis Statement

The last part of the writing topic asks you to support the position you put forward in your thesis statement. Well-developed ideas are crucial when you are making an argument because you will have to be clear, logical, and thorough if you are to be convincing. As you work through the exercises below, you will generate much of the 4Cs material you will need when you draft your essay's body paragraphs.

writing topic's last part:

Write an essay in which you develop your own position; you may use your own experiences, observations, and examples from readings, including "Practicing Medicine Can Be Grimm Work."

Complete each section of this prewriting activity; your responses will become the material you will use in the next stage—planning and writing the essay.

1. As you begin to develop your own examples as the basis for your thesis statement, make a list of the fairy tales that you are familiar with, and, for each tale, jot down as many lessons you can think of that the tale teaches us. Include the tales that are provided at the end of this assignment unit.

2. Now go down your list again, and, this time, for each lesson, include the specific part of the plot that demonstrates the lesson. Fairy tales often teach more than one lesson, so spend some time with each tale to explore what a reader of the tale might draw from it. For example, Cinderella's stepmother tells her that, if she finishes her housework, she may go with them to the ball; but later, when Cinderella tells her that her chores are finished, her stepmother does not keep her word. We learn from this that lying is unfair and wrong, and that we should treat one another with kindness and fairness. Do any other tales carry this lesson or message? What other lessons can be found in fairy tales?

Once you've listed your specific examples and done some speculative freewriting about the meaning or significance of each, carefully look over all that you have written. Try to group your ideas into categories. Then, give each category a label. In other words, cluster ideas that seem to have something in common and, for each cluster, identify that shared quality by giving it a title.

3. Now that you have worked with some specific tales, consider whether they influence your thinking. As an adult, do you think that they provide a meaningful source of knowledge that can be helpful or meaningful when we meet life's challenges? At this point, you should do some more freewriting and see in what direction your ideas take you. Are fairy tales too unrealistic to be of help to adults? Do you think they are merely entertainment for children?

Now look back at your working thesis statement. Have your views changed now that you've thought more extensively about the issue? If so, think now about the position you want to take. You will have a chance to revise it in the next activity. Whatever position you will take in your essay, you will have to refer to specific fairy tales and the lessons they teach. Take time now to explain below how each category and its examples connect to your thesis statement. You will use these details for the next stage.

Revising Your Thesis Statement

Now that you have spent some time working out your ideas more systematically and developing some supporting evidence for the position you want to take, look again at the working thesis statement you crafted earlier and see if it is still accurate. As your first step, look again at the writing topic, and then write your original working thesis on the lines that follow it.

writing topic:

How have fairy tales influenced Valerie Gribben, especially as she learned to be a doctor? Do you share her belief in the power of fairy tales to help us deal with the experiences in our lives? Write an essay in which you develop your own position; you may use your own experiences, observations, and examples from readings, including "Practicing Medicine Can Be Grimm Work."

Working Thesis Statement:

_____

_____

Take some time now to see if you want to revise your thesis statement. Remember that your thesis statement must respond to the second part of the writing topic, but also take into consideration the writing topic as a whole. The first part of the writing topic identifies the issue that is up for debate, and the last part of the writing topic reminds you that, whatever position you take on the issue, you must support it with specific evidence.

There is a good chance that some revision of your thesis is necessary. Sometimes only a word or phrase must be added or deleted; other times, the thesis statement must be significantly rewritten, as either the subject section or the claim portion or both are inaccurate. Use the following questions to reexamine it now to ensure that it is fully developed, clear, and accurate:

a. Does the thesis directly identify Gribben's argument about the way fairy tales provide support for life's experiences?

b. Do you make clear your opinion regarding this connection?

c. Is your thesis well punctuated, grammatically correct, and precisely worded?

Add any missing elements, correct the grammar errors, and refine the wording. Then, write your polished thesis on the lines below. Try to look at it from your readers' perspective. Is it strong and interesting?

Hint

Be sure that your thesis presents a clear position; it should not be a statement that shows you haven't yet made up your mind and are still considering two or more options or possibilities.

Planning and Drafting Your Essay

Now that you have examined Gribben's argument and thought at length about your own views, draft an essay that responds to all parts of the writing topic. Use the material you developed in the above activities to compose your draft, and then exchange drafts with a classmate and use the peer review activity to revise your draft.

Getting started on the draft is often the hardest part of the writing process because this is where you move from exploring and planning to getting your ideas down in a unified, coherent shape. You may not be in the habit of outlining or planning your essay before you begin drafting it, and some of you may avoid outlining altogether. If you haven't been using an outline as you move through the writing process, try using it this time. Creating an outline will give you a clear and coherent structure for incorporating all of the ideas you have developed in the preceding pages. It will also show you where you may have gone off track, left logical holes in your reasoning, or failed to develop one or more of your paragraphs.

Your outline doesn't have to use Roman numerals or be highly detailed. Just use an outline form that suits your style and shows you a bird's-eye view of your argument. Below is a form that we think you will find useful. Consult the academic essay diagram in Part 1 of this book, too, to remind yourself of the conventional form of a college essay and its basic parts.

I. Introductory Paragraph

    A. An opening sentence that gives the reading selection's title and author and begins to answer the first part of the writing topic:

        _____

        _____

        _____

    B. Main points to include in the directed summary:

        1.

        2.

        3.

        4.

C. Write out your thesis statement. (Look back to "Revising Your Thesis Statement," where you reexamined and refined your working thesis statement.) It should clearly state whether you agree with Gribben's claim about the connection between the lessons in fairy tales and human experiences.

_____

_____

II. Body Paragraphs

A. The paragraph's one main point that supports the thesis statement:

_____

1. Controlling idea sentence:

_____

_____

2. Corroborating details:

_____

_____

_____

_____

3. Careful explanation of why the details are relevant:

_____

_____

_____

_____

4. Connection to the thesis statement:

_____

_____

_____

B. The paragraph's one main point that supports the thesis statement:

_____

    1. **C**ontrolling idea sentence:

    _____

    _____

    2. **C**orroborating details:

    _____

    _____

    _____

    3. **C**areful explanation of why the details are relevant:

    _____

    _____

    _____

    _____

    4. **C**onnection to the thesis statement:

    _____

    _____

    _____

C. The paragraph's one main point that supports the thesis statement:

_____

    1. **C**ontrolling idea sentence:

    _____

    _____

2. Corroborating details:

_____

_____

_____

_____

3. Careful explanation of why the details are relevant:

_____

_____

_____

_____

_____

4. Connection to the thesis statement:

_____

_____

_____

D. The paragraph's one main point that supports the thesis statement:

_____

1. Controlling idea sentence:

_____

_____

2. Corroborating details:

_____

_____

_____

_____

3. **C**areful explanation of why the details are relevant:

_____

_____

_____

_____

_____

4. **C**onnection to the thesis statement:

_____

_____

_____

Repeat this form for any remaining body paragraphs.

III. Conclusion

A. Type of conclusion to be used (see "Conclusions" in Part 1):

_____

B. Key words or phrases to include:

_____

Getting Feedback on Your Draft

Use the following guidelines to give a classmate feedback on his or her draft. Read the draft through first, and then answer each of the items below as specifically as you can.

Name of draft's author: _____

Name of draft's reader: _____

The Introduction

1. Within the opening sentences:
   a. Gribben's first and last name are given.   yes   no
   b. The reading selection's title is given and
      placed within quotation marks.   yes   no

2. The opening contains a summary that:

   a. explains the connection Gribben believes exists
      between fairy tales and human experiences   yes   no
   b. identifies <u>at least one</u> specific example she uses
      to illustrate this connection   yes   no

3. The opening provides a thesis that makes clear
   the draft writer's opinion regarding Gribben's claim.   yes   no

If you circled yes in #3 above, copy the thesis below as it is written. If you circled no, explain to the draft writer what information is needed to make the thesis complete.

_____

_____

_____

The Body

1. How many paragraphs are in the body of this essay? _____

2. To support the thesis, this number is   sufficient   not enough

3. Do body paragraphs contain the 4Cs?

   Paragraph 1   Controlling idea sentence   yes   no
                  Corroborating details   yes   no

		yes	no
	Careful explanation of why the details are relevant	yes	no
	Connection to the thesis statement	yes	no
Paragraph 2	Controlling idea sentence	yes	no
	Corroborating details	yes	no
	Careful explanation of why the details are relevant	yes	no
	Connection to the thesis statement	yes	no
Paragraph 3	Controlling idea sentence	yes	no
	Corroborating details	yes	no
	Careful explanation of why the details are relevant	yes	no
	Connection to the thesis statement	yes	no
Paragraph 4	Controlling idea sentence	yes	no
	Corroborating details	yes	no
	Careful explanation of why the details are relevant	yes	no
	Connection to the thesis statement	yes	no
Paragraph 5	Controlling idea sentence	yes	no
	Corroborating details	yes	no
	Careful explanation of why the details are relevant	yes	no
	Connection to the thesis statement	yes	no

(Continue as needed.)

4. Identify any of the body paragraphs that are underdeveloped (too short).

_____

5. Identify any of the body paragraphs that fail to support the thesis.

_____

6. Identify any of the body paragraphs that are redundant or repetitive.

_____

7. Suggest any ideas for additional body paragraphs that might improve this essay.

_____

_____

_____

The Conclusion

1. Does the final paragraph avoid introducing new ideas
   and examples that really belong in the body of the essay?   yes   no

2. Does the conclusion provide closure (let readers know
   that the end of the essay has been reached)?   yes   no

3. Does the conclusion leave readers with an
   understanding of the significance of the argument?   yes   no

   State in your own words what the draft writer considers to be important about
   his or her argument.

   _____

   _____

   _____

4. Identify the type of conclusion used (see the guidelines for conclusions in Part 1).

   _____

Editing

1. During the editing process, the writer should pay attention to the following
   problems in sentence structure, punctuation, and mechanics:

   fragments
   fused (run-on) sentences
   misplaced and dangling modifiers
   comma splices
   misplaced, missing, and unnecessary commas
   misplaced, missing, and unnecessary apostrophes
   incorrect quotation mark use
   capitalization errors
   spelling errors

2. While editing, the writer should pay attention to the following areas of grammar:

   verb tense
   subject-verb agreement
   irregular verbs
   pronoun type
   pronoun reference
   pronoun agreement
   noun plurals
   prepositions

Final Draft Checklist

Content:

- My essay has an appropriate title.
- I provide an accurate summary of Gribben's argument concerning the connection between fairy tales and life.
- My thesis states a clear position that can be supported by evidence.
- I have enough paragraphs and argument points to support my thesis.
- Each body paragraph is relevant to my thesis.
- Each body paragraph contains the 4Cs.
- I use transitions whenever necessary to connect ideas.
- The final paragraph of my essay (the conclusion) provides readers with a sense of closure.

Grammar, Punctuation, and Mechanics:

- I use the present tense to discuss Gribben's argument and examples.
- I use verb tenses correctly to show the chronology of events.
- I have verb tense consistency throughout my sentences and paragraphs.
- I have checked for subject-verb agreement in all of my sentences.
- I have revised all fragments and mixed or garbled sentences.
- I have repaired all fused (run-on) sentences and comma splices.
- I have placed a comma after introductory elements (transitions and phrases) and all dependent clauses that open a sentence.
- If I present items in a series (nouns, verbs, prepositional phrases), they are parallel in form.
- If I include material spoken or written by someone other than myself, I have correctly punctuated it with quotation marks, using the MLA style guide's rules for citation.
- If I include material spoken or written by someone other than myself, I have included a works cited list that follows the MLA style guide's rules for citation.

Reviewing Your Graded Essay

After your instructor has returned your essay, you may have the opportunity to revise your paper and raise your grade. Many students, especially those whose essays receive nonpassing grades, feel that their instructors should be less "picky" about grammar and should pass the work on content alone. However, most students at this level have not yet acquired the ability to recognize quality writing, and they do not realize that content and writing actually cannot be separated in this way. Experienced instructors know that errors in sentence structure, grammar, punctuation, and word choice either interfere with content or distract readers so much that they lose track of content. In short, good ideas badly presented are no longer good ideas; to pass, an essay must have passable writing. So even if you are not submitting a revised version of this essay to your instructor, it is important that you review your work carefully in order to understand its strengths and weaknesses. This sheet will guide you through the evaluation process.

You will want to continue to use the techniques that worked well for you and to find strategies to overcome the problems that you identify in this sample of your writing. To recognize areas that might have been problematic for you, look back at the scoring rubric in this book. Match the numerical/verbal/letter grade received on your essay to the appropriate category. Study the rubric's explanation for your grade.

Write a few sentences below in which you identify your problems in each of the following areas. Then, suggest specific changes you could make that would improve your paper. Don't forget to use your handbook as a resource.

1. **Grammar/punctuation/mechanics**

    My problem:

    My strategy for change:

2. **Thesis/response to assignment**

    My problem:

    My strategy for change:

3. Organization

My problem:

My strategy for change:

4. Paragraph development/examples/reasoning

My problem:

My strategy for change:

5. Assessment

In the space below, assign a grade to your paper using the rubric in Part1 of this book. In other words, if your instructor assigned your essay a grade of *High Fail*, you might give it the letter grade you now feel the paper warrants. If your instructor used the traditional letter grade to evaluate the essay, choose a category from the rubric in this book, or any other grading scale that you are familiar with, to show your evaluation of your work. Then, write a short narrative explaining your evaluation of the essay and the reasons it received the grade you gave it.

Grade: _____

Narrative: _____

_____

_____

_____

_____

Extending the Discussion: Considering Other Viewpoints

Reading Selections

"Briar Rose" by the Grimm Brothers

"Hansel and Gretel" by the Grimm Brothers

"The Goose-Girl" by the Grimm Brothers

"Cap o' Rushes" an English Fairy Tale

"Cinderella; or, The Little Glass Slipper" by Charles Perrault

"Cinderella" by the Grimm Brothers

"Fairy Tales Are Good for Children" by G. K. Chesterton

"Change and Sexuality: Ursula and Ariel as Markers of Metamorphosis in *The Little Mermaid*" by Paul Beehler

"The Moral of the Story" by Alice Abler

"The World of Myths and Fairy Tales" by Julius E. Heuscher

Briar Rose

THE GRIMM BROTHERS

Jacob Ludwig Carl Grimm and his brother Wilhelm Carl Grimm were born in Hanau, Germany, in the late 1700s. Both brothers studied law at the University of Marburg, but it was their scholarly work on linguistics, folklore, and medieval studies that resulted in their most famous work, a two-volume collection of German legends titled Kinder- und Hausmärchen (Children's and Household Tales)*. The collection went through six editions during the Grimm brothers' lifetime.*

A king and queen once upon a time reigned in a country a great way off, where there were in those days fairies. Now this king and queen had plenty of money, and plenty of fine clothes to wear, and plenty of good things to eat and drink, and a coach to ride out in every day; but though they had been married many years they had no children, and this grieved them very much indeed. But one day as the queen was walking by the side of the river, at the bottom of the garden, she saw a poor little fish, that had thrown itself out of the water, and lay gasping and nearly dead on the bank. Then the queen took pity on the little fish, and threw it back again into the river; and before it swam away it lifted its head out of the water and said, "I know what your wish is, and it shall be fulfilled, in return for your kindness to me— you will soon have a daughter." What the little fish had foretold soon came to pass; and the queen had a little girl, so very beautiful that the king could not cease looking on it for joy, and said he would hold a great feast and make merry, and show the child to all the land. So he asked his kinsmen, and nobles, and friends, and neighbors. But the queen said, "I will have the fairies also, that they might be kind and good to our little daughter." Now there were thirteen fairies in the kingdom; but as the king and queen had only twelve golden dishes for them to eat out of, they were forced to leave one of the fairies without asking her. So twelve fairies came, each with a high red cap on her head, and red shoes with high heels on her feet, and a long white wand in her hand: and after the feast was over they gathered round in a ring and gave all their best gifts to the little princess. One gave her goodness, another beauty, another riches, and so on till she had all that was good in the world.

Just as eleven of them had done blessing her, a great noise was heard in the courtyard, and word was brought that the thirteenth fairy was come, with a black cap on her head, and black shoes on her feet, and a broomstick in her hand: and presently up she came into the dining-hall. Now, as she had not been asked to the feast she was very angry, and scolded the king and queen very much, and set to work to take her revenge. So she cried out, "The king's daughter shall, in her fifteenth year, be wounded by a spindle, and fall down dead." Then the twelfth of the friendly fairies, who had not yet given her gift, came forward, and said that the evil wish must be fulfilled, but that she could soften its mischief; so her gift was, that the king's daughter, when the spindle wounded her, should not really die, but should only fall asleep for a hundred years.

However, the king hoped still to save his dear child altogether from the threatened evil; so he ordered that all the spindles in the kingdom should be bought up and burnt. But all the gifts of the first eleven fairies were in the meantime fulfilled; for the princess was so beautiful, and well behaved, and good, and wise, that everyone who knew her loved her.

It happened that, on the very day she was fifteen years old, the king and queen were not at home, and she was left alone in the palace. So she roved about by herself, and looked at all the rooms and chambers, till at last she came to an old tower, to which there was a narrow staircase ending with a little door. In the door there was a golden key, and when she turned it the door sprang open, and there sat an old lady spinning away very busily. "Why, how now, good mother," said the princess; "what are you doing there?" "Spinning," said the old lady, and nodded her head, humming a tune, while buzz! went the wheel. "How prettily that little thing turns round!" said the princess, and took the spindle and began to try and spin. But scarcely had she touched it, before the fairy's prophecy was fulfilled; the spindle wounded her, and she fell down lifeless on the ground.

However, she was not dead, but had only fallen into a deep sleep; and the king and the queen, who had just come home, and all their court, fell asleep too; and the horses slept in the stables, and the dogs in the court, the pigeons on the house-top, and the very flies slept upon the walls. Even the fire on the hearth left off blazing, and went to sleep; the jack stopped, and the spit that was turning about with a goose upon it for the king's dinner stood still; and the cook, who was at that moment pulling the kitchen-boy by the hair to give him a box on the ear for something he had done amiss, let him go, and both fell asleep; the butler, who was slyly tasting the ale, fell asleep with the jug at his lips: and thus everything stood still, and slept soundly.

A large hedge of thorns soon grew round the palace, and every year it became higher and thicker; till at last the old palace was surrounded and hidden, so that not even the roof or the chimneys could be seen. But there went a report through all the land of the beautiful sleeping Briar Rose (for so the king's daughter was called): so that, from time to time, several kings' sons came, and tried to break through the thicket into the palace. This, however, none of them could ever do; for the thorns and bushes laid hold of them, as it were with hands; and there they stuck fast, and died wretchedly.

After many, many years, there came a king's son into that land, and an old man told him the story of the thicket of thorns, and that a beautiful palace stood behind it, and that a wonderful princess, called Briar Rose, lay in it asleep, with all her court. He told, too, that he had heard from his grandfather that many, many princes had come, and had tried to break through the thicket, but that they had all stuck fast in it, and died. Then the young prince said, "All this shall not frighten me; I will go and see this Briar Rose." The old man tried to hinder him, but he was bent upon going.

Now that very day the hundred years were ended; and as the prince came to the thicket he saw nothing but beautiful flowering shrubs, through which he went with ease, and they shut in after him as thick as ever. Then he came at last to the palace, and there in the court lay the dogs asleep; and the horses were standing in the stables; and on the roof sat the pigeons fast asleep, with their heads under their wings. And when he came into the palace, the flies were sleeping on the walls; the spit was standing still; the butler had the jug of ale at his lips, going to drink a draught; the maid sat with a fowl in her lap ready to be plucked; and the cook in the kitchen was still holding up her hand, as if she was going to beat the boy.

Then he went on still farther, and all was so still that he could hear every breath he drew; till at last he came to the old tower, and opened the door of the little room in which Briar Rose was; and there she lay, fast asleep on a couch by the window. She looked so beautiful that he could not take his eyes off her, so he stooped down and gave her a kiss. But the moment he kissed her she opened her eyes and awoke, and smiled upon him; and they went out together; and soon the king and queen also awoke, and all the court, and gazed on each other with great wonder. And the horses shook themselves, and the dogs jumped up and barked; the pigeons took their heads from under their wings, and looked about and flew into the fields; the flies on the walls buzzed again; the fire in the kitchen blazed up; round went the jack, and round went the spit, with the goose for the king's dinner upon it; the butler finished his draught of ale; the maid went on plucking the fowl; and the cook gave the boy the box on his ear.

And then the prince and Briar Rose were married, and the wedding feast was given; and they lived happily together all their lives long.

Discussion Questions

1. Discuss the ways that magic plays a part in the life of Briar Rose from her conception to her marriage.

2. Discuss the behavior of the thirteenth fairy. How might her role in the fairy tale be helpful to Gribben in her medical practice?

3. Discuss the coincidence of the prince's arriving on the very day the hundred years are ended and kissing Briar Rose as she awakens from her trance. Do you think this event in the fairy tale reinforces a harmful myth about romantic love, or is it merely presenting a satisfying ending? Explain your position.

Hansel and Gretel

THE GRIMM BROTHERS

Jacob Ludwig Carl Grimm and his brother Wilhelm Carl Grimm were born in Hanau, Germany, in the late 1700s. Both brothers studied law at the University of Marburg, but it was their scholarly work on linguistics, folklore, and medieval studies that resulted in their most famous work, a two-volume collection of German legends titled Children's and Household Tales. *The collection went through six editions during the Grimm brothers' lifetime.*

Hard by a great forest dwelt a poor wood-cutter with his wife and his two children. The boy was called Hansel and the girl Gretel. The man had little to bite and to break, and once when great dearth fell on the land, he could no longer procure even daily bread. Now when he thought over this by night in his bed, and tossed about in his anxiety, he groaned and said to his wife: "What is to become of us? How are we to feed our poor children, when we no longer have anything even for ourselves?" "I'll tell you what, husband," answered the woman, "early to-morrow morning we will take the children out into the forest to where it is the thickest; there we will light a fire for them, and give each of them one more piece of bread, and then we will go to our work and leave them alone. They will not find the way home again, and we shall be rid of them." "No, wife," said the man, "I will not do that; how can I bear to leave my children alone in the forest—the wild animals would soon come and tear them to pieces." "O, you fool!" said she, "then we must all four die of hunger, you may as well plane the planks for our coffins," and she left him no peace until he consented. "But I feel very sorry for the poor children, all the same," said the man.

The two children had also not been able to sleep for hunger, and had heard what their step-mother had said to their father. Gretel wept bitter tears, and said to Hansel: "Now all is over with us." "Be quiet, Gretel," said Hansel, "do not distress yourself, I will soon find a way to help us." And when the old folks had fallen asleep, he got up, put on his little coat, opened the door below, and crept outside. The moon shone brightly, and the white pebbles which lay in front of the house glittered like real silver pennies. Hansel stooped and stuffed the little pocket of his coat with as many as he could get in. Then he went back and said to Gretel: "Be comforted, dear little sister, and sleep in peace, God will not forsake us," and he lay down again in his bed. When day dawned, but before the sun had risen, the woman came and awoke the two children, saying: "Get up, you sluggards! We are going into the forest to fetch wood." She gave each a little piece of bread, and said: "There is something for your dinner, but do not eat it up before then, for you will get nothing else." Gretel took the bread under her apron, as Hansel had the pebbles in his pocket. Then they all set out together on the way to the forest. When they had walked a short time, Hansel stood still and peeped back at the house, and did so again and again. His father said: "Hansel, what are you looking at there and staying behind for? Pay attention, and do not forget how to use your legs." "Ah, father," said Hansel, "I am looking at my little white cat, which is sitting up on the roof, and wants to say good-bye to me." The wife said: "Fool, that is not your little cat, that is the morning sun which is shining on the chimneys." Hansel, however, had not been looking back at the cat, but had been constantly throwing one of the white pebble-stones out of his pocket on the road.

When they had reached the middle of the forest, the father said: "Now, children, pile up some wood, and I will light a fire that you may not be cold." Hansel and Gretel gathered brushwood together, as high as a little hill. The brushwood was lighted, and when the flames were burning very high, the woman said: "Now, children, lay yourselves down by the fire and rest, we will go into the forest and cut some wood. When we have done, we will come back and fetch you away."

Hansel and Gretel sat by the fire, and when noon came, each ate a little piece of bread, and as they heard the strokes of the wood-axe they believed that their father was near. It was not the axe, however, but a branch which he had fastened to a withered tree which the wind was blowing backwards and forwards. And as they had been sitting such a long time, their eyes closed with fatigue, and they fell fast asleep. When at last they awoke, it was already dark night. Gretel began to cry and said: "How are we to get out of the forest now?" But Hansel comforted her and said: "Just wait a little, until the moon has risen, and then we will soon find the way." And when the full moon had risen, Hansel took his little sister by the hand, and followed the pebbles which shone like newly-coined silver pieces, and showed them the way.

They walked the whole night long, and by break of day came once more to their father's house. They knocked at the door, and when the woman opened it and saw that it was Hansel and Gretel, she said: "You naughty children, why have you slept so long in the forest—we thought you were never coming back at all!" The father, however, rejoiced, for it had cut him to the heart to leave them behind alone.

Not long afterwards, there was once more great dearth throughout the land, and the children heard their mother saying at night to their father: "Everything is eaten again, we have one half loaf left, and that is the end. The children must go, we will take them farther into the wood, so that they will not find their way out again; there is no other means of saving ourselves!" The man's heart was heavy, and he thought: "It would be better for you to share the last mouthful with your children." The woman, however, would listen to nothing that he had to say, but scolded and reproached him. He who says A must say B, likewise, and as he had yielded the first time, he had to do so a second time also.

The children, however, were still awake and had heard the conversation. When the old folks were asleep, Hansel again got up, and wanted to go out and pick up pebbles as he had done before, but the woman had locked the door, and Hansel could not get out. Nevertheless he comforted his little sister, and said: "Do not cry, Gretel, go to sleep quietly, the good God will help us."

Early in the morning came the woman, and took the children out of their beds. Their piece of bread was given to them, but it was still smaller than the time before. On the way into the forest Hansel crumbled his in his pocket, and often stood still and threw a morsel on the ground. "Hansel, why do you stop and look round" said the father, "go on." "I am looking back at my little pigeon which is sitting on the roof, and wants to say good-bye to me," answered Hansel. "Fool!" said the woman, "that is not your little pigeon, that is the morning sun that is shining on the chimney." Hansel, however, little by little, threw all the crumbs on the path.

The woman led the children still deeper into the forest, where they had never in their lives been before. Then a great fire was again made, and the mother said: "Just sit there, you children, and when you are tired you may sleep a little; we are going into the forest to cut wood, and in the evening when we are done, we will come and fetch you away." When it was noon, Gretel shared her piece of bread with Hansel, who had scattered his by the way. Then they fell asleep and evening passed, but no one came to the poor children. They did not awake until it was dark night, and Hansel comforted his little sister and said: "Just wait, Gretel, until the moon rises, and then we shall see the crumbs of bread which I have strewn about, they will show us our way home again." When the moon came they set out, but they found no crumbs, for the many thousands of birds which fly about in the woods and fields had picked them all up.

Hansel said to Gretel: "We shall soon find the way," but they did not find it. They walked the whole night and all the next day too from morning till evening, but they did not get out of the forest, and were very hungry, for they had nothing to eat but two or three berries, which grew on the ground. And as they were so weary that their legs would carry them no longer, they lay down beneath a tree and fell asleep.

It was now three mornings since they had left their father's house. They began to walk again, but they always came deeper into the forest, and if help did not come soon, they must die of hunger and weariness. When it was mid-day, they saw a beautiful snow-white bird sitting on a bough, which sang so delightfully that they stood still and listened to it. And when its song was over, it spread its wings and flew away before them, and they followed it until they reached a little house, on the roof of which it alighted; and when they approached the little house they saw that it was built of bread and covered with cakes, but that the windows were of clear sugar. "We will set to work on that," said Hansel, "and have a good meal. I will eat a bit of the roof, and you Gretel, can eat some of the window, it will taste sweet." Hansel reached up above, and broke off a little of the roof to try how it tasted, and Gretel leant against the window and nibbled at the panes. Then a soft voice cried from the parlor:

"Nibble, nibble, gnaw,
Who is nibbling at my little house?"

The children answered:

"The wind, the wind,
The heaven-born wind,"

and went on eating without disturbing themselves. Hansel, who liked the taste of the roof, tore down a great piece of it, and Gretel pushed out the whole of one round window-pane, sat down, and enjoyed herself with it. Suddenly the door opened, and a woman as old as the hills, who supported herself on crutches, came creeping out. Hansel and Gretel were so terribly frightened that they let fall what they had in their hands. The old woman, however, nodded her head, and said:

"Oh, you dear children, who has brought you here. Do come in, and stay with me. No harm shall happen to you." She took them both by the hand, and led them into her little house. Then good food was set before them, milk and pancakes, with sugar, apples, and nuts. Afterwards two pretty little beds were covered with clean white linen, and Hansel and Gretel lay down in them, and thought they were in heaven.

The old woman had only pretended to be so kind; she was in reality a wicked witch, who lay in wait for children, and had only built the little house of bread in order to entice them there. When a child fell into her power, she killed it, cooked and ate it, and that was a feast day with her. Witches have red eyes, and cannot see far, but they have a keen scent like the beasts, and are aware when human beings draw near. When Hansel and Gretel came into her neighborhood, she laughed with malice, and said mockingly: "I have them, they shall not escape me again!" Early in the morning before the children were awake, she was already up, and when she saw both of them sleeping and looking so pretty, with their plump and rosy cheeks, she muttered to herself: "That will be a dainty mouthfull." Then she seized Hansel with her shriveled hand, carried him into a little stable, and locked him in behind a grated door. Scream as he might, it would not help him. Then she went to Gretel, shook her till she awoke, and cried: "Get up, lazy thing, fetch some water, and cook something good for your brother, he is in the stable outside, and is to be made fat. When he is fat, I will eat him." Gretel began to weep bitterly, but it was all in vain, for she was forced to do what the wicked witch commanded.

And now the best food was cooked for poor Hansel, but Gretel got nothing but crab-shells. Every morning the woman crept to the little stable, and cried: "Hansel, stretch out your finger that I may feel if you will soon be fat." Hansel, however, stretched out a little bone to her, and the old woman, who had dim eyes, could not see it, and thought it was Hansel's finger, and was astonished that there was no way of fattening him. When four weeks had gone by, and Hansel still remained thin, she was seized with impatience and would not wait any longer. "Now, then, Gretel," she cried to the girl, "stir yourself, and bring some water. Let Hansel be fat or lean, to-morrow I will kill him, and cook him." Ah, how the poor little sister did lament when she had to fetch the water, and how her tears did flow down her cheeks! "Dear God, do help us," she cried. "If the wild beasts in the forest had but devoured us, we should at any rate have died together." "Just keep your noise to yourself," said the old woman, "it won't help you at all."

Early in the morning, Gretel had to go out and hang up the cauldron with the water, and light the fire. "We will bake first," said the old woman, "I have already heated the oven, and kneaded the dough." She pushed poor Gretel out to the oven, from which flames of fire were already darting. "Creep in," said the witch, "and see if it is properly heated, so that we can put the bread in." And once Gretel was inside, she intended to shut the oven and let her bake in it, and then she would eat her, too. But Gretel saw what she had in mind, and said: "I do not know how I am to do it; how do I get in?" "Silly goose," said the old woman. "The door is big enough; just look, I can get in myself!" and she crept up and thrust her head into the oven. Then Gretel gave her a push that drove her far into it, and shut the iron door, and fastened the bolt. Oh then she began to howl quite horribly, but Gretel ran away, and the godless witch was miserably burnt to death.

Gretel, however, ran like lightning to Hansel, opened his little stable, and cried: "Hansel, we are saved! The old witch is dead!" Then Hansel sprang like a bird from its cage when the door is opened. How they did rejoice and embrace each other, and dance about and kiss each other! And as they had no longer any need to fear her, they went into the witch's house, and in every corner there stood chests full of pearls and jewels. "These are far better than pebbles!" said Hansel, and thrust into his pockets whatever could be got in, and Gretel said: "I, too, will take something home with me," and filled her pinafore full. "But now we must be off," said Hansel, "that we may get out of the witch's forest."

When they had walked for two hours, they came to a great stretch of water. "We cannot cross," said Hansel, "I see no footplank, and no bridge." "And there is also no ferry," answered Gretel, "but a white duck is swimming there; if I ask her, she will help us over." Then she cried:

> "Little duck, little duck, dost thou see,
> Hansel and Gretel are waiting for thee?
> There's never a plank, or bridge in sight,
> Take us across on thy back so white."

The duck came to them, and Hansel seated himself on its back, and told his sister to sit by him. "No," replied Gretel, "that will be too heavy for the little duck; she shall take us across, one after the other." The good little duck did so, and when they were once safely across and had walked for a short time, the forest seemed to be more and more familiar to them, and at length they saw from afar their father's house. Then they began to run, rushed into the parlor, and threw themselves round their father's neck. The man had not known one happy hour since he had left the children in the forest; the woman, however, was dead. Gretel emptied her pinafore until pearls and precious stones ran about the room, and Hansel threw one handful after another out of his pocket to add to them. Then all anxiety was at an end, and they lived together in perfect happiness.

Discussion Questions

1. Why do their mother and father leave Hansel and Gretel in the woods alone? Relate some of the possible modern day scenarios of child abandonment, similar to those you have seen on the news, that Gribben might encounter. In what ways might the contemporary cases seem similar to "Hansel and Gretel"? In what ways are they different?

2. Discuss some of the medical cases Gribben mentions that might cause her to reflect on the story of "Hansel and Gretel." What in particular about this fairy tale might seem pertinent to her?

3. Do you think this fairy tale could provide comfort to doctors like Gribben and to readers like yourself? Explain your view.

The Goose-Girl

THE GRIMM BROTHERS

There once lived an old queen whose husband had been dead for many years, and she had a beautiful daughter. When the princess grew up she was promised in marriage to a prince who lived far away. When the time came for her to be married, and she had to depart for the distant kingdom, the old queen packed up for her many costly vessels and utensils of silver and gold, and trinkets also of gold and silver, and cups and jewels, in short, everything that belonged to a royal dowry, for she loved her child with all her heart.

She likewise assigned to her a chambermaid, who was to ride with her, and deliver her into the hands of the bridegroom. Each received a horse for the journey. The princess's horse was called Falada, and could speak. When the hour of departure had come, the old mother went into her bedroom, took a small knife and cut her fingers with it until they bled. Then she held out a small white cloth and let three drops of blood fall into it. She gave them to her daughter, saying, "Take good care of these. They will be of service to you on your way."

Thus they sorrowfully took leave of one another. The princess put the cloth into her bosom, mounted her horse, and set forth for her bridegroom. After they had ridden for a while she felt a burning thirst, and said to her chambermaid, "Dismount, and take my cup which you have brought with you for me, and get me some water from the brook, for I would like a drink."

"If you are thirsty," said the chambermaid, "get off your horse yourself, and lie down near the water and drink. I won't be your servant."

So in her great thirst the princess dismounted, bent down over the water in the brook and drank; and she was not allowed to drink out of the golden cup. Then she said, "Oh, Lord," and the three drops of blood answered, "If your mother knew this, her heart would break in two." But the king's daughter was humble. She said nothing and mounted her horse again. They rode some miles further. The day was warm, the sun beat down, and she again grew thirsty. When they came to a stream of water, she again called to her chambermaid, "Dismount, and give me some water in my golden cup," for she had long ago forgotten the girl's evil words.

But the chambermaid said still more haughtily, "If you want a drink, get it yourself. I won't be your servant."

Then in her great thirst the king's daughter dismounted, bent over the flowing water, wept, and said, "Oh, Lord," and the drops of blood again replied, "If your mother knew this, her heart would break in two."

As she was thus drinking, leaning over the stream, the cloth with the three drops of blood fell from her bosom and floated away with the water, without her taking notice of it, so great were her concerns. However, the chambermaid saw what had happened, and she rejoiced to think that she now had power over the bride, for by losing the drops of blood, the princess had become weak and powerless.

When she wanted to mount her horse again, the one that was called Falada, the chambermaid said, "I belong on Falada. You belong on my nag," and the princess had to accept it.

Then with many harsh words the chambermaid ordered the princess to take off her own royal clothing and put on the chambermaid's shabby clothes. And in the end the princess had to swear under the open heaven that she would not say one word of this to anyone at the royal court. If she had not taken this oath, she would have been killed on the spot. Falada saw everything, and remembered it well.

The chambermaid now climbed onto Falada, and the true bride onto the bad horse, and thus they traveled onwards, until finally they arrived at the royal palace. There was great rejoicing over their arrival, and the prince ran ahead to meet them, then lifted the chambermaid from her horse, thinking she was his bride.

She was led upstairs, while the real princess was left standing below. Then the old king looked out of the window and saw her waiting in the courtyard, and noticed how fine and delicate and beautiful she was, so at once he went to the royal apartment, and asked the bride about the girl she had with her who was standing down below in the courtyard, and who she was.

"I picked her up on my way for a companion. Give the girl some work to do, so she won't stand idly by."

However, the old king had no work for her, and knew of nothing else to say but, "I have a little boy who tends the geese. She can help him." The boy was called Kürdchen (Little Conrad), and the true bride had to help him tend geese.

Soon afterwards the false bride said to the young king, "Dearest husband, I beg you to do me a favor." He answered, "I will do so gladly."

"Then send for the knacker, and have the head of the horse which I rode here cut off, for it angered me on the way." In truth, she was afraid that the horse might tell how she had behaved toward the king's daughter.

Thus it happened that faithful Falada had to die. The real princess heard about this, and she secretly promised to pay the knacker a piece of gold if he would perform a small service for her. In the town there was a large dark gateway, through which she had to pass with the geese each morning and evening. Would he be so good as to nail Falada's head beneath the gateway, so that she might see him again and again?

The knacker's helper promised to do that, and cut off the head, and nailed it securely beneath the dark gateway. Early in the morning, when she and Conrad drove out their flock beneath this gateway, she said in passing, "Alas, Falada, hanging there!"

Then the head answered:

> Alas, young queen, passing by,
> If this your mother knew,
> Her heart would break in two.

Then they went still further out of the town, driving their geese into the country. And when they came to the meadow, she sat down and unbound her hair which was of pure gold. Conrad saw it, was delighted how it glistened, and wanted to pluck out a few hairs. Then she said:

> Blow, wind, blow,
> Take Conrad's hat,
> And make him chase it,
> Until I have braided my hair,
> And tied it up again.

Then such a strong wind came up that it blew Conrad's hat across the fields, and he had to run after it. When he came back, she was already finished combing and putting up her hair, so he could not get even one strand. So Conrad became angry, and would not speak to her, and thus they tended the geese until evening, and then they went home.

The next morning when they were driving the geese out through the dark gateway, the maiden said, "Alas, Falada, hanging there!"

Falada answered:

> Alas, young queen, passing by,
> If this your mother knew,
> Her heart would break in two.

She sat down again in the field and began combing out her hair. When Conrad ran up and tried to take hold of some, she quickly said:

> Blow, wind, blow,
> Take Conrad's hat,
> And make him chase it,
> Until I have braided my hair,
> And tied it up again.

Then the wind blew, taking the hat off his head and far away. Conrad had to run after it, and when he came back, she had already put up her hair, and he could not get a single strand.

Then they tended the geese until evening.

That evening, after they had returned home, Conrad went to the old king and said, "I won't tend geese with that girl any longer."

"Why not?" asked the old king.

"Oh, because she angers me all day long."

Then the old king ordered him to tell what it was that she did to him. Conrad said, "In the morning when we pass beneath the dark gateway with the flock, there is a horse's head on the wall, and she says to it, 'Alas, Falada, hanging there!' And the head replies:

> 'Alas, young queen, passing by,
> If this your mother knew,
> Her heart would break in two.'"

Then Conrad went on to tell what happened at the goose pasture, and how he had to chase his hat.

The old king ordered him to drive his flock out again the next day. As soon as morning came, he himself sat down behind the dark gateway, and heard how the girl spoke with Falada's head. Then he followed her out into the country and hid himself in a thicket in the meadow. There he soon saw with his own eyes the goose-girl and the goose-boy bringing their flock, and how after a while she sat down and took down her hair, which glistened brightly. Soon she said:

> Blow, wind, blow,
> Take Conrad's hat,
> And make him chase it,
> Until I have braided my hair,
> And tied it up again.

Then came a blast of wind and carried off Conrad's hat, so that he had to run far away, while the maiden quietly went on combing and braiding her hair, all of which the king observed. Then, quite unseen, he went away, and when the goose-girl came home in the evening, he called her aside, and asked why she did all these things.

"I am not allowed to tell you, nor can I reveal my sorrows to any human being, for I have sworn under the open heaven not to do so, and if I had not so sworn, I would have been killed."

He urged her and left her no peace, but he could get nothing from her. Finally he said, "If you will not tell me anything, then tell your sorrows to the iron stove there," and he went away. So she crept into the iron stove, and began to cry sorrowfully, pouring out her whole heart. She said, "Here I sit, abandoned by the whole world, although I am the daughter of a king. A false chambermaid forced me to take off my royal clothes, and she has taken my place with my bridegroom. Now I have to do common work as a goose-girl. If my mother knew this, her heart would break in two."

The old king was standing outside listening by the stovepipe, and he heard what she said. Then he came back inside, and asked her to come out of the stove. Then they dressed her in royal clothes, and it was marvelous how beautiful she was.

The old king summoned his son and revealed to him that he had a false bride who was only a chambermaid, but that the true one was standing there, the one who had been a goose-girl. The young king rejoiced with all his heart when he saw her beauty and virtue. A great feast was made ready to which all the people and all good friends were invited.

At the head of the table sat the bridegroom with the king's daughter on one side of him, and the chambermaid on the other. However, the chambermaid was deceived, for she did not recognize the princess in her dazzling attire. After they had eaten and drunk, and were in a good mood, the old king asked the chambermaid as a riddle, what punishment a person deserved who had deceived her master in such and such a manner, then told the whole story, asking finally, "What sentence does such a person deserve?"

The false bride said, "She deserves no better fate than to be stripped stark naked, and put in a barrel that is studded inside with sharp nails. Two white horses should be hitched to it, and they should drag her along through one street after another, until she is dead."

"You are the one," said the old king, "and you have pronounced your own sentence. Thus shall it be done to you."

After the sentence had been carried out, the young king married his true bride, and both of them ruled over their kingdom in peace and happiness.

Discussion Questions

1. How is nature portrayed in "The Goose-Girl"? Compare it to the portrayal of nature in "Hansel and Gretel."

2. What advice does the goose-girl's mother give her when she leaves home? What results from her failure to heed her mother's advice?

3. What specific actions by the goose-girl lead to the tale's happy ending? How is justice defined by this ending?

4. How do you think Gribben would talk about this tale? What aspects in this tale might she find relevant to her own life experiences? With a classmate, discuss the relevance of this tale to your own experiences and then share your views with the class.

Cap o' Rushes

Reading Selection

AN ENGLISH FAIRY TALE

Once upon a time, there was a very rich gentleman who had three daughters. One day, he thought he'd find out how much they loved him. So he said to the first, "How much do you love me, my dear?"

"Why," she said, "as much as I love life itself."

"That's good," he said.

Then said to the second, "How much do you love me, my dear?"

"Why," she said, "better than all of the world."

Finally, he said to the third, "How much do you love me, my dear?"

"Why, I love you as fresh meat loves salt," she said.

This answer infuriated him.

"You don't love me at all," he said, "you can't live in this house anymore."

So she went away a great distance until she came to a fen. There she gathered some rushes and made them into a cloak with a hood to cover her from head to foot and to hide her fancy clothes. Then she continued on until she came to a grand house.

"Do you want a maid?" she asked.

"No," the servants answered.

"I don't have anywhere to go," she said, "and I don't need any money. I'll do any sort of work."

"Okay," they said, "You can wash all of the dishes." So she stayed and washed the pots and scraped the saucepans and did all of the dirty work. Because she gave no name, they called her Cap o' Rushes.

One day there was to be a great dance nearby, and the servants went. They invited her too, but Cap o' Rushes said she was too tired to go.

But when everyone else had gone, she took off her cloak, cleaned herself up, and went to the dance. And no one was as beautifully dressed as she.

Well, who should be at the dance but her master's son. He fell in love with her the minute he set eyes on her. He wouldn't dance with anyone else.

But before the dance was done, Cap o' Rushes crept off home and put her cloak back on. When the other maids came back, she pretended to be asleep.

From *English Fairy Tales* by Joseph Jacobs, 1890.

The next morning they said to her, "You missed something grand!"

"What was that?" she asked.

"The most beautiful lady you'll ever see, dressed in the fanciest clothes. The young master, he never took his eyes off her."

"Well, I should have liked to have seen her," said Cap o' Rushes.

"There's to be another dance this evening, and perhaps she'll be there."

But Cap o' Rushes said she was too tired to go with them to the dance. Once they had gone, though, she took off he cloak once again and cleaned herself, and away she went to the dance.

The master's son had been hoping to see her. He danced with no one else and never took his eyes off her. But, before the dance was over, she crept away. When the maids came back, she pretended to be asleep.

The next day they said to her again, "Well, Cap o' Rushes, you should have been there to see the lady. The young master never took his eyes off her."

"Well," she said, "I should liked to have seen her."

They said, "There's a dance again this evening. You must go with us, for she's sure to be there."

That evening, Cap o' Rushes said she was too tired to go. But when they had gone, she took off her cloak, cleaned herself, and away she went to the dance.

The master's son was so happy when he saw her. When she wouldn't tell him her name, or where she came from, he gave her a ring and told her if he didn't see her again he would die.

Before the dance was over, she slipped off. When the maids came home, she pretended to be asleep with her cap o' rushes on.

The next day they said to her, "There, Cap o' Rushes, you didn't come last night, and now you won't see the lady, for there's no more dances."

"That's too bad," she said.

The master's son tried every way to find out where the lady had gone, but he had no luck. Finally, he took ill to his bed because he was so lovesick.

"Make some porridge for the young master," the maids said to the cook. "He's dying for the love of the lady."

The cook had started making the porridge when Cap o' Rushes came in.

"What are you doing?" she asked.

"I'm going to make some porridge for the young master," said the cook, "for he's dying for love of the lady."

"Let me make it," said Cap o' Rushes.

The cook wouldn't agree at first, but at last she said yes. And Cap o' Rushes made the porridge. When it had finished cooking, she slipped the ring into it before the cook took it upstairs.

The young man ate the porridge and then saw the ring at the bottom of the bowl.

"Who made this porridge?" he asked the cook.

"I did," said the cook, lying because she was frightened.

"No, you didn't," he said. "Tell me who made it!"

"Well, then, it was Cap o' Rushes," the cook said.

"Send her here," he said.

When Cap o' Rushes came, he asked, "Did you make my porridge?"

"Yes, I did," she said.

"Where did you get this ring?" he asked.

"From the person who gave it to me," she said. And she took off her cap o' rushes, and there she was in her beautiful clothes.

Well, the master's son quickly got well, and they were to be married right away. It was to be a very grand wedding. Cap o' Rushes's father was asked. But she had never told anybody who she was.

Before the wedding, she went to the cook, and said, "I want you to dress every dish without a bit of salt."

"That'll be rather nasty," said the cook.

"That doesn't matter," she replied.

The wedding day came and they were married. After the ceremony, all of the guests sat down to eat. When they tried the meat, it was so tasteless they couldn't eat it. Cap o' Rushes's father tried first one dish, then another, and then burst out crying.

"What is the matter?" asked the master's son.

"I had a daughter and when I asked her how much she loved me, she said, 'As much as fresh meat loves salt.' I kicked her out of the house, for I thought she didn't love me. Now I see she loved me best of all. She may be dead for all I know."

"No, Father, here she is!" said Cap o' Rushes. And she went up to him, put her arms around him, and gave him a giant bear hug.

And they were all happy forever after.

Discussion Questions

1. What similarities and differences do you notice between this tale and the familiar version of "Cinderella"?

2. Discuss the difference of agency in the characters of Cinderella and Cap o' Rushes. Which character is more self-sufficient? Which character seems more in line with our contemporary view of women? Which character or story do you prefer? Explain.

3. Describe the behavior of the father at the beginning and end of this tale. Do you think that Cap o' Rushes contributed in any way to her banishment? What could or should she have done to prevent her punishment?

4. List the characters in this fairy tale and explain how Gribben might qualify them as one of what she calls the "eternal cast of characters."

Cinderella; or, The Little Glass Slipper

Reading Selection

CHARLES PERRAULT

Charles Perrault was born in 1628 and died in 1703. He was a French author and a member of l'Académie française. He is known for his foundational work with what was at that time a new literary genre, the fairy tale. His best-known tales include "Little Red Riding Hood," "The Sleeping Beauty," and "Cinderella," which is presented here. The Brothers Grimm rewrote many of Perrault's stories, and Disney adapted some of them into films.

Once there was a gentleman who married, for his second wife, the proudest and most haughty woman that was ever seen. She had, by a former husband, two daughters of her own, who were, indeed, exactly like her in all things. He had likewise, by another wife, a young daughter, but of unparalleled goodness and sweetness of temper, which she took from her mother, who was the best creature in the world.

No sooner were the ceremonies of the wedding over but the stepmother began to show herself in her true colors. She could not bear the good qualities of this pretty girl, and the less because they made her own daughters appear the more odious. She employed her in the meanest work of the house. The girl scoured the dishes, tables, etc., and cleaned madam's chamber, and those of misses, her daughters. She slept in a sorry garret, on a wretched straw bed, while her sisters slept in fine rooms, with floors all inlaid, on beds of the very newest fashion, and where they had looking glasses so large that they could see themselves at their full length from head to foot.

The poor girl bore it all patiently, and dared not tell her father, who would have scolded her; for his wife governed him entirely. When she had done her work, she used to go to the chimney corner, and sit down there in the cinders and ashes, which caused her to be called Cinderwench. Only the younger sister, who was not so rude and uncivil as the older one, called her Cinderella. However, Cinderella, notwithstanding her coarse apparel, was a hundred times more beautiful than her sisters, although they were always dressed very richly.

It happened that the king's son gave a ball, and invited all persons of fashion to it. Our young misses were also invited, for they

From *The Fairy Tales of Charles Perrault* by Charles Perrault, 1922.

cut a very grand figure among those of quality. They were mightily delighted at this invitation, and wonderfully busy in selecting the gowns, petticoats, and hair dressing that would best become them. This was a new difficulty for Cinderella; for it was she who ironed her sister's linen and pleated their ruffles. They talked all day long of nothing but how they should be dressed.

"For my part," said the eldest, "I will wear my red velvet suit with French trimming."

"And I," said the youngest, "shall have my usual petticoat; but then, to make amends for that, I will put on my gold-flowered cloak, and my diamond stomacher, which is far from being the most ordinary one in the world."

They sent for the best hairdresser they could get to make up their headpieces and adjust their hairdos, and they had their red brushes and patches from Mademoiselle de la Poche.

They also consulted Cinderella in all these matters, for she had excellent ideas, and her advice was always good. Indeed, she even offered her services to fix their hair, which they very willingly accepted. As she was doing this, they said to her, "Cinderella, would you not like to go to the ball?"

"Alas!" said she, "you only jeer me; it is not for such as I am to go to such a place."

"You are quite right," they replied. "It would make the people laugh to see a Cinderwench at a ball."

Anyone but Cinderella would have fixed their hair awry, but she was very good, and dressed them perfectly well. They were so excited that they hadn't eaten a thing for almost two days. Then they broke more than a dozen laces trying to have themselves laced up tightly enough to give them a fine slender shape. They were continually in front of their looking glass. At last the happy day came. They went to court, and Cinderella followed them with her eyes as long as she could. When she lost sight of them, she started to cry.

Her godmother, who saw her all in tears, asked her what was the matter.

"I wish I could. I wish I could." She was not able to speak the rest, being interrupted by her tears and sobbing.

This godmother of hers, who was a fairy, said to her, "You wish that you could go to the ball; is it not so?"

"Yes," cried Cinderella, with a great sigh.

"Well," said her godmother, "be but a good girl, and I will contrive that you shall go." Then she took her into her chamber, and said to her, "Run into the garden, and bring me a pumpkin."

Cinderella went immediately to gather the finest she could get, and brought it to her godmother, not being able to imagine how this pumpkin could help her go to the ball. Her godmother scooped out all the inside of it, leaving nothing but the rind. Having done this, she struck the pumpkin with her wand, and it was instantly turned into a fine coach, gilded all over with gold.

She then went to look into her mousetrap, where she found six mice, all alive, and ordered Cinderella to lift up a little the trapdoor. She gave each mouse, as it went out, a little tap with her wand, and the mouse was that moment turned into a fine horse, which altogether made a very fine set of six horses of a beautiful mouse-colored dapple gray.

Being at a loss for a coachman, Cinderella said, "I will go and see if there is not a rat in the rat trap that we can turn into a coachman."

"You are right," replied her godmother. "Go and look."

Cinderella brought the trap to her, and in it there were three huge rats. The fairy chose the one which had the largest beard, touched him with her wand, and turned him into a fat, jolly coachman, who had the smartest whiskers that eyes ever beheld.

After that, she said to Cinderella, "Go again into the garden, and you will find six lizards behind the watering pot. Bring them to me."

She had no sooner done so but her godmother turned them into six footmen, who skipped up immediately behind the coach, with their liveries all bedaubed with gold and silver, and clung as close behind each other as if they had done nothing else their whole lives. The fairy then said to Cinderella, "Well, you see here an equipage fit to go to the ball with; are you not pleased with it?"

"Oh, yes," she cried; "but must I go in these nasty rags?"

Her godmother then touched her with her wand, and, at the same instant, her clothes turned into cloth of gold and silver, all beset with jewels. This done, her godmother gave her a pair of glass slippers, the prettiest in the whole world. Being thus decked out, she got up into her coach; but her godmother, above all things, commanded her not to stay past midnight, telling her, at the same time, that if she stayed one moment longer, the coach would be a pumpkin again, her horses mice, her coachman a rat, her footmen lizards, and that her clothes would become just as they were before.

She promised her godmother to leave the ball before midnight; and then drove away, scarcely able to contain herself for joy. The king's son, who was told that a great princess, whom nobody knew, had arrived, ran out to receive her. He gave her his hand as she alighted from the coach, and led her into the hall, among all the company. There was immediately a profound silence. Everyone stopped dancing, and the violins ceased to play, so entranced was everyone with the singular beauties of the unknown newcomer.

Nothing was then heard but a confused noise of, "How beautiful she is! How beautiful she is!"

The king himself, old as he was, could not help watching her, and telling the queen softly that it was a long time since he had seen so beautiful and lovely a creature.

All the ladies were busied in considering her clothes and headdress, hoping to have some made next day after the same pattern, provided they could find such fine materials and as able hands to make them.

The king's son led her to the most honorable seat, and afterwards took her out to dance with him. She danced so very gracefully that they all more and more admired her. A fine meal was served up, but the young prince ate not a morsel, so intently was he busied in gazing on her.

She went and sat down by her sisters, showing them a thousand civilities, giving them part of the oranges and citrons which the prince had presented her with, which very much surprised them, for they did not know her. While Cinderella was thus amusing her sisters, she heard the clock strike eleven and three-quarters, whereupon she immediately made a courtesy to the company and hurried away as fast as she could.

Arriving home, she ran to seek out her godmother, and, after having thanked her, she said she could not but heartily wish she might go to the ball the next day as well, because the king's son had invited her.

As she was eagerly telling her godmother everything that had happened at the ball, her two sisters knocked at the door, which Cinderella ran and opened.

"You stayed such a long time!" she cried, gaping, rubbing her eyes and stretching herself as if she had been sleeping; she had not, however, had any manner of inclination to sleep while they were away from home.

"If you had been at the ball," said one of her sisters, "you would not have been tired with it. The finest princess was there, the most beautiful that mortal eyes have ever seen. She showed us a thousand civilities, and gave us oranges and citrons."

Cinderella seemed very indifferent in the matter. Indeed, she asked them the name of that princess; but they told her they did not know it, and that the king's son was very uneasy on her account and would give all the world to know who she was. At this Cinderella, smiling, replied, "She must, then, be very beautiful indeed; how happy you have been! Could not I see her? Ah, dear Charlotte, do lend me your yellow dress which you wear every day."

"Yes, to be sure!" cried Charlotte; "lend my clothes to such a dirty Cinderwench as you are! I should be such a fool."

Cinderella, indeed, well expected such an answer, and was very glad of the refusal; for she would have been sadly put to it, if her sister had lent her what she asked for jestingly.

The next day the two sisters were at the ball, and so was Cinderella, but dressed even more magnificently than before. The king's son was always by her, and never ceased his compliments and kind speeches to her. All this was so far from being tiresome to her, and, indeed, she quite forgot what her godmother had told her. She thought that it was no later than eleven when she counted the clock striking twelve. She jumped up and fled, as nimble as a deer. The prince followed, but could not overtake her. She left behind one of her glass slippers, which the prince picked up most carefully. She reached home, but quite out of breath, and in her nasty old clothes, having nothing left of all her finery but one of the little slippers, the mate to the one that she had dropped.

The guards at the palace gate were asked if they had not seen a princess go out. They replied that they had seen nobody leave but a young girl, very shabbily dressed, and who had more the air of a poor country wench than a gentlewoman.

When the two sisters returned from the ball, Cinderella asked them if they had been well entertained, and if the fine lady had been there.

They told her, yes, but that she hurried away immediately when it struck twelve, and with so much haste that she dropped one of her little glass slippers, the prettiest in the world, which the king's son had picked up; that he had done nothing but look at her all the time at the ball, and that most certainly he was very much in love with the beautiful person who owned the glass slipper.

What they said was very true; for a few days later, the king's son had it proclaimed, by sound of trumpet, that he would marry her whose foot this slipper would just fit. They began to try it on the princesses, then the duchesses and all the court, but in vain; it was brought to the two sisters, who did all they possibly could to force their foot into the slipper, but they did not succeed.

Cinderella, who saw all this, and knew that it was her slipper, said to them, laughing, "Let me see if it will not fit me."

Her sisters burst out laughing, and began to banter with her. The gentleman who was sent to try the slipper looked earnestly at Cinderella, and, finding her very handsome, said that it was only just that she should try as well, and that he had orders to let everyone try.

He had Cinderella sit down, and, putting the slipper to her foot, he found that it went on very easily, fitting her as if it had been made of wax. Her two sisters were greatly astonished, but then even more so, when Cinderella pulled out of her pocket the other slipper, and put it on her other foot. Then in came her godmother and touched her wand to Cinderella's clothes, making them richer and more magnificent than any of those she had worn before.

And now her two sisters found her to be that fine, beautiful lady whom they had seen at the ball. They threw themselves at her feet to beg pardon for all the ill treatment they had made her undergo. Cinderella took them up, and, as she embraced them, said that she forgave them with all her heart, and wanted them always to love her.

She was taken to the young prince, dressed as she was. He thought she was more charming than before, and, a few days after, married her. Cinderella, who was no less good than beautiful, gave her two sisters lodgings in the palace, and that very same day matched them with two great lords of the court.

Moral: Beauty in a woman is a rare treasure that will always be admired. Graciousness, however, is priceless and of even greater value. This is what Cinderella's godmother gave to her when she taught her to behave like a queen. Young women, in the winning of a heart, graciousness is more important than a beautiful hairdo. It is a true gift of the fairies. Without it nothing is possible; with it, one can do anything.

Another moral: Without doubt it is a great advantage to have intelligence, courage, good breeding, and common sense. These and similar talents come only from heaven, and it is good to have them. However, even these may fail to bring you success, without the blessing of a godfather or a godmother.

Discussion Questions

1. What qualities, as the heroine of this tale, does Cinderella possess? Do you think that Cinderella, as well as being the heroine, is heroic? Explain.

2. Cinderella's biological mother is dead. Who are the other two mother figures in this tale? What do you think children might learn about life from each of these quasi-mothers?

3. Discuss some elements of this story that could provide any reader—children, doctors, or other adults—with comfort.

Cinderella

THE GRIMM BROTHERS

A rich man's wife became sick, and when she felt that her end was drawing near, she called her only daughter to her bedside and said, "Dear child, remain pious and good, and then our dear God will always protect you, and I will look down on you from heaven and be near you." With this she closed her eyes and died.

The girl went out to her mother's grave every day and wept, and she remained pious and good. When winter came, the snow spread a white cloth over the grave, and when the spring sun had removed it again, the man took himself another wife.

This wife brought two daughters into the house with her. They were beautiful, with fair faces, but evil and dark hearts. Times soon grew very bad for the poor stepchild.

"Why should that stupid goose sit in the parlor with us?" they said. "If she wants to eat bread, then she will have to earn it. Out with this kitchen maid!"

They took her beautiful clothes away from her, dressed her in an old gray smock, and gave her wooden shoes. "Just look at the proud princess! How decked out she is!" they shouted and laughed as they led her into the kitchen.

There she had to do hard work from morning until evening, get up before daybreak, carry water, make the fires, cook, and wash. Besides this, the sisters did everything imaginable to hurt her. They made fun of her and scattered peas and lentils into the ashes for her, so that she had to sit and pick them out again. In the evening when she had worked herself weary, there was no bed for her. Instead she had to sleep by the hearth in the ashes. And because she always looked dusty and dirty, they called her Cinderella.

One day it happened that the father was going to the fair, and he asked his two stepdaughters what he should bring back for them.

"Beautiful dresses," said the one.

"Pearls and jewels," said the other.

"And you, Cinderella," he said, "what do you want?"

"Father, break off for me the first twig that brushes against your hat on your way home."

So he bought beautiful dresses, pearls, and jewels for his two stepdaughters. On his way home, as he was riding through a green thicket, a hazel twig brushed against him and knocked off his hat. Then he broke off the twig and took it with him. Arriving home, he gave his stepdaughters the things that they had asked for, and he gave Cinderella the twig from the hazel bush.

Cinderella thanked him, went to her mother's grave, and planted the branch on it, and she wept so much that her tears fell upon it and watered it. It grew and became a beautiful tree.

Cinderella went to this tree three times every day, and beneath it she wept and prayed. A white bird came to the tree every time, and whenever she expressed a wish, the bird would throw down to her what she had wished for.

Now it happened that the king proclaimed a festival that was to last three days. All the beautiful young girls in the land were invited, so that his son could select a bride for himself. When the two stepsisters heard that they too had been invited, they were in high spirits.

They called Cinderella, saying, "Comb our hair for us. Brush our shoes and fasten our buckles. We are going to the festival at the king's castle."

Cinderella obeyed, but wept, because she too would have liked to go to the dance with them. She begged her stepmother to allow her to go.

"You, Cinderella?" she said. "You, all covered with dust and dirt, and you want to go to the festival? You have neither clothes nor shoes, and yet you want to dance!"

However, because Cinderella kept asking, the stepmother finally said, "I have scattered a bowl of lentils into the ashes for you. If you can pick them out again in two hours, then you may go with us."

The girl went through the back door into the garden, and called out, "You tame pigeons, you turtledoves, and all you birds beneath the sky, come and help me to gather:

The good ones go into the pot,
The bad ones go into your crop."

Two white pigeons came in through the kitchen window, and then the turtledoves, and finally all the birds beneath the sky came whirring and swarming in, and lit around the ashes. The pigeons nodded their heads and began to pick, pick, pick, pick. And the others also began to pick, pick, pick, pick. They gathered all the good grains into the bowl. Hardly one hour had passed before they were finished, and they all flew out again.

The girl took the bowl to her stepmother, and was happy, thinking that now she would be allowed to go to the festival with them.

But the stepmother said, "No, Cinderella, you have no clothes, and
you don't know how to dance. Everyone would only laugh at you."

Cinderella began to cry, and then the stepmother said, "You may
go if you are able to pick two bowls of lentils out of the ashes for me
in one hour," thinking to herself, "She will never be able to do that."

The girl went through the back door into the garden, and called
out, "You tame pigeons, you turtledoves, and all you birds beneath
the sky, come and help me to gather:

The good ones go into the pot,
The bad ones go into your crop."

Two white pigeons came in through the kitchen window, and then
the turtledoves, and finally all the birds beneath the sky came whirring and swarming in, and lit around the ashes. The pigeons nodded
their heads and began to pick, pick, pick, pick. And the others also
began to pick, pick, pick, pick. They gathered all the good grains
into the bowls. Before a half hour had passed they were finished, and
they all flew out again.

The girl took the bowls to her stepmother, and was happy, thinking that now she would be allowed to go to the festival with them.

But the stepmother said, "It's no use. You are not coming with us,
for you have no clothes, and you don't know how to dance. We would
be ashamed of you." With this she turned her back on Cinderella,
and hurried away with her two proud daughters.

Now that no one else was at home, Cinderella went to her mother's grave beneath the hazel tree, and cried out:

Shake and quiver, little tree,
"Throw gold and silver down to me."

Then the bird threw a gold and silver dress down to her, and slippers
embroidered with silk and silver. She quickly put on the dress and
went to the festival.

Her stepsisters and her stepmother did not recognize her. They
thought she must be a foreign princess, for she looked so beautiful in
the golden dress. They never once thought it was Cinderella, for they
thought that she was sitting at home in the dirt, looking for lentils in
the ashes.

The prince approached her, took her by the hand, and danced
with her. Furthermore, he would dance with no one else. He never

let go of her hand, and whenever anyone else came and asked her to dance, he would say, "She is my dance partner."

She danced until evening, and then she wanted to go home. But the prince said, "I will go along and escort you," for he wanted to see to whom the beautiful girl belonged. However, she eluded him and jumped into the pigeon coop. The prince waited until her father came, and then he told him that the unknown girl had jumped into the pigeon coop.

The old man thought, "Could it be Cinderella?"

He had them bring him an ax and a pick so that he could break the pigeon coop apart, but no one was inside. When they got home, Cinderella was lying in the ashes, dressed in her dirty clothes. A dim little oil-lamp was burning in the fireplace. Cinderella had quickly jumped down from the back of the pigeon coop and had run to the hazel tree. There she had taken off her beautiful clothes and laid them on the grave, and the bird had taken them away again. Then, dressed in her gray smock, she had returned to the ashes in the kitchen.

The next day when the festival began anew, and her parents and her stepsisters had gone again, Cinderella went to the hazel tree and said:

"Shake and quiver, little tree,
Throw gold and silver down to me."

Then the bird threw down an even more magnificent dress than on the preceding day. When Cinderella appeared at the festival in this dress, everyone was astonished at her beauty. The prince had waited until she came, then immediately took her by the hand, and danced only with her. When others came and asked her to dance with them, he said, "She is my dance partner."

When evening came, she wanted to leave, and the prince followed her, wanting to see into which house she went. But she ran away from him and into the garden behind the house. A beautiful tall tree stood there, on which hung the most magnificent pears. She climbed as nimbly as a squirrel into the branches, and the prince did not know where she had gone. He waited until her father came, then said to him, "The unknown girl has eluded me, and I believe she has climbed up the pear tree."

The father thought, "Could it be Cinderella?" He had an ax brought to him and cut down the tree, but no one was in it. When they came to the kitchen, Cinderella was lying there in the ashes as usual, for she had jumped down from the other side of the tree, had taken the beautiful dress back to the bird in the hazel tree, and had put on her gray smock.

On the third day, when her parents and sisters had gone away, Cinderella went again to her mother's grave and said to the tree:

"Shake and quiver, little tree,
Throw gold and silver down to me."

This time the bird threw down to her a dress that was more splendid and magnificent than any she had yet had, and the slippers were of pure gold. When she arrived at the festival in this dress, everyone was so astonished that they did not know what to say. The prince danced only with her, and whenever anyone else asked her to dance, he would say, "She is my dance partner."

When evening came, Cinderella wanted to leave, and the prince tried to escort her, but she ran away from him so quickly that he could not follow her. The prince, however, had set a trap. He had had the entire stairway smeared with pitch. When she ran down the stairs, her left slipper stuck in the pitch. The prince picked it up. It was small and dainty, and of pure gold.

The next morning, he went with it to the man, and said to him, "No one shall be my wife except for the one whose foot fits this golden shoe."

The two sisters were happy to hear this, for they had pretty feet. With her mother standing by, the older one took the shoe into her bedroom to try it on. She could not get her big toe into it, for the shoe was too small for her. Then her mother gave her a knife and said, "Cut off your toe. When you are queen you will no longer have to go on foot."

The girl cut off her toe, forced her foot into the shoe, swallowed the pain, and went out to the prince. He took her on his horse as his bride and rode away with her. However, they had to ride past the grave, and there, on the hazel tree, sat the two pigeons, crying out:

"Rook di goo, rook di goo!
There's blood in the shoe.
The shoe is too tight,
This bride is not right!"

Then he looked at her foot and saw how the blood was running from it. He turned his horse around and took the false bride home again, saying that she was not the right one, and that the other sister should try on the shoe. She went into her bedroom, and got her toes into the shoe all right, but her heel was too large.

Then her mother gave her a knife, and said, "Cut a piece off your heel. When you are queen you will no longer have to go on foot."

The girl cut a piece off her heel, forced her foot into the shoe, swallowed the pain, and went out to the prince. He took her on his horse as his bride and rode away with her. When they passed the hazel tree, the two pigeons were sitting in it, and they cried out:

"Rook di goo, rook di goo!
There's blood in the shoe.
The shoe is too tight,
This bride is not right!"

He looked down at her foot and saw how the blood was running out of her shoe, and how it had stained her white stocking all red. Then he turned his horse around and took the false bride home again.

"This is not the right one, either," he said. "Don't you have another daughter?"

"No," said the man. "There is only a deformed little Cinderella from my first wife, but she cannot possibly be the bride."

The prince told him to send her to him, but the mother answered, "Oh, no, she is much too dirty. She cannot be seen."

But the prince insisted on it, and they had to call Cinderella. She first washed her hands and face clean, and then went and bowed down before the prince, who gave her the golden shoe. She sat down on a stool, pulled her foot out of the heavy wooden shoe, and put it into the slipper, and it fitted her perfectly.

When she stood up, the prince looked into her face, and he recognized the beautiful girl who had danced with him. He cried out, "She is my true bride."

The stepmother and the two sisters were horrified and turned pale with anger. The prince, however, took Cinderella onto his horse and rode away with her. As they passed by the hazel tree, the two white pigeons cried out:

"Rook di goo, rook di goo!
No blood's in the shoe.
The shoe's not too tight,
This bride is right!"

After they had cried this out, they both flew down and lit on Cinderella's shoulders, one on the right, the other on the left, and remained sitting there.

When the wedding with the prince was to be held, the two false sisters came, wanting to gain favor with Cinderella and to share her good fortune. When the bridal couple walked into the church, the older sister walked on their right side and the younger on their left side, and the pigeons pecked out one eye from each of them. Afterwards, as they came out of the church, the older one was on the left side, and the younger one on the right side, and then the pigeons pecked out the other eye from each of them. And thus, for their wickedness and false-hood, they were punished with blindness as long as they lived.

- Source: Jacob and Wilhelm Grimm, "Aschenputtel," *Kinder- und Hausmärchen* [*Children's and Household Tales—Grimms' Fairy Tales*], 7th edition (Göttingen: Verlag der Dieterichschen Buchhandlung, 1857), no. 21, pp. 119-26.
- The Grimms' source: Dorothea Viehmann (1755-1815), and other sources.
- This tale, in a different version, was included in the first edition of *Kinder- und Hausmärchen* (1812). It was substantially revised for the second edition (1819).
- Translated by D. L. Ashliman. © 2001-2006.
- Aarne-Thompson-Uther type 510A.

Discussion Questions

1. The Brothers Grimm collected folk tales that had been passed down through generations. Because these stories were shared orally rather than written down, small changes occurred in each retelling. Identify details that are different in this version of "Cinderella" from the one you are familiar with from childhood or from the Disney movie version. Explain your reasons for preferring one version over the other.

2. Discuss this version's use of the natural world to propel the plot. Do you think that the character of Cinderella in this version is different from the Cinderella in other versions because in the Grimm's version, nature, rather than a magical person such as the fairy godmother, champions her cause?

3. Considering Gribben's claim that she finds comfort in fairy tales, which version of "Cinderella" do you think she would prefer, the one above by the Grimm brothers, or the one that precedes it by Perrault? Why?

Fairy Tales Are Good for Children

Essay

G. K. CHESTERTON

G. K. Chesterton (1874-1936), born in England, was a highly respected author of many novels, poems, and essays.

I find that there really are human beings who think fairy tales bad for children. I do not speak of the man in the green tie, for him I can never count truly human. But a lady has written me an earnest letter saying that fairy tales ought not to be taught to children even if they are true. She says that it is cruel to tell children fairy tales, because it frightens them. You might just as well say that it is cruel to give girls sentimental novels because it makes them cry. All this kind of talk is based on that complete forgetting of what a child is like that has been the firm foundation of so many educational schemes. If you kept bogeys and goblins away from children, they would make them up for themselves. One small child in the dark can invent more hells than Swedenborg [a Swedish scientist and mystic]. One small child can imagine monsters too big and black to get into any picture, and give them names too unearthly and cacophonous to have occurred in the cries of any lunatic. The child, to begin with, commonly likes horrors, and he continues to indulge in them even when he does not like them. There is just as much difficulty in saying exactly where pure pain begins in his case, as there is in ours when we walk of our own free will into the torture-chamber of a great tragedy. The fear does not come from fairy tales; the fear comes from the universe of the soul.

The timidity of the child and the savage is entirely reasonable; they are alarmed at this world because this world is a very alarming place. They dislike being alone because it is verily and indeed an awful idea to be alone. Barbarians fear the unknown for the same reason that Agnostics worship it—because it is a fact. Fairy tales, then, are not responsible for producing in children fear, or any of the shapes of fear; fairy tales do not give the child the idea of the evil or the ugly; that is in the child already, because it is in the world already. Fairy tales do not give a child his first idea of bogey. What fairy tales give the child is his first clear idea of the possible defeat of bogey. The baby has known the dragon intimately ever since he had an imagination. What the fairy tale provides for him is a St. George to kill the dragon.

Exactly what the fairy tale does is this: It accustoms him through a series of clear pictures to the idea that these limitless terrors have a limit, that these shapeless enemies have enemies in the knights of God, that there is something in the universe more mystical than darkness and stronger than strong fear. When I was a child, I stared at the darkness until the whole black bulk of it turned into one dark giant taller than heaven. If there was one star in the sky, it only made him a Cyclops. But fairy tales restored my mental health, for the next day I read an authentic account of how a giant with one eye, of quite equal dimensions, had been baffled by a little boy like me (of similar inexperience and even lower social status) by means of a sword, some bad riddles, and a brave heart. Sometimes the sea at night seemed as dreadful as any dragon. But then I was acquainted with many youngest sons and little sailors to whom a dragon or two was as simple as the sea.

Take the most horrible of the Grimms' tales in incident and imagery, the excellent tale of "The Boy Who Could Not Shudder," and you will see what I mean.[1] There are some living shocks in that tale. I remember specially a man's legs which fell down the chimney by themselves and walked about the room, until they were rejoined by the severed head and body which fell down the chimney after them. That is very good. But the point of the story and the point of the reader's feelings is not that these things are frightening, but the far more striking fact that the hero was not frightened at them. The most fearful of all these fearful wonders was his own absence of fear. He slapped the bogeys on the back and asked the devils to drink wine with him; many a time in my youth, when stifled with some modern morbidity, I have prayed for a double portion of his spirit. If you have not read the end of his story, go and read it; it is the wisest thing in the world. The hero was at last taught to shudder by taking a wife, who threw a pail of cold water over him. In that one sentence, there is more of the real meaning of marriage than in all the books about sex that cover Europe and America.

At the four corners of a child's bed stand Perseus and Roland, Sigurd and St. George.[2] If you withdraw the guard of heroes, you are not making him rational; you are only leaving him to fight the devils

---

[1] Also known as "A Tale about the Boy Who Went Forth to Learn What Fear Was" (and similar titles).

[2] These heroes are not fairy-tale characters, so Chesterton is confusing fairy tales with myths and legends.

alone. For the devils, alas, we have always believed in. The hopeful element in the universe has in modern times continually been denied and reasserted; but the hopeless element has never for a moment been denied.

Discussion Questions

1. What reason does Chesterton say that a well-meaning woman gave to him in a letter for banning the teaching of fairy tales? What other reasons, that neither she nor Chesterton nor Gribben mentions, have you heard about or thought of for keeping these stories away from children?

2. Why does Chesterton believe it is impossible to protect children from scary things? If you were a parent, would you try to keep your child from ever being afraid? What things would you do to make him or her feel safe?

3. Why does Chesterton think that childhood fears are reasonable? What things were you afraid of as a child? Was your fear realistic? How do you think Chesterton would judge the reasonableness of your fear?

4. According to Chesterton, how do fairy tales help children to cope with fear in real life? How did a fairy tale about a boy and a giant help Chesterton? How does he relate "The Boy Who Could Not Shudder" to real life?

Change and Sexuality: Ursula and Ariel as Markers of Metamorphosis in *The Little Mermaid*

Essay

Paul Beehler

Dr. Paul Beehler is a faculty member in the University Writing Program and also teaches in the School of Business Administration at the University of California, Riverside.

Even after some twenty years, Disney's *The Little Mermaid* (1989) is perceived as one of the "new classics," and many copies of the DVD can be found in libraries throughout the world.[1] Indeed, Disney, in August of 2008, saw fit to produce and release the second sequel to *The Little Mermaid—The Little Mermaid: Ariel's Beginning*—in an attempt to capitalize upon the renewed interest around the characters and concept. Even more recent is the debut of Disney's *World of Color*, a production Disney released in its California Adventure theme park on June 11, 2010. Offering a keenly prominent position specifically for Ariel, Disney's *World of Color* is the culmination of a highly technical show that relies extensively on animation, lights, lasers, and water cannons. With the span of time comes a greater appreciation (and in this case greater verve for the work) as well as a certain perspective that can be applied through criticism.[2] That Ariel, the protagonist of *The Little Mermaid*, undergoes a profound metamorphosis in both Disney's and Hans Christian Andersen's versions of the fairy tale is undisputed. Laura Sells, in a chapter entitled "Where

---

[1]Indeed, according to <www.the-numbers.com/movies/1989/LMERM-DVD.php>, three releases of *The Little Mermaid* have taken place: November 15, 1989; November 14, 1997; and December 7, 1999. During the last period that the DVD was released from the vault, sales were epic: 6,290,363 copies were sold for a total of $95,266,221 between October 8, 2006, and December 3, 2006. What is more astounding is that these sales numbers only apply to the DVD and not Blu-ray nor VHS (which reported over four million copies sold in the first week alone of the rerelease). The recent release (late August of 2008) of the second sequel that showcases Ariel, *The Little Mermaid: Ariel's Beginning* (2008), is certain to ignite sales and reinvigorate interest once again in *The Little Mermaid* and all its accompanying lore.

[2]Recently, I polled my students to get an anecdotal sense of how pervasive *The Little Mermaid* is with an audience that is removed from the film in time by a full generation. To my surprise, all of the women in my class demonstrated an impressive familiarity with the film, even to the point that some spontaneously broke out into song. The men seemed aware of the film, but much less so.

Do the Mermaids Stand," is perhaps one of the more vocal critics of the film, and she directly identifies the theme of change as she positions the film, and specifically Ariel, in a feminist discourse. After considering Barbara Bush's use of mermaid imagery when speaking to a group of Wellesley students, Sells asserts that "*The Little Mermaid* reflects some of the tensions in American feminism between reformist demands for access, which leave in place the fixed and complementary definitions of masculine and feminine gender identities, and radical refigurings of gender that assert symbolic change as preliminary to social change" (177). Change in the film is seemingly desirable, inevitable, and essential, but what Sells only tangentially mentions (and this is an argument generally found wanting in the field) is the intense scrutiny regarding the agent of that change, Ursula—a self-proclaimed "witch." A study of the actual change and its political/feminist ramifications is most certainly a productive conversation, but a complete exegesis of *The Little Mermaid* must move beyond the transformation into a broader argument regarding the catalyst for such change. This odyssey, an investigation that has thus far eluded critics, is essential to any plenary appreciation of the work, so the character Ursula requires close scrutiny if one is to fully appreciate Ariel and her role.

Historically, the experienced and prurient widow was a seminal component of the Early Modern witch, but the other common image of the sixteenth- and seventeenth-century English witch is equally important: that of the young unmarried temptress. Ostracized and banned from society, witches who were in part identified as unattached women scratched out a living in the outskirts of villages by offering counsel and herbs to other women as a form of *uenificium*. Those women who tended to women, especially in matters of reproduction and birth, routinely faced the hazards of witch hunts. Their powers could be officially indicted under *maleficium*. The formal profession of midwife offered an especially tempting target for those zealots interested in prosecuting witches through forces such as King James and the *Malleus Malifecarum*. Here was a group of women who offered assistance with birth, abortion, and contraception—these women were frequently present in the lives of other women during crucial periods of feminine transition; for their efforts, they were occasionally rewarded with fines, imprisonment, scorn, and even execution. Like these historical witches, Ursula serves as a midwife to assist Ariel during her process of transformation, and Ariel stands before a crossroads: Will she be fashioned in the image of Ursula, or will she assume the role of young temptress/witch? Essentially, Ariel finds herself poised between the two primary roles of witch: On one hand, Ariel faces the possibility of assuming the position of a seductively threatening woman, while on the other hand, the heroine may, under the tutelage of Ursula, refashion her identity into the witch who has knowledge of sex and can manipulate society through this position of power. Neither form of the feminine nightmare is suitable, especially for an ascending princess of Ariel's magnitude. Indeed, Ariel must simultaneously divorce herself from her current form while avoiding the undue influence and auspices of Ursula. Bruno Bettelheim sums up the situation of Disney's heroine best when he argues that with every fairy tale's end the hero has mastered all trials and despite them remained true to himself, or in successfully undergoing them has achieved his true selfhood. He has become an autocrat in the best sense of the word—a self-ruler, a truly autonomous person, not a person who rules over others (127).

Ariel requires Ursula's guidance to achieve, ultimately, a new form that serves as a delicately tempered hybrid of the sexual witch and the experienced matron/witch; however, Ariel extricates herself in the final moments of the film to claim, at least in relation to Ursula, the ostensible role of Bettelheim's autocrat. Would that such a role enjoyed some traction; unfortunately, in Ariel's case, the heroine's liberty is perhaps more ephemeral than even that of a common mayfly because she quickly delivers herself to the much-anticipated wedding nuptials.

Ariel's role as seductress or matron has yet to be determined when *The Little Mermaid* opens. Her breasts are those of a budding adolescent, and this image benefits from a certain intensity with Ariel's line, "I'm sixteen years old. I'm not a child." Ariel's line is delivered in one of the opening scenes, and she openly declares that she is not a child; indeed, the audience does not know what she is just yet, and this is where the female threat is poised. Ariel's physical body—that of mermaid or human—is as ambiguous as her role in the film. Is she a girl or a woman? Does she reside in the water or on land? Is she the matron or the seductress? The movie can essentially be read as a journey for the protagonist, a journey that results in the birth of her identity and then a renunciation of identity, an act that yields to a solidification of her position in society. This birth is appropriately mired in the image of water and forcefully moves upwards towards the concretely defined surface of land. Of greatest consequence is that this process can only be negotiated with the aid of Ursula, the midwife witch, and Ursula harbors her own agenda. Chris Richards, in his essay "Room to Dance: Girls' Play and *The Little Mermaid*," addresses the dramatic binaries that stand before Ariel at the moment she considers the flotsam of the human world:

> Ariel's song sets out a series of binary oppositions and it is through these that her yearning is constructed. Her desire is animated by the distance between the treasured, but lifeless, objects in her cavern and the vibrant mobility of life on two legs shared by the people on land. The wish to be part of that world above, from which her physical form appears irrevocably to exclude her, is expressed in terms which divide her fishy attributes from those which might be associated with maturity and sexuality. (144)

The transformation of forms and the binaries present in the film are also powerfully communicated through the image of the breast. Ariel's scanty clothing reveals, upon her introduction, shapely and youthful breasts. Like the other mermaids, she has a single tail with no vaginal opening. She is, at one and the same time, oddly seductive and disturbingly asexual: Richards' binary is potently communicated through such an image. The camera is trained on Ariel throughout her opening sequences, and she becomes the object of "the gaze" because the young mermaid with her scantily clad breasts and "V" shaped scales around her navel is an unapproachable seductress who, without some form of physical transformation, is incapable of assuming the role of mother. Ariel faces a dilemma of the greatest magnitude: Will she maintain her current form, thereby becoming a nexus of frustrating and threatening actions to society and the larger audience as a whole, or will the worlds below and above conspire against her by consigning her to the acceptable and controlled role of matron? In other words, the audience confronts a question of identity regarding the little mermaid: Will Ariel frustrate society by retaining social power through the traits of sexual seduction, or will society find a comedic resolution by robbing Ariel of any social force by extricating the seductive and replacing such characteristics with the role of wife and, eventually, mother? Disney's heroine actively struggles with this role of identity, and Ariel must decide whether she will subvert or reinforce the power structure before her. Ariel becomes a malleable object hidden deep beneath the waters of the subconscious, and she serves as a frustration which must ultimately be resolved in the course of the film.

When Disney's film concludes, Ariel is poised to assume the role of queen by kissing Prince Eric in a wedding ceremony; her ascension to the role of queen requires, in part, that she, to use Bettelheim's terminology, has "gained mature adulthood" (128), and this act is steeped in the mystique of "what sex consists of; that is the secret of adults which [s]he wishes to discover" (128). Through Ursula's intimate guidance, Ariel has mastered the secret power of sex: She now physically signals the profound transformation through her covered breast, a breast that neither intimidates nor threatens society. Ariel is no longer the seductress/witch, nor has she overshot her mark to become the sexually knowledgeable witch; instead, Ariel enjoys but a brief existence in the role of autocrat only to accept her position as society and Prince Eric define it—that is, as a function of deference. When the film concludes, Ariel's existence as an independent force is tragically best characterized as momentary in nature.

Ariel's nudity and the unfettered breast, upon the conclusion of Disney's film, are deftly exchanged for a series of dresses and clothing that fully efface any seductive trace of Ariel's breast. With the single exception of a brief retransformation of Ariel into a mermaid (which, interestingly enough, enables Prince Eric to again express his amorous desires), the images of Ariel's breast become increasingly stifled and controlled until Disney offers its final image of the heroine: Ariel in a wedding dress. Even when King Triton, in the final moments of the film, extends his trident to transfigure his daughter one last time from mermaid to human, Ariel emerges from the ocean not as an unclothed woman, but as an enchanting female donning a luminescent gown. This emergence is significantly different from the earlier resurrection of Ariel that revealed a nude heroine. No chance is afforded for the emergence of the autocrat as Ariel runs into the arms and subsequent protection of Prince Eric. Ariel's sleeveless gown is then, in a single moment, replaced with the image of Ariel in her wedding dress, a piece of clothing that almost entirely eclipses Ariel's body—even white gloves hide Ariel's hands. The movie, as well as Ariel's transfiguration, comes to an irrefutable conclusion, and Ariel assumes her contained position in society—a position that comes at the cost of her independence and sexual expressiveness. In Andersen's conclusion, Ariel meets a less tragic ending in that she is released upon the sea as bubbles and so meets a physical demise, but her identity and determinism remain intact. Acts of violence and social transgressions, while not resolved in a comfortable manner, are at least recognized, and a clear sense of loss is conveyed. Disney's more comic ending, at least in the sense of a Shakespearean comedy, is in many ways much more disturbing because Ariel is physically passed from her father, King Triton, to her husband, Prince Eric. The final minutes of the film suggest that Ariel's window to fulfill the role of autocrat may indeed have been very brief if, alas, it ever existed in this world of illusion.

Works Cited

Andersen, Hans Christian. *"The Little Mermaid" and Other Stories*. Trans. R. Nisbet Bain. Lawrence and Bullen: London, 1893. Print.

Bettelheim, Bruno. *The Uses of Enchantment: The Meaning and Importance of Fairy Tales*. New York: Vantage Books, 1989. Print.

The Little Mermaid. Dir. Ron Clements and John Musker. Perf. Samuel E. Wright, Jodi Benson, Pat Carroll, and Kenneth Mars. Disney Feature Animation, 1989. DVD.

The Little Mermaid: Ariel's Beginning. Dir. Peggy Holmes. Perf. Jodi Benson, Sally Field, Jim Cummings, and Samuel E. Wright. Disney Toon Studios, 2008. DVD.

"The Little Mermaid—DVD Sales." *The Numbers: Box Office Data, Movies Stars, Idle Speculation*. Nash Information Services, LLC, n.d. Web. 3 Sept. 2008. <http://www.the-numbers.com/movies/1989/LMERM-DVD.php>.

Richards, Chris. "Room to Dance: Girls' Play and *The Little Mermaid*." *In Front of the Children*. Ed. Cary Bazalgette and David Buckingham. London: British Film Institute, 1995. 141-50. Print.

Sells, Laura. "Where Do the Mermaids Stand?: Voice and Body in *The Little Mermaid*." *From Mouse to Mermaid: The Politics of Film, Gender, and Culture*. Ed. Elizabeth Bell, Lynda Haas, and Laura Sells. Bloomington: Indiana University Press, 1995. 175-92. Print.

Discussion Questions

1. What role, according to Paul Beehler, does Ursula play in Ariel's transformation from mermaid to human? What is the historical context in which he places this role? Why does Ariel need to be guided by and to divorce herself from Ursula? Explain your reasons for accepting or rejecting Beehler's exploration of Ursula's role.

2. According to Beehler, what relationship exists between Ariel's identity, her transformation, and society? Why do you think the same basic argument applies to all, some, or no modern brides?

3. Discuss the necessity and implications of the physical changes Ariel undergoes.

4. Although Disney films aren't fairy tales per se, do you think that Gribben's discussion of fairy tales applies in the same way to *The Little Mermaid?* Explain.

5. In *The Little Mermaid*, Ariel must rely upon a nonbenevolent witch to reach her goal. How does Ariel's ability to get the help she needs differ from that of the Cinderella character in Grimm, Perault, and "Cap o' Rushes? What similarities and differences do you notice in these various portrayals of female agency and those who help them? What real-life messages might Gribben draw from one or more of these portrayals?

The Moral of the Story

Essay

ALICE ABLER

Alice Abler is a student at College of the Redwoods in Arcata, California, where she is a music major.

Between "once upon a time" and "happily ever after" lies a timeless, ever-changing world, where everything is possible and dreams do come true. Countless fairy tales with infinite variations, usually conveying moral, social, or political lessons through skillful narrative and interesting characters, have existed throughout history and throughout the world. Consider Aesop's fables, the basis for so many of our contemporary moral stories. The still-popular tales have lived on for more than two millennia, exemplifying extraordinary power and longevity. Other early influences on our literary tradition abound: Cinderella stories, for example—distressed damsels losing diminutive footwear—are found in ancient Egypt and ninth-century China.

The nature of this genre seems to invite evolution. Originally, these deceptively simple stories were passed orally from generation to generation. As the printed word became more accessible, the tales became somewhat less mutable for a time. Today, the images we see on the movie screen have firmly implanted themselves in our minds and have all but supplanted the originals. More significant than the changes themselves, however, is what the evolution of the fairy tale tells us about ourselves and our changing society.

The origins of the fairy tales we know today are found in sources as varied as mythology and the Bible. Common themes can be found in most cultures, whether through commonality of experience or because the tales themselves traveled with both conquerors and conquered. Globetrotting folktales were used sometimes to educate and sometimes to frighten children (and adults) into compliance, graphically warning of the consequences for wrong actions.

As the centuries passed, virtue and a sense of morality ebbed and flowed, both in real life and in the tales that accompanied mankind on the journey. Among medieval peasants, folktales passed from those older and more experienced to younger adults and children as moral lessons for life. Many take place during the hero's or heroine's passage from childhood to adulthood, often ending in marriage. Along this fantastic path are not only challenges to be overcome but warnings: the perils of being alone in the woods, the potential pitfalls of physical attractiveness, the dangers of being naïve.

The stories often addressed subjects in veiled terms. According to folklore researcher and retired professor D. L. Ashliman, "Many fairy tales owe their longevity to an ability to address tabooed subjects in a symbolic manner" (97). It is not surprising, therefore, to learn how many of these seemingly benign tales have descended from darker stories involving themes of adultery, incest, cannibalism, rape, murder, and mutilation.

As Italy emerged from the medieval period and embraced the Renaissance, one of Europe's first known written story collections was being conceived by Giovanni Francesco Straparola, often considered the father of the literary fairy tale. In 1550, Straparola first published a collection of stories told within the framework of a greater story. These bawdy literary romps, which reflected the relaxed morality of the time, were clearly not meant for children. By writing as though the stories were told by a group of ladies and gentlemen, Straparola was able to justify his use of shocking vernacular language. This pretext allowed the stories to be accepted by the educated classes in Italy and later throughout Europe, anesthetizing them to vulgarity in literature.

Straparola's influence is seen in later European writings, including those of his fellow countryman Giambattista Basile (ca. 1576–1632). Basile's posthumously published collection of fifty stories followed in the same tradition. His timeless social commentaries highlighted the shortcomings of those who descended to the depths for wealth, power, and fame. Included are early versions of classic fables we would recognize today.

Half a century later, Charles Perrault and his contemporaries took some of the earlier European peasant tales and massaged them until they were more suited to the aristocratic salon set of seventeenth-century France, where storytelling was considered an important social art. He customized the stories and added new ones, often making a point of showcasing the difficulties and the challenges of his time. A collection of Perrault's stories was published in 1697, subtitled *Contes de ma Mere l'Oye* (literally *Tales of My Mother the Goose*). Gone was much of the violence, but added was the subtle sexual innuendo expected in the popular culture of the period. Our modern "Cinderella," "Little Red Riding Hood," "Sleeping Beauty," "Bluebeard," "Puss in Boots" and others are easily recognized in Perrault's writings.

His work was characterized by typically French actions and light-hearted humor; for example, Cinderella, with undeniable *savoir faire*, drops her slipper on purpose. And when Perrault's prince finds the sleeping beauty, who has been slumbering for a century in the woods, one of the first things he notices is her out-of-style clothing. The wicked queen, mother of the prince, upon discovering the clandestine marriage of the pair and their subsequent offspring, orders one of her grandchildren to be cooked for dinner. But not just any recipe will do: The gourmand requests that the child be served with a classic *sauce Robert*.

A rhyme telling a moral at the end of Perrault's stories came later. His warning to young girls about the nature of wolves, for instance, leaves no doubt that he was not referring to canines in "Little Red Riding Hood." One English translation reads:

> *Little girls, this seems to say,*
> *Never stop upon your way,*
> *Never trust a stranger-friend;*
> *No one knows how it will end.*
> *As you're pretty so be wise;*
> *Wolves may lurk in every guise.*
> *Handsome they may be, and kind,*
> *Gay, and charming—never mind!*
> *Now, as then, 'tis simple truth—*
> *Sweetest tongue has sharpest tooth!*

Perrault's social circle included Marie-Catherine d'Aulnoy, who published her own stories in an anthology titled *Contes de Fées* (*Fairy Tales*), and the term lives on.

According to historian Marina Warner in *Wonder Tales*, many of d'Aulnoy's stories and similar "Beauty and the Beast" tales were based on the classic fable of Cupid and Psyche. The common thread, fear of an unknown or brutish groom, struck a chord with the women of France, who were beginning to challenge the traditional balance of power and the common practice of arranged marriages (8). Warner states, "Though the message is largely lost on today's audience, thoroughly accustomed to choosing not just one partner but several, the French wonder tale was fighting for social emancipation and change on grounds of urgent personal experience" (Warner 9)."

The objects of these stories went beyond weddings and women's issues. The indiscretions and warmongering of the king and his courtesans were also subtly spoofed in the veiled satires, sometimes resulting in exile for the authors.

Using stories for political ends was not limited to the French. Neither, obviously, did biblical values tend to be an overriding theme. But often as not, the changing tales did reflect each society's prevailing interpretations of religious themes. Anti-Semitic blood libel stories—the later-debunked tales of ritual murders and drinking of Christian children's blood by Jews—were started by early Christian zealots and propagated during the Crusader era. These tales were found throughout Europe and encouraged in Martin Luther's Germany, and later they even appeared in a well-known collection of folktales.

The Romantic period of the early nineteenth century saw a growing fascination with a glorified primitive or peasant culture. Germany was mostly recovered from the effects of the Thirty Years War, which had left a third of the population dead and the rest struggling with famine and disease. Stepparents and early death had been facts of life for much of the population, and the folktales reflected that reality. The stage was set for the work of Jacob and Wilhelm Grimm, known for their work in promoting a common German culture and language. Today, the world at large recognizes the brothers Grimm as the authors of what may well be the best-known anthology of fairy tales, translated into more than 160 languages.

The brothers collected tales from friends and acquaintances, some of whom were fluent in French and intimately familiar with the popular *fées*. The Grimms declared the tales pure, original and German, yet they were conflated from the writings of Perrault and his contemporaries, from the anthologies of Basile, and from storytellers of the Middle East, Asia, and elsewhere. Even with the multicultural influences, however, their stories demonstrated a distinct Germanic flair.

Despite claims of wanting to retain literary purity, the brothers changed the stories over the years. Their earliest manuscript dates from 1810, with various revisions being published from 1812 to 1857 (the last edition being the basis for most of the translated Grimm tales we have today). Each revision took away some of the sexual overtones and gruesome violence against the innocent (though not against wrongdoers), and added lessons in their brand of Christian morality. This sometimes altered the stories in a dramatic way: for example, Snow White's jealous biological mother from the first edition became a vain stepmother in later editions, changing the theme from a complex mother-daughter rivalry to a much simpler moral lesson against vanity.

Meanwhile, in Puritan England, where the child mortality rate was high, the fear of eternal damnation for unprepared children had been a driving force in the popularity of instructive literature such as John Bunyan's *Pilgrim's Progress*. And those in the privileged, literate classes had tried to restrict the nature of children's literature to stories that reinforced class distinctions, such as the upper class feeling charitable toward the poor, who always reacted humbly and knew their place in society. The wealthy saw danger in fairy tales encouraging upward social mobility by suggesting, for example, that a peasant could marry into the aristocracy and live happily ever after.

But the eighteenth century saw changes in English society, with a growing and increasingly literate middle class carrying newfound discretionary income, a budding children's culture, and money to be made in commercial endeavors. Before long, dozens of volumes of fairy tales were translated from European languages and turned into inexpensive books, which the children of the working class devoured. In response, the fairy tales underwent dramatic changes, nearly eliminating the fantasy and including even stronger moral lessons, with strained, sometimes unintentionally humorous results.

Onto this post-Puritan stage stepped Thomas Bowdler, whose surname became immortalized as a verb after 1818 when he published his sanitized and paraphrased version of Shakespeare, titled *The Family Shakespeare*. Bowdlerization was the answer for those who believed suitable literature was to be purely didactic and devoid of fantasy. Piety and virtue were esteemed and enforced, so in books that otherwise ran the risk of being banned outright, material deemed objectionable was deleted or purified.

George Cruikshank, a popular illustrator of the Grimms' translations and Charles Dickens's works, became an outspoken moral revisionist in the straitlaced Victorian era. When he tried to turn Cinderella into a promotional tome for teetotalism, however, it was more than Dickens, who was raised on fairy tales, could quietly bear.

In *Social Dreaming: Dickens and the Fairy Tale*, Elaine Ostry remarks that Dickens:

> helped establish the fairy tale as respectable, artistic, and critical of society. He adhered to one vital aspect of the fairy-tale tradition: the use of the fairy tale to influence the way people acted as social beings. For Dickens and many other writers before and after him, the fairy tale was an essential voice of the nation that carried with it cultural messages. For him, the fairy tale had the power, or magic, to effect social transformations. (26)

His 1853 "Frauds on the Fairies" counterattacked bowdlerization's forced revisions with a satirical Cinderella story reworked to be politically correct in that era, 140 years before James Finn Garner did the same with his tongue-in-cheek bestseller, *Politically Correct Bedtime Stories*.

The furor died, and fairy tales continued their slow evolution. *My Book House*, a popular set from the early twentieth century, included classic literature, fables, fairy tales, and stories with historical themes. In keeping with the prevailing ideals of the time, the six-volume anthology was intended to be educational as well as entertaining. The fairy tales included were still somewhat sanitized versions, most notably eliminating all traces of wicked parents. Contributing factors included increased longevity and the exaltation of motherhood as women became more able to choose the size of their families. The romantic ideal was that each child was wanted and precious in the eyes of the parents.

The popularity of literature for children and ethereal art featuring children by a new generation of artists and illustrators, including Jessie Willcox Smith and Maxfield Parrish, helped pave the way for the next major change: the Disney fairy-tale-to-film phenomenon.

Walt Disney's film *Snow White and the Seven Dwarfs* (1937) broke new ground as the first American full-length animated musical feature. Disney knew his audience—a country that had been through both a world war and an economic depression in one generation. The social and political messages were softened, and the stories were changed to enhance their entertainment value. The project consumed more time and resources than anyone could have expected at the time—nearly $1.5 million was an astronomical sum in the midst of the Great Depression. It was a huge risk and a huge commercial success, as people went without necessities to buy 83 minutes of escape.

Snow White was followed by *Pinocchio*, *Cinderella*, and *Sleeping Beauty*. These fairy tale movies, produced before Disney's death in 1966, were of the same formula, usually involving an adolescent hero/heroine desperately in need of outside help. These movies are done in the spirit of the Grimm versions, but without the violence and harshness. Romantic themes, cheery musical interludes, and comic relief before the happy ending became the norm. Villains died or were otherwise disposed of as a result of their own actions, preventing the blemishing of the pristine character of the hero or heroine. These sunny revisions avoided the unpleasant realities addressed in the earlier tales but also diminished the ability of the hero or heroine to triumph over greater adversity. Yet it was exactly what the paying public of that era wanted, especially for their children.

The late 1960s and 70s saw a surge of interest in women's rights in the Western world as the Equal Rights Amendment gained approval in the United States. Australian-born Helen Reddy's feminist anthem "I Am Woman" hit the top of the US Billboard charts in 1972. In this atmosphere, the Disney-formula heroines were increasingly criticized for their wide-eyed docility. By 1989, the passive princess of the past reemerged in the form of Ariel, an empowered teenage mermaid taking charge and not listening to anyone—not even her father. Two years later, a beautiful bookworm named Belle tamed the beast and became the new standard for girls everywhere. This calculated reworking of the female protagonist both echoed then-current feelings about femininity and shaped the attitudes of young fans worldwide. More significant and far-reaching is the prevailing trend within these reworked fairy tales of people not looking to a higher authority for guidance but attempting to find solutions from within themselves.

With globalization, full-length animated movies have become today's standard for fairy tales worldwide. Often forgotten are the deeper meanings and lessons of some of the earlier versions, as well as the moralistic revisions of the brothers Grimm. If fairy tales have been a social gauge through the ages, then today's tales suggest that Western society has shifted even further from supporting biblical values and principles to embracing the concepts of relative morality and self-sufficiency.

The dual forces of cause and effect have been consistently at work through the ages. The mutable fairy tale has always been both an unrelenting influence on society and a mirror of society. From oral tradition, through the literary fairy tale, and now to cinema—we can only imagine what new medium will carry fairy tales to the next generations and what influential messages they will instill.

One thing is certain, however. The current trend in popular fairy tales toward moral ambivalence suggests that the foreseeable future looks disturbingly amoral.

Works Cited

Ashliman, D.L. "Incest in Indo-European Folktales." *The Greenwood Encyclopedia of Folktales and Fairy Tales*. 3 vols. Ed. Donald Haase. Westport: Greenwood Press, 2008. Print.

Ostry, Elaine. *Social Dreaming: Dickens and the Fairy Tale. Studies in Major Literary Authors Series*. Ed. William Cain. New York: Routledge Press, 2002. Print.

Warner, Marina, ed. *Wonder Tales*. Gordonsville, Virginia: Farrar Straus & Giroux, 1996. Print.

Discussion Questions

1. Discuss the origins of the fairy tale. What does this information suggest to you about human nature and culture?

2. What, according to the author, were the social/political goals of the fairy tale in Puritan England, the Romantic period, the Victorian period, and after World War II? What social/political messages are provided by fairy tales in the versions popular today? What are some new ideas you think might be embraced by versions of fairy tales in the future?

3. How do you think Valerie Gribben would respond to the history of fairy tales that Alice Abler describes? Would knowing about the way fairy tales changed over time reduce or enhance their value for her in any way? Why or why not?

The World of Myths and Fairy Tales

Essay

JULIUS E. HEUSCHER

We can never exhaust the depths of myths and fairy tales—of that we may be certain; but then neither can anyone else. And a cupped handful of the fresh waters of life is sweeter than a whole reservoir of dogma, piped and guaranteed. (188)

-Heinrich Zimmer

There are many tasks we would never undertake if we were aware of all the difficulties and problems, of all the work and frustrations they would entail. Thus, while the uncertainty of the future fills us with deep anxiety, it equally emboldens us through a permissive attitude which hides many of the obstacles lying ahead. I might never have tackled the wide field of myths and fairy tales, with its manifold aspects and ramifications, if I had known beforehand what an enormous number of these narrations exist all over the world, and how excellent some of the literature concerning the subject is. I was naïvely unaware of all this, like the youngest of the three brothers whom the fairy tale king sends out into the world to accomplish a seemingly impossible task. Yet, as in the case of this youngest brother, it was just this naïve lack of prejudice which gave me both the incentive to meet the problems which arose out of my research and the freedom to find answers.

Some years ago, when my curiosity for the meaning of fairy tales was reawakened, I did not feel the need to scan any of the collections of myths and folk tales. On the contrary, I sensed that a few, or even only one, of the genuine folk-fairy tales would open the door to the world of these wondrous stories. Indeed, the spiritual realities, the metaphysical ideas reflected in the images of myths and fairy tales are not nearly as fragmented as our variegated material environment. J. W. Goethe expresses this magnificently when he has Faust exclaim in regard to the "world of the spirit": "How everything weaves itself into the whole (pattern), / How each part lives and works in each other part! / How Heavenly forces ascend and descend / Handing each other the golden vessels, /

Penetrating from Heaven through the earth / Upon grace-scented wings, / All resounding harmoniously through all!" (42). Thus, I surmised that a completely unprejudiced, a truly *phenomenologic* approach to a single fairy tale would reveal not just a significant fragment, but a whole view of the human being.

And though, during subsequent years, I had reason to read a good many folk tales and myths, this initial, naïve attitude was not all wrong. I found confirmation of my original belief in the following statement by Joseph Campbell, who has written excellently and widely on the subject: "The wonder is that the characteristic efficacy to touch and inspire deep creative centers dwells in the smallest nursery fairy tale—as the flavor of the ocean is contained in a droplet, or the whole mystery of life within the egg of a flea" (2).

An old Indian fairy tale analyzed by the prominent, late indologist, Heinrich Zimmer, reaches the same conclusion. In this story, titled *The King and the Corpse*, the once prominent and self-assured king finds himself in a nightmarish, graveyard-like, dark region. Here he must answer the riddles contained in the twenty-five riddle-fairy-tales told to him by the spirit in the corpse which he patiently carries back and forth through the bleak night. Each one of these tales is so complete, so perfect in itself, that it is universally celebrated when the king, after several more trials, has regained his throne, mightier and wiser than before. Even Shiva, "the great god, overlord of all the Spectres and Demons," does them honor. And thus, the story announces in the end that "whoever recites with sincere devotion even a *single one* (of the riddle tales) shall be free from sin" (Zimmer 209).

The last quotation is of the deepest significance. It points towards the intimate relationship between the tale and the one who receives the tale. On the one hand, the "**truthfulness**" of the fairy tale is not simply objectively given, but depends upon the ability of the listener to *perceive* the truth. The German expression for perceiving, *wahrnehmen*, literally meaning *to take the truth*, refers to this interrelationship between the objective truth and the faculties of the observer. This is largely the reason for the differing interpretations of the same fairy tale or myth by various qualified students. Rather than seeing the differing interpretations as erroneous, we may try to recognize them as the particular truths which the observer has been able to grasp among the wealth of meanings harmoniously interacting in the images of the story.

On the other hand, the intimate relationship between the tale and the listener or reader purifies the person. As he becomes able *to recite with sincere devotion* the tale, as he is led to experience the truth contained in it, he is simultaneously purified of sin. This is of utmost importance. Genuine understanding cannot be a merely intellectual process; rather, it goes hand in hand with an emotional cleansing process. The tale cleans the soul, and the purification of the soul, in turn, is necessary for the fuller comprehension of the tale. Here we must remember that, like the epos, the fairy tales were originally narrated by adults for adults. It is only during the past two centuries that fairy tales have been confined, more and more, to the children's world. And even the epos lost much of its former influence upon the adult listeners.

Yet, just as the mythic drama was seen by the Greeks as a purifying, cathartic mystery and not merely as entertainment, so is the fairy tale to be viewed not just as a pastime for the child but also as a fare which helps our young listener. In these overly rationalistic times, the fairy tale and myth have remained an indispensable nourishment which can strengthen the non-intellectual soul forces, the emotions and impulses, of the growing child. All the techniques of child rearing, helpful as they may be with particular problems, cannot offer an adequate substitute for this necessary food of the child's soul. But even to the adult, the lecture of myths, heroic epos, and fairy tales may become a healthy compensation against the overly technologic and rational world in which we live. Thus, R. Steiner tells us that James Thurber became so engrossed in his delightful fairy tale of *The Thirteen Clocks* that he kept on rewriting it until his friends figuratively tore it out of his hands; and in a modern play we see the serious scientist periodically seeking solace and harmony in the simple cottage of an elderly couple, listening to the fairy tales spontaneously flowing from the woman's lips (166).

By gaining a deeper understanding, a greater respect for these stories, the parent will be able to read or tell them to his child at the proper time and in a manner which, rather than creating fears, will commune the hidden meaning. Elaborating on some of the preceding remarks, we might say that the truth contained in the fairy tale is *not* relative, but that it becomes alive and operative in the *relationship* between the story, the parent, and the child. And the purification of the narrator and listener, resulting from experiencing the meaning of the tale, makes them progressively more capable of perceiving ever new truths. In other words, the narration itself becomes, as Joseph Campbell tells us, a more and more transparent "Mask of God" that allows an experience of the invisible and ineffable (25).

I have been digressing from the assertion that *one* single tale may open our eyes to the inner world of the growing and groping human being, as well as to the deeper meanings of human existence and evolution. Now one should add that, especially in our times, the need is felt to illuminate the various truths from *many* viewpoints. We are so thoroughly conditioned by modern natural-scientific methods that usually require numerous repetitive observations in order to achieve statistically valid conclusions, that it becomes difficult for us to accept fully the truths that can be gathered from a single observation. This may well have been a substantial reason for my continued interest in ever new folk narrations.

The brothers Grimm, in spite of all their respect and love for the German fairy tales, were not completely aware of what enormous spiritual treasures their stories contained. However, they sensed this need for a reawakening of the human spirit and recognized that the disclosure of many spiritual truths was still reserved for the future. So they placed at the end of their fairy tale collection the story of "The Golden Key." It is the story of the poor youth who, in midwinter, goes with his sleigh into the forest to gather some wood. Almost frozen from the cold, he tries to start a fire; and in the process, he finds under the snow a little golden key. As he digs deeper, he finds an iron box which can be opened by the key: "And now"—so finishes this tale—"we must wait until the box is unlocked . . . then we shall find out what marvelous things are in it" (Meyer 124). This story reminds me to be modest, patient and humble.

Cinderella does not shrink from joy nor from physical reality. In fact, hardly any task could be more down to earth than that of separating the lentils from the ashes. Yet this menial task that she performs humbly and modestly seems to emphasize her ability to isolate even out of the spent ashes something that is nourishing and life-giving. The white doves help her in this. The doves, rather than being of physical help, portray spiritual assistance exactly opposite to the laws of the material world: We read that on the first day of the celebration, Cinderella is challenged to separate one potful of lentils from the ashes in two hours, and that she accomplishes this—with the birds' help—in one hour. Yet when challenged the second time, she finishes twice this task in only half the time. From a spiritual viewpoint, the physical tasks cannot ever become impossible; the greater the hardship, the greater the help. This fairy tale underscores that only the young individual who willingly faces the challenges of our material existence, but who also is keeping faith with her noble origin, becomes capable of solving even those tasks that at first seem insurmountable.

The natural scientist, the materialist, the atheist forget that even they derive their experience of existence (as well as their ability to function as human beings) from the meaning that they connect with their work and with their ideas, even though they are inclined to deny the reality of any meaningfulness. They cannot, however, be discounted or ignored, since they play a very essential role in the journey of humanity through the "wintry forest." In the fairy tale, we have seen this orientation toward death (and away from values and meaningfulness), toward animalism and materialism in the guise of some sorcerers, witches, and dwarfs, of stepmothers and stepsisters, of the haughty maid and other apparently maleficent beings. They laugh about God, but they serve His purposes. Goethe has made this the principal theme of his *Faust*, where the devil Mephistopheles is "a part of that force which always desires evil and always creates good" (54). I regret that my accounts of various fairy tales and epos have not always reflected the richness of my inner experience and that this experience often has only been able to grasp a small part of the variegated meaningfulness of these narrations.

Works Cited

Campbell, Joseph. *The Hero with a Thousand Faces*. Ed. C. Schuddekopf. New York: Meridian Books, 1956. Print.

Goethe, J. W. *Faust*. Berlin: C. Schuddekopf, n.d. Print.

Meyer, R. *Die Weisheit der Deutschen Volksmarchen*. Stuttgart: Verlag der Christengemeinschaft, 1935. Print.

Steiner, R. *Die Pforte der Einweihung*. Dornach, Switzerland: Phil.-Anthrop. Verlag, 1935. Print.

Zimmer, H. *The King and the Corpse*. New York: Meridian Books, 1960. Print.

Discussion Questions

1. Explain the ways Julius E. Heuscher's failure to grasp the monumental task he was undertaking was essential to his ultimate success. Tell about something you accomplished that you would never have begun had you known of the difficulties involved.

2. Discuss the way Heuscher's claim, that fairy tales provide an "intellectual process" and an "emotional cleansing process," is relevant to the study of medicine. Think back to the reasons Valerie Gribben believes they help her as a doctor. Do you think they could help you in your future career?

3. Discuss the lesson the author learns from the fairy tale "The Golden Key." How is this lesson different from the one Gribben says that fairy tales teach? How would Heuscher account for the different interpretation Gribben might offer of any fairy tale?

Assignment #6

"Connectivity and Its Discontents"

We hope you have come to see the value in doing extensive prewriting as you work to build a draft of your essay. By now you should be familiar with the prewriting strategies in *Write It*. For this assignment, decide which are most beneficial to your writing and critical thinking style, and customize them to maximize their benefits. Just be sure not to omit a thorough examination of Sherry Turkle's ideas and your own before you formulate your thesis statement and offer your supporting evidence.

Turkle is concerned about the impact that she believes cell phones are having on our personal relationships. Be sure to keep an open mind as you consider her argument. The prewriting activities in this unit will guide you to explore your experience and observations carefully and thoughtfully before you take a position on the issue her essay presents. Also, keep in mind the importance of responding directly to the writing topic that follows "Connectivity and Its Discontents," and the importance of having a clear and well-supported thesis statement as you develop, shape, and revise your essay.

Connectivity and Its Discontents

Essay

SHERRY TURKLE

Sherry Turkle is a professor of the Social Studies of Science and Technology at the Michigan Institute of Technology (MIT). She is the founder and director of the MIT Initiative on Technology and Self, and a licensed clinical psychologist. She has published a trilogy of books in her field, and the following excerpt comes from the third book in the sequence, Alone Together *(2011).*

Online connections were first conceived as a substitute for face-to-face contact, when the latter was for some reason impractical: Don't have time to make a phone call? Shoot off a text message. But very quickly, the text message became the connection of choice. We discovered the network—the world of connectivity—to be uniquely suited to the overworked and overscheduled life it makes possible. And now we look to the network to defend us against loneliness even as we use it to control the intensity of our connections. Technology makes it easy to communicate when we wish, and to disengage at will.

A few years ago at a dinner party in Paris, I met Ellen, an ambitious, elegant young woman in her early thirties, thrilled to be working at her dream job in advertising. Once a week, she would call her grandmother in Philadelphia using Skype, an Internet service that functions as a telephone with a Web camera. Before Skype, Ellen's calls to her grandmother were costly and brief. With Skype, the calls are free and give the compelling sense that the other person is present—Skype is an almost real-time video link. Ellen could now call more frequently: "Twice a week and I stay on the call for an hour," she told me. It should have been rewarding; instead, when I met her, Ellen was unhappy. She knew that her grandmother was unaware that Skype allows surreptitious multitasking. Her grandmother could see Ellen's face on the screen but not her hands. Ellen admitted to me, "I do my e-mail during the calls. I'm not really paying attention to our conversation." Ellen's multitasking removed her to another place. She felt that her grandmother was talking to someone who was not really there. During their Skype conversations, Ellen and her grandmother were more connected than they had ever been before, but at the same time, each was alone. Ellen felt guilty and confused: She knew that her grandmother was happy, even if their intimacy was now, for Ellen, another task among multitasks.

I have often observed this distinctive confusion: These days, whether you are online or not, it is easy for people to end up unsure if they are closer together or further apart. I remember my own sense of disorientation the first time I realized that I was "alone together." I had traveled an exhausting thirty-six hours to attend a conference on advanced robotic technology held in central Japan. The packed grand ballroom was Wi-Fi enabled: The speaker was using the Web for his presentation, laptops were open throughout the audience, fingers were flying, and there was a sense of great concentration and intensity. But not many in the audience were attending to the speaker. Most people seemed to be doing their e-mail, downloading files, and surfing the Net. The man next to me was searching for a *New Yorker* cartoon to illustrate his upcoming presentation. Every once in a while, audience members gave the speaker some attention, lowering their laptop screens in a kind of curtsy, a gesture of courtesy.

Outside, in the hallways, the people milling around me were looking past me to virtual others. They were on their laptops and their phones, connecting to colleagues at the conference going on around them and to others around the globe. There but not there. Of course, clusters of people chatted with each other, making dinner plans, "networking" in that old sense of the word, the one that implies having a coffee or sharing a meal. But at this conference, it was clear that what people mostly want from public space is to be alone with their personal networks. It is good to come together physically, but it is more important to stay tethered to our devices. I thought of Sigmund Freud's idea that communities have the power to both shape and subvert us, and a psychoanalytic pun came to mind: "connectivity and its discontents."

The phrase comes back to me months later as I interview management consultants who seem to have lost touch with their best instincts for what makes them competitive. They complain about the BlackBerry revolution, yet accept it as inevitable while decrying it as corrosive. They say they used to talk to each other as they waited to give presentations or took taxis to the airport; now they spend that time doing e-mail. Some tell me they are making better use of their "downtime," but they argue without conviction. The time that they once used to talk as they waited for appointments or drove to the airport was never downtime. It was the time when far-flung global teams solidified relationships and refined ideas.

In corporations, among friends, and within academic departments, people readily admit that they would rather leave a voicemail or send an e-mail than talk face-to-face. Some who say "I live on my iPhone" are forthright about avoiding the "real-time" commitment of a phone call. The new technologies allow us to "dial down" human contact, to titrate its nature and extent. I recently overheard a conversation in a restaurant between two women. "No one answers the phone in our house anymore," the first woman proclaimed with some consternation. "It used to be that the kids would race to pick up the phone. Now they are up in their rooms, knowing no one is going to call them, and texting and going on Facebook, or whatever, instead." Parents with teenage children will be nodding at this very familiar story in recognition and perhaps a sense of wonderment that this has happened, and so quickly. We've sacrificed conversation for mere connection.

Writing Topic

According to Turkle, what is the problem with our growing reliance on technological communication in our personal and professional lives? Do you agree with her? Be sure to support your position with specific evidence; this evidence may be taken from your personal experience, your observations, or your reading, including the reading from this course.

Vocabulary Check

You will want to be sure that you understand the key vocabulary terms below and the way Turkle uses them in "Connectivity and Its Discontents." Words can have a variety of meanings, or they can have specialized meanings in certain contexts. Look up the definitions of the following words. Then, choose the meaning that you think Turkle intended when she selected that particular word. Explain the way the meaning or concept behind the definition is key to understanding his argument.

1. *discontent (noun)*

    definition: _____

    _____

    explanation: _____

    _____

    _____

    _____

2. *connection*

    definition: _____

    _____

    explanation: _____

    _____

    _____

    _____

3. *conceive*

definition: _____

_____

explanation: _____

_____

_____

_____

4. *intensity*

definition: _____

_____

explanation: _____

_____

_____

_____

5. *disengage*

definition: _____

_____

explanation: _____

_____

_____

_____

6. *surreptitious*

   definition: _____

   _____

   explanation: _____

   _____

   _____

   _____

7. *intimacy*

   definition: _____

   _____

   explanation: _____

   _____

   _____

   _____

8. *distinctive*

   definition: _____

   _____

   explanation: _____

   _____

   _____

   _____

9. *disorientation*

   definition: _____

   _____

   explanation: _____

   _____

   _____

   _____

10. *exhaust (verb)*

    definition: _____

    _____

    explanation: _____

    _____

    _____

    _____

11. *concentration*

    definition: _____

    _____

    explanation: _____

    _____

    _____

    _____

12. *courtesy*

   definition: _____

   _____

   explanation: _____

   _____

   _____

   _____

13. *mill (verb)*

   definition: _____

   _____

   explanation: _____

   _____

   _____

   _____

14. *subvert*

   definition: _____

   _____

   explanation: _____

   _____

   _____

   _____

15. *psychoanalytic*

    definition: _____

    _____

    explanation: _____

    _____

    _____

    _____

16. *instinct*

    definition: _____

    _____

    explanation: _____

    _____

    _____

    _____

17. *solidify*

    definition: _____

    _____

    explanation: _____

    _____

    _____

    _____

18. *refined*

    definition: _____

    _____

    explanation: _____

    _____

    _____

    _____

19. *titrate*

    definition: _____

    _____

    explanation: _____

    _____

    _____

    _____

20. *sacrifice*

    definition: _____

    _____

    explanation: _____

    _____

    _____

    _____

Questions to Guide Your Reading

Answer the following questions so you can gain a thorough understanding of "Connectivity and Its Discontents."

Paragraph 1

According to Turkle, what was the original purpose of online communications? How was the purpose subverted?

Paragraph 2

Why did Ellen become unhappy with her Skype calls to her grandmother?

Paragraphs 3-4

What does Turkle mean when she uses the phrase "alone together"? What experience aided her recognition of this state of communal aloneness?

Paragraph 5

How did technology change the "downtime" of the management consultants Turkle interviewed?

Paragraph 6

In what ways have the many groups that Turkle identifies eliminated opportunities for face-to-face contact from their lives?

Prewriting for a Directed Summary

The first part of the writing topic that follows "Connectivity and Its Discontents" asks you about a central idea from Turkle's essay. To answer this part of the writing topic, you will want to write a *directed* summary, meaning one that responds specifically to the writing topic's first question.

first part of the writing topic:

According to Turkle, what is the problem with our growing reliance on technological communication in our personal and professional lives?

 Hint

Don't forget to look back to Part 1's "Guidelines for Writing a Directed Summary."

Focus Questions

1. How has the original purpose of online communication changed, according to Turkle?

2. What role does she believe we expect the network to play in our lives today?

3. Why does Turkle believe that the use of Skype or other online methods for communication in our personal lives can produce feelings of discontent?

4. How does Turkle explain the impact of technological communication on our wants and behaviors in public spaces?

5. What does Turkle believe to be the ultimate cost of online communication?

Developing an Opinion and Working Thesis Statement

The second part of the writing topic for "Connectivity and Its Discontents" asks you to take a position of your own on the issue that concerns Turkle. Your response to this part of the writing topic will become the thesis statement of your essay, so it is important to spend some time ensuring that it reflects the position you want to take. Do you think that our connections with one another are being damaged or diminished by our increasing use of technology, such as cell phones and Skype, to communicate with one another?

> writing topic's second part:
>
> *Do you agree with her?*

In order to make your position clear to readers, state it early in your essay, preferably at the end of your introductory paragraph. A clear thesis statement, one that takes a position on the impact of technology on our connections with one another, will unify your essay and allow it to effectively communicate with readers.

It is likely that you aren't yet sure what position you want to take in your essay. If this is the case, go on to the next section and work on developing your ideas through specific evidence drawn from your experience. Then, you will be asked to reexamine the working thesis statement you write here and see if you want to revise it based on the discoveries you made when you explored your ideas more systematically.

1. Use the following thesis frame to identify the basic elements of your working thesis statement:

   a. What is the issue of "Connectivity and Its Discontents" that the writing topic asks you to consider?

   _____

   b. What is Turkle's opinion about that issue?

   _____

   c. What is your opinion about the issue, and will you agree or disagree with Turkle?

   _____

   _____

   _____

2. Now use the elements you isolated in the thesis frame to write a thesis statement. You may have to revise it several times until it captures your ideas clearly.

_____

_____

Prewriting to Find Support for Your Thesis Statement

The last part of the writing topic asks you to support the position you put forward in your thesis statement. Well-developed ideas are crucial when you are making an argument because you will have to be clear, logical, and thorough if you are to be convincing. As you work through the exercises below, you will generate much of the 4Cs material you will need when you draft your essay's body paragraphs.

writing topic's last part:

Be sure to support your position with specific evidence; this evidence may be taken from your personal experience, your observations, or your reading, including the reading from this course.

Complete each section of this prewriting activity; your responses will become the material you will use in the next stage—planning and writing the essay.

1. Turkle believes that the amount of quality time we spend talking with one another is significantly decreasing as we opt to use technology such as text messaging and the Internet to communicate with one another. Consider the personal conversations you have in a typical week. Perhaps make a list of the people—especially friends and family members—you spoke with face-to-face or voice-to-voice in an extended conversation. Following each, add a couple of words indicating the main reason for the conversation and your feeling about it—positive, negative, or neutral. Now make a list of the people—especially friends and family members—you interacted with using some form of technology that did not involve personal contact, again adding the purpose and tone of the communication.

   Now examine your two lists and consider whether they support or conflict with Turkle's argument. Consider first whether your communication with others takes place personally or electronically. Do you use one significantly more often than the other? If so, why? When you want to get in touch with someone, what determines the method you use? Are these experiences mostly satisfying, or do they support Turkle's point that we are becoming more and more isolated from one another? Do some freewriting to explore your thoughts.

Once you've listed your specific examples and done some speculative freewriting about the meaning or significance of each, carefully look over all that you have written. Try to group your ideas into categories. Then, give each category a label. In other words, cluster ideas that seem to have something in common and, for each cluster, identify that shared quality by giving it a title.

2. Now broaden your focus. Consider the culture of academia, business, and society at large. No one would disagree that technology has significantly increased efficiency by providing easier, less time-consuming ways to communicate with one another. But do you think that the price of this greater efficiency has increased isolation? Have the potential richness and warmth of our communications disappeared as we've come to rely primarily on technology? List several examples of the ways we interact in academia, business, and society at large. Then, freewrite to explore your thoughts.

Once you've written your ideas, look them over carefully. Try to group your ideas into categories. Then, give each category a label. In other words, cluster ideas that seem to have something in common and, for each cluster, identify that shared quality by giving it a name.

3. Once you've created topics by clustering your ideas into categories, go through them and pick two or three specific ones to develop in your essay. Make sure that they are relevant to your thesis and that they have enough substance to be compelling to your reader. Then, in the space below, briefly summarize each item. Take some time to explain how each category and its items connect to your thesis statement. You will use these details for the next stage.

Revising Your Thesis Statement

Now that you have spent some time working out your ideas more systematically and developing some supporting evidence for the position you want to take, look again at the working thesis statement you crafted earlier and see if it is still accurate. As your first step, look again at the writing topic, and then write your original working thesis on the lines that follow it.

writing topic:

According to Turkle, what is the problem with our growing reliance on technological communication in our personal and professional lives? Do you agree with her? Be sure to support your position with specific evidence; this evidence may be taken from your personal experience, your observations, or from reading, including the reading from this course.

Working Thesis Statement:

_____

_____

_____

Often, after extensive prewriting and focused thought, you will find that the working thesis statement is no longer an accurate reflection of what you plan to say in your essay. You may need to add or change a word or phrase in the subject or the claim. Or, you may decide that the thesis statement must be completely rewritten so that it takes a very different position on the issue. Take some time now to see if you want to revise your thesis statement. Remember that your thesis statement must respond to the second part of the writing topic, but also take into consideration the writing topic as a whole. The first part of the writing topic identifies the issue that is up for debate, and the last part of the writing topic reminds you that, whatever position you take on the issue, you must support it with specific evidence.

Use the following questions to ensure that your thesis statement is fully developed, clear, and accurate:

a. Does the thesis directly identify Turkle's concern that our increasing use of technology to communicate with one another is eroding the quality of our personal relationships?

b. Do you make clear your opinion regarding this connection?

c. Is your thesis well punctuated, grammatically correct, and precisely worded?

Add any missing elements, correct the grammar errors, and refine the wording. Then, write your polished thesis on the lines below. Try to look at it from your readers' perspective. Is it strong and interesting?

Hint

Be sure that your thesis presents a clear position; it should not be a statement that shows you haven't yet made up your mind and are still considering two or more options or possibilities.

_____

_____

_____

Planning and Drafting Your Essay

Now that you have examined Turkle's argument and thought at length about your own views, draft an essay that responds to all parts of the writing topic. Use the material you developed in the above activities to compose your draft, and then exchange drafts with a classmate and use the peer review activity to revise your draft.

Getting started on the draft is often the hardest part of the writing process because this is where you move from exploring and planning to getting your ideas down in a unified, coherent shape.

You may not be in the habit of outlining or planning your essay before you begin drafting it, and some of you may avoid outlining altogether. If you haven't been using an outline as you move through the writing process, try using it this time. Creating an outline will give you a clear and coherent structure for incorporating all of the ideas you have developed in the preceding pages. It will also show you where you may have gone off track, left logical holes in your reasoning, or failed to develop one or more of your paragraphs.

Your outline doesn't have to use Roman numerals or be highly detailed. Just use an outline form that suits your style and shows you a bird's-eye view of your argument. Below is a form that we think you will find useful. Consult the academic essay diagram in Part 1 of this book, too, to remind yourself of the conventional form of a college essay and its basic parts.

I. Introductory Paragraph

   A. An opening sentence that gives the reading selection's title and author and begins to answer the first part of the writing topic:

   _____

   _____

   _____

   B. Main points to include in the directed summary:

   1.

   2.

   3.

   4.

C. Write out your thesis statement. (Look back to "Revising Your Thesis Statement," where you reexamined and refined your working thesis statement.) It should clearly state whether you agree with Turkle's claim about the damaging effect technology is having on our connections with one another.

_____

_____

_____

II. Body Paragraphs

A. The paragraph's one main point that supports the thesis statement:

_____

1. Controlling idea sentence:

_____

_____

2. Corroborating details:

_____

_____

_____

_____

3. Careful explanation of why the details are relevant:

_____

_____

_____

_____

_____

4. Connection to the thesis statement:

_____

_____

_____

B. The paragraph's one main point that supports the thesis statement:

_____

1. Controlling idea sentence:

_____

_____

2. Corroborating details:

_____

_____

_____

_____

3. Careful explanation of why the details are relevant:

_____

_____

_____

_____

_____

4. Connection to the thesis statement:

_____

_____

_____

C. The paragraph's one main point that supports the thesis statement:

_____

1. **C**ontrolling idea sentence:

_____

_____

2. **C**orroborating details:

_____

_____

_____

_____

3. **C**areful explanation of why the details are relevant:

_____

_____

_____

_____

_____

4. **C**onnection to the thesis statement:

_____

_____

_____

D. The paragraph's one main point that supports the thesis statement:

_____

1. **C**ontrolling idea sentence:

_____

_____

2. **C**orroborating details:

_____

_____

_____

_____

3. **C**areful explanation of why the details are relevant:

_____

_____

_____

_____

_____

4. **C**onnection to the thesis statement:

_____

_____

_____

Repeat this form for any remaining body paragraphs.

III. Conclusion

A. Type of conclusion to be used (see "Conclusions" in Part 1):

_____

B. Key words or phrases to include:

_____

Getting Feedback on Your Draft

Use the following guidelines to give a classmate feedback on his or her draft. Read the draft through first, and then answer each of the items below as specifically as you can.

Name of draft's author: _____

Name of draft's reader: _____

The Introduction

1. Within the opening sentences:
   a. Turkle's first and last name are given.   yes   no
   b. The reading selection's title is given and
      placed within quotation marks.   yes   no

2. The opening contains a summary that:
   a. summarizes Turkle's claim that we are becoming
      more and more dependent on technology
      to communicate   yes   no
   b. explains the impact that Turkle believes this
      dependence is having on our personal relationships   yes ·   no
   c. explains why our increasing dependence on technology
      to communicate with one another concerns her   yes   no

3. The opening provides a thesis that makes clear the
   draft writer's opinion regarding Turkle's argument.   yes   no

If you circled yes in #3 above, copy the thesis below as it is written. If you circled no, explain to the draft writer what information is needed to make the thesis complete.

_____

_____

_____

The Body

1. How many paragraphs are in the body of this essay? _____
2. To support the thesis, this number is   sufficient   not enough

3. Do body paragraphs contain the 4Cs?

Paragraph 1	Controlling idea sentence	yes	no
	Corroborating details	yes	no
	Careful explanation of why the details are relevant	yes	no
	Connection to the thesis statement	yes	no
Paragraph 2	Controlling idea sentence	yes	no
	Corroborating details	yes	no
	Careful explanation of why the details are relevant	yes	no
	Connection to the thesis statement	yes	no
Paragraph 3	Controlling idea sentence	yes	no
	Corroborating details	yes	no
	Careful explanation of why the details are relevant	yes	no
	Connection to the thesis statement	yes	no
Paragraph 4	Controlling idea sentence	yes	no
	Corroborating details	yes	no
	Careful explanation of why the details are relevant	yes	no
	Connection to the thesis statement	yes	no
Paragraph 5	Controlling idea sentence	yes	no
	Corroborating details	yes	no
	Careful explanation of why the details are relevant	yes	no
	Connection to the thesis statement	yes	no

(Continue as needed.)

4. Identify any of the body paragraphs that are underdeveloped (too short).

_____

5. Identify any of the body paragraphs that fail to support the thesis.

_____

6. Identify any of the body paragraphs that are redundant or repetitive.

_____

7. Suggest any ideas for additional body paragraphs that might improve this essay.

_____

_____

_____

The Conclusion

1. Does the final paragraph avoid introducing new ideas
   and examples that really belong in the body of the essay?   yes   no

2. Does the conclusion provide closure (let readers know
   that the end of the essay has been reached)?   yes   no

3. Does the conclusion leave readers with an
   understanding of the significance of the argument?   yes   no

   State in your own words what the draft writer considers to be important about his or her argument.

   _____

   _____

   _____

4. Identify the type of conclusion used (see the guidelines for conclusions in Part 1).

   _____

Editing

1. During the editing process, the writer should pay attention to the following problems in sentence structure, punctuation, and mechanics:

   fragments
   misplaced and dangling modifiers
   fused (run-on) sentences
   comma splices
   misplaced, missing, and unnecessary commas
   misplaced, missing, and unnecessary apostrophes
   incorrect quotation mark use
   capitalization errors
   spelling errors

2. While editing, the writer should pay attention to the following areas of grammar:

verb tense
subject-verb agreement
irregular verbs
pronoun type
pronoun reference
pronoun agreement
noun plurals
prepositions

Final Draft Checklist

Content:

- My essay has an appropriate title.
- I provide an accurate summary of Turkle's argument concerning the damaging effects of technology on our personal relationships.
- My thesis states a clear position that can be supported by evidence.
- I have enough paragraphs and argument points to support my thesis.
- Each body paragraph is relevant to my thesis.
- Each body paragraph contains the 4Cs.
- I use transitions whenever necessary to connect ideas.
- The final paragraph of my essay (the conclusion) provides readers with a sense of closure.

Grammar, Punctuation, and Mechanics:

- I use the present tense to discuss Turkle's argument and examples.
- I use verb tenses correctly to show the chronology of events.
- I have verb tense consistency throughout my sentences and paragraphs.
- I have checked for subject-verb agreement in all of my sentences.
- I have revised all fragments and mixed or garbled sentences.
- I have repaired all fused (run-on) sentences and comma splices.
- I have placed a comma after introductory elements (transitions and phrases) and all dependent clauses that open a sentence.
- If I present items in a series (nouns, verbs, prepositional phrases), they are parallel in form.
- If I include material spoken or written by someone other than myself, I have correctly punctuated it with quotation marks, using the MLA style guide's rules for citation.
- If I include material spoken or written by someone other than myself, I have included a works cited list that follows the MLA style guide's rules for citation.

Reviewing Your Graded Essay

After your instructor has returned your essay, you may have the opportunity to revise your paper and raise your grade. Many students, especially those whose essays receive nonpassing grades, feel that their instructors should be less "picky" about grammar and should pass the work on content alone. However, most students at this level have not yet acquired the ability to recognize quality writing, and they do not realize that content and writing actually cannot be separated in this way. Experienced instructors know that errors in sentence structure, grammar, punctuation, and word choice either interfere with content or distract readers so much that they lose track of content. In short, good ideas badly presented are no longer good ideas; to pass, an essay must have passable writing. So even if you are not submitting a revised version of this essay to your instructor, it is important that you review your work carefully in order to understand its strengths and weaknesses. This sheet will guide you through the evaluation process.

You will want to continue to use the techniques that worked well for you and to find strategies to overcome the problems that you identify in this sample of your writing. To recognize areas that might have been problematic for you, look back at the scoring rubric in this book. Match the numerical/verbal/letter grade received on your essay to the appropriate category. Study the explanation given on the rubric for your grade.

Write a few sentences below in which you identify your problems in each of the following areas. Then, suggest specific changes you could make that would improve your paper. Don't forget to use your handbook as a resource.

1. **Grammar/punctuation/mechanics**

   My problem:

   My strategy for change:

2. **Thesis/response to assignment**

   My problem:

   My strategy for change:

3. Organization

My problem:

My strategy for change:

4. Paragraph development/examples/reasoning

My problem:

My strategy for change:

5. Assessment

In the space below, assign a grade to your paper using the rubric in Part 1 of this book. In other words, if your instructor assigned your essay a grade of *High Fail*, you might give it the letter grade you now feel the paper warrants. If your instructor used the traditional letter grade to evaluate the essay, choose a category from the rubric in this book, or any other grading scale that you are familiar with, to show your evaluation of your work. Then, write a short narrative explaining your evaluation of the essay and the reasons it received the grade you gave it.

Grade: _____

Narrative: _____

_____

_____

_____

_____

Extending the Discussion:
Considering Other Viewpoints

Reading Selections

"Cognitive Surplus" by Clay Shirky

"The Facebook Machine of Impoverishment: One Click at a Time" by Ninetta Papadomichelaki and Lash Keith Vance

"The Net and Fundamentalism" by Douglas Rushkoff

"Addicted to Technology" by Gary Small, MD, and Gigi Vorgan

"The Final Showdown between In-Person and Cyberspace Relationships" by John Suler

"Technology's Impact on Social Relationships" by Tom Dellner

Cognitive Surplus

Essay

CLAY SHIRKY

Clay Shirky writes and teaches about the social effects of Internet technology. He is interested especially in the way culture shapes the Internet and the Internet shapes culture. He graduated from Yale with a BA in fine art and currently teaches at New York University's graduate telecommunications program. His essays have appeared in Business 2.0, *the* New York Times, *the* Wall Street Journal, *the* Harvard Business Review, *and* Wired.

Americans watch roughly two hundred *billion* hours of TV every year. That represents about two thousand Wikipedia projects' worth of free time annually. Even tiny subsets of this time are enormous: We spend roughly a hundred million hours every weekend just watching commercials. This is a pretty big surplus. People who ask "Where do they find the time?" about those who work on Wikipedia don't understand how tiny that entire project is, relative to the aggregate free time we all possess. One thing that makes the current age remarkable is that we can now treat free time as a general social asset that can be harnessed for large, communally created projects, rather than as a set of individual minutes to be whiled away one person at a time.

Society never really knows what to do with any surplus at first. (That's what makes it a surplus.) For most of the time when we've had a truly large-scale surplus in free time—billions and then trillions of hours a year—we've spent it consuming television because we judged that use of time to be better than the available alternatives. Sure, we could have played outdoors or read books or made music with our friends, but we mostly didn't because the thresholds to those activities were too high compared to just sitting and watching. Life in the developed world includes a lot of passive participation: At work we're office drones; at home we're couch potatoes. The pattern is easy enough to explain by assuming we've wanted to be passive participants more than we have wanted other things. This story has been, in the last several decades, pretty plausible; a lot of evidence certainly supported this view, and not a lot contradicted it.

But now, for the first time in the history of television, some cohorts of young people are watching TV less than their elders. Several population studies—of high school students, broadband users, YouTube users—have noticed the change, and their basic observation is always the same: Young populations with access to fast, interactive media are shifting their behavior away from media that presuppose pure consumption. Even when they watch video online, seemingly a pure analog to TV, they have opportunities to comment on the material; to share it with their friends; to label, rate, or rank it; and, of course, to discuss it with other viewers around the world. As Dan Hill notes in a much-cited online essay, "Why *Lost* Is Genuinely New Media," the viewers of that show weren't just viewers—they collaboratively created a compendium of material related to that show called (what else?) *Lostpedia*. Even when they are engaged in watching TV, in other words, many members of the networked population are engaged with one another, and this engagement correlates with behaviors other than passive consumption.

The choices leading to reduced TV consumption are at once tiny and enormous. The tiny choices are individual; someone simply decides to spend the next hour talking to friends or playing a game or creating something instead of just watching. The enormous choices are collective ones, an accumulation of those tiny choices by the millions; the cumulative shift toward participation across a whole population enables the creation of a *Wikipedia*. The television industry has been shocked to see alternative uses of free time, especially among young people, because the idea that watching TV was the best use of free time, as ratified by the viewers, has been such a stable feature of society for so long. Believing that the past stability of this behavior meant it would be a stable behavior in the future as well turned out to be a mistake.

As long as the assumed purpose of media is to allow ordinary people to consume professionally created material, the proliferation of amateur-created stuff will seem incomprehensible. What amateurs do is so, well, unprofessional— lolcats as a kind of low-grade substitute for the Cartoon Network. But what if, all this time, providing professional content isn't the only job we've been hiring media to do? What if we've also been hiring it to make us feel connected, engaged, or just less lonely? What if we've always wanted to produce as well as consume, but no one offered us that opportunity?

The pleasure in *You can play this game too* isn't just in the making; it's also in the sharing. The phrase "user-generated content," the current label for creative acts by amateurs, really describes not just personal but also social acts. Lolcats aren't just user-generated; they are user-shared. The sharing, in fact, is what makes the making fun—no one would create a lolcat to keep for themselves.

The atomization of social life in the twentieth century left us so far removed from participatory culture that when it came back, we needed the phrase "participatory culture" to describe it. Before the twentieth century, we didn't really have a phrase for participatory culture; in fact, it would have been something of a tautology. A significant chunk of culture was participatory—local gatherings, events, and performances—because where else could culture come from? The simple act of creating something with others in mind and then sharing it with them represents, at the very least, an echo of that older model of culture, now in technological raiment. Once you accept the idea that we actually like making and sharing things, however dopey in content or poor in execution, and that making one another laugh is a different kind of activity from being made to laugh by people paid to make us laugh, then in some ways the Cartoon Network is a low-grade substitute for lolcats.

Media in the twentieth century were run as a single event: consumption. The animating question of media in that era was *If we produce more, will you consume more?* The answer to that question has generally been yes, as the average person consumed more TV with each passing year. But media are actually like a triathlon, with three different events: People like to consume, but they also like to produce and to share. We've always enjoyed all three of those activities, but until recently, broadcast media rewarded only one of them.

Evidence accumulates daily that if you offer people the opportunity to produce and to share, they'll sometimes take you up on it, even if they've never behaved that way before and even if they're not as good at it as the pros. That doesn't mean we'll stop mindlessly watching TV. It just means that consumption will no longer be the only way we use media. And any shift, however minor, in the way we use a trillion hours of free time a year is likely to be a big deal.

One reason we have such a hard time thinking about cultural change as enabled by new communications tools is that the egocentric view is the wrong way to approach it. The chance that anyone with a camera will come across an event of global significance is simply the number of witnesses of the event times the percentage of them that have cameras. That first number will fluctuate up and down depending on the event, but the second number—the number of people carrying cameras—rose from a few million worldwide in 2000 to well over a billion today. Cameras are now embedded in phones, increasing the number of people who have a camera with them all the time.

We've seen the effects of this new reality dozens of times: the London transport bombings in 2005, the Thai coup in 2006, the police killing of Oscar Grant in Oakland in 2008, the post-election Iranian unrest in 2009—all these events and countless more were documented with camera phones and then uploaded for the world to see. The chance that someone with a camera will come across an event of global significance is rapidly becoming the chance that such an event has any witnesses at all. Those kinds of changes in scale mean that formerly improbable events become likely, and that formerly unlikely events become certainties. Whereas we previously relied on professional photojournalism to document such events, we are increasingly becoming one another's infrastructure.

Even that, though, doesn't yet describe what we could do with the cognitive surplus, because the way we put our collective talents to work is a social issue, not solely a personal one. Because we have to coordinate with one another to get anything out of our shared free time and talents, using cognitive surplus isn't just about accumulating individual preferences. The culture of the various groups of users matters enormously for what they expect of one another and how they work together. The culture in turn will determine how much of the value that we get out of the cognitive surplus will be merely communal (enjoyed by the participants, but not of much use for society at large) and how much of it will be civic. (You can think of *communal* versus *civic* as paralleling *lolcats* versus *Ushahidi*.)[1]

We've already learned some lessons from successful uses of cognitive surplus, lessons that can guide us as more of that surplus is used in more important ways. The cognitive surplus, newly forged from previously disconnected islands of time and talent, is just raw material. To get any value out of it, we have to make it mean or do things. We,

---

[1]Ushahidi was a blog site developed to help citizens of Kenya track outbreaks of ethnic violence during the 2007 elections. The blog was started by a Kenyan political activist, Ory Okolloh, and her site became a popular critical source of first-person reporting.

collectively, aren't just the source of the surplus; we are also the people designing its use, by our participation and by the things we expect of one another as we wrestle together with our new connectedness.

The old view of online as a separate space, cyberspace, apart from the real world, was an accident of history. Back when the online population was tiny, most of the people you knew in your daily life weren't part of that population. Now that computers and increasingly computerlike phones have been broadly adopted, the whole notion of cyberspace is fading. Our social media tools aren't an alternative to real life, they are part of it. In particular, they are increasingly the coordinating tools for events in the physical world, as in Cheonggyecheon Park. People concerned about digital media often worry about the decay of face-to-face contact, but in Seoul, the most wired (and wireless) place on earth, the effect was just the opposite. Digital tools were critical to coordinating human contact and real-world activity. The old idea that media are a domain relatively separate from "the real world" no longer applies to situations like the mad cow protests in South Korea, or indeed to any of the myriad ways people are using social media to arrange real-world action.

Discussion Questions

1. How has the use of surplus time been changing in recent years? What, according to Clay Shirky, does the change suggest about the desirability of passive consumption?

2. When you have free time, how do you prefer to spend it? Is your choice active or passive? After reading the other articles in this unit, tell why you feel pleased or displeased with your favorite free time activity now that you have read Turkle and Shirky.

3. What does Shirky believe accounts for the popularity of websites with "user-generated content"? How do you think Turkle would answer Shirky's concern about the reasons people visit such sites?

4. Explain the "shift" in media that Shirky identifies. What are some examples he gives of the ways this shift is revising our infrastructure? Give some examples of your own of possible revisions.

The Facebook Machine of Impoverishment: One Click at a Time

Essay

Ninetta Papadomichelaki and Lash Keith Vance

Keith Vance and Ninetta Papadomichelaki are faculty members in the University Writing Program at the University of California, Riverside. They have published Compass: Paths to Effective Reading *and* Compass: Guidebook to English Grammar.

There has never been a more powerful communication tool to bring together so many so quickly so elegantly, conquering distance, culture, and economic disparity with a single click. It is the great equalizer; it is the missing connective tissue that people have lacked in a global village where everyone seems to be in flux, moving from place to place and job to job. It is the constant presence, a reminder of our place—and connection—to others in the world even if that exists only as bits and bytes in the ether.

In the age of social media, Facebook is the unsurpassed and unchallenged king. With over 1.55 billion active accounts by 2016, one service, one site has reached out to nearly 20% of the population of the world—and according to *Statista.com*, over 1.3 billion of those users access, post, and parse Facebook pages on their cell phones (Number). The numbers are astounding. According to the PEW Research Center, by 2015 some 72% of all Internet users utilized Facebook, with the highest usage appearing in the 18-29 group (Duggan). It cuts across class boundaries, gender barriers, and race. The only place it seems not to hold total sway is age because the older people are, the less likely they are to use this kind of social medium for communication.

Beyond the connections that it grants peer-to-peer and friend-to-friend, Facebook is even credited as being the primary communication tool for the Arab Spring, that time of revolution and hope from 2010-2011 in the Middle East, where tyrannical governments fell and activists communicated the time, manner, and place of demonstrations through Mark Zuckerberg's creation (Storck; Chebib). And one doesn't have to wait on the front lines of a revolution to see the merits of Facebook. Its defenders are quick to claim that it allows people to stay connected in a topsy-turvy world; it keeps families and friends a click away; it disseminates information to those who need it.

But so many of us have jumped on the Facebook bandwagon that perhaps we haven't thought through the potentially insidious drawbacks to this omnipresent technology. Indeed, while we have changed Facebook and made it the juggernaut that it is, how has Facebook changed us? Surely our overloaded bandwagon is not traversing a one-way street? Contrary to the claims of deeper social interaction, Facebook has become much less about communicating *between* people and far more about communicating an image *to* people.

Sometimes the conveyed image is an accident. Take the example of a couple who constantly post pictures of the gourmet food they create, the fancy restaurants they frequent, or the eclectic wine they enjoy. At first blush, their image in the Facebook universe is that of bragging sybarites—or more charitably—epicureans, people strongly inclined to the physical pleasure of food. Not only do these people just cook, eat, drink, and spend inordinate amounts of money on culinary pleasures, but they also brag about it as well. Little would a Facebook audience know that this couple also enjoy reading, attending the theater, and donating time to a local charity. What this particular audience sees of the couple is a fragment of the whole picture, hyper-focusing on the recipes and wealth sufficient to provide lobster on a regular basis.

Like many others who underestimate the power of Facebook as an image maker or breaker, this couple have an accidental image problem of their own making, and they do not even know it, nor do they consider the ramifications of these postings that showcase their love for creative cooking. Indeed, Facebook users often inadvertently tell a story they wish they could later redact: those bachelor party photos that were posted at 3:00 AM, an admission of cheating on a boyfriend or girlfriend, an angry posting about an employer. . . . Once these postings have a digital life of their own, this information and images can seemingly never be euthanized.

These are unfortunate instances when the digital life of one's shame or partial reality may outlive them. But what of the millions of users who safeguard or even alter their image for the sake of self-promotion? That would be the flipside of the Facebook coin that allows such deep self-editing that there is very little room for authenticity, let alone honesty. And this is not even about those extreme cases of "catfishing" through fraudulent representation of oneself. We are talking about the casual "airbrushing" that Facebook allows its users on a daily basis. Just as many strategically edit a résumé or curriculum vitae in order to apply for a job, many Facebook users intentionally post material specific to the image they wish to project: the editing of pictures to the point of flawlessness, the editing of postings to the point of extreme political correctness or lack thereof, the editing of comments to the point of dishonesty. It's all part of the self-editing machine.

In this era of personal-image glory, Facebook allows its users to be extremely calculative and narcissistic about their idealized projections to the world. As a result, many users cannot function without the omnipresence of their Facebook audience in mind. Inadvertently, this leads to people who are less concerned about their real selves and instead more concerned with how the "self" is projected and perceived by others. In psychoanalysis, this would be called an awareness of the "other"; we would like to call it narcissistic manipulation.

Indeed, even if we try to control the message of our posts, ultimately what we upload is all about the "*I*." Look at what *I'm* doing. How cool am *I* to be skydiving over Palm Springs? Wouldn't you like to be *me*, skiing in the Alps with Jacques Frost bringing *me* a warm mug of hot chocolate to ward off the chill? Instead of enjoying the now and what, Facebook users often agonize about posting the where and the when for "friends" to see and admire, as evidenced by the frenzy of selfies at concerts, amusement parks, all kinds of events. For many, Facebook has become the medium by which the "*I*" keeps up appearances, crying into the machine code of zeros and ones for all to pay attention to just how cool the "*I*" is. At the same time, narcissism's co-conspirator, insecurity, leads to a digital and improved form of "keeping up with the Joneses." Posters may want to show everyone else what they think, what they do, or just how living the good life looks, yet doubt is as old as time, and many people routinely troll the Facebook posts of their "friends," to examine what those "friends" are up to and compare whether that's better, hipper, cooler. In the olden days, this would be called gossip. Nowadays, it's called social media, and it has inveigled its way deep into the heart of all social discourse.

On the surface, Facebook promotes the idea of a connected society, with people staying in contact with friends whom they normally would have lost to the sands of time or even making new, life-long ones. The technology may allow for keeping in contact with others, but at most it may allow for maintaining a friendship that was already well established through personal contact (i.e., spending time together, talking, phone calls, etc.). Is it likely, given the narcissistic format of Facebook and the lack of sustained discussion, that new friendships really spring up? Instead of creating deep connections among people, Facebook has impoverished friendship at its very core: It has altered the definition of friend.

As of 2015, over half of Facebook users had more than 200 friends while 15% had more than 500 (Duggan). Again, the number of friends seems to be directly related to one's age, with older users having 30 or fewer friends. But just how many friends can a person possibly have? It turns out that friendships are not infinite—at least in number if not in degree. Research studies by British anthropologist Robin Dunbar have shown that the human brain has distinct limits on the neocortical processing capacity as evidenced through brain mapping as well as through other ethnographical literature (34). In other words, humans are really only capable (brain-wise) of knowing, recognizing, and being able to associate with about 150 people in a particular social group. This means that we cannot realistically have 150 bosom buddies with whom we share our innermost thoughts over a beer. Instead, the number is much lower for the friends, with whom people hold a special social bond.

Words do mean something still, yet the idea of friendship in the traditional sense has been gutted and transformed by Facebook for an entire generation. By Facebook default, everyone is a "friend." If you want to communicate with people on Facebook, you have to become "friends." In many awkward cases, friend requests are sent and accepted without any further comment, and they are just a code for access to a person's projected Facebook world, not an opportunity for any further communication through dialogue and exchange of ideas. That simple "friend request" has drained interpersonal communication skills even from common courtesy. In our own experience, we have often received these requests from old school mates or people we have not seen in years. Even though we all grew up in an era of no social media, the people from our past seem to have fallen victim to Facebook's new etiquette. They send these requests void of any message that would seem appropriate, such as "Hey, how are you? I thought of you the other day as I was looking at our high-school year book. How is life treating you? I would love to catch up." Instead, even the people in our generation often resort to the clicking of the "Friend Request" button, forsaking any other form of verbal communication or real social interaction. Or is this dry clicking of the button the new social reality? It is frightful to think so.

At the same time, the term "friend" is loosely used for everyone who is granted access to the user's little Facebook kingdom. In real life, it would seem immature if not pretentious to refer to all of our peers, coworkers, or acquaintances as "friends." Yet in the Facebook world, it is the norm. One cannot overtly label another as an acquaintance, client, or close friend, for this would prove uncomfortable or be deemed rude. While it is possible to create different lists of people in order to limit the number of incoming announcements from their Facebook walls, at present there is no way to overtly categorize someone as anything other than friend. The would-be client, the mere acquaintance, the informational group, or the person you have known since kindergarten are all labeled the same. For close, personal, "real" friends, it is possible to navigate a number of menus in order to allow these privileged few access to the inner sanctum, but this *is not* the default. And who actually bothers to limit the newsfeed that others see?

For the younger users, collecting friends on Facebook has become a way to demonstrate social wealth and popularity, as the numerous articles from the *Huffington Post* to the *LA Times* indicate (Dunbar; Williams; Knapton; Mohan). Even the average number of "likes" one receives on a particular posting feeds the friendship and popularity machines. Fifty or more likes on a post must mean your friend pool is strong and robust; five or fewer could be an indication of your low social stature. But doesn't this striving for popularity by collecting friends as a form of currency debase the whole idea of friendship—lasting bonds built through shared experiences, attachments, affinity, rapport, understanding? The matter grows more mysterious with deeper discussion. When asked about the hyperbolic number of friends they have on Facebook, students often respond, "These aren't true friends." Yet their "true" friends are also on Facebook and also part of the crowd subscribing to their newsfeed. It's a convoluted mess that not only devalues friendship at its very core but also distorts the idea of friendship, especially for the younger generation who may grow up applying themselves mostly to gaining Facebook prestige through "friend" numbers, instead of investing time and energy into the cultivation of fewer but deeper social ties that constitute authentic friendships.

As a medium to disseminate information, Facebook is unsurpassed. Perhaps this is why so many businesses and news outlets have flocked to it with such glee. And its role of providing a forum for information and planned action in political movements across the globe is well known. The Arab Spring in 2011 may well not have happened without Facebook or another social media site of similar stature. Perhaps this is the very reason that China, Iran, and a handful of other countries have significantly limited their citizens' access to the service.

Unlike TV news, which is a one-sided medium in which information is relayed from sender to receiver, from news station to viewer, Facebook is hailed as part of Web 2.0, where viewers have morphed from passive consumers of material to active producers of it. As good as Facebook is in distributing news, it falls flat in terms of real, substantive communication among its members. Ironically, there is a steady impoverishment and debasement of real exchanges of ideas, debates, and communication that occurs, and not just in the lack of etiquette. For example, if a person posts a link, a video, and pictures of the pitiable state of refugees fleeing a war-torn country like Syria, the Ukraine, or any number of other hotspot areas around the world, what normally happens? In the case of our unfortunate refugee, what can other viewers of the page do? They can press "Like," post a comment, and/or share the link with their cohort of Facebook users. Although Facebook does offer a platform and prime opportunity for discussion, what happens when a tablet-wielding viewer sees these posts? Most press a button and are too lazy or cagey to comment and start a discussion.

Pressing the "Like" button when viewing the picture of the three-year-old boy refugee who was washed up on the shore after the failed attempt to cross from Turkey to Greece seems oxymoronic, moronic, if not callous. If you "Like" this picture, what does that say about you? Does that reveal your cruel heart that rejoices at the misfortune of others? Of course, Facebook masterminds are now considering adding "Dislike" to expand the options of human expression, lest we forget the hundreds of free emoticons available to the Facebook users. Maybe a sad yellow face or the one with the tear trickling down its cheek? Don't worry: you can post them both and add an angry face too. Wouldn't that be more appropriate for the dead boy? Isn't that good enough before you keep scrolling through your newsfeed? Hardly.

Serious conversation is curtailed by the all-too-easy selection of buttons; people may be aware of important issues should they be posted at all, but these moments quickly pass by the onslaught of additional posts. The opportunity for meaningful dialogue is lost not only by the presence of the buttons that seem to say everything and nothing, but also by the sheer nature of people having to parse so many posts. Maybe Facebook will create a button called "Empathy and Compassion" so that we can all express the sentiment without actually having to write anything. That ought to keep the machine running smoothly, with plenty of time to parse hundreds of posts without getting bogged down in any one in particular.

Facebook is a marvelous tool for presenting information, whether that be about the political proposals of presidential candidates or the last gourmet meal you ate. It's all information. More importantly, it's the same sort of informational relationship: sender and receiver. Yet social media, hailed as the connective tissue that binds us together, should be reevaluated and reinterpreted. Facebook comes with a cost—at least how we currently tend to use this technology. It has affected the way we relate to others and portray ourselves; it has altered our very definition of friendship. Finally, though the platform for communication and discussion exists, though we have ways of intimately connecting to long-lost friends or an ability to make new ones, though we all could become active Web 2.0 participants, Facebook and social media in their current form have not lived up to the hype. Maybe Mark Zuckerberg will develop a "Discussion" button that will, with a click, fill in for all the effort, mental processing, and self-reflection that a real discussion would normally take.

Works Cited

Chebib, Nadine Kassem, and Rabia Minatullah Sohail. "The Reasons Social Media Contributed to the 2011 Egyptian Revolution." International Journal of Business Research and Management 2.3 (2011): 1-24. Print.

Duggan, Maeve. *Mobile Messaging and Social Media 2015*. Washington, D.C.: Pew Research Center, 2015. Print.

Dunbar, Robin. *How Many Friends Does One Person Need?: Dunabar's Number and Other Evolutionary Quirks*. Boston: Harvard University Press, 2010. Print.

Knapton, Sarah. "Facebook Users Have 155 Friends—but Would Trust Just Four in a Crisis." *Telegraph*. Telegraph Media Group Limited, 20 Jan. 2016. Web. 25 Apr. 2016.

Mohan, Geoffrey. "Facebook Is a Bummer, Study Says." *Los Angeles Times*. Los Angeles Times, 14 Aug. 2014. Web. 24 Apr. 2016.

"Number of Monthly Active Facebook Users Worldwide as of 1st Quarter 2016 (in Millions)." *Statista*. Statista, Inc., n.d. Web. 25 May 2016. <http://www.statista.com/statistics/264810/number-of-monthly-active-facebook-users-worldwide/>.

Storck, Madeline. "The Role of Social Media in Political Mobilisation: A Case Study of the January 2011 Egyptian Uprising." Diss. University of St. Andrews, 2011. Print.

Williams, Casey. "Only 4 of Your Facebook Friends Really Matter, New Study Finds: Your Facebook Friend Count Is a Sad, Empty Lie." *Huffington Post*. TheHuffingtonPost.com, Inc., 25 Jan. 2016. Web. 22 Apr. 2016.

Discussion Questions

1. Identify the positive functions that Facebook performs, according to Papadomichelaki and Vance. What other items can you add to this list? Give an example of a way the results of each of these functions could be achieved better or differently.

2. Explain the authors' description of Facebook as a "self-editing machine." Why do you believe or not believe that the medium itself encourages dishonesty? What other ways do people engage in the same kind of self-editing that the authors say occurs on Facebook?

3. Why do the authors believe that Facebook has altered the definition of "friendship"? If you worked for Facebook, what changes would you make in its format and language to address this problem?

4. Turkle focuses on Skype and e-mail in the examples she uses in her article. Using Facebook as an example, write a paragraph that Turkle would be able to cite as support for her point of view.

The Net and Fundamentalism

Douglas Rushkoff

Douglas Rushkoff is an American theorist, writer, columnist, lecturer, graphic novelist, and documentarian. He earned his BA from Princeton and his MA from California Institute of the Arts, and he wrote a PhD dissertation in media studies at Utrecht University. One of his many books, Coercion *(1999), explores the potential benefits and dangers inherent in cyberculture and analyzes market strategies that work to make people act on instinct rather than common sense. His most recent book,* Present Shock: When Everything Happens Now *(2013), analyzes several kinds of rapid and profound change that are a unique part of today's technological world, and the effects of constant and rapid change on our lifestyles and social interactions.*

I saw a bumper sticker on a minivan in Wisconsin last week that read: "In case of rapture, this car will be empty!" I suppose that means that my car shall remain occupied. But I am less troubled by the supposed inevitability of my damnation than the delight with which those Milwaukee passengers seemed to be anticipating Armageddon. They're looking forward to the apocalypse!

This is what happens when people take the stories their religions offer a bit too literally. Sure enough, the narratives of the Bible, like those of many other religious texts, tell a version of the history of the human race—from God's creation of the universe, through the life and death of a messiah, right on to the end of everything and the tallying of the score. In that paradigm, if you subscribe to the right story and follow the rules, all you have to do is hang in there and wait for the ending, and you'll be saved. Best of all, the real quandaries of human existence—questions such as where do we come from, what is the right way to live, and where do we go when we die—are all preordained, a closed book.

But these kinds of stories were developed back before the days of interactive media. When you're part of a captive, passive audience without keyboards or even joysticks, the only way out of a story is to wait. You have to accept the storyteller's solution because it's the only one being told in your tribe—either that, or reject the story altogether and risk damnation. This was the sad fate of poor infidels like me until pretty recently. Thanks to the Internet, we now have a way out of the story: We can write our own endings. The interactive medium is, at its core, an invitation to talk back. The online world is one in which we are entitled to voice our own opinions, however much they might contradict the status quo. We are challenged to reflect on the stories we're being told, even create our own versions—and our own sacred truths.

What a terrific weapon the Internet gives us against extreme fundamentalism. And just in time. We're now facing religion's darkest implications, violence done by true believers blindly following the unilateral decrees of their leaders. For fundamentalists are simply people who insist that their religion's narrative become everyone else's literal truth. Interactive media tend to loosen up those fixed narratives by allowing users to contribute their own ideas to the story. Try giving a sermon in an AOL chat room or a list of commandments on the *Yahoo! Internet Life* bulletin boards. The people you're preaching to won't remain silent—at all. The ministers I know who have taken their messages online have had to reassess their roles as mediators of faith and accept new ones as partners in spiritual learning. When religion is practiced on the Internet, participants quickly realize that we're all in this together.

The Internet undermines the blind obedience of fundamentalism by offering alternative points of view, promoting pluralism, and encouraging feedback. Not that this concept is all that new. While the fundamentalist priests of ancient Israel sacrificed animals on the altar, those interested in hypertext were sitting around a table arguing together as they wrote the Talmud. While fundamentalist Muslims were declaring their first holy wars, liberals in old Baghdad were sharing wine and finding common ground with similarly inclined Christians and Jews. Today, the Internet deconstructs the narratives that religions use to explain the world, while inviting people from every race and culture to participate in the conversation. No wonder fundamentalists are upset.

In this context, the entire personal computing revolution starts to look like a new sort of spiritual movement. Is it coincidental that these technologies were developed in California's Bay Area, the breeding ground for alternative spiritual practices? Or that the first easily networkable personal computer was conceived by a practicing

Buddhist, Steve Jobs? And Jobs didn't call it an Apple for nothing. The personal computer was the forbidden fruit—a way of accessing the Tree of Knowledge, and an affront to those who would sequester any information from the formerly little people. Thanks to the geek, the meek would indeed inherit the earth.

In the beginning, however, darkness was on the face of the waters. The realms of computing and, even more so, networking, were unfamiliar turf. They were hard to navigate, and harder still to design. It's no wonder that many Silicon Valley firms were forced to rely on the skills of many strange young members of the counterculture, rebels who—like Moses, Buddha, Jesus, and the Prophet Mohammed—saw a new and radically different way of bringing people together to understand the world.

Those of us lucky enough to get online in the early years were struck by how plastic, fluid, and malleable the digital world could be. Online communities have no real form—they are the ever-changing consensus reality of their members. A person's value in an interactive conversation is not his or her ability to listen and obey but the capacity to hear, process, and then express. The interactive universe does not exist without the active participation of its people—and this participation is the ongoing act of creation itself. Talk about playing God.

There are a few faiths in which congregants are invited to participate in the creation and interpretation of the underlying narrative. Certain Jewish sects spurn answers in favor of more questions and interpretation; Quakers enjoy a dogma-free, town-meeting-style Sabbath. Most religious traditions, though, simply treat their believers as a "mass" who must depend on priests or ministers for access to the "story." But just as the Internet has led patients to information about alternative medical treatments (often against doctor's orders), it has given congregants something in the spiritual realm that is very rare—the ability to find alternative stories about who we are, who made us, and why. More important than any one story we may have discovered or written, the experience of sifting through them all and writing our own has changed our relationship to religion, perhaps forever. The Internet is anathema to unitary narrative. If you want to understand life only as a story etched in stone, you had better stay away.

Every early culture composed stories—myths—to explain the basic facts of existence. For centuries, we have understood our world—even our sciences—as being somehow authored: that things were set in motion by someone or something. We cling to the belief that our existence proceeds by design. That's why Darwin's theory of natural selection was such a threat to our narrative understanding of the world, and why creationists resist its implications to this day. But even those of us who believe in evolution have been able to impose a kind of narrative on top of it in which we imagine matter and life to be groping steadily and consciously toward complexity, with evolution itself as the agent of that grand authorial entity we dearly hope exists.

Now our computers are forcing us to entertain new, even less linear models for why things happen. One of these models, described in Steven Johnson's new book, *Emergence*, explores the way everything from ant colonies to ancient cities finds its order. It turns out that queen ants issue no decrees, and ancient cities still in existence today had no official planners. The necessary preconditions must exist, but it now appears that life, organisms, communities, and order arise— emerge, in other words—from the bottom up. There is no central story, yet there is radical change and something that, if it isn't intelligence, has often been mistaken for it.

And what is the chief prerequisite for emergence to occur? You guessed it: networking. Interconnectivity is what allows an "it" to become a "they." Instead of acting on its own, each atom, molecule, cell, organism, or community can act as part of a larger complex—a networked being. Almost anyone who has been online has seen evidence of emergent behavior. Just watch the way communities form around reviewers on *Amazon.com*, or the way opinions pile on to discussions at *Slashdot.org*, or the way fan websites spring up about the latest sci-fi movie.

Consider what the Net has done to television. The current TV season is littered with so-called reality shows. We're fed up with authored stories; we'd rather see programs that are authored by their participants: real people (for the most part) in unscripted (for the most part) situations. This is because we no longer think of ourselves as actors working from a script, but as cocreators, responsible for the collective development of our world. The experience of democracy, free markets, free speech, and an interactive media space has made us reluctant to live by decree. Fundamentalism—the notion that our world is completely ordained and that our job is simply to follow the rules—does not jibe with our newfound experience of collective will.

This doesn't mean that God needn't exist—just that we may be more partnered with the Almighty than we at first presumed.

Narrative is not the enemy as long as we understand that any given narrative is not more important than any other. Thanks to the interconnected nature of the Net, that doesn't mean all narratives are equally obscure, but rather that all narratives are equally vital. We live in a universe where a butterfly's wing-flaps can cause a hurricane halfway around the world, a universe where a couple of loose cannons in the Middle East can create two of the world's most practiced religions. Every time we participate in the ongoing reality creation of the Net, we shape our world in ways we can't begin to understand.

The Internet teaches us to see the value of diversity and plurality. All the opinions of all the people matter. Fundamentalism teaches that there is only one path, one story, and one author. Whether they are attacking the free market, women's rights activists, civil libertarians, or homosexuals, and whether they are using purchased airwaves or hijacked airplanes, such fundamentalists are fighting a losing battle.

For we are the network, and we will include them—which is how we will win.

Discussion Questions

1. How does the Internet, as Douglas Rushkoff believes, give us "a terrific weapon" against extreme fundamentalism"? What counterargument might be used to suggest that the Internet supports extreme fundamentalism?

2. Explain Rushkoff's observation that the digital world is "malleable." Give some examples you have witnessed of the way that online technologies have changed in form.

3. Rushkoff talks about human connections through technology in very different ways than Turkle does. How do you think that he might respond to Turkle's concerns? What point in Rushkoff's argument do you think offers the strongest counterargument for Turkle's argument? Explain why you chose that topic, and then discuss how strong you think it is in refuting Turkle.

Addicted to Technology

Essay

GARY SMALL, MD, AND GIGI VORGAN

*Gary Small is a professor of psychiatry and the director of the UCLA Longevity Center at the Semel Institute for Neuroscience & Human Behavior. *Scientific American* magazine named him one of the world's leading innovators in science and technology. Dr. Small lectures throughout the world and has written several books, including a* New York Times *best seller,* The Memory Bible. *The following piece is an excerpt from his book* iBrain, *written with co-author and wife Gigi Vorgan. She is also a screenwriter and actress and has appeared in numerous television shows and feature films.*

When we think of addiction, we usually associate it with alcoholism or drug abuse. However, the same neural pathways in the brain that reinforce dependence on those substances can lead to compulsive technology behaviors that are just as addictive and potentially destructive. Almost anything that people like to do—eat, shop, gamble—has the potential for psychological and physiological dependence. But the access, anonymity, and constancy of the Internet have helped create several new forms of compulsive behavior fueled by the World Wide Web and other digital technologies.

Whether we're watching reality TV or googling for old TV show theme songs, the brain and other organs automatically react to the video monitor's novel and staccato stimuli. The heart rate slows, the blood vessels in the brain dilate, and blood flows away from the major muscles. This physiological reaction helps the brain focus on the mental stimulus. The rapid change and flow of visual stimuli can shift our orienting response into overdrive—we continue staring at the screen, but eventually we experience fatigue rather than continued mental stimulation. After a computer or television marathon, concentration abilities are diminished, and many people report a sense of depletion—as if the energy has been "sucked out of them." Despite these side effects, computers and the Internet are hard to resist, and our brains—especially young ones—can get hooked rapidly. Sales of video games are stronger than ever.

Internet addicts report feeling a pleasurable mood burst or "rush" from simply booting up their computer, let alone visiting their favorite websites—just as shopping addicts get a thrill from scanning sale ads, putting their credit cards in their wallets, and setting out on a spending spree. These feelings of euphoria, even before the actual acting out of the addiction occurs, are linked to brain chemical changes that control behaviors ranging from a seductive psychological draw to a full-blown addiction. The brain-wiring system that controls these responses involves the neurotransmitter dopamine, a brain messenger that modulates all sorts of activities involving reward, punishment, and exploration.

Dopamine is responsible for the euphoria that addicts chase, whether they get it from methamphetamine, alcohol, or Internet gambling. The addict becomes conditioned to compulsively seek, crave, and recreate the sense of elation while offline or off the drug. Whether we are knocking back a few whiskeys or whipping out the credit cards, dopamine transmits messages to the brain's pleasure centers, causing addicts to want to repeat those actions over and over again, even if the addict no longer experiences the original pleasure and is aware of negative consequences.

The mental reward stimulation of the dopamine system is a powerful pull that nonaddicts feel as well. Studies of volunteers rapt in addictive video games show that gamers continue to play despite multiple attempts to distract them. The dopamine system allows them to tolerate noise and discomfort extremely well. Previous research has shown that both eating and sexual activity drive up dopamine levels. One can only imagine the intensity of the dopamine bursts produced from an interactive video game with a sexual theme (and they're out there).

As Internet addiction takes hold, the brain's executive region, known as the anterior cingulate, loses ground. This is an area in the front part of the brain that is responsible for decision-making and judgment. Intervention for these addictions involves not only holding the dopamine system at bay but also strengthening these anterior neural circuits.

Internet addiction afflicts people from all walks of life: homemakers in their thirties and forties, teenagers, business people in their fifties and older, college students, and even kids under ten. Everyone is at risk to get hooked on Web applications. In February 2007, the *Los Angeles Times* reported that after working nineteen stellar years for a large computer company, a man was fired for visiting sexual chat rooms during his breaks. The man, married with two children, claimed that the chat room visits helped ease the stress he had continued to experience since the Vietnam War. At the time of the news report, he was suing the company for wrongful termination.

Many kids and teens may not exactly be addicted, but the pull of new technology can cloud their judgment. The anterior cingulate in their brains often loses out to the dopamine rush they get from text messaging with their friends. Teenagers' text messaging while driving has caused thousands of fatal car accidents across the United States. Although text messaging is much more distracting than merely talking on a cell phone, as of July 2007, only a handful of states in this country had outlawed text messaging while driving.

Business executives have found another reason to keep their BlackBerrys in hand—an embedded game called BrickBreaker. Attorneys, bankers, hedge fund managers, and other marketing and financial executives have reportedly "caught" Brickmania, wherein the player moves a paddle left and right with the thumb to bounce a ball so it demolishes bricks at the top of the screen. Players have been found to exchange strategies in chat rooms, brag about their high scores, and gossip about BrickBreaker idols who have scored over a million points. Executives have admitted to playing during conference calls and sports events, and some have become so obsessed with BrickBreaker that they've had to remove the game from their handheld device because they could not control the urge to play during work hours.

A recent Stanford University study found that up to fourteen percent of computer users reported neglecting school, work, family, food, and sleep in order to remain online. The Internet is fast becoming the entertainment and information medium of choice, and it could soon become more popular than traditional television.

It has been reported that college students with difficulties adjusting to campus life may use the Internet to escape everyday stress. Rather than face the challenges of face-to-face social life, they feel a greater sense of control by using social networking sites, e-mail, instant messages, and chat rooms. More than eighteen percent of college students are pathological Internet users, and fifty-eight percent report that their excessive Internet use has disrupted their studying and classroom attendance and also lowered their grade point average.

It is not the Internet itself that is addictive, but rather the specific application of choice. People can get hooked on database searching, online dating, Web shopping, porn sites, or even checking their e-mail. Others become compulsive online gamblers, stock traders, gamers, or instant message senders.

Part of the appeal of new technology is the sense of control it gives us. The direct and instant command we have over our computers empowers us. We have the power to turn our computers on and off whenever we feel like it; we can make them stand by, hibernate, or reboot. We can gauge the pace of our communications, or not communicate at all if we wish. But for individuals at risk for addiction, the computer and Internet can provide a false sense of control. The screen, keyboard, and mouse become extensions of the individual—a hardware/software link to the global, Internet-connected world. Compulsive users report feeling a sense of liberation and anonymity online, so they often say or write things they might not otherwise reveal about their personal lives. Some users get a thrill from making up completely false personalities. What some Internet users don't realize is that once you put your thoughts and feelings into words on the Web, they are public forever—and accessible not just to friends and family members but also to work associates, job recruiters, and people without your best interests in mind.

Whether we are blogging or Internet shopping, addictive behaviors get people into all kinds of trouble, not just job-related trouble. Addiction doesn't happen overnight—habit-forming behavior patterns build gradually. Usually, an individual begins Internet use casually, but eventually the emotional charge and the amount of time spent online progress, and the brain needs a stronger dopamine boost. Soon, a psychological dependence on the Internet develops, causing the person to experience discomfort when not online, while at the same time the person may be developing tolerance to the effects of being online. The user may then feel the need for more time online or possibly more exciting online sites. Pathological Internet users typically start out in complete denial that they have any problem controlling their online activity. Although the amount of time spent on the computer is usually considerable, the disorder has as much to do with whether the behavior interferes with the person's everyday life by disrupting his or her job, family life, or social activities.

The driving force of addiction depends on the individual. Genetics plays a role. Some people inherit a tendency to get hooked on almost anything, and the Internet supports various forms of addictive behavior that often occur offline as well, such as gambling, eating, and shopping. Others are looking for an escape from depression, anxiety, boredom, or interpersonal conflict. Peer pressure spurs many young people to get hooked on interactive online activities involving chat rooms, social networks, or virtual games.

Addiction experts have proposed criteria for Internet addiction disorder that include mood changes, tolerance, withdrawal symptoms. and relapse. Some experts estimate that ten percent of Internet users meet these criteria for addiction, which are similar to those for gambling and shopping addictions, wherein the user is addicted to a process rather than a substance such as drugs, alcohol, tobacco, or food. However, whereas a substance abuser strives for complete abstinence (except for food), an Internet addict more often tries to attain moderation. Recently, the American Medical Association recommended additional study to determine whether video gaming and Internet addictions should be considered official diagnostic categories.

Internet addicts typically spend forty or more hours each week online in addition to online work time. If you calculate the number of hours needed to eat, work, travel, dress, and bathe, that leaves approximately four to five hours a night for sleep before a person hops back on the computer. Most addicts lie about it to others and tend to get defensive when family and friends question the amount of time they spend online. These addicts routinely experience apathy, depression, anxiety, restlessness, fatigue, irritability, and clouded thinking.

Internet addiction has physical side effects as well. Too much time at a computer display terminal can lead to muscle strain, eye discomfort, and headaches. Letters appear less precise and not as sharply defined when viewed on a video screen rather than a printed page. Screen contrast levels are often less than optimal; moreover, reflections and glare from the screen can make it even harder to see. Repetitive mouse use can cause tendinitis and muscle cramping in the hands and upper arms. Because vision and joint mobility generally decline with age, older people are more sensitive to these kinds of physical symptoms, although with continual use they can occur at any age. One recent study found that more than two hours of daily computer use was significantly associated with neck, shoulder, and low back pain in adolescents.

Proposed Criteria for Internet Addiction Disorder

The following specific criteria must be present:

Preoccupation: The individual thinks about previous online activity or constantly anticipates the next online session.

Tolerance: Longer periods online are needed for the person to feel satisfied.

Lack of Control: The person is unable to cut back on or stop online activities.

Withdrawal: Attempts to decrease or stop Internet use lead to restlessness, irritability, and other mood changes.

Staying Online: The user repeatedly remains online longer than originally intended.

In addition, at least one of the following criteria must be present as well:

Risk of Functional Impairment: Internet use has jeopardized a job, educational or career opportunity, or important relationship.

Concealment: The user lies to others in order to hide his or her Internet activities.

Escape: The individual goes online to relieve uncomfortable feelings, escape problems, or not deal with personal relationships.

Discussion Questions

1. Discuss the physiological effects of technology addiction. Apart from the addictive activities that Gary Small and Gigi Vorgan mention in their article, tell about a time you experienced a "rush" that may have been the result of dopamine production.

2. What do the authors believe to be "part of the appeal of new technology"? Do you think this appeal might be a particularly important one for college students to understand? Why or why not?

3. Look at the box that lists the specific and optional criteria for diagnosing Internet use as an addiction disorder. How would this information support or contradict Turkle's argument that Internet use causes isolation? Give an example from your own experience, readings, observations, or even hearsay about the life of someone addicted to technology.

The Final Showdown between In-Person and Cyberspace Relationships; or, Can I Hold You in Cyberspace?

Essay

JOHN SULER

John Suler is a clinical psychologist and professor of psychology at Rider University. He specializes in Internet research and the development of online groups and communities. The following reading is from his online hypertext book The Psychology of Cyberspace *(1999).*

Whether you like it or not, cyberspace has become the new frontier in social relationships. People are making friends, colleagues, lovers, and enemies on the Internet. The fervor with which many people have pursued this new social realm is matched by a backlash reaction from the skeptics. Relationships on the Internet aren't really real, some people say— not like relationships in the real world. Socializing in cyberspace is just a cultural fad, a novelty, a phase that people go through. The critics say it can't compare to real relationships—and if some people prefer communicating with others via wires and circuits, there must be something wrong with them. They must be addicted. They must fear the challenging intimacy of real relationships. Is this true? Is it true that "real" relationships are intrinsically superior to relationships in cyberspace? Or might relationships in cyberspace in fact be better? Here is the showdown for us to explore.

But first, let's settle on some terms. What exactly should we call relationships in cyberspace and relationships in the "real" world? Right off the bat, I'm going to discard the term "real" because it already biases our discussion in favor of relationships in the physical world. Whether or not those relationships are more "real" is the very issue at hand. The same is true of "virtual relationships" because the word "virtual" implies that those relationships are somehow less-than or not quite up to snuff. Some people like to say "face-to-face relationships" (ftf, f2f). I'm not particularly thrilled by that term either, because video conferencing on the Internet surely allows people to present their faces to each other. We could say "physical relationships," although that conjures up images of wrestling and sex. I like "in-person relationships" because it captures the feeling of physical presence without necessarily getting physical. I doubt that even when holographic multimedia communication arrives, perhaps many years from now, we will ever say that we meet our Internet acquaintances "in person." So it seems like a term that safely falls outside the realm of cyberspace. We can even abbreviate it nicely as IP and IPR.

Now, we need a term for cyberspace relationships. How about "cyberspace relationships"—aka, CSR? I like the word "cyberspace." It conjures up feelings of place, location, and spatial interaction. People do indeed experience cyberspace as containing places where they go and meet others. Rather than highlighting the fact that cyberspace is controlled by computers, I like to emphasize instead that it is a psychological and social space.

With terms in hand, we're back to the showdown. Which is better? IPR or CSR? The key word here is "relationships." One approach to understanding that phenomenon is to examine the various pathways by which people communicate with and connect to each other—by the specific mechanisms for "relating." On the most fundamental level, we can compare IPR and CSR according to how people connect via the five senses:

> hearing the other
> seeing the other
> touching the other
> smelling the other
> tasting the other

The first—hearing—involves that basic human skill for language, which isn't necessarily auditory. So, before getting to the five senses, let's back up a notch to examine language.

A powerful way that people connect to each other is through words. In the beginning, CSR relied mostly on language conveyed through typed text—mostly e-mail and newsgroups posts. Even today, typed-text accounts for a very large majority of communication over the Internet. There are at least three distinct advantages of these text-mediated relationships over IPR.

1. The interaction is asynchronous. It doesn't occur in "real time," so you can respond to your net-mate whenever you wish, at whatever pace you wish. That gives you time to think about what you want to say and to compose your reply exactly the way you want. This comes in very handy for those awkward or emotional situations in a relationship. Unlike IPR,

you're never on the spot to reply immediately. You can think it through first, do a little research or soul-searching, if you wish. My advice for those very emotional moments is to compose a message, wait at least twenty-four hours, reread your message, modify it if necessary, and THEN send it off. This wait-and-revise strategy can do wonders in averting impulsiveness, embarrassment, and regret.

2. The written dialogues of CSR may involve different mental mechanisms than in-person talk. It may reflect a distinct cognitive style that enables some people to be more expressive, subtle, organized, or creative in how they communicate. Some people feel that they can express themselves better in the written word. Surely, there have been truly great authors and poets who sounded bumbling or shallow during IP conversation.

3. Text-mediated relationships enable you to record the interactions by saving the typed-text messages. Essentially, you can preserve large chunks of the relationship with your net-mate, maybe even the entire relationship if you communicated only via typed-text. At your leisure, you can review what you and your partner said, cherish important moments in the relationship, and reexamine misunderstandings and conflicts. This kind of reevaluation of the relationship is impossible in IPR, where you almost always have to rely on the vagaries of memory. In fact, if you want to get downright philosophical about it, you could make the argument that your complete archive of text communications with your net-mate *is* the relationship with that person, perfectly preserved in bits and bytes. It's not unlike a novel, which isn't a record of characters and plot, but rather *is* the characters and plot.

The big disadvantage of text-driven relationships is what's missing *vis-à-vis* IPR. There are no voices, facial expressions, or body language to convey meaning and emotion. That issue takes us to the first of the five senses—hearing.

Listen carefully. The human voice is rich in meaning and emotion. A sharp edge to someone's words can rouse your suspicion or anger. Just the sound of a loved one's voice can be enough to create feelings of comfort and joy. Singing—one of the most expressive of human activities—powerfully unites people. In CSR mediated by text only, both obvious and subtle nuances in voice pitch and volume are completely absent. And singing is impossible (unless you consider the mutual recitation of lyrics as singing—which some onliners do).

Advocates of text-driven CSR do have a comeback to this criticism. Lacking auditory and visual cues, the e-mail message or newsgroup post can be productively ambiguous in tone. When reading that typed message, there is a strong tendency to project—sometimes unconsciously—your own expectations, wishes, anxieties, and fears into what the person wrote. Psychoanalytic thinkers call this transference. Your distorting the person's intended meaning could lead to misunderstandings and conflict. It could stimulate countertransference reactions from your Internet partner. On the other hand, if you discuss your (mis)perceptions with your friend, you are revealing underlying (perhaps unconscious) elements of how you think and feel. In a sense, you are being more real with the other person, allowing a deeper relationship to form. Of course, this more rich and meaningful relationship will develop only when people are mature enough to talk about and work through those projections and transferences with each other.

An entirely different comeback for cyberspace advocates is that one's voice CAN be heard via the Internet. It's only a matter of time before audio-streaming becomes perfected to the point where it matches the quality of IPR. In fact, conversing in cyberspace may have some distinct advantages. If you so desire, conversations easily could be saved and replayed—which isn't possible in IPR, unless you're carrying a tape recorder. When we use software programs, nuances in voice pitch and volume can be examined more carefully for subtle emotions and meaning. Programs also could allow you to modify your voice as you transmit it. If you want to speak in the voice of Bill Clinton, Arnold Schwarzenegger, or Daffy Duck, so be it. Or you can add in any auditory special effect you desire in order to embellish your words—"Pomp and Circumstance," explosions, quacks.

As we'll see over and over again, a unique feature of CSR is the ability to use imagination and fantasy to shape the way in which you desire to present yourself. This can be a fascinating and revealing dimension to a relationship.

Seeing is believing. I could write this section on seeing almost word for word as I wrote the previous section on hearing. The human face and body language are rich in meaning and emotion. Critics of text-only communication in cyberspace complain that all these visual cues are missing, hence making the relationship ambiguous and depleted. Advocates of text-driven CSR again could reply that this ambiguity creates an opportunity to explore one's transference reactions, thereby enriching the relationship. They also may praise its level playing field. Appearances—such as gender, race, and whether you are "attractive" or not—are irrelevant. Everyone has an equal voice and is judged by the same standards: their words. Some claim that text-only talk carries you past the distracting superficial aspects of a person's existence and connects you more directly to their mind and personality.

Like audio-streaming, video transmissions will eventually make face-to-face meetings both practical and realistic, with the added feature of making it possible for you to LOOK like Bill Clinton, Arnold Schwarzenegger, or Daffy Duck, if you so choose. The multimedia chat environments where people use "avatars" to represent themselves is the first step in this opportunity to present yourself visually in any form you desire. It's the perfect way to express all sorts of things about your personality. You also can interact with others in any of an almost limitless variety of visual scenes. Want to meet your friend at the bottom of the ocean, or on a space station, or in the Oval Office? No problem. There is a big disadvantage, though, of audio/visual cyberspace meetings involving three or more people who can see each other only on computer screens. The subtle body language of who is looking and gesturing at whom is lost. Eventually, holographic meetings will solve that problem.

Can I hold you in cyberspace? Humans need physical contact with each other. Infants sink into depression and die without it. How parents interact physically with them becomes a cornerstone of their identity and well-being. Adults deprived of tactile contact for long periods will tell you just how depriving it feels. In day-to-day relationships, never underestimate the power of a handshake, a pat on the back, a hug, or a kiss.

On this level of human relating, cyberspace falls short, way short. In multimedia chat communication, there are some vague hints of physical contact, as when you snuggle up your avatar next to someone else's. But this is a far cry from the in-person counterpart. Unfortunately, it's not very likely that CSR—even holographic ones—will ever develop kinesthetic capabilities, unless technology figures out how to accurately record someone's caress and transmit that digital record into the other's nervous system. You can argue until the cows come home about how you can psychologically and emotionally embrace someone through words alone, but the bottom line is that you can't and probably never will be able to hold your loved one in cyberspace.

In the physical, tactile, spatial world, we also can DO things with people. We can play tennis, go for a walk, eat dinner together. Doing things with people creates bonds. It creates a history to the relationship. Are these things possible in CSR? Sort of. In multimedia environments, we can "meet" people at some specified site and move with them from one visual setting to another. It feels a bit like "going places" with them. There also are lots of games we can play with others via the Internet—games that sometimes have an imaginary physical feeling to them. That's "doing" something, isn't it?

While doing things with others certainly is possible on the Internet, it doesn't have as powerful a physical, tactile, or spatial feeling as activities in IPR. Almost anything you can do with someone in cyberspace you can also do with them in person, simply by the fact that they can be sitting side-by-side with you while you do it. But the reverse isn't true—everything you can do with someone in person can't be duplicated in cyberspace. That's a big disadvantage for CSR. The scent of perfume, hair, clothes, skin. Smell brings us very close to the other. It stirs up powerful emotional reactions. The sense of taste brings us closer still. It's the sensation of lovers. One might say that smell and taste are rather "primitive" interpersonal sensations, but both are the cornerstones of deep intimacy—maybe because they ARE so primitive, so fundamental. In addition to touch, smell and taste are the primary ways an infant connects to its mother. It is one's very first, essential relationship that serves as the prototype for all later relationships in one's life.

On this level of relating, a CSR once again falls flat on its noseless, tongueless face. Will computers ever be able to duplicate smells and tastes and then accurately transmit those sensations to another person hundreds and thousands of miles away? Don't hold your breath. As with tactile sensations, when it comes to the smelling/tasting dimension of intimate relationships, IPR wins hands down over CSR.

Rarely in IPR do we connect to the other person by one sense alone. At the very least, we see and hear simultaneously. During more intimate relating, we see, hear, touch, smell, and maybe even taste. The complex and subtle interactions among all that sensory input far exceeds the interpersonal meaning we can extract from any one of them alone. Mother Nature was pretty clever in giving us eyes, ears, skin, noses, and tongues—all interconnected in marvelous ways that science still doesn't fully understand. Those clusters of sensations make for relationships that are highly robust in emotion and meaning.

As Internet technology improves, auditory and visual sensations will be more effectively coordinated with each other. But even with unlimited bandwidth and highly imaginative code, we'll never see all five sensations integrated as in IPR. In CSR, the five senses tend to be dissociated, and that's a double-edged sword. On the one hand, the rich interpersonal qualities afforded by the five senses are lost, resulting in human encounters that may run a bit on the stale side. On the other hand, extracting out some sensory modes—like vision or voice—creates unique ways to interact with others. E-mail and typed chat can be rather fascinating styles of developing a relationship. The sensory limitations can fuel the imagination and lead to creative patterns of communicating that are not found in IPR.

Sometimes we humans connect to each other in ways that seem to defy the traditional laws of sense impressions. Whether we call it telepathy, empathy, or intuition, we seem to know what others are thinking or feeling without being aware of just how we know it. Some people think that we reach those conclusions based on an unconscious detection of subtle qualities in voice, body language, or things said between the lines. If that's the case, then sensory information indeed is influencing how we experience the other. We just don't realize how exactly we're being subliminally influenced.

Curiously, people report that even in the stripped-down sensory world of CSR—like text-only chat—others sometimes sense what you are thinking and feeling, even when you haven't said anything to that effect. Do they detect your mood or state of mind from some subtle clue in what or how you typed? Are they picking up on some seemingly minor change in how you typically express yourself? Or does their empathy reach beyond your words appearing on the screen? Perhaps they are in tune with your mind via some pathway that neither psychology nor computer technology can fully explain. If that kind of intuitive connection really exists, then the differences between IPR and CSR become rather insignificant. On that mysterious level, human relating transcends sense organs and microchips.

So what's the outcome of the final showdown? Which is better: IPR or CSR? It's a loaded question since "better" is an ambiguous term. Better for what? There are distinct advantages to the time-stretching, distance-shortening, and potentially fantasy-driven dimensions of CSR. On the other hand, IPRs have the advantage of touch, smell, taste, the complex integration of all the five senses, and a more robust potential to "do things with" other people.

So is the showdown a draw? People can and will continue to argue for their side of the debate. As for me, the acid test is a very simple one. As much as I respect and enjoy cyberspace relationships, I would be very unhappy if I could ONLY relate to my family and closest friends via the Internet, even if sophisticated visual/auditory technology made it seem like actually being there with them. Cyberspace relating is a wonderful supplement to IPR, but in the long run, it's not ultimately fulfilling as a substitute, especially when it comes to our most intimate relationships. Most people who develop close friendships and romances in cyberspace eventually want and need to meet their friend or lover in person. And once they've done that, returning to cyberspace-relating often feels at least a tiny bit flat and incomplete.

In an ideal world, we could have it both ways. We could develop our relationships in person and in cyberspace, thereby taking advantage of each realm. But we don't always have the luxury of ideal circumstances. There will be some people whom we can only or mostly meet in person, and others only or mostly via the Internet. In the not-too-distant future, most people will have three types of social lives that will be distinct but overlapping. We'll have friends, colleagues, and lovers whom we know only in person, those whom we know only via the Internet, and those whom we know both in person and online.

Variety is the spice of life.

Discussion Questions

1. What are the advantages and disadvantages of cyberspace relationships discussed in this article? Explain reasons and circumstances when you would or would not prefer to engage in a long-term cyberspace-only relationship with someone.

2. According to this article, what are the advantages and disadvantages of in-person relationships? List people in your life with whom you have only an in-person relationship, and explain the reasons you never communicate via technology.

3. According to John Suler, who wins the "final showdown" between IPR and CSR? Explain the outcome the author considers "ideal." Do you think Turkle would be satisfied with this ideal? Why or why not?

4. Copy Suler's thesis statement—or compose one, if necessary— for his argument. Does the essay have a traditional academic, an hourglass, or a funnel structure? What kind of readership does he seem to be targeting? When deciding on a structure for his argument, do you think he made the best choice? Why?

5. Look through the essay again and find three or four examples where Suler uses informal language—for example, colloquial expressions, idioms, and subject matter not found in formal academic writing. Discuss the effect of this informal language on the overall impression of his essay, and, ultimately, on his success in persuading his readers. If you were Suler's editor, would you advise him to make revisions before the essay was included in a college textbook? Justify your decision.

Technology's Impact on Social Relationships

Essay

Tom Dellner

Tom Dellner is an editor of university publications at CalSouthern, a completely online university, and he serves on the editorial staffs of several internationally distributed magazines. His work has appeared in a wide variety of consumer and trade publications, including Bloomberg/BusinessWeek, Men's Health, Golf Digest, Rolling Stone, Online Strategies, *and* Links Magazine. *He's also a marketing communications expert.*

My relationship with technology and social media is a little like my relationship with fast food. I enjoy it immensely and find it semi-addictive, but deep down, I wonder what it's doing to me.

Our collective cultural embrace of the Internet, social media, and the litany of mobile devices represents a massive shift in human behavior. Family members text one another from different rooms in the same house. We move about with ear buds in our ears or our thumbs working a mobile keyboard—or both. At any public place with an Internet connection, we sit by ourselves, digesting media along with our coffee and scones, or engaging in communication with perhaps thousands of friends or connections—just not the person seated across the table.

This has to be doing something to us, right? It must have some sort of impact on family and other relationships, correct? If you're like me, you have an uneasy feeling that whatever the impact is, it's probably not good. Dr. Keith Hampton has some of the same questions and concerns. But he articulates them far better—and he also knows the answers. At the 2011 American Association for Marriage and Family Therapy Annual Conference, Dr. Hampton—a communications professor at the University of Pennsylvania and the principal author of the Pew Research study "Social Networking Sites and Our Lives"—delivered a fascinating presentation titled "Technology in Family and Social Relations: The Good, the Bad, and the Data."

Here's how Dr. Hampton articulated our concerns about technology and relationships: We're afraid that people are becoming more and more isolated as they increasingly engage with their computers and mobile devices. We're worried that we are substituting these activities for traditional social behaviors and that our real-life social networks are shrinking and becoming less diverse as we cluster into and communicate with groups of trusted, like-minded others. We wonder if our relationships will lose intimacy as we rely more on technology-driven communication and less on face-to-face conversation.

As noted above, Dr. Hampton has been working closely with the Pew Research Center on its Internet and American Life Project. He says that, while the digital age is still relatively new and its impact on relationships is still evolving, the current data are both consistent and surprising. As it turns out, the research does indicate that digital technologies are changing the nature of community and the structure of relationships, but not in the negative ways outlined above.

I'll be conducting an in-depth interview with Dr. Hampton soon, but here's a quick summary of what his research has revealed: It's true that today people report having fewer close relationships or confidants. However, there's no evidence establishing a connection between technology use and the decrease in the size of our core networks. In fact, users of the Internet and mobile devices tend to report more close relationships, as well as more diversity within these close relationships, than non-users. And avid Facebook users reported ten percent more close ties than average Internet users.

Looking beyond the groups of closest confidants, researchers have found that Internet and technology users tend to have more social ties in what they term the "parochial realm" (e.g., relationships such as those formed around neighborhoods, the workplace, churches, volunteer organizations, clubs, etc.) than those who don't engage with the Internet and technology. Internet and Facebook users also say they receive higher levels of social support from their friends, as compared to those who don't use this technology. And there's no indication that heavy Internet users participate in fewer traditional, face-to-face social activities—in fact, they seem to do so at a greater rate.

Dr. Hampton cautions that, as I noted above, the social and relational implications of technology use are still evolving, and he is quick to note that the context of the surveys may have impacted the data. However, the research suggests that users of technology tend to have more social relationships and that these relationships are more supportive and more diverse.

So for now, we can return to our Facebook accounts, guilt free.

Discussion Questions

1. Describe Tom Dellner's "gut feeling" about the impact of the Internet on his life. Describe the way you feel when you think about your own relationship with technology. Explain your reasons for feeling the same as or different from Dellner regarding the impact of technology.

2. Explain why Dr. Keith Hampton found his research results "surprising." How might his data impact Turkle's argument? What aspects of his study, pointed out by Hampton himself, would be useful as a counterargument to the conclusions he draws from his research?

3. After reading Turkle, Hampton, and other authors in this unit, will you change the amount of time you spend on the Internet, or the way in which you use it for communication? Why or why not?

with heavy internet users
tend to have a wide social
networking
- They're more involved in
activities
- Know many people from
many places.
- Relationships are more
supportive and diverse
- Anti-Turkle.

Assignment 7

Arguments through Literature: "The Monkey Garden"

This assignment will show you how to recognize arguments in fiction writing. After looking at an example based on an excerpt from Mary Shelley's novel *Frankenstein*, you will be asked to write an essay in response to a writing topic based on a short story by Sandra Cisneros, "The Monkey Garden." Again in this unit, prewriting pages follow Cisneros's story, and by now, we hope that you have worked out a personal writing process through the prewriting pages in *Write It*'s assignment units.

This assignment is somewhat different from Assignments 1–6 because it asks you to work with a short story rather than a reading selection that overtly makes and supports an argument. In this assignment, you will learn how to recognize an argument made through metaphor, as works of fiction carry messages that readers can recognize, messages that make us think as we test their significance in terms of our own lives. The prewriting exercises that follow "The Monkey Garden" will help you to understand the story's argument—based on your own interpretation of the story—and respond to the writing topic with an effective essay of your own.

Understanding and Responding to Arguments in Literature

One way to talk about literature is to uncover the arguments it makes, arguments that are presented and supported through the elements of the story it tells. An argument is a kind of discussion in which reasons are advanced for (or against) some value or ethical position, often to influence or change people's ideas and actions. The first step to discussing literature as argument is to understand the way literature works *representationally*. In other words, readers are meant to see a fictional story and its characters as dramatizing general human experiences that all of its readers will recognize and understand. Authors hope to use the devices of fiction to capture a representation of life that is insightful and that rings true for readers.

For example, even though Shakespeare's *Romeo and Juliet* is a centuries-old story of two young lovers in a small town in Italy who cannot marry because of an old feud between their families, readers today understand that it is also about the experience of love and the ethical dilemmas we face when our individual desires conflict with the demands of people who have authority over us. We interpret the argument in *Romeo and Juliet* when we decide what the work is saying about this particular ethical dilemma. Those of you who know this play, what do you think it is arguing? That love is more important than duty? That love put over duty to others leads to tragedy? What details about the plot or characters in this play make you answer the way that you have? As you answer these questions, you begin to see *Romeo and Juliet* as a form of argument. Even though you and your classmates may have different answers, many of your answers may be equally compelling if each of you can bring out the elements in the play that support your interpretation. One of the reasons that we continue to read works such as *Romeo and Juliet* is that they encourage us to discuss and question our experiences and our beliefs as individuals and as members of human society.

Works of fiction contain one or more themes—in other words, issues and ideas very similar to those in prose essays such as "In Defense of Masks" and "Reading and Thought." Instead of stating arguments directly as prose essays do, however, fiction takes positions on human concerns indirectly, through the tools of fiction. Sometimes authors will have a narrator present a "thesis statement" in a fairly straightforward manner, but more often the thesis will be implied through the events and characters of the story. Here is a set of strategies that you can use when analyzing the arguments in fiction:

1. List the main characters in the story. Briefly summarize their words and actions. What do these things suggest about their personalities and relationships with each other?

2. Identify the main conflict in the story. What is the subject or issue of the conflict? What more general issue is the story *representing* with this conflict?

3. Identify the two or more sides of the conflict. Looking back at the characters you listed in #1, what does each character contribute to the conflict through his or her words or actions? Look carefully at the evidence that each character (including the narrator) presents, and try to determine how the evidence is being linked to support a position.

4. Look over what you wrote for #2 and #3, and then try to state the argument that the story and its characters are representing. This time, try to state the argument in general terms that readers can apply to their own lives.

5. Identify how the story resolves the conflict. This resolution leads directly to the thesis statement, or the story's position in the argument.

Read the following chapter taken from Mary Shelley's *Frankenstein*. Pay attention to the conflict between Dr. Frankenstein, who is narrating, and his creation, the creature that he has abandoned. Then use these five steps to see the chapter as an argument. Remember that these steps are guides and are meant to be used with flexibility. For instance, sometimes you might merge the first two steps or you might want to rearrange the steps in a way that meets your needs.

Chapter IX from Mary Shelley's *Frankenstein*

Essay

The being finished speaking and fixed his looks upon me in expectation of a reply. But I was bewildered, perplexed, and unable to arrange my ideas sufficiently to understand the full extent of his proposition. He continued—

"You must create a female for me, with whom I can live in the interchange of those sympathies necessary for my being. This you alone can do; and I demand it of you as a right which you must not refuse."

The latter part of his tale had kindled anew in me the anger that had died away while he narrated his peaceful life among the cottagers, and, as he said this, I could no longer suppress the rage that burned within me.

"I do refuse it," I replied; "and no torture shall ever extort a consent from me. You may render me the most miserable of men, but you shall never make me base in my own eyes. Shall I create another like yourself, whose joint wickedness might desolate the world? Begone! I have answered you; you may torture me, but I will never consent."

"You are in the wrong," replied the fiend; "and, instead of threatening, I am content to reason with you. I am malicious because I am

Excerpt from *Frankenstein* by Mary Shelley, 1818.

miserable; am I not shunned and hated by all mankind? You, my creator, would tear me to pieces, and triumph; remember that, and tell me why I should pity man more than he pities me? You would not call it murder, if you could precipitate me into one of those ice-rifts, and destroy my frame, the work of your own hands. Shall I respect man, when he contemns me? Let him live with me in the interchange of kindness, and, instead of injury, I would bestow every benefit upon him with tears of gratitude at his acceptance. But that cannot be; the human senses are insurmountable barriers to our union. Yet mine shall not be the submission of abject slavery. I will revenge my injuries: if I cannot inspire love, I will cause fear; and chiefly towards you, my arch-enemy because my creator, do I swear inextinguishable hatred. Have a care: I will work at your destruction, nor finish until I desolate your heart, so that you curse the hour of your birth."

A fiendish rage animated him as he said this; his face was wrinkled into contortions too horrible for human eyes to behold; but presently he calmed himself, and proceeded—

"I intended to reason. This passion is detrimental to me; for you do not reflect that you are the cause of its excess. If any being felt emotions of benevolence towards me, I should return them an hundred and an hundred fold; for that one creature's sake, I would make peace with the whole kind! But I now indulge in dreams of bliss that cannot be realized. What I ask of you is reasonable and moderate; I demand a creature of another sex, but as hideous as myself: the gratification is small, but it is all that I can receive, and it shall content me. It is true, we shall be monsters, cut off from all the world; but on that account we shall be more attached to one another. Our lives will not be happy, but they will be harmless, and free from the misery I now feel. Oh! my creator, make me happy; let me feel gratitude towards you for one benefit! Let me see that I excite the sympathy of some existing thing; do not deny me my request!"

I was moved. I shuddered when I thought of the possible consequences of my consent; but I felt that there was some justice in his argument. His tale, and the feelings he now expressed, proved him to be a creature of fine sensations; and did I not, as his maker, owe him all the portion of happiness that it was in my power to bestow? He saw my change of feeling, and continued—

"If you consent, neither you nor any other human being shall ever see us again: I will go to the vast wilds of South America. My food is not that of man; I do not destroy the lamb and the kid, to glut my appetite; acorns and berries afford me sufficient nourishment.

My companion will be of the same nature as myself, and will be content with the same fare. We shall make our bed of dried leaves; the sun will shine on us as on man, and will ripen our food. The picture I present to you is peaceful and human, and you must feel that you could deny it only in the wantonness of power and cruelty. Pitiless as you have been towards me, I now see compassion in your eyes; let me seize the favorable moment, and persuade you to promise what I so ardently desire."

"You propose," replied I, "to fly from the habitations of man, to dwell in those wilds where the beasts of the field will be your only companions. How can you, who long for the love and sympathy of man, persevere in this exile? You will return, and again seek their kindness, and you will meet with their detestation; your evil passions will be renewed, and you will then have a companion to aid you in the task of destruction. This may not be; cease to argue the point, for I cannot consent."

"How inconstant are your feelings! But a moment ago you were moved by my representations, and why do you again harden yourself to my complaints? I swear to you, by the earth which I inhabit, and by you that made me, that, with the companion you bestow, I will quit the neighborhood of man, and dwell, as it may chance, in the most savage of places. My evil passions will have fled, for I shall meet with sympathy; my life will flow quietly away, and, in my dying moments, I shall not curse my maker."

His words had a strange effect upon me. I compassionated him, and sometimes felt a wish to console him; but when I looked upon him, when I saw the filthy mass that moved and talked, my heart sickened, and my feelings were altered to those of horror and hatred. I tried to stifle these sensations; I thought, that as I could not sympathize with him, I had no right to withhold from him the small portion of happiness that was yet in my power to bestow.

"You swear," I said, "to be harmless, but have you not already shown a degree of malice that should reasonably make me distrust you? May not even this be a feint that will increase your triumph by affording a wider scope for your revenge?"

"How is this? I thought I had moved your compassion, and yet you still refuse to bestow on me the only benefit that can soften my heart, and render me harmless. If I have no ties and no affections, hatred and vice must be my portion; the love of another will destroy the cause of my crimes, and I shall become a thing of whose existence every one will be ignorant. My vices are the children of a forced solitude that I abhor; and my virtues will necessarily arise when I live in communion with an equal. I shall feel the affections of a sensitive being, and become linked to the chain of existence and events, from which I am now excluded."

I paused some time to reflect on all he had related, and the various arguments which he had employed. I thought of the promise of virtues which he had displayed on the opening of his existence, and the subsequent blight of all kindly feeling by the loathing and scorn which his protectors had manifested towards him. His power and threats were not omitted in my calculations: A creature who could exist in the ice caves of the glaciers, and hide himself from pursuit among the ridges of inaccessible precipices, was a being possessing faculties it would be vain to cope with. After a long pause of reflection, I concluded, that the justice due both to him and my fellow-creatures demanded of me that I should comply with his request. Turning to him, therefore, I said—

"I consent to your demand, on your solemn oath to quit Europe for ever, and every other place in the neighborhood of man, as soon as I shall deliver into your hands a female who will accompany you in your exile."

"I swear," he cried, "by the sun, and by the blue sky of heaven, that if you grant my prayer, while they exist you shall never behold me again. Depart to your home, and commence your labors; I shall watch their progress with unutterable anxiety; and fear not but that when you are ready I shall appear."

Saying this, he suddenly quitted me, fearful, perhaps, of any change in my sentiments. I saw him descend the mountain with greater speed than the flight of an eagle, and quickly lost him among the undulations of the sea of ice.

His tale had occupied the whole day; and the sun was upon the verge of the horizon when he departed. I knew that I ought to hasten my descent towards the valley, as I should soon be encompassed in darkness; but my heart was heavy, and my steps slow. The labor of winding among the little paths of the mountains, and fixing my feet firmly as I advanced, perplexed me, occupied as I was by the emotions which the occurrences of the day had produced. Night was far advanced, when I came to the half-way resting-place, and seated myself beside the fountain. The stars shone at intervals, as the clouds passed from over them; the dark pines rose before me, and every here and there a broken tree lay on the ground: it was a scene of wonderful solemnity, and stirred strange thoughts within me. I wept bitterly;

and, clasping my hands in agony, I exclaimed, "Oh! stars, and clouds, and winds, ye are all about to mock me: If ye really pity me, crush sensation and memory; let me become as nought; but if not, depart, depart and leave me in darkness."

These were wild and miserable thoughts; but I cannot describe to you how the eternal twinkling of the stars weighed upon me, and how I listened to every blast of wind, as if it were a dull ugly siroc on its way to consume me.

Morning dawned before I arrived at the village of Chamounix; but my presence, so haggard and strange, hardly calmed the fears of my family, who had waited the whole night in anxious expectation of my return.

The following day we returned to Geneva. The intention of my father in coming had been to divert my mind, and to restore me to my lost tranquility; but the medicine had been fatal. And, unable to account for the excess of misery I appeared to suffer, he hastened to return home, hoping the quiet and monotony of a domestic life would by degrees alleviate my sufferings from whatsoever cause they might spring.

For myself, I was passive in all their arrangements; and the gentle affection of my beloved Elizabeth was inadequate to draw me from the depth of my despair. The promise I had made to the demon weighed upon my mind, like Dante's iron cowl on the heads of the hellish hypocrites. All pleasures of earth and sky passed before me like a dream, and that thought only had to me the reality of life. Can you wonder, that sometimes a kind of insanity possessed me, or that I saw continually about me a multitude of filthy animals inflicting on me incessant torture, that often extorted screams and bitter groans?

By degrees, however, these feelings became calmed. I entered again into the every-day scene of life, if not with interest, at least with some degree of tranquility.

Writing Topic

Explain the moral dilemma that the creature presents to Dr. Frankenstein in this chapter. Do you think Dr. Frankenstein's decision to give the creature what he asks for is justifiable? Is he correct when he chooses to satisfy the needs of the creature and to protect his own well-being, even if his decision may put others at risk? Be sure to support your response with concrete examples that come from your own experiences, observations, and readings.

Strategies for Identifying an Argument in Literature

As in earlier chapters of *Write It*, you will use the answers you fill in here when you write a directed summary in response to the first part of the writing topic for this assignment:

> first part of the writing topic:
>
> *Explain the moral dilemma that the creature presents to Dr. Frankenstein in this chapter.*

This question asks you to look at this chapter from a particular point of view. The monster makes specific demands on Frankenstein, demands that force Frankenstein to make a choice. To answer this first part of the writing topic, you will have to summarize the conflicting aspects of the two possible choices he has.

Begin by looking for the elements of argument in this chapter. You will remember from working on the prose essays in the previous chapters that argument works by putting together and linking evidence to support a conclusion. Unlike essays such as "Practicing Medicine Can Be Grimm Work" and "Reading and Thought" where writers present their views directly, for this assignment you will have to determine how the story presents an argument and supports it using plot and characters. What position does the monster represent? What evidence does the monster link together to support his demand? What position does Frankenstein ultimately represent? What evidence does he link together to support his decision? We can use, with some flexibility, the five steps we listed above to help isolate and identify the argument.

1. List the main characters in the story. Briefly summarize their words and actions. What do these things suggest about their personalities and relationships with each other?

   In this short excerpt, there are two characters:

   <u>Dr. Frankenstein</u>: He is the scientist responsible for creating the creature. When the creature requests that Dr. Frankenstein make a mate so that he won't be lonely, Frankenstein feels torn. On the one hand, he has compassion for the creature's miserable existence and concludes "that the justice due both to him and my fellow-creatures demanded of me that I should comply with his request." At the same time, Frankenstein worries about the consequences of having two monsters (and possibly their offspring) in the world. Dr. Frankenstein is revealed to be a man capable of reason who wants to make the best decision possible in an impossible situation.

   <u>The creature</u>: He is a monster created in a laboratory by Dr. Frankenstein. The creature admits that he is motivated by malice and a thirst for revenge. He both loves Frankenstein as a father and resents him for not loving the creature as a son. The creature argues with Frankenstein and attempts to convince him

to comply with his request. The creature seems miserable, desperate, and yet hopeful that Dr. Frankenstein will be willing and able to help him.

2. Identify the main conflict in the story. What is the subject or issue of the conflict? What more general issue is the story *representing* with this conflict?

The moral dilemma in this story is easy to see. Dr. Frankenstein cannot decide whether to grant or deny the creature's request. It is clear that Frankenstein is torn because, while he recognizes compelling aspects to the monster's plea, he also recognizes the interests of society and how they conflict with the interests of the creature. Is it right to consider the needs of the individual when there is the possibility that they conflict with the needs of the group? This is the conflict presented to us *representationally* in this chapter of *Frankenstein*, a conflict that all of us have probably experienced in our lives to some degree. We may find similar situations develop with our family, friends, and authority figures, or in politics, health care, science, business, and law—in fact, it is a conflict that we as a society must struggle with every day.

3. Identify the two or more sides of the conflict. Looking back at the characters you listed in #1, what does each character contribute to the conflict through his or her words or actions? Look carefully at the evidence that each character (including the narrator) presents, and try to determine how the evidence is being linked to support a position.

The creature wants his creator, Victor Frankenstein, to create a mate for him because he is lonely. He is shunned by others because he is different and cannot live happily in isolation. The creature has responded to this treatment with violence, even murder, but insists that his violence has been an unavoidable response to being rejected and shunned because of his ugliness. He wants a mate for companionship, and insists that this will dispel his violent tendencies so that he will no longer be a threat to others. He insists on his right to have a companion and, the story says, the "interchange of those sympathies necessary for [his] being."

Dr. Frankenstein, on one hand, feels responsible for the creature's happiness because he has created him. He understands the suffering of the creature and respects the creature's desire for a solution to its suffering. He finds hope in the creature's claim that, if it has a mate, it will no longer be a threat to anyone. Frankenstein also knows that, if he doesn't grant the creature's request, it will "work at [his] destruction" and make his life miserable. On the other hand, Frankenstein also recognizes valid reasons for rejecting the creature's request. He fears the creature's violent tendencies, and he understands the suffering the creature has brought to others. Bringing another creature into existence may double the threat and open the possibility for the creatures to reproduce themselves and thereby increase the violence and discord. Frankenstein cannot satisfy both the creature and the larger society of people. He must sacrifice the interests of one or the other. He struggles to resolve this moral dilemma: Does he try to provide for the monster, or does he try to provide for the larger community?

4. Look over what you wrote for #2 and #3, and then try to state the argument that the story and its characters are representing. This time, try to state the argument in general terms that readers can apply to their own lives.

How much consideration does Dr. Frankenstein owe his creation, the creature? Should Frankenstein's concern about the creature's potential harm to society outweigh his responsibility for the creature's well-being? The creature represents the position that, if individual needs are met, the group will be better, but if they're not met, everyone will suffer. The group has to be willing to make some sacrifice for the needs of the individual. If we don't pay attention to individuals, we might become heartless. After all, groups are made up of individuals.

But if we always decide for the individual, fairness may disappear because those who can demand the loudest or with the most influence could get unfair consideration at the cost of everyone else. As far as possible, we should try to provide everyone with the opportunity for a good life, and this can only be done by making the best decisions for the greatest number of people. Individuals have to see that they must give some things up if we are to live together in harmony.

5. Identify how the story resolves the conflict. This resolution leads directly to the thesis statement, or the story's position in the argument.

We can't tell how the novel as a whole resolves the conflict just by looking at one chapter. We can, however, see a chain of evidence in this chapter that shows both sides of the argument, and we can think of the chapter as a kind of "whole" as we respond to the assignment.

Developing an Opinion and Working Thesis Statement

The second part of the writing topic that follows the chapter from *Frankenstein* asks you to take a position of your own:

second part of the writing topic:

Do you think Dr. Frankenstein's decision to give the creature what he asks for is justifiable? Is he correct when he chooses to satisfy the needs of the creature and to protect his own well-being, even if his decision may put others at risk?

Do you agree with Frankenstein's viewpoint, which we've identified to be that the needs of the few outweigh the needs of the many? To answer this, you would simply use the thesis frame (which you should recognize from previous chapters of this book) to formulate a thesis statement. As you may have done in previous chapters of *Write It*, if you're not sure what position you want to take, do some prewriting to develop your ideas, and then come back to writing a working thesis statement.

a. What is the issue of the *Frankenstein* excerpt that the writing topic asks you to consider? In other words, what is the main topic the excerpt is about?

   Whether we should act in the interest of the individual or the interest of the group.

b. What is Dr. Frankenstein's position on that issue?

   He acts in his own interest rather than in the interest of the group.

c. What is your position on the issue; that is, will you agree or disagree with Dr. Frankenstein?

   _____

   _____

   _____

The last part of the writing topic asks you to support the argument you put forward in your thesis statement:

   Last part of the writing topic:

   Be sure to support your response with concrete examples that come from your own experiences, observations, and readings.

If you had to write this essay, the majority of it would be devoted to supporting the position you took in your thesis statement. You would do some prewriting to explore your ideas and develop your supporting topics; then, you would use an outline to plan and draft your essay. As you can see, even though finding arguments in literature requires you to read with a somewhat different perspective, you can use the same steps of the writing process that you have worked with throughout the writing assignments in *Write It*.

The *Frankenstein* example is a discussion between two characters that is easily recognizable as a debate, so the argument is fairly clear. But what happens when this is not the case? How do you find the argument when you are asked to look at narration that includes description of characters and setting, but no extended dialogue that carries a debate? Go on to the next pages and try out the five steps using a short story, Sandra Cisneros's "The Monkey Garden."

The Monkey Garden

Sandra Cisneros

Sandra Cisneros is a Mexican-American writer, author, and poet born in Chicago. She earned her BA from Loyola University and her MFA at the University of Iowa. She has taught at many colleges and universities, including the University of California and the University of Michigan. "The Monkey Garden" is taken from her best-known novel, The House on Mango Street *(1984).*

The monkey doesn't live there anymore. The monkey moved—to Kentucky—and took his people with him. And I was glad because I couldn't listen anymore to his wild screaming at night, the twangy yakkety-yak of the people who owned him. The green metal cage, the porcelain table top, the family that spoke like guitars. Monkey, family, table. All gone.

And it was then we took over the garden we had been afraid to go into when the monkey screamed and showed its yellow teeth.

There were sunflowers big as flowers on Mars and thick cocks-combs bleeding the deep red fringe of theater curtains. There were dizzy bees and bow-tied fruit flies turning somersaults and humming in the air. Sweet sweet peach trees. Thorn roses and thistle and pears. Weeds like so many squinty-eyed stars and brush that made your ankles itch and itch until you washed with soap and water. There were big green apples hard as knees. And everywhere the sleepy smell of rotting wood, damp earth, and dusty hollyhocks thick and perfumy like the blue-blond hair of the dead.

Yellow spiders ran when we turned rocks over, and pale worms blind and afraid of light rolled over in their sleep. Poke a stick in the sandy soil, and a few blue-skinned beetles would appear, an avenue of ants, so many crusty ladybugs. This was a garden, a wonderful thing to look at in the spring. But bit by bit, after the monkey left, the garden began to take over itself. Flowers stopped obeying the little bricks that kept them from growing beyond their paths. Weeds mixed in. Dead cars appeared overnight like mushrooms. First one and then another and then a pale blue pickup with the front windshield missing. Before you knew it, the monkey garden became filled with sleepy cars.

Things had a way of disappearing in the garden, as if the garden itself ate them, or, as if with its old-man memory, it put them away and forgot them. Nenny found a dollar and a dead mouse between two rocks in the stone wall where the morning glories climbed, and once when we were playing hide-and-seek, Eddie Vargas laid his head beneath a hibiscus tree and fell asleep there like a Rip Van Winkle until somebody remembered he was in the game and went back to look for him.

This, I suppose, was the reason why we went there. Far away from where our mothers could find us. We and a few old dogs who lived inside the empty cars. We made a clubhouse once on the back of that old blue pickup. And besides, we liked to jump from the roof of one car to another and pretend they were giant mushrooms.

Somebody started the lie that the monkey garden had been there before anything. We liked to think the garden could hide things for a thousand years. There beneath the roots of soggy flowers were the bones of murdered pirates and dinosaurs, the eye of a unicorn turned to coal.

This is where I wanted to die and where I tried one day, but not even the monkey garden would have me. It was the last day I would go there.

Who was it that said I was getting too old to play the games? Who was it I didn't listen to? I only remember that when the others ran, I wanted to run too, up and down and through the monkey garden, fast as the boys, not like Sally who screamed if she got her stockings muddy.

I said, Sally, come on, but she wouldn't. She stayed by the curb talking to Tito and his friends. Play with the kids if you want, she said, I'm staying here. She could be stuck-up like that if she wanted to, so I just left.

It was her own fault too. When I got back, Sally was pretending to be mad . . . something about the boys having stolen her keys. Please give them back to me, she said punching the nearest one with a soft fist. They were laughing. She was too. It was a joke I didn't get.

I wanted to go back with the other kids who were still jumping on cars, still chasing each other through the garden, but Sally had her own game.

One of the boys invented the rules. One of Tito's friends said you can't get the keys back unless you kiss us, and Sally pretended to be mad at first, but she said yes. It was that simple.

I don't know why, but something inside me wanted to throw a stick. Something wanted to say no when I watched Sally going into the garden with Tito's buddies all grinning. It was just a kiss, that's all. A kiss for each one. So what, she said.

Only how come I felt angry inside. Like something wasn't right. Sally went behind that old blue pickup to kiss the boys and get her keys back, and I ran up three flights of stairs to where Tito lived. His mother was ironing shirts. She was sprinkling water on them from an empty pop bottle and smoking a cigarette.

Your son and his friends stole Sally's keys and now they won't give them back unless she kisses them and right now they're making her kiss them, I said all out of breath from the three flights of stairs.

Those kids, she said, not looking up from her ironing.

That's all?

What do you want me to do, she said, call the cops? And kept on ironing.

I looked at her a long time, but couldn't think of anything to say, and ran back down the three flights to the garden where Sally needed to be saved. I took three big sticks and a brick and figured this was enough.

But when I got there, Sally said go home. Those boys said leave us alone. I felt stupid with my brick. They all looked at me as if *I* was the one that was crazy and made me feel ashamed.

And then I don't know why, but I had to run away. I had to hide myself at the other end of the garden, in the jungle part, under a tree that wouldn't mind if I lay down and cried a long time. I closed my eyes like tight stars so that I wouldn't, but I did. My face felt hot. Everything inside hiccupped.

I read somewhere in India there are priests who can will their heart to stop beating. I wanted to will my blood to stop, my heart to quit its pumping. I wanted to be dead, to turn into the rain, my eyes to melt into the ground like two black snails. I wished and wished. I closed my eyes and willed it, but when I got up, my dress was green and I had a headache.

I looked at my feet in their white socks and ugly round shoes. They seemed far away. They didn't seem to be my feet anymore. And the garden that had been such a good place to play didn't seem mine either.

Writing Topic

How does the narrator's alienation by the end of the story present us with a critique of gender roles? Do you think this critique is valid? Be sure to support your position with concrete evidence taken from your own experiences, including your observations and readings.

Vocabulary Check

Good writers choose their words carefully so that their ideas will be clear. Therefore, it is important to think about a story's key vocabulary terms and the way they are used by the author. Words can have a variety of meanings, or they can have specialized meanings in certain contexts. Look up the definitions of the following words or phrases from "The Monkey Garden." Choose the meaning that you think gives the most insight to the story. Then explain the way the meaning or concept behind the definition is key to understanding the story's argument.

porcelain

definition: _____

_____

_____

explanation: _____

_____

_____

Rip Van Winkle

definition: _____

_____

_____

explanation: _____

_____

_____

cockscomb

definition: _____

_____

_____

explanation: _____

_____

_____

Questions to Guide Your Reading

Paragraph 1

What are the things that have disappeared, and how does the narrator of the story feel about their absence?

Paragraph 2

What happens to the garden after the disappearance? Why?

Paragraphs 3–4

What natural things occupy the garden now? What things start to appear that seem out of place in a garden?

Paragraph 5

What kinds of things become lost in the garden?

Paragraph 6

If strange things appear and other things get lost in this garden, what reason does the narrator give for its popularity?

Paragraph 7
What rumor is told about the garden? Is there any truth in it? Why do you think this lie is circulated? Why would anyone believe it?

Paragraph 8
What does the narrator try to do in the garden? Is she successful? How does she feel about the garden after that day?

Paragraph 9
What is the relationship between growing up and going to the garden?

Paragraphs 10–14
Who is Sally? What does the narrator want Sally to do? What does Sally do instead? How does the narrator feel about what Sally is doing?

Paragraphs 15–19
Whom does the narrator ask for help? What kind of response does she get?

Paragraphs 20–21

What plan does the narrator have next? Does it work? Why? How does she feel then?

Paragraphs 22–23

Then where does the narrator go, and what does she do? What emotions is she experiencing?

Paragraph 24

In the end, what changes have occurred in the way the narrator feels about herself, the garden, and the other children? Has the story established any relationship between her feelings and her age and gender?

Prewriting for a Directed Summary

You will find that providing thorough answers to these questions will help you write a clear and accurate *directed* summary that responds to the first part of the writing topic.

> first part of the writing topic:
>
> *How does the narrator's alienation by the end of the story present us with a critique of gender roles?*

For this assignment, you are working with a short story, so you should use the five steps for identifying an argument in literature.

1. List the main characters in the story. Briefly summarize their words and actions. What do these things suggest about their personalities and relationships with each other?

2. Identify the main conflict in the story. What is the subject or issue of the conflict? What more general issue is the story *representing* with this conflict?

3. Identify the two or more sides of the conflict. Looking back at the characters you listed in #1, what does each character contribute to the conflict through his or her words or actions? Look carefully at the evidence that each character (including the narrator) presents, and try to determine how the evidence is being linked to support a position.

4. Look over what you wrote for #2 and #3, and then try to state the argument that the story and its characters are representing. This time, try to state the argument in general terms that readers can apply to their own lives.

5. Identify how the story resolves the conflict. This resolution leads directly to the thesis statement, or the story's position in the argument.

Developing an Opinion and Working Thesis Statement

The second question in the writing topic that follows "The Monkey Garden" asks you to take a position of your own:

> second part of the writing topic:
>
> *Do you think this critique is valid?*

Now that you have done some careful prewriting and have systematically developed your thoughts, you are ready to formulate a working thesis statement that responds to this part of the writing topic. What argument does the story as a whole make about the subject of gender roles? At this point in your thinking, will you agree or disagree with this argument? In other words, does the message of the story *as you have interpreted it* reflect your own view on gender roles? If not, what position do you want to take on the subject of gender roles and their influence on us?

To formulate your position and thesis statement, keep in mind the way "The Monkey Garden" defines gender roles. For help, review what you discovered in "Questions to Guide Your Reading."

Because these ideas may be new to you, it is possible that you aren't yet sure what position you want to take in your essay. If this is the case, you can explore your ideas on a blank page of this book, or go on to the next section and work on developing your ideas through examples drawn from your experience. Then you will be directed to come back to the working thesis statement you have written here and work on revising it, if necessary, based on the discoveries you made when you explored your ideas more systematically.

1. Use the following thesis frame to identify the basic elements of your thesis statement:

    a. What is the issue in "The Monkey Garden" that the first part of the writing topic asks you to consider?

    _____

    b. What is the story's point of view on that issue?

    _____

    c. What is your position on the issue, and will you agree or disagree with the story's view?

_____

_____

_____

2. Now use the elements you isolated in 1a, b, and c of the thesis frame to write a thesis statement. You may have to revise it several times until it captures your idea clearly.

_____

_____

Prewriting to Find Support for Your Thesis Statement

The last part of the writing topic asks you to support the argument you put forward in your thesis statement:

last part of the writing topic:

Be sure to support your position with concrete evidence taken from your own experiences, including your observations and readings.

Use the following questions to help develop examples you might use to support your thesis statement.

Hint

Complete each section of this prewriting activity; your responses will become the material you will use in the next stage—planning and writing the essay.

---

1. As you begin to develop your own examples, consider the influence of gender roles in your own life. In the space below, list or freewrite about personal experiences (either concerning you, your friends, or your family) when you or someone you know was expected to behave or look a certain way because of gender. Think about your own identity and your hopes and aspirations to see if they are tied to your own, your family's, or society's expectations based on your gender. Feel free to include any experience, however minor or incidental.

   Once you've written your ideas, look them over carefully. Try to group your ideas into categories. Then give each category a label. In other words, cluster ideas that seem to have something in common and, for each cluster, identify that shared quality by giving it a name.

2. Now broaden your focus; list or freewrite about examples from your studies, your readings, and your knowledge of current events. Think, too, about the readings you have done in some of your other classes or in your free time. Do any of them offer examples of the influence of gender roles that you may be able to use?

Once you've written your ideas, look them over carefully. Try to group your ideas into categories. Then give each category a label. In other words, cluster ideas that seem to have something in common and, for each cluster, identify that shared quality by giving it a name.

3. Once you've created topics by clustering your ideas into categories, go through them and pick two or three specific ones to develop in your essay. Make sure that they are relevant to your thesis and that they have enough substance to be compelling to your readers. Then, in the space below, briefly summarize each item.

Once you've decided which categories and items on your lists you will use in your essay, take some time to explain below how each category and its items connect to your thesis statement.

Revising Your Thesis Statement

Now that you have spent some time working out your ideas more systematically and developing some supporting evidence for the position you want to take, look again at the working thesis statement you crafted earlier to see if it is still accurate. As your first step, look again at the writing topic, and then write your original working thesis on the lines that follow it. Remember that your thesis statement must answer the second question, but take into consideration the writing topic as a whole. The first question in the topic identifies the issue that is up for debate, and the last question reminds you that, whatever position you take on the issue, you must be able to support it with specific examples.

second part of the writing topic:

How does the narrator's alienation by the end of the story present us with a critique of gender roles? Do you think this critique is valid? Be sure to support your position with concrete evidence taken from your own experiences, including your observations and readings.

Working Thesis Statement:

_____

_____

_____

Take some time now to see if you want to revise your thesis statement. Often, after extensive prewriting and focused thought, you will find that the working thesis statement is no longer an accurate reflection of what you plan to say in your essay. Sometimes only a word or phrase must be added or deleted; other times, the thesis statement must be significantly rewritten, as either or both the subject and the claim portions are inaccurate.

After examining your working thesis statement and completing any necessary revisions, check it one more time by asking yourself the following questions:

a. Does the thesis directly identify the argument about gender roles that "The Monkey Garden" presents?

b. Do you make clear your opinion about the way gender roles define us?

If you answered "no" to either of these questions, then rewrite your thesis statement so that it is fully developed.

_____

_____

Planning and Drafting Your Essay

Now that you have examined the argument in "The Monkey Garden" and thought at length about your own views, draft an essay that responds to all parts of the writing topic. Use the material you developed in this section to compose your draft, and then exchange drafts with a classmate and use the peer review that follows to revise your draft. Don't forget to review Part 1, especially "The Conventional Academic Essay Structure," for further guidance on the essay's conventional structure.

Getting started on the draft is often the hardest part of the writing process because this is where you move from exploring and planning to getting your ideas down in writing and in a unified, coherent shape. Creating an outline will give you a basic structure for incorporating all the ideas you have developed in the preceding pages. An outline will also give you a bird's-eye view of your essay and help you spot problems in development or logic. The form below is modeled on Part 1's "The Conventional Academic Essay Structure," and it is meant to help you create an outline or writing plan before you begin drafting your essay.

Creating an Outline for Your Draft

I. **Introductory Paragraph**

A. An opening sentence that gives the story's title and author and begins to answer the first part of the writing topic:

_____

_____

_____

B. Main points to include in the directed summary:

1.

2.

3.

4.

C. Look up "Revising Your Thesis Statement," where you wrote a polished and accurate statement of your position on gender roles and their influence on us. Copy it on the line below. It should clearly agree or disagree with the argument in "The Monkey Garden" about gender roles, and it should state a clear position using your own words.

_____

_____

II. Body Paragraphs

   A. The paragraph's one main point that supports the thesis statement:

     _____

      1. **C**ontrolling idea sentence:

        _____

        _____

      2. **C**orroborating details:

        _____

        _____

        _____

      3. **C**areful explanation of why the details are relevant:

        _____

        _____

        _____

        _____

        _____

      4. **C**onnection to the thesis statement:

        _____

   B. Subject of the paragraph: _____

      1. **C**ontrolling idea sentence:

        _____

        _____

      2. **C**orroborating details:

        _____

        _____

        _____

3. Careful explanation of why the details are relevant:

_____

_____

_____

_____

_____

4. Connection to the thesis statement:

_____

C. Subject of the paragraph: _____

1. Controlling idea sentence:

_____

2. Corroborating details:

_____

_____

_____

3. Careful explanation of why the details are relevant:

_____

_____

_____

_____

_____

4. Connection to the thesis statement:

_____

D. Subject of the paragraph: _____

    1. **C**ontrolling idea sentence:

      _____

    2. **C**orroborating details:

      _____

      _____

      _____

    3. **C**areful explanation of why the details are relevant:

      _____

      _____

      _____

      _____

      _____

    4. **C**onnection to the thesis statement:

      _____

III. Conclusion

A. Type of conclusion to be used:

    _____

B. Key words or phrases to include:

    _____

Getting Feedback on Your Draft

Use the following guidelines to give a classmate feedback on his or her draft. Read the draft through first, and then answer each of the items below as specifically as you can. Be sure to have a classmate fill out a review sheet for your draft. Look carefully at the responses he or she made to your draft, and use them to revise your essay.

Name of draft's author: _____

Name of draft's reader: _____

Introduction

1. Within the opening sentences,
   a. the author is correctly identified by first and last name   yes   no
   b. the short story's title is included and placed within
      quotation marks   yes   no

2. The opening contains a summary that
   a. explains the narrator's alienation at the end
      of "The Monkey Garden"   yes   no
   b. explains the story's critique of gender roles   yes   no

3. The opening provides a thesis that
   a. states whether the story's critique of gender roles is valid   yes   no
   b. takes a position on gender roles   yes   no

If the answers to 3 above are yes, state the thesis below as it is written. If the answer to one or both of these questions is no, explain to the draft's writer what information is needed to make the thesis complete.

Body

1. How many paragraphs are in the body of this essay? _____

2. To support the thesis, this number is   sufficient   not enough

3. Do body paragraphs contain the 4Cs?

Paragraph 1	Controlling idea sentence	yes	no
	Corroborating details	yes	no
	Careful explanation of why the details are relevant	yes	no
	Connection to the thesis statement	yes	no

Paragraph 2	Controlling idea sentence	yes	no
	Corroborating details	yes	no
	Careful explanation of why the details are relevant	yes	no
	Connection to the thesis statement	yes	no
Paragraph 3	Controlling idea sentence	yes	no
	Corroborating details	yes	no
	Careful explanation of why the details are relevant	yes	no
	Connection to the thesis statement	yes	no
Paragraph 4	Controlling idea sentence	yes	no
	Corroborating details	yes	no
	Careful explanation of why the details are relevant	yes	no
	Connection to the thesis statement	yes	no
Paragraph 5	Controlling idea sentence	yes	no
	Corroborating details	yes	no
	Careful explanation of why the details are relevant	yes	no
	Connection to the thesis statement	yes	no
	(Continue as needed.)		

4. Identify any of the above paragraphs that are not fully developed (too short).

   _____

5. Identify any of the above paragraphs that fail to support the thesis.

   _____

6. Identify any of the above paragraphs that are redundant or repetitive.

   _____

7. Suggest any ideas for additional paragraphs that might improve this essay.

   _____

Conclusion

1. Does the draft's conclusion contain any material that should have been developed in the body of the essay?

   a. examples   yes   no

   b. new ideas   yes   no

2. Does the conclusion provide closure (let the reader know that the end of the essay has been reached)?   yes   no

3. Does the conclusion leave the reader with an understanding of the significance of the argument?   yes   no

   State in your own words what the writer considers to be important about his or her argument.

   _____

   _____

4. Identify the type of conclusion used (see the guidelines for conclusions in Part 1).

Revision

1. During revision, the writer should pay attention to the following problems in sentence structure, punctuation, and mechanics:

   comma splices
   misplaced, missing, and unnecessary commas
   fragments
   run-on sentences
   misplaced, missing, and unnecessary apostrophes
   incorrect quotation mark use
   capitalization errors
   spelling errors
   dangling and misplaced modifiers

2. During revision, the writer should pay attention to the following areas of grammar:

   verb tense
   subject-verb agreement
   irregular verbs
   pronoun type
   pronoun reference
   pronoun agreement
   noun plurals
   prepositions

Final Draft Checklist

Content:

- My essay has an appropriate title.
- I provide an accurate summary of the position on the topic set out by "The Monkey Garden."
- My thesis contains a claim that can be supported with concrete evidence.
- I have a sufficient number of paragraphs and argument points to support my thesis.
- Each body paragraph is relevant to my thesis.
- Each body paragraph contains the 4Cs.
- I use transitions whenever necessary to connect paragraphs and ideas to each other.
- The final paragraph of my essay (the conclusion) provides the reader with a sense of closure.

Grammar, Punctuation, and Mechanics:

- I use the present tense to discuss the author's arguments and examples.
- All of my verb tense shifts are correct and necessary to the shifts in time.
- I have verb tense consistency throughout my sentences and paragraphs.
- I have checked for subject-verb agreement in all of my sentences.
- My sentences are punctuated correctly.
- If I present items in a series (nouns, verbs, prepositional phrases), they are parallel in form.
- If I include material spoken or written by someone other than myself, I have correctly punctuated it with quotation marks, using the MLA style guide's rules for citation.

Reviewing Your Graded Essay

After your essay has been graded by your instructor, you may have the opportunity to revise your paper and raise your grade. Even if you are not submitting a revised version of this essay to your instructor, it is important that you review your work carefully in order to understand its strengths and weaknesses. This sheet will guide you through the evaluation process.

You will want to continue to use the techniques that worked well for you and to find strategies to overcome the problems that you identify in this sample of your writing. In order to help yourself recognize areas that might have been problematic for you, look back at the scoring rubric in this book. Match the numerical/verbal/letter grade received on your essay to the appropriate category. Study the explanation given on the rubric for your grade.

Write a few sentences below in which you identify your problems in each of the following areas. Then, suggest specific changes you could make that would improve your paper. Don't forget to use your handbook as a resource.

1. **Grammar/punctuation/mechanics**
   My problem:

   My strategy for change:

2. **Thesis/response to assignment**
   My problem:

   My strategy for change:

3. **Organization**
   My problem:

   My strategy for change:

4. **Paragraph development/examples/reasoning**
   My problem:

   My strategy for change:

5. Assessment

In the space below, assign a grade to your paper using a rubric other than the one used by your instructor. In other words, if your instructor assigned your essay a grade of *High Fail*, you might give it the letter grade you now feel the paper warrants. If your instructor used the traditional letter grade to evaluate the essay, choose a category from the rubric in this book, or any other grading scale that you are familiar with, to show your evaluation of your work. Then write a short narrative explaining your evaluation of the essay and the reasons it received the grade you gave it.

Grade: _____

Narrative: _____

_____

_____

_____

_____

Case Studies

Part 3 contains three reading selections and, following each, four or five essays written by students like you. Using the sample scoring rubric in Part 1, score each of the student essays. Then, discuss each with your classmates, focusing on each essay's strengths and weaknesses.

Case Study #1

Dwight Macdonald's "Reading and Thought"

The following case study uses Macdonald's essay "Reading and Thought," which you will remember from Part 2. The essay is reproduced here, followed by five timed-writing essays written by students just like you. Read Macdonald's essay and the five student essays that respond to the topic question that follows it. Examine each student essay for its strengths and weaknesses. A set of study questions at the end will help you evaluate its success. Then, use the scoring rubric in Part 1 to give each essay a score.

Reading and Thought

Essay

DWIGHT MACDONALD

Dwight Macdonald (1906-82), was a part of the New York intellectuals of his time, and became famous for his attacks on middlebrow culture. He frequently carried on his debate in essays published in magazines such as the Partisan Review, the New Yorker, Esquire, *and the magazine he edited in the 1940s,* Politics.

Henry Luce[1] has built a journalistic empire on our national weakness for being "well-informed." *Time* attributes its present two-million circulation to a steady increase, since it first appeared in 1925, in what it calls "functional curiosity." Unlike the old-fashioned idle variety, this is a "kind of searching, hungry interest in what is happening everywhere—born not of an idle desire to be entertained or amused, but of a solid conviction that the news intimately and vitally affects the lives of everyone now. Functional curiosity grows as the number of educated people grows."

The curiosity exists, but it is not functional since it doesn't help the individual function. A very small part of the mass of miscellaneous facts offered in each week's issue of *Time* (or, for that matter, in the depressing quantity of newspapers and magazines visible on any large newsstand) is useful to the reader; they don't help him make more money, take some political or other action to advance his interests, or become a better person. About the only functional gain (though the *New York Times*, in a recent advertising campaign, proclaimed that reading it would help one to "be more interesting") the reader gets out of them is practice in reading. And even this is a doubtful advantage. *Time*'s educated people read too many irrelevant words—irrelevant, that is, to any thoughtful idea of their personal interests, either narrow (practical) or broad (cultural).

Imagine a similar person of, say, the sixteenth century, confronted with a copy of *Time* or the *New York Times*. He would take a whole day to master it, perhaps two, because he would be accustomed to take the time to think and even to feel about what he read; and he could take the time because there *was* time, there being comparatively little to

---

[1]The publisher of *Time* magazine until his death in 1967.

read in that golden age. (The very name of Luce's magazine is significant: *Time*, just because we don't have it.) Feeling a duty—or perhaps simply a compulsion—at least to glance over the printed matter that inundates us daily, we have developed of necessity a rapid, purely rational, classifying habit of mind, something like the operations of a Mark IV calculating machine, making a great many small decisions every minute: read or not read? If read, then take in this, skim over that, and let the rest go by. This we do with the surface of our minds, since we "just don't have time" to bring the slow, cumbersome depths into play, to ruminate, speculate, reflect, wonder, *experience* what the eye flits over. This gives a greatly extended coverage to our minds, but also makes them, compared to the kind of minds similar people had in past centuries, coarse, shallow, passive, and unoriginal.

Such reading habits have produced a similar kind of reading matter, since, except for a few stubborn old-fashioned types—the handcraftsmen who produce whatever is written today of quality, whether in poetry, fiction, scholarship, or journalism—our writers produce work that is to be read quickly and then buried under the next day's spate of "news" or the next month's best seller; hastily slapped-together stuff that it would be foolish to waste much time or effort on either writing or reading. For those who, as readers or as writers, would get a little under the surface, the real problem of our day is how to *escape* being "well-informed," how to resist the temptation to acquire too much information (never more seductive than when it appears in the chaste garb of duty), and how in general to elude the voracious demands on one's attention enough to think a little.

Writing Topic

According to MacDonald, what is the nature of the "printed matter that inundates us daily," and what connection does this kind of reading have with thought? What do you think about the position he takes here? Be sure to support your argument with specific examples based on your observations and experiences; you may also draw on your reading, including the supplementary readings in this unit.

Student 1

Henry Lace, publisher of time magazine, says that educated people have developed a "functional curiosity" that compels people who think they are educated to read. Henry Luce go on by saying that news, print, articles, novels, etc. intimately affect our daily lives and those who compose of it. But, according to Dwight MacDonald in "Reading and Thought" the only advantageous gain we receive when reading an article, passage, novel, etc. is simply the practice of reading. Dwight continues and states that the connection between reading and thought is time. Dwight concludes saying that we read it and then it becomes irrelevant, old news, instead of thinking about it or challenging ourselves with it. And that is why reading is only practice.

I agree with Dwight MacDonald, reading today is only practice. A lot of the time all we do is read it and then put it on the shelf, dump it, and repeat that process. I realize that I do the same thing, read & dump, with readings, that I could care less about. I am assigned in some of my classes. Reading without mediation is just reading, meaningless. But when we read and think or think throughout the reading, we finish with meaning. The next couple of paragraphs will be example of reading without thought and then reading with thought.

This last summer I took a Sociology class. In eight weeks I had to read two books, the text book and "Lies My Teacher told me." To say the least it was a little overwhelming, but in the end I was able to read the two books. Read, all I did was quickly read through the two books, which caused an absence of the real meaning in the two books. All I gained was practice and the practice was beneficial, but meaning is far more enhancing to the reader. Meaning gives us perspective and broadens our narrow point of views. Because we can attach meaning to life, not practice.

Reading with thought is far more beneficial to us. For example, I love the book of Ecclesiasties in the Bible. It is full of depressing poetry and in the end it gives the meaning of life. I have read Exxlesiasties on numerous occasions. I have attached value to it and believe that no matter how many time I read it, I will catch something new or will be reminded of something important. for me reading Ecclesiasties is far more than practice, instead it has importance and meaning to it. I can't read it without thinking about. Reading is important to us but when we think and mediate on the reading it turns into something else. Something meaning full.

Reading without thought is merely practice. But when reading and thought are combined the result is meaning. It puts value on reading. I think that everyone should think about the reading, and they should read Ecclesiasties.

Assessment Questions

1. Does this essay answer the first part of the writing topic?

2. Does this essay have a thesis that answers the second part of the writing topic?

3. Does this essay develop the thesis with supporting examples? Evaluate the effectiveness of these examples.

4. Are there significant errors in grammar that limit the essay's effectiveness? In other words, as you read the essay, did you notice several mistakes in the way the sentences are written?

5. Using the conventional standards presented in the scoring rubric in Part 1 of this book, what score does this essay deserve? Explain.

Student 2

According to Dwight MacDonald in <u>Reading and Thought</u>, he talks about the difference of reading from old ages to today, and how in the past people had the time to read and think and imagine what the person was reading. Whereas, today we don't have time to take a book and really get in depth of the story. Dwight says that how we read is functional curiosity. He said that we only read because of what is happening in todays life and us wanting to inquire information. What we read today only is to receive information. We read with ease. However, a person from the older ages would take much longer because of their reading skill and wanting to experiance their reaiding material, Dwight also says that people now only wright to be read quickly and then thrown away never to be seen again. He makes a point to say that the problem we have is we want to be well informed and we need to resist that, so as we read we can think, experiance, and reflect.

Reading styles have changed from old times to today. According to Dwight MacDonald we read alot, but only to inquire information, and we don't ruminate, reflect, or even experiance what we read and we give no thought to our readings. In materials that I have read I have only read them because I had to or else because I wanted to get some information. I understand Dwight, because many people read for those few reasons. It's even fewer who read to imagine, experiance, and visuallize themselves there. An example of this is, In high school many of the books I read were because I had to, and even while I read I skimed over the material. Another example of this is when I have had a project were it required me to gather information I only read the important parts just to wright it down on my paper. Finally, I would read, but I would the newspaper only because something had happen near by my city and I wanted to know what was going on.

In high school I read many materials such as <u>Raisin in the Sun</u>, <u>How to Kill a Mocking Bird</u>, <u>Mice of Men</u>, but although I read those stories I never thought of myself as a character or even to be there. I read the story, but most of my time skimed over the material. The reson for that is like Dwight said only to inquire information. I remember very little from the stories. I only read enough and only thought enough to be able to answer the questions ons on the test.

A second example, is that I only pick up a book or a magazine to read when I'm looking for information. Also in highschool I only read when it required me to have resources or get answers to a question. Many of my readins were long so I would look for only the part I needed, so I never took the time to imagine myself there. Many of my fellow classmates would do the same There was really not one person that would take their time and effort to read and enjoy the book.

Finally, any material that I would read would be in my spare time, and the matieral I would read was not for my enjoyment. It would be like Dwight said to know whats happing like he called it to be well informed. I would get the newspaper and read what was going on. The section that I would read more often would be the local. Only because I cared more about what was going on in my city or near by. Reading the newspaper does not give us the affect of exireanceing something it just gives us the information, and numers of people read for that same exact reason.

In conclusion, I understand what Dwight MacDonald is saying that many people now and day do not care to take their time and redd something enjoyable, and not just to read but see themselves there or be involved with the story. Now when we read, we do not have any thought in our reading only the purpose to know more and be well informed, So in my next reading I will enjoy what I'm reading and become one of the main characters.

Assessment Questions

1. Does this essay answer the first part of the writing topic?

2. Does this essay have a thesis that answers the second part of the writing topic?

3. Does this essay develop the thesis with supporting examples? Evaluate the effectiveness of these examples.

4. Are there significant errors in grammar that limit the essay's effectiveness? In other words, as you read the essay, did you notice several mistakes in the way the sentences are written?

5. Using the conventional standards presented in the scoring rubric in Part 1 of this book, what score does this essay deserve? Explain.

Student 3

In Dwight MacDonald's essay, "Reading and Thought," Dwight states that because our society no longer has the time to read, our minds are becoming similar to that of people in the past centuries. Meaning, although we have advanced far beyond the people in the past, the limitation we set upon our reading time is holding the advancement of our thought process back because we no longer take the time to think about what we have read. Dwight also states that the problem with today's people is that we tend to avoid long readings, and we do not hold enough attention to even think the slightest bit.

Personally, I agree with Dwight because I do feel our society is becoming less intelligent due to the fact we do not read as much. Over time the less we read the more stagnant our minds become, and the more stagnant our minds become the less original intellect is outputted. Most people today have replaced their reading time with other various types of stimuli, such as watching television or playing video games; however, such stimuli does not produce one's own vision or original thought, thus limiting their own power of thoughts and opinions.

Based on my personal experience, I also noticed the decrease in my intellectual capacity because of the lack of reading. After I graduated high school in 2004, I decided to take a couple years off in order to focus just on my businesses. While running my businesses, such as my liquor stores and my clothing line, I realized after awhile that my mind was not working as effieciently as it had before. At times, I even found myself just staring into space without a single thought on my mind. It turns out while running my business, I was always so occupied that I never took the time to do any decent reading. Even when I would go over contracts, it would usually be a quick skim over what I deemed important and I just ignored the rest. Then I even found it incredibly difficult to produce new and original marketing campains, which completely shocked me because I was known for producing amazing marketing ideas. I soon realized that my lack of thought in general was due to the fact that my brain was not being stimulated as it should be by way of reading. I knew this to be true because when I realized my thought process was becoming stagnant, I immediately started to pick up research journals on business and marketing, and I began to read through them diligently. After a couple days of constant and thoughtful reading, I noticed a huge difference in the way I thought because I was filled with so many new ideas about business and marketing campaigns.

Another example of how reading and thought go hand in hand is one pertaining to my ex-girlfriend's mom's foster kids. My ex-girlfriend's mom, Emma, constantly takes in and raises foster kids for a living. I remember two foster kids specifically whom I helped take care of Eric and Jessika. Eric and Jessika are brother and sister who grew up in many broken homes. Because they were raised under such harsh conditions, they rarely focused on their education. One activity they hated to do the most was reading. I noticed, because their lack of reading, that they hardly ever came up with their own original ideas or opinions. In fact, when we asked them what they wanted to do for leisure, they both kept saying, "whatever he/she wants to do." When we got into details about asking them of their likes and dislikes, one sibling would respond the same as the other sibling, again no original thought. Because reading helps stimulate one's own thoughts and opinions, Eric and Jessika did not seem to have either.

In essence, reading has a direct influence over one's thoughts. If an individual were to go without reading for a good amount of time, there is a real high possibility that their minds will become stagnant and vapid. If we want our society to keep progressing with new and original ideas, we must then continue to make time for reading. Especially with the younger generation of kids, we must keep them reading. Since the younger generation is our future, we want to make sure that life as we know it does not become so dull and unoriginal due to lack of new ideas brought on by the lack of reading.

Assessment Questions

1. Does this essay answer the first part of the writing topic?

2. Does this essay have a thesis that answers the second part of the writing topic?

3. Does this essay develop the thesis with supporting examples? Evaluate the effectiveness of these examples.

4. Are there significant errors in grammar that limit the essay's effectiveness? In other words, as you read the essay, did you notice several mistakes in the way the sentences are written?

5. Using the conventional standards presented in the scoring rubric in Part 1 of this book, what score does this essay deserve? Explain.

Student 4

The Loss of Reading

In "Reading and Thought," by Dwight MacDonald, MacDonald states that reading is not the same as it was in the past eras. MacDonald states that reading should involve deep analysis of what had been read, reflection, and experience what the eye flits over (MacDonald). MacDonald directly quotes the publisher of Time Magazine Henry Luce, when he says that, "Functional curiosity grows as the number of educated people grows," but MacDonald contradicts this statement saying that curiosity isn't functional because it does not help the individual function (MacDonald). MacDonald also explains that one of the reason why we do not embrace the gift of reading is because we simply do not have the time. Another reason given is that the writers of newspapers, magazines, and other forms of literature that are not of the academy, actually produce work that are meant to be read quickly and set aside (MacDonald).

I agree on MacDonald's claim that reading has been neglected. A reader should embrace the gift of reading, and be humble that there are so many things available to be read. In the past times, there wasn't anything to be read. A library did not exist in the colonial times, the internet was not invented, and there weren't books produced everyday for the average people. I believe that many people have forgotten that reading is a gift and a privelage. Analyzing, reflecting, and just breaking down a piece of Literature in order to find the true hidden message in a book is what makes life important. Now, all that is produced in the newspapers and magazines are gossip and "How to's." In my opinion, I think the celebrity magazine sells more than the actual newspapers. I also believe that most adults read newspapers to find deals on merchandise and coupons rather than to find out the polls in elections.

With all the gossip and scandals going around on celebrities, there isn't anything to be analized and reflected on what has been read. Whenever I talk with my friends they always seem to know whether or not Brad Pitt and Angelina Jolie adopted a new child, but they didn't seem to know what the local news headline was. Except for a few, most of my friends didn't even know what the local newspaper was called. The fact that gossip is more popular than world news shows how low the academic level has dropped for the average people.

Coupons and deals are always a great find, they save you a lot of money and teach you to spend money unwisely. My friend Angela Bae used to search for coupons every Sunday in her newspapers. She would bring the newspaper to work and just cut out coupons and throw everything else away. By everything, I mean everything, even the actual newspaper. She would never read about what was going on in the world, but she would always read about what was on sale this week. She wouldn't even be able to tell you if we were in war, or with what country. It has been forgotten that reading is a gift and also that having a lot of things to read is a gift.

I believe that both the publishers and readers have forgotten what reading and analizing means. Most that are produced are work that are to be buried under gossip and coupons, instead of what is of importance like world news, politics, and local news. MacDonald specifically states that our mind asks one question, "read or not read?" necaise we tell our selves that we do not have time to read and give thought (MacDonald). Reading has been dumped into the vast black hole along with the one-hit wonders, poodle skirt, shoulder pads, and many other things that are not useful in today's daily life. Gossip, scandals, and coupons seem to be more important than political issues. This shows how uneducated the world is becoming because we have forgotten the true meaning of reading, that reading is to break down the book or article and produce deep thoughts and reflection.

Assessment Questions

1. Does this essay answer the first part of the writing topic?

2. Does this essay have a thesis that answers the second part of the writing topic?

3. Does this essay develop the thesis with supporting examples? Evaluate the effectiveness of these examples.

4. Are there significant errors in grammar that limit the essay's effectiveness? In other words, as you read the essay, did you notice several mistakes in the way the sentences are written?

5. Using the conventional standards presented in the scoring rubric in Part 1 of this book, what score does this essay deserve? Explain.

Student 5

The Time It Takes for Reading and Thought

According to Dwight MacDonald's "Reading and Thought," he believes the connection between reading and thought is time. That it takes time to read and to think no matter what someone is looking at. Books, magazines, and even newspapers will always take time to look over to understand what it says.

I believe that MacDonald is taking the right position here. I do agree that it takes time to read and think. When I open a book, I want to know what I am getting myself into. When I start to write the perfect essay, I have to think a lot about what I am going to write. In this essay, I am going to discuss how much time it takes me to read and think.

Reading opens my eyes to so many different things. For example, in one book I can be an airline pilot flying to Africa or a young boy on a desert island. But before I can go to those places, I have to take the time to read the book. I have to take the time to understand what I am reading. If I do not understand the book, then I will have no idea what is going on in the book. Another thing that takes time when reading is looking up words I do not understand. I have to get a dictionary and look up a word so I can understand what the author is trying to say. If I do not take the time for that, then I will not understand that part in the book. Finally, it takes time to put it in my own words. If I ever wanted to tell my mother about the book, I would have to put it in words that she would have to read the book herself. This is why I believe it takes time to read because I have to understand whay I am reading, I have to look up the words I do not know to find what they mean, and put it into my own words so I can understand the book or story better.

Another thing that takes time is writing the perfect essay. The essay has a lot of steps to it that will take a lot of time. It only takes a lot of time to write the perfect essay. One step is called brainstorming. During my brainstorming phrase, I have to think about what I going to write. I would also take the time to think about the questions I need to answer. Last, I have to write down my ideas before they leave my brain. Another step is outlining my essay. I have to take the time to see what order I will write the information in. it also takes time to list the ideas down. That's for me to know what things I am going to write about. Another step is writing the essay down onto the paper. Al the time it takes to put it into my own words. It takes a lot of time to think about what words I would want to use. Last, it takes a lot of time to check my essay for mistakes. I have to make sure my grammar is correct. I have to make my spelling is correct. If I messed up anytime in the essay, I have to change it to make it make sense. That is why I believe it takes a lot of time to think when I want to write the perfect essay.

That is why I agree with MacDonald. I believe time is the connection between reading and thought. There are so many things I need to think about reading and thinking. No matter what, everyone takes time in life to think about the choices he is going to make and the time to read to get ahead in life.

Assessment Questions

1. Does this essay answer the first part of the writing topic?

2. Does this essay have a thesis that answers the second part of the writing topic?

3. Does this essay develop the thesis with supporting examples? Evaluate the effectiveness of these examples.

4. Are there significant errors in grammar that limit the essay's effectiveness? In other words, as you read the essay, did you notice several mistakes in the way the sentences are written?

5. Using the conventional standards presented in the scoring rubric in Part 1 of this book, what score does this essay deserve? Explain.

Case Study #2

Susan Sontag's "Why We Take Pictures"

The following case study uses Sontag's essay "Why We Take Pictures," which you will remember from Part 2. The essay is reproduced here, followed by four timed-writing essays written by students just like you. Read Sontag's essay and the sample student essays that respond to the topic question that follows it. Examine each student essay for its strengths and weaknesses. A set of study questions at the end will help you evaluate its success. Then, use the scoring rubric in Part 1 to give each essay a score.

Why We Take Pictures

SUSAN SONTAG

Susan Sontag received her BA from the College of the University of Chicago and did graduate work in philosophy, literature, and theology at Harvard University and Saint Anne's College, Oxford. She was an American writer, teacher, and human rights activist. Her stories and essays have appeared in newspapers, magazines, and literary publications all over the world, and her books have been translated into thirty-two languages. The following essay comes from one of her best-known works, On Photography *(1978).*

The age when taking photographs required a cumbersome and expensive contraption—the toy of the clever, the wealthy, and the obsessed—seems remote indeed from the era of sleek pocket cameras that invite anyone to take pictures. The first cameras, made in France and England in the early 1840s, had only inventors and buffs to operate them, and taking photographs had no clear social use. Recently, photography has become almost as widely practiced an amusement as sex and dancing. For most people, photography is mainly a social rite, but it can also be a defense against anxiety and a tool of power.

Memorializing the achievements of individuals considered as members of families, as well as of other groups, is the earliest popular use of photography. For at least a century, the wedding photograph has been as much a part of the ceremony as the prescribed verbal formulas. Cameras go with family life. According to a sociological study done in France, most households have a camera, but a household with children is twice as likely to have at least one camera as a household in which there are no children. Not to take pictures of one's children, particularly when they're small, is a sign of parental indifference, just as not turning up for one's graduation picture is a gesture of adolescent rebellion.

Through photographs, each family constructs a portrait-chronicle of itself—a portable kit of images that bears witness to its connectedness. It hardly matters what activities are photographed so long as photographs get taken and are cherished. Photography became a rite of family life just when, in the industrializing countries of Europe and America, the very institution of the family started undergoing radical surgery. As that claustrophobic unit—the nuclear family—was being carved out of a much larger family aggregate, photography came along to memorialize, to restate symbolically, the imperiled continuity and vanishing extendedness of family life. Those ghostly traces, photographs, supply the token presence of the dispersed relatives. A family's photograph album is generally about the extended family—and, often, is all that remains of it.

As photographs give people an imaginary possession of a past that is unreal, they also help people to take possession of space in which they are insecure. Thus, photography develops in tandem with one of the most characteristic of modern activities: tourism. For the first time in history, large numbers of people regularly travel out of their habitual environments for short periods of time. It seems to them positively unnatural to travel for pleasure without taking a camera along: Their photographs will offer indisputable evidence that the trip was made, that the program was carried out, that fun was had. Photographs document sequences of consumption carried on outside of the view of family, friends, and neighbors. The camera makes real what one is experiencing, and the compulsion to use it doesn't fade when people travel more. Taking photographs fills the same need for the cosmopolitans accumulating photograph-trophies of their boat trip up the Nile or their fourteen days in China as it does for less-traveled vacationers taking snapshots of Disneyland or Niagara Falls.

Besides being a way of certifying experience, taking photographs is also a way of refusing it—by limiting experience to a search for the photogenic, by converting experience into an image, a souvenir. Travel becomes a strategy for accumulating photographs. The very activity of taking pictures is soothing, and assuages general feelings of disorientation that are likely to be exacerbated by travel. Most tourists feel compelled to put the camera between themselves and whatever is remarkable that they encounter. Unsure of other responses, they take a picture. This gives shape to their experience: They stop, take a photograph, and move on. This activity especially appeals to Americans and other people handicapped by a ruthless work ethic. Using a camera appeases the anxiety that work-driven people feel about not working when they are on vacation and supposed to be having fun. They have something to do that is a friendly imitation of work: They can take pictures.

Writing Topic

According to Sontag, in what ways can taking pictures be a defense against anxiety, and sometimes even a tool of power? Do you agree with her analysis? Be sure to support your argument with specific examples; these examples can be taken from your own experience and observations or anything you have read, especially the readings from this course.

Student 1

Let's Take a Selfie!

In a 1978 essay from her book, *On Photography*, humanitarian activist, Susan Sontag discusses the universal access and increased use of cameras in American culture, arguing that capturing experience is not the sole purpose of the camera. Instead, Sontag makes the assertion that cameras can grant the user relief from anxiety and a sense of power in situations where they feel like they have no control. Sontag argues that in unfamiliar environments the photographer is granted an illusion of control through the practice of composition, thus neutralizing any anxiety they might have felt about being an alien in an environment. Furthermore, she claims that a photograph can create an impression of togetherness in a family, even if it is forged. The implications that Sontag claims are that we are so indulged in taking pictures and it becomes problematic when we constantly try to manipulate reality. I, however, disagree with Sontag because I believe that the camera in fact accentuates how powerless we are and increases anxiety. Photographs often display an unachievable beauty, can be lost control of its images on the web, and there is constant social pressure in taking a perfect photo.

Taking the perfect selfie is a staple in social media. Unfortunately, selfies advocate an often-unattainable form of beauty. Photographs, overall, have put an emphasis on the importance of one's image. For example in the essay *What Your Selfies Say About You Are Your Selfies Ruining Your Relationship?* research psychologists, Peggy Drexler explains how selfies are "a manifestation of society's obsession with looks." When posting pictures online, pictures are often modified through photoshop and filters bringing confidence to the person who posts the image. Nevertheless, the need to edit and modify one's picture only emphasizes their insecurity. With techniques such as Photoshop and filters, we continue to advocate and idealize a beauty that is not there. We falsely advertise an appearance gained through the fixations of photoshop and filters. In fact, many celebrities who are praised for their selfie taking posts such as Kim Kardashian West normalize an ideal beauty that was often achieved through physical alterations. Thus, making the ideal beauty harder for various women to achieve and as a result, women turn to filters to better their virtual image. The inability to achieve the ideal beauty, despite the many tools set on photographs, only displays how powerless an individual is physically not virtually. Throughout recent years the manifestation of self-images have influenced an ideal form of beauty, and by being so easily influenced and becoming insecure again accentuates how powerless an individual really is. Perhaps the tools set for images have the vast amount of power given its influence on American culture. It is evident that people who are insecure/ weak minded would hide behind the camera because they realize how they cannot achieve that look in person. Overall, today people tend to maneuver images to give the perception they want to present, however, this is only temporary and it is only in a matter time that one has to confront reality of what they truly look like. While Sontag argues that photographs give families the ability to manipulate togetherness, I argue photographs demonstrate that the families are powerless because they resort to a cameras rather than changing the family itself.

Everything you post online will be there forever. Social media constitutes taking images, updating statuses, and sharing stories. Unfortunately once someone posts something online, an image for instance, can no longer be erased. For example in the essay *A 1,000 Pictures for a Million Words*, faculty member in the University writing program in the University of California Riverside, Lash Keith discusses how as adolescents teens are diverted to post images of them drinking on Facebook. Keith adds that in the future these images will have negative effects on adolescents because once any image is uploaded there is a "loss of control over the image." Now a day, teenagers have no discretion about their private lives and most of their private moments are captured in images and posted on social media e.g. Facebook. It is often difficult to erase images/photographs once uploaded on the Internet, especially with screenshots being available to people. Because of screenshots, images can now be saved on other people's cellphones. Ultimately, when someone shares a picture on the Internet they have lost control of the picture and is available for anyone to modify it as they wish. In terms of losing power, once a picture is posted online there is a loss of power and no longer is that picture only yours. Evidently, social media apps have risen in popularity and now various people, like myself, take images with the purpose of posting it online. Although many will argue that the camera gives you the power to post a picture online to share with others, posting pictures online only reduces the control over that image and you will no longer have power over it.

Posting the perfect image is key in the world of social media. There is a social pressure into taking a picture that captures your greatest assets, in best lighting, at the perfect angle. So the question arises whether Sontag's argument about cameras relieving anxiety is in fact true. For example, in the reading she explains that a camera reduces anxiety by granting us power to control an unfamiliar place. Nonetheless, the work required to take an image is an aspect that needs to be further analyzed. For example, when I am taking pictures, after countless amounts of pictures, I become anxious because the images do not come out the way I want them to. To put this into perspective, when I visited the Getty, Los Angeles' popular art museum, it was almost impossible not to take a picture of the beauty that surrounded me. However, one does not simply point the camera to the attraction and snap a picture, in fact when someone is taking a picture one analyzes, evaluates, and criticizes the quality of the picture. At times I was blocked by crowds of people, had to bend my body at a certain angle, and would try to avoid the glare of the glass where the art was displayed. The effort itself caused me emotional and physical distress. When I am taking a picture I feel a pressure into taking a perfect picture of my surroundings and of myself. Even after I post a picture, I become more anxious because I start wondering whether or not people will appreciate the quality of my picture. The need for acceptance from others is what makes people anxious when taking pictures. Lastly, I am very fastidious when it comes to taking pictures, so I become anxious when I am unable to take a "perfect" picture.

In conclusion, the use of cameras have risen since Sontag published her book; thus, making cameras more relevant in American culture. Photographs promote beauty expectations that are inaccessible to many behind a camera lens. The social media trend highlights how accessible "our" images are and the need to post a high quality picture makes us nervous. Overall, despite being able to capture a moment with a camera, a camera is causing a distorted reality for many.

Assessment Questions

1. Does this essay answer the first part of the writing topic?

2. Does this essay have a thesis that answers the second part of the writing topic?

3. Does this essay develop the thesis with supporting examples? Evaluate the effectiveness of these examples.

4. Are there significant errors in grammar that limit the essay's effectiveness? In other words, as you read the essay, did you notice several mistakes in the way the sentences are written?

5. Using the conventional standards presented in the scoring rubric in Part 1 of this book, what score does this essay deserve? Explain.

Student 2

Photography and the Act of Picture Taking

In her 1978 essay from her book "On Photography", author and Humanitarian Susan Sontag discusses the increased use of cameras in the American lifestyle, arguing that photography is more than just a simple act to complete, but deals with anxiety and power in a larger spectrum. Sontag makes this assertion by discussing the changes in the typical American family lifestyle and by explaining how the practice of taking pictures has engulfed itself in today's culture. Anxiety, according to Sontag, is something experienced when we visit unfamiliar places and our day-to-day tasks are taken away from us in places where people do not know how to behave. Furthermore, she claims that the photographer can take control over specific situations that once caused anxiety by using it as a type of power. The implications of Sontag's claim state that because of photography family households have changed and is able to transform reality, in a way where it can help reduce anxiety and give people a sense of power. In today's day and age technology has had many advancements, that we may have more anxiety and less power when it comes to taking pictures.

Regarding this argument, I feel as though certain aspects have changed. The act of taking pictures has become more convenient because essentially every person that owns a cellphone has a camera within their pocket. So things may have become more accessible in a way that could be either positive or negative within when we think about the way that it is being talked about. Because things are made to be more accessible, it may not be such a big deal to feel as though you need to take pictures, but they are constantly taken because there is this sense of convenience just because it is made to be something that can be easily done whether or not it is something that is extremely important.

When it comes to the reduction of anxiety, I feel as though the importance or significance of taking pictures is no longer there. Since cellphone cameras are so accessible, instead of being worried about feeling uncomfortable within an unfamiliar place or situation people no longer care because their phone carries what "home" can represent to them. So essentially, their home, which could be a safety blanket, is always at their fingertips. Cellphones have so much data that there is no use in feeling that you are in a place where you do not belong because you can remind yourself of things that remind you of home, but at the same time people are so worried about remaining connected to home that they feel anxious about the fact that they constantly have to worry about trying to stay connected. This relates to the essay written by Lash Keith Vance, "A 1,000 Picture for a Million Words" because he talks about how there is this "barrier" that is created between what it happening and the picture taker. This is essentially stating how there is a person trying to capture the perfect moment, so all of their time is being wasted. By constantly taking pictures, people are missing out on the certain environments and are unable to experience what is happening. I feel as though this can cause more anxiety because if someone is constantly taking their time in a specific environment to take pictures for the perfect shot, then there is a chance that they could think that they essentially missed out on the experience. Missing the experience all because of a picture can cause more anxiety than trying to find the perfect picture.

Reducing anxiety also has to deal with work. But once again because the cellphone is so accessible, people are not concerned with having to make a job out of having to take pictures. Reason being is because they now have access to everything they would normally do at the tip of their fingers since technology has given us the opportunity to make things that were once inconvenient, the opportunity to be accessed quite easily. But there is a sense of power to being able to take pictures or work at one's convenience. If I were to relate work to the selfie, while referring to the Saltz essay "Art at Arm's Length: A History of the Selfie" we could see that there are some similarities that take power away. The one thing makes me strongly agree with power is that because of the amount of options to fix, filter or change the state of an original picture, people have the power to make you believe you look a certain when, when you actually do not. Then there is the idea that people with power can make you feel like you need to look a certain way or give you the idea that you need to buy something in order to look like them. This directly explains how there are certain people who can directly make you think something just from a picture that has no direct correlation to themselves. And if the picture was of themselves, then they are giving you this false idea of what they are actually supposed to be like.

When it comes to anxiety, what is not taken into consideration is how cellphones are there for our convenience. If work and pictures are constantly there whenever we needed them, we may feel anxious and constantly feel the need to check things and take pictures when we are not in an uncomfortable state. The Saltz essay talks about Kim Kardashian and the types of pictures that she takes, but there is always a purpose to why she is posting certain things, one of those reasons being publicity. Because of paparazzi, her power to make people believe she looks a certain way or does certain things no longer exists, in the same way with work. Because people are taken out of the work environment and feel as though picture taking can be a type of work, we are taking away the power that we would normally have when trying to enjoy ourselves which can cause anxiety.

The power of the photograph also deals with something that can make a family look ideal, but is that a sense of power if you are misrepresenting something? Peggy Drexler, a research psychologist and author of the essay "What Your Selfies

Say About You Are your selfies ruining your relationships?" talks about how being people are so fixated on capturing the perfect picture. Photographs can capture what people want you to think is the way an ideal family should look instead of actually being able to do things that would make you a real ideal family. If photographs are wanted or need to be taken, it would be considered to be so much more genuine and real if they were taken at a time when the family is actually connected and doing something to enjoy each other's presence. The power is taken away in today's day and age because in order to seem ideal, you have to do the most or too much in order to "prove" to people that they are a specific type of family.

In the end, because of technology there is this sense of something being taken away because you are not able to experience something directly because you are too busy trying to capture the perfect moment. This also relating to power because there is no perfect moment other than being able to experience the moment at that direct time because it can never be experienced in the same way again. As Sontag explains, photography can make one feel as though they have a grasp on life and what they are trying to perceive that their life is like. Although there are reasons to believe that photography can reduce anxiety and give a sense of power, there are too many advancements in technology for there to be such a simple task to do these things.

Assessment Questions

1. Does this essay answer the first part of the writing topic?

2. Does this essay have a thesis that answers the second part of the writing topic?

3. Does this essay develop the thesis with supporting examples? Evaluate the effectiveness of these examples.

4. Are there significant errors in grammar that limit the essay's effectiveness? In other words, as you read the essay, did you notice several mistakes in the way the sentences are written?

5. Using the conventional standards presented in the scoring rubric in Part 1 of this book, what score does this essay deserve? Explain.

Student 3

The Power to Taking Pictures

Often when people are asked by others "if you could have any type of power you want, what could it be?", some people could immediately think of the power rich people have due to monetary influences. Other people, such as teenagers or young adults, may immediately think of power as the ones seen on television, such as being able to control an element of nature or being able to fly through the sky and have supernatural strength. However, what most people do not realize when they are asked this question is that every one of them have a tool that gives them power right inside their small pocket. In a 1978 essay from her book "On Photography", human rights activist Susan Sontag discusses the increase use of cameras in the America culture, arguing that photography can not only help reduce anxiety, but also grant us power. Sontag makes this assertion by discussing the changes in America lives and by the way tourism has changed with the use of a camera. Anxiety, according to Sontag, is the extreme stress experienced when people enter an unfamiliar place or do something beyond his or her comfort zone. Furthermore, she claims that the photographer can use the camera to impose lies onto us and reshape the reality within the photographs. The implications of Sontag's claim are our experience, and therefore our reality, can be easily manipulated and reshaped through the use of the camera. I agree with Sontag that taking pictures is a tool of power and can relieve anxiety because the act of taking pictures allows us to cement a moment, relieve anxiety, and turn a fabrication into the truth.

Taking a picture gives us the power to cement a moment. To cement a moment means that we create a solid, tangible proof that the moments we had experience in that event did occur. For example, recently, my officers and I went to Big Bear Lake for a retreat. During our time hiking up the Castle Rock Trail, most of the officers took photographs using our phone camera. Most photographs are of a few officers sitting or standing on top of the tall rocks that we climbed. Some are of us playing with the leftover snow and having a small snowball fight. Others are of the beautiful scenery around us when we were on top of the rocks. These photographs allows us to remember the memorable events that have occurred. By pressing the shutter button on the cameras, we are using turning the camera into a tool of power by allowing us to capture these precious moments and solidifying the events into something tangible that can be printed or put into the digital world.

Not only does taking pictures allow us to capture precious moments in time, it also allows an anxious person to do something to distract and relieve him or her of the situation. For example, a friend of mine name Kenma has a minor case of social anxiety. Although he often prefers to stay indoors, he could occasionally go to a social event held by his club to try to get out of his comfort zone to try new activities and to spend time with his friends. However, during these events, there were times when all the noise and people become too loud, which starts giving him a migraine and making him feel light headed. It is during those moments that he also starts feeling as if the space around him is enclosing on him and his anxiety level starts to rise up slowly. During those times, he could take his phone out and unlock the phone screen, turn on the camera app, and will start taking pictures of nearby scenery that catches his eyes or of his friends that are socializing at the moment. By taking pictures using his smartphone, Kenma is giving himself a distraction away from all the harsh noises and loud people. The motion of taking pictures is a familiar action, which gives him a semblance of peace. Taking pictures makes sure that his attention is away from all the noise and on how he wants the photos to turn out. By intentionally blocking out all the deafening noises, he is able to feel a bit more relaxed and less anxious. In this way, the act of taking photographs can be used as a tool to relieve anxiety in a person.

Taking pictures does not only help reduce anxiety in the photographer, it also gives the photographer the power to turn a deception into the truth by reshaping the reality within the photo. This can be illustrated by art historian Debra Brehmer's article "Every Portrait Tells a Lie." In her article, the Debra Brehmer tells us that there was a time in her past where the her whole family has to take a family photograph together. The photograph that was taken shown a family that is intimate and close. However, in reality, that is far from the truth. Brehmer's brother and the author did not get along very well. According to the author, the brother was mean to her and the author did not like standing near him and smiling when the photo was getting taken. In addition, her father was a cold distant figure in the author's life, but the the exact opposite of the relationship was portrayed in the photograph. In actuality, Brehmer's family was not a closely knit group of people. What was portrayed in the photograph, however, was that the family was very close, which is the reality the photographer decides to create. By taking a picture, it gives the photographer the power to turn that lie into reality inside that photograph. If people were to look at the reality within the photograph, the first impression they will get is that the family is a very intimate and devoted. Even if people were to closely observe the photo, the only observation they will gain is that everyone in the photograph gets along with each other and the observers will never know how much of a the reality in the photo is a lie.

Sontag think that the power of taking photograph are not a good influence on us since we can, and are, essentially trying to reshape our own reality by using a camera to take photos. By taking pictures, it gives the photographer the power to transform deception into the truth. What is actually happening in the real life situation may not be what is shown in the picture. By taking a picture that does not portray what is actually happening in reality, the photographer reshapes the lie into the reality the photographer wants people to view. However, in my opinion, using a camera to take picture is not always a horrible influence. Taking photographs can give the anxious photographer a small semblance of peace and the act of doing something familiar can help diminish anxiety. In addition, the act of taking photographs also gives the photographer the power to capture a moment in time. By using a camera to take pictures, the person is creating a tangible piece of proof that the moment he or she has experienced does in fact exist and had occurred. Therefore, before you start thinking what type of power you could like to gain if you could gain the power, you may want to check inside your pockets and realize that you do have power as a photographer as long as you have a camera on hand.

Assessment Questions

1. Does this essay answer the first part of the writing topic?

2. Does this essay have a thesis that answers the second part of the writing topic?

3. Does this essay develop the thesis with supporting examples? Evaluate the effectiveness of these examples.

4. Are there significant errors in grammar that limit the essay's effectiveness? In other words, as you read the essay, did you notice several mistakes in the way the sentences are written?

5. Using the conventional standards presented in the scoring rubric in Part 1 of this book, what score does this essay deserve? Explain.

Student 4

"It is more than just a picture"

Today, photography has reached a new level in which it no longer documents moments in time, but creates a fantasized lifestyle and identity. In a 1978 essay, from her book "On Photography," humanitarian activist Susan Sontag discusses the increase of cameras in society, arguing that photography can reduce anxiety and grant us power. According to Sontag, anxiety is produced by the unfamiliarity of places and the unusual change in people's everyday work ethic one aspires. Furthermore, she claims that photography can manipulate reality to gain control and power over previous events or experiences one struggles. The implications of Sontag's claim are that photography does not equal documentation but transforms reality.

Sontag argues that through a picture one can decrease the emotional feeling of anxiety and the act of taking a picture one can obtain power and control; in addition, today Sontag's argument continues to be true due to the increase of portable phone cameras and social media that through every photography and every picture taken anxiety and power is embedded to create an idealized reality and image.

It has become simple to capture a moment in an instant with the portable cameras cellular phones have installed in the previous years. When attending a concert it no longer involves swaying lighters in the air to the beat of a slow song, but the flash of the phone camera that is seizing the moment. People have the tendency to capture the social moment to remember or to show off to friends the experience. It is a way to reduce anxiety of other people's judgement and also diminishes the agitation of the individual because capturing the moment is a memory and experience of a lifetime. Yet, will the memory or experience be remembered? From one's perspective, there is no experience if one is always worried about seizing the moment. One is unable to tell the actual emotion and feeling if the only physical activity they remember is how much it hurt to keep their hands up in the air to take pictures. The only power or control they have is if they want to remember the off camera experience, or the pictures and videos they have captured on their phones. In the essay, "A 1,000 Pictures for a million Words," Lash Vance states "Forget the real experience; preserve on the idealized one." It demonstrates how our cellular devices are a distraction to the reality because people are constantly taking out their phones to record only what they want to share and remember.

Social media has advanced that its main purpose to keep family members and friends connected no longer is important, but to convey a fake reality. Many individuals post pictures of themselves with expensive brand name clothing or pictures of themselves in luxurious settings, usually inspired by celebrities. The picture portrays an illusion to viewers that the person is well-off or rich and able to offer such materials and trips. It also conveys the idea the person is of status. For the person who took the picture it reduces anxiety of how other people may view his or her reality. The reality may possibly be that he or she works more than forty-five hours week, in a minimum wage job, in order to purchase the things he or she wants. The high-quality material is an influence that reduces the angst in the person, which they gain confidence because it provides the feeling of having class. The ability to fake a reality creates power and control in the person to manipulate his or her struggles. It demonstrating for the viewer an illusionistic perspective of luxury the person might be living. By posting these types of photos it conveys a fantasized reality they want to live in, but cannot offered.

The social network of Instagram has been the main network for posting adventurous, motivational, funny, and inspiring pictures. It has become the network to post selfies and body transformation photos that can be manipulated. Many men and women, with the portable phone cameras, have been able to edit a photo by adding filters and cropping out certain part of the photograph to make it a great photo. The idea behind the picture is that individuals have control and power by adding a filter or cropping out aspects of a photo because it hides acne, blemishes, or even a part of the body the individual is insecure about. It reduces anxiety in the individual because the imperfections are not being shown and they are living up to the ideal beauty standards society has input in people's minds. In the essay, "What Your Selfies Say About You," a researcher psychologist Peggy Drexler claims by stating "And yet selfies are also a manifestation of society's obsession with looks and its ever narcissistic embrace." Peggy gives a valid point for today society that picture taking and photographs are only being taken because we think we "look good." People have become so obsessed with the idea of being "camera-ready" because it reduces anxiety in the person. They know they will be prepared for any photographic moment. Not only does it reduce anxiety but it gives them the ability to have control of the photograph being taken because they know what angle they should pose for every photo taken. For example, many body builders or individuals who are losing weight tend to post transformation photos on Instagram to hype up their self-esteem. If one were to lurk into their account they would find that they are all recent photos of their progress, and no old photos of the person before the transformation. The old photos provide anxiety in the individual because of the insecurity of their own body. The recent photo minimizes the anxiety they feel because they may be receiving positive and motivational comments the gives them confidence. Confidence is the power the individual has built and adapted towards the camera because they discover the love for themselves and the camera that capturing the moment has become necessary. Although, there is nothing wrong in being confident and loving oneself, but it has become the standardized beauty of men and women in society.

By possessing a moment through a photograph and creating an idealized lifestyle and image it can be influential and motivational to people; however, it defeats the reality and identity of the person. The time Sontag wrote the essay, in 1978, the children of that generation might have been looking at their grandparents photos and might find the lack of a smile or activity, which could be compared to passport or identification photos. Perhaps, our future grandchildren will encounter photos of today's era and find photos with dog filters and possibly question the real life story behind the pictures. However, will we have the ability to remember them if the only memory storage was not our brains, but our phones. In addition, the photos hide the true story that the individual is living, all due to the idea that people have become so worried about other people's judgement and criticism about the way of living life and what is considered to be beautiful. But what is the right way of living life? And what is considered beautiful? It has become difficult to express our real thoughts and struggles without the fear of other people's judgement.

Assessment Questions

1. Does this essay answer the first part of the writing topic?

2. Does this essay have a thesis that answers the second part of the writing topic?

3. Does this essay develop the thesis with supporting examples? Evaluate the effectiveness of these examples.

4. Are there significant errors in grammar that limit the essay's effectiveness? In other words, as you read the essay, did you notice several mistakes in the way the sentences are written?

5. Using the conventional standards presented in the scoring rubric in Part 1 of this book, what score does this essay deserve? Explain.

Case Study #3

Rebecca Solnit's "Walking and the Suburbanized Psyche"

The following case study uses Solnit's essay "Walking and the Suburbanized Psyche," which you will remember from Part 2. The essay is reproduced here, followed by four timed-writing essays written by students just like you. Read Solnit's essay and the sample student essays that respond to the topic question that follows it. Examine each student essay for its strengths and weaknesses. A set of study questions at the end will help you evaluate its success. Then, use the scoring rubric in Part 1 to give each essay a score.

Walking and the Suburbanized Psyche

Rebecca Solnit

Rebecca Solnit is an art critic and a writer. Her work reflects her interest in the history of the American West, and in environmental issues that threaten our environment and fail to foster communal, artistic, and personal life. The following is from her book Wanderlust: A History of Walking (2000).

Freedom to walk is not of much use without someplace to go. There is a sort of golden age of walking that began late in the eighteenth century and, I fear, expired some decades ago, a flawed age more golden for some than others, but still impressive for its creation of places in which to walk and its valuation of recreational walking. This age peaked around the turn of the twentieth century, when North Americans and Europeans were as likely to make a date for a walk as for a drink or meal. Walking was a sort of sacrament and a routine recreation, and walking clubs flourished. At that time, nineteenth-century urban innovations such as sidewalks and sewers were improving cities not yet menaced by twentieth-century speedups, and rural developments such as national parks and mountaineering were in first bloom. Perhaps 1970, when the US Census showed that the majority of Americans were—for the first time in the history of any nation—suburban, is a good date for this golden age's tombstone. Suburbs are bereft of the natural glories and civic pleasures of those older spaces, and suburbanization has radically changed the scale and texture of everyday life, usually in ways inimical to getting about on foot. This transformation has happened in the mind as well as on the ground. Ordinary Americans now perceive, value, and use time, space, and their own bodies in radically different ways than they did before. Walking still covers the ground between cars and buildings and the short distances within the latter, but walking as a cultural activity, as a pleasure, as travel, as a way of getting around, is fading, and with it goes an ancient and profound relationship between body, world, and imagination.

The history of the suburbs is the history of fragmentation. The twentieth-century American suburb reached a new level of fragmentation when cars made it possible to place people's homes ever farther from work, stores, public transit, schools, and social life. To illustrate how suburbs designed with curving streets and cul-de-sacs vastly expand distances, Philip Langdon gives the example of an Irvine, California, subdivision where, in order to reach a destination only a quarter mile away as the crow flies, the traveler must walk or drive more than a mile. These American suburbs are built with a diffuseness that the unenhanced human body is inadequate to cope with. Suburbanization has radically changed the scale and texture of everyday life, usually in ways inimical to getting about on foot. There are many reasons suburban sprawls generally make dull places to walk, and a large subdivision can become numbingly repetitive at three miles an hour instead of thirty or sixty.

But this transformation has happened in the mind as well as on the ground. The suburbanization of the American mind has made walking increasingly rare even when it is effective. Walking can become a sign of powerlessness or low status, and new urban and suburban design disdains the walker. Walking is no longer, so to speak, how many people think. Even in San Francisco, which is very much a "walking city," people have brought this suburbanized consciousness to their local travel, or so my observations seem to indicate. I routinely see people drive and take the bus for remarkably short distances, often distances that could be covered more quickly by foot. During one of my city's public transit crises, a commuter declared he could *walk* downtown in the time it took the streetcar, as though walking was some kind of damning comparison—but he had apparently been traveling from a destination so near downtown that he could've walked every day in less than half an hour. Once, I made my friend Maria—a surfer, biker, and world traveler—walk the half mile from her house to the shops and restaurants on Sixteenth Street, and she was pleased to realize how startlingly close they were. It had never occurred to her before that they were accessible by foot. Last Christmas season, the parking lot of the hip outdoor equipment store in Berkeley was full of drivers idling their engines and waiting for a parking space, while the streets around were full of such spaces. Apparently, shoppers weren't willing to walk two blocks to buy their outdoor gear. People have a kind of mental radius of how far they are willing to go on foot, a radius that seems to be shrinking. In defining neighborhoods and shopping districts, planners say this walking distance is about a quarter mile, the distance that can be walked in five minutes. But sometimes it hardly seems to be fifty yards.

More recent developments have been more radical in their retreat from communal space: We are in a new era of walls, guards, and security systems, and of architecture, design, and technology intended to eliminate or nullify public space. Urbanity and automobiles are antithetical in many ways, for a city of drivers is only a dysfunctional suburb of people shuttling from private interior to private interior. Cars have encouraged the diffusion and privatization of space, as shopping malls replace shopping streets, public buildings become islands in a sea of asphalt, civic design lapses into traffic engineering, and people mingle far less freely and frequently. Jane Holtz Kay, in her book on the impact of cars, *Asphalt Nation*, writes of a study that compared the lives of ten-year-olds in a walkable Vermont small town and an unwalkable southern California suburb. The California children watched four times as much television because the outdoor world offered them few adventures and destinations. And a recent study of the effects of television on Baltimore adults concluded that the more local news television, with its massive emphasis on sensational crime stories, local people watched, the more fearful they were, and the more discouraged they were from going out. These developments have made it less necessary to go out into the world, and have accommodated the deterioration of public space and social conditions.

Nature's occasional inconveniences resulting from biological and meteorological factors are now seen as drawbacks. Progress consists of the transcendence of time, space, and nature by the train and later the car, airplane, and electronic communications. But eating, resting, moving, experiencing the weather, are primary experiences of being embodied. To view them as negative is to condemn biology and the life of the senses, and severs human perception, expectation, and action from the organic world in which our bodies exist. Alienation from nature can be seen as an estrangement from natural spaces. Musing takes place in a kind of meadowlands of the imagination, a part of the imagination that has not yet been plowed, developed, or put to any immediately practical use. Time spent there is not work time, and without that time the mind becomes sterile, dull, domesticated. The fight for free space—for wilderness and for public space—must be accompanied by a fight for free time to spend wandering in that space. Otherwise, the individual imagination will be bulldozed over for the chain-store outlets of consumer appetite, true-crime titillations, and celebrity crises.

Walking has been one of the constellations in the starry sky of human culture, a constellation whose three stars are the body, the imagination, and the wide-open world. This constellation called walking has a history, the history trod out by all those poets and philosophers and insurrectionaries, by jaywalkers, streetwalkers, pilgrims, tourists, hikers, mountaineers, but whether it has a future depends on whether those connecting paths are traveled still.

Writing Topic

What, according to Solnit, will be lost if walking continues to be devalued by our society? Do you agree with her? Be sure to support your position with specific evidence. This evidence may come from your experience, your observations, or your reading, especially the reading from this course.

Student 1

Walking is Life

In the article "Walking and the Suburbanized Psyche", Rebecca Solnit talks about how the value of walking has changed over the years. Before suburbs flourished, walking was valuable and was part of culture. Solnit gives reasons that walking connects the body, the outside world, and the mind. Since the suburbs came into existence ,everything changed including people who became segregated and driftied apart from their communities. Individuals now see walking as something less, a low status and powerless activity. Over the years, people have lost the pleasure of walking. Walking is now seen as something useless to the world. People don'tr even care about nature. Solnit also mentions that we have lost imagination because kids are staying in to watch television and not going outside to play. Without walking and exploring the world we could lose all of our senses and without our senses we become dull. Walking is a great tool for maintaining good health. I agree with Solnit walking improves our imagination, our body, and our world.

Walking can help a person love and embrace nature more than just driving a car from one place to another. I remember when in January my roommate and I went to visit the Botanic gardens. As we were going to the garden we got lost at first but, then we found our way. Entering the garden we did not know what to expect so we started to walk. When we were walking in the garden it was amazing how everything looked. There weren't that much blooming flowers but it was still nice. Not only did it look nice and wonderful but also it smelled nice and fresh. As we continued through the path there were extraordinary sites. I loved the view, It felt really special and amazing at the same time. Then we came upon a place full of plants which was beautiful as well. Everything looked so natural and beautiful. I felt relaxed and refreshed. This walk through the garden relieved me from stress and cleared my mind for a while. When we finished taking a walk through the garden I started to appreciate nature and everything around me. I was very pleased that I went to the garden that day. I visit the garden from time to time now. I learned to love nature by just walking around through the Botanic Gardens.

Walking is very beneficial to the body because it can lead you to a healthy body. I never thought that my life would change completely by just walking. It all started in the summer of 2014 to be exact, I started to gain weight tremendously. So my weight started to affect my health. It came to the point that it was difficult for me to breathe, be active and feel good about myself. Then came the year 2015 and I was still overweight. Starting mid-July of 2015 I started to work and my family noticed that I was losing weight. When I was working I would walk a lot so it helped me to lose weight. Now, I walk every single day before I go to class and after I finish all my classes. Because I walk now I feel healthier and I can breathe easily. I feel more confident about myself, walking has made me feel incredibly good and has made me healthier.

In conclusion, walking is very beneficial because it can help support a healthy mind and body. Walking is beneficial. While walking a person can release any trouble, so it relaxes your mind and body. When people walk, they are able to think about ideas that can help them become a better person. Walking is a great tool for therapy when a person is feeling depressed or feeling outraged. I believe walking should be classified as enriching and powerful.

Assessment Questions

1. Does this essay answer the first part of the writing topic?

2. Does this essay have a thesis that answers the second part of the writing topic?

3. Does this essay develop the thesis with supporting examples? Evaluate the effectiveness of these examples.

4. Are there significant errors in grammar that limit the essay's effectiveness? In other words, as you read the essay, did you notice several mistakes in the way the sentences are written?

5. Using the conventional standards presented in the scoring rubric in Part 1 of this book, what score does this essay deserve? Explain.

Student 2

Walking Creates a Healthy Body, world, and Imagination

In the article called "Walking and the Suburbanized Psyche," Rebecca Solnit, the author, argues that, with the development of suburbanization, walking has been devalued by modern society, and this has led to many disadvantages: efficient exercise, connection with society and other people, and free spaces for human being's imagination and creativity. AS she has pointed out in her essay, under the influence of fragmentation and subdividing, people's homes are further from their working places. Schools, stores, public areas, and so on, so people are more likely to go by car rather than by foot, and this makes people lose a connection with their community. Meanwhile, the distance today's people are willing to walk is much shorter than before, and walking is considered as a low status way of getting around, so many people give up walking as their primary way to go from place to place. For example, in Berkeley, some drivers prefer to waste time waiting for a parking space at the hip outdoor equipment store instead of parking on another street, which was full of empty spaces. In addition, people spend more time staying in private places, like shopping malls and homes, rather than staying in public areas like streets and parks, so public spaces and social conditions has worsened. Moreover, modern transportation cuts people off from nature, which is a free space for human imagination. I agree with Solnit that not walking limits not just our bodies, but our world, and our imaginations,

First, there is a connection between walking and the world because walking can help people keep contact with their neighborhood and know their communities. Without walking people easily loose connection with society and become indifferent to many things. For example, know people are less likely to visit their neighbors. Often, they don't even know their neighbors' names. Last semester, my friend who lived in an American home never visited her classmate who lived less than half a mile from that residence. Influenced by the suburbanization of the American mind, my friend thought it too far to walk to see her classmate, so she stayed at home and watched television or communicated on her iphone, In contrast, when I was in China, my best friend and I liked walking to the library and parks around our community every weekend. On a way to these public spaces, my friend shared some things which had happened to her in school and introduced many good books to me. Sometimes we could find some just opened shops on the road and had delicious food there. Based on my experience, walking promotes communication and builds people's relationships. Moreover, there is a great difference between America and China in construction of sidewalks. Americans build wider lanes by shortening pathways and making people arrive quickly at destinations, but this reduces time spent connecting, while China sets many resting places, like pavilions, where pedestrians can talk with others and local retired people can play chess with their neighbors. Therefore, waling can help people connect with society and build connections to the world.

In addition, walking can strengthen people's imagination and creativity because walking is a good way for people to experience nature, and it gives people free time and space to imagine and create. Human beings are a part of nature, so, if people are always far away from nature, they wil fail to get inspiration. When people experience real life and nature, their thinking expands. Every day I walk from campus to my apartment, and this 20 minute distance makes my life more interesting and peaceful. If I took a bus to go home, I would never have known the group of high school students who have baseball training in the field, or smelled the pomegranate flowers blooming in early spring, and so on. Getting in touch with nature is good for my imagination and creativity. Last month was my aunt's birthday, and I didn't want to buy a normal cake from a supermarket for her, so I had a colorful rainbow cake by myself, and this idea came from the beautiful rainbow I saw after a rain when I was walking home. Nature opens up my imagination and strengthens my creativity. In her article, Solnit also argues that people need free space to muse which can help them develop imagination and creativity. People need to be part of the world, not just customers in a store. Therefore, walking helps people bond with nature and use their imaginations.

In conclusion, Solnit mentions that suburbanization has made people devalue walking, and this has contributed to the loss of many benefits. Besides a healthy body, walking provides a fuller world and a playground for the imagination.

Assessment Questions

1. Does this essay answer the first part of the writing topic?

2. Does this essay have a thesis that answers the second part of the writing topic?

3. Does this essay develop the thesis with supporting examples? Evaluate the effectiveness of these examples.

4. Are there significant errors in grammar that limit the essay's effectiveness? In other words, as you read the essay, did you notice several mistakes in the way the sentences are written?

5. Using the conventional standards presented in the scoring rubric in Part 1 of this book, what score does this essay deserve? Explain.

Student 3

Essay #2

The essay "Walking and Suburbanized Psyche" written by Rebecca Solnit, explains the rise of suburbs and the way transportation has changed the way people think about walking, as well as how people manage time and space. The growth of suburbs is one of the main things that changed how people think about walking. Most people want to take the fastest route They want to complete things on time, rather than enjoy themselves by walking as a cultural activity or pleasure. Solnit explains because the suburbs are too repetitive, so the landscape itself is repetitive and that makes it uninteresting for people to walk around the suburb and enjoy themselves. People with vehicles or public transportations loose the sense of distance, making them not feel like walking even a short distance, like to school or to the gym. With no one out walking and really "communicating" we loose the sence of a community. Solnit believes that the society will be lost if walking continues to be devalued, people will lose connections to nature, health, freedom, imagination and creativity.

I agree with Solnit that the society will loose if walking continues to be devalued by the community because of technological growth. People no longer need to walk to any place., They take a bus, ride a bike, or even skate to their destination. In addition, people forget about what they are doing if they happen to take transportations to their destination instead of walking. They don't notice the people and the beauty of nature as they ride along. Riding to school, work, or even to the gym makes many people think about what they are going to do later on or something they might not have done yet. For example, if we happen to go to the gym on the way there we could be thinking about which body part should we be working out today, or driving from home to work makes one think about when is the boss going to pay them so that one could pay their bills etc... Walking instead of riding would increase one's imagination. For example, one of the famous artists Yayoi Kusama, gets her inspiration by walking through parks and clearing her mind. Walking could also give us chances to smile at other people and have a sense of community, instead of riding alone in our car and getting angry at traffic.

Transportations use is very common in today's soecity. Human's don't have to walk no more, they could stay indoors of houses or use cars to avoid nature. Walking connects humans to nature. Without it we are not going to be aware of what's around us in the nature. Walking is also a really good exercise. By walking thirty minutes without taking any transportation one will lose 112 calories each day says one of the formal health clinics. By walking we are connected to people and nature together; it would really encourage us to think about nature and our bodies even more. This movement will also encourage us and inspire us to start moving instead of staying in front of the computer.

Another thing, if people start getting used to transportations and suburbanization people will lose their freedom. One could walk to any destination they wanted, but if one agrees to use transport one would have to follow the restrictions and rules of the transport they are taking. For example, a friend of mine wasn't able to meet me on time for an appointment because he had to wait for the bus He should have walked to the restaurant and not made me wait. The bus schedule messed up his and my appointment time. This shows that we lose the freedom of what we are able to accomplish and we can't be spontaneous and have new experiences.

I believe walking will make us think about the values of our society. Kids who live in an unwalkable place will tend to watch television more than kids who live in a walkable place. This example shows us that more walking will inspire people to go around places just to stay relaxed, or think about things. I believe walking is a really important part of life. It gives us nature, health, freedom, imagination and creativity.

Assessment Questions

1. Does this essay answer the first part of the writing topic?

2. Does this essay have a thesis that answers the second part of the writing topic?

3. Does this essay develop the thesis with supporting examples? Evaluate the effectiveness of these examples.

4. Are there significant errors in grammar that limit the essay's effectiveness? In other words, as you read the essay, did you notice several mistakes in the way the sentences are written?

5. Using the conventional standards presented in the scoring rubric in Part 1 of this book, what score does this essay deserve? Explain.

Student 4

The Loss of Walking

In "Walking and The Suburbanized Psyche" argues the people have devalued the meaning and benefits of walking. In her argument she describs there is a lost between the profound relationship between body, world, and imagination. Solnit believes that people lose their senses and contact with the world by avoiding to walk outside and be inside doors. The connection Solnit mentions referring to people and nature itself. It will causes a loss in social skills to strain future relationships. Individuals also lose the freedom of imagination by being trapped into a prison filled with consumer appetite, true crime titillations, and celebrity crisis.. People need to follow Solnit's opinion by understanding walking can bring many benefits such as mental improvements, intellectual imagination, and an inseparable connection with the world.

Yes walking can bring a physical benefits but a lot of the positives come from mental improvements. A perfect example of this would be my mother. As a child I grew up going to the park almost every other day. I thought I went so much so

I wouldn't get bored or because my mother really knew I loved going there, but I came to realize my mother would only take me to the park because it was a mental break from the duties she had. I remember her telling me she needed to walk outdoors to release stress that she carried not only on her but my father's as well. She mentioned how walking with or without her friends kept her sane and calm. Being a mother is the hardest job to do because she not only takes responsibility for herself but also for another human being. For her walking helped improve her mental strength by simply embracing the nature of the world or the people on her side. Walking also gave her the opportunity to think how she could resolve issues she would run into the house.

The loss of leisure walking has cause my cousin to lose her creative ways. In a sense she is a character that repeats the same things taught on TV. I feel bad to see her lost that touch of creativity because out of every member in our family she was the most creative one. I always asked her if she would like to walk around the neighborhood with me but she always turned me down for another episode of her addiction. It not only impacted her imagination but also her skills of life.

Furthermore my cousin started to loss her social skills and went from being an extrovert to being an introvert. Solnit explains people start to lost their connection with the world by living their lives inside a box blocking them from it. My cousin demonstrates that by not being able to communicate well with other human beings also being afraid of the beauty of nature. Her life has always been focused on a screen that demonstrates negativity of our society that she forgets walking isn't just an unsafe action it's a must do activity that brings out a great improvement with the relationship to the world. My friends who usually walk with me explained to me because they walk almost everyday they build a stronger connection with many others and a healthier life with nature. Stories like my brother meeting his girlfriend at the park while both of them walk their dogs exemplify the benefits of living life outside one's house. Walking should not be seen as a burden but viewed as a helpful to better someone's connection to life and the world.

With attention to Solnit's and my opinion, walking is a great sense of action that humans need to start including in their everyday life. People will start to lose their ability to grow mentally by staying indoors instead of walking outside. Also they will loss the chance to be able to improve their lives. Walking isn't just a form of action it's a way of living. Therefore, Solnit and I do believe if people keep living their life without walking, then they are sure to lose all of the things I mentioned in this essay.

Assessment Questions

1. Does this essay answer the first part of the writing topic?

2. Does this essay have a thesis that answers the second part of the writing topic?

3. Does this essay develop the thesis with supporting examples? Evaluate the effectiveness of these examples.

4. Are there significant errors in grammar that limit the essay's effectiveness? In other words, as you read the essay, did you notice several mistakes in the way the sentences are written?

5. Using the conventional standards presented in the scoring rubric in Part 1 of this book, what score does this essay deserve? Explain.

A Glossary of Key Terms

annotation
a comment, underline, or other marking made on or in the margins of a reading to help critically evaluate the text

conclusion
the closing section of an essay that may restate the thesis and its supporting points, or offer the reader an emotional appeal or interesting anecdote that gracefully signals the end of an essay

drafting
a stage of the writing process where a writer develops and organizes the ideas in a paper in an effort to present the essay's points with clarity and effectiveness

editing
the stage in the writing process where work is checked for grammatical and mechanical errors

freewriting
an activity in which the writer quickly puts down on paper random thoughts and ideas on a topic as a method of discovery

handbook
a text that guides the writer through the various stages of writing and provides complete information on the grammar, mechanics, and conventions of written English

index
an alphabetical list of all subjects mentioned in the text, followed by the page numbers on which those subjects appear

introduction
the opening paragraph(s) of an essay that provide a context for the material that follows

outline
a brief list of an essay's thesis statement, main points, main supporting ideas, and specific details

paragraph
related sentences grouped around a central idea or thought

peer review
an activity structured by a set of criteria for students to evaluate one another's writing during the writing process in an effort to guide revision

post-grade evaluation
a process where a writer, after receiving instructor feedback on a paper, determines patterns of weakness and strength in his or her writing and formulates a plan for improvement

prewriting
invention techniques or strategies—such as clustering, freewriting, or listing—for exploring ideas about a topic

revising
the process of rethinking and rewriting the initial draft

scoring rubric
a guide for evaluating the strengths and weaknesses of an essay

summary
a short presentation in the writer's own words of the argument and main points of a reading

table of contents
a topical list at the beginning of a text that shows at a glance the text's chapters and subjects and the pages on which they are located

thesis statement
a sentence (or sentences) found in an essay's introduction that gives the essay's central argument, the perspective or idea that locks the other components of the essay together

timed essay
usually a response to a question or topic written in a supervised setting in a designated amount of time

topic sentence
the sentence in a paragraph that states the paragraph's main point

transition
a word, phrase, or device used to provide a connection between sentences or paragraphs

Index